Raymond of the Times

Courtesy of Mrs. Seymour Holbrook

Henry Jarvis Raymond

Raymond

OF THE

TIMES

FRANCIS BROWN

W · W · NORTON & COMPANY · INC · *New York*

PRINTED IN THE UNITED STATES OF AMERICA
FOR THE PUBLISHERS BY THE VAIL-·BALLOU PRESS

FOR
MARY, VICKI, and SCOTTY

Contents

Illustrations

Raymond of the Times

CHAPTER
1

Seward, Weed & Greeley

IN THE dusty, littered *Evening Journal* office at Albany, New York, two men labored long hours through the hot summer days of 1838. One of them was Thurlow Weed, the tall, robust editor of the *Journal*, who was about to cement his power as the Whig dictator of New York by electing his friend, William Henry Seward, to the governorship. The other man, sandy-haired, near-sighted, stooped, and somewhat disheveled, was Horace Greeley. He too was an editor.

Thurlow Weed had just passed forty. He had been born to poverty and had worked in a blacksmith's shop, on shipboard, and in a printing house before he risked his first editorial venture when scarcely old enough to vote. Shrewd, well-informed, he was a fighter and an organizer and was fast giving his *Evening Journal* the largest circulation of any political paper in the country. He wrote slowly, with difficulty, yet his pen had a brilliant pungency that placed him among the nation's most gifted editorial writers. Men said that in politics Thurlow Weed was none too scrupulous, that he was indeed a dictator; the charges followed him all the days of his life. His friends found him good-natured, generous, sympathetic. "I had no idea," Seward once said, "that dictators were such amiable creatures." A suave and ingratiating diplomat, the handsome Weed possessed a subtle power to influence others that explained in part the political strength he was gathering.

He was rising to power at a moment of political change. Martin Van Buren, who had hardly settled in the White House when a business panic swept the land, had inherited from Andrew Jackson, his patron and predecessor, the first well-organized party in American history. He had also inherited the political democracy which Jackson had embodied, the sense of equality that was installing manhood suffrage in state after state, that was making public office elective and stirring in broadclothed city merchants and in ragged frontiersmen political interest and partisanship. As never before, politics drew men to great rallies and processions and to speechmaking by orators who threw time to the winds as they unfolded sonorous periods.

Martin Van Buren, like Jackson, was a Democrat. Opposed to him and his party were the Whigs, who had come into being in 1832 under the name of National Republicans and the leadership of Henry Clay. The party coat was of many colors, covering Southern slaveholders and anti-slavery Northerners, anti-Masons, anti-foreigners, those who favored and those who opposed strong government at Washington. Manufacturers who wanted a protective tariff supported the Whigs; Louisiana sugar planters joined the party for the same reason. Bankers, North and South, who hated Jackson's financial policies and particularly his destruction of the Bank of the United States, found a place in the youthful Whig organization so long to be regarded as the party of "property and talents." Within that organization Thurlow Weed was building himself a career.

In 1838 he had not known Horace Greeley long. Weed and other New York Whigs had been impressed, as that year's state elections drew near, with the need for a campaign paper which would "furnish to every person within the State of New York a complete summary of political intelligence, at a rate which shall place it absolutely within the reach of every man who will read it." The Whig Central Committee agreed to sponsor the project and leading politicians promised to finance it. Weed set out to find a suitable editor. He had one in mind.

He had been reading for some time a weekly journal—the *New-Yorker*, it was called—that since March, 1834, had been bringing to a small public summaries of political and general news and a diversity of literary material that ranged from book reviews and verse to reprints from American and foreign periodicals. The political news, despite the partisanship of the period, was both accurate and objective, and while the editorials often bristled with Whiggery, the paper as a whole gave an impression of modesty and candor. Who the editor of the weekly might be, Weed had no knowledge, but whoever he was, there, thought the "Dictator," was the man to edit the projected Whig campaign organ. He sought him out, and so it was that Thurlow Weed first met Horace Greeley of the *New-Yorker*.

Greeley was twenty-eight and, like Weed, his roots were in poverty. Born a New England farmer's son, he had been a farm hand before he became a printer. His education was largely what he had given himself, but that education was considerable, and from the day he turned editor to publish the *New-Yorker* he showed a maturity that usually belongs only to older men. Though his little paper gained considerable circulation, the subscribers sorely tried the editor. "They took my journal, and probably read it," he complained. "They promised to pay for it, and defaulted, leaving me to pay my paper-maker, type-founder, journeyman, etc., as I could." The panic of 1837 had only made matters worse, inducing a chronic shortage of funds in the *New-Yorker* office. Yet Greeley pushed ahead, even though it meant that he both edited his paper and set type for its issues. It was at the type-case that Weed found him when he called with the proposal for a campaign organ.

Greeley quickly accepted, although the post would require his presence at Albany the greater part of every week, to the considerable damage, perhaps, of the *New-Yorker*. Yet he was glad of the opportunity Weed offered, and in the deep cold of the 1838 winter he set out for Albany, arriving, after a three-day journey from New York by stage and sleigh, at the *Evening Journal* office where the new paper was to be published. Greeley suggested its name, the *Jeffersonian*, and Whigs approved, although their political principles were more akin to the conservatism of Alexander Hamilton than to the liberalism of Thomas Jefferson.

The first issue was dated March 3, 1838, and during ensuing weeks a new sort of party journal was laid before the public. Shrill partisanship had no place in the *Jeffersonian*. Instead, Greeley filled its pages with general political news, with Congressional speeches, with articles on political subjects, for he "aimed," he said, "to convince and win by candor and moderation, rather than overbear by passion and vehemence." Publication of the paper marked the beginning of the political firm of Seward, Weed & Greeley.

One August day that summer, an eager, energetic boy—he was eighteen, but, small and frail, looked younger—called at the *Journal* office. He introduced himself. He was Henry J. Raymond, a student from the University of Vermont at Burlington, where he had just witnessed the conferring of an honorary degree upon Silas Wright, United States Senator from New York. He thought the news might interest the *Journal*, but to his chagrin and disappointment Weed and Greeley were pleased not at all and were, though both the *Journal* and the *New-Yorker* later published the item, considerably disgusted, for Silas Wright was a leading Democrat and a foeman whose steel they feared. Raymond, ashamed of his political ignorance but unabashed, settled down to conversation with Greeley, with whom he had already had correspondence. He liked him at this first face-to-face meeting, and remembered afterward that the young editor was "not very much devoted to ceremonious observances."

When Raymond that August day walked from the *Journal* office into the shade of the elms along Albany's State Street, he had not seen the last of Greeley and Weed, nor they of him. In the years ahead, when Raymond had grown to manhood, their lives crossed and recrossed. Their conflicting ambitions helped to shape the history of New York and of the nation, for the three were destined to achieve a fame and reputation that gave each such a prominence as none could have foreseen when Raymond brought to Albany the news of Silas Wright's degree.

With Greeley as teacher, Raymond was to learn the journalist's craft, to start his own paper, the New York *Times*. They were to be associates, friends, and then, parting, bitter political and professional rivals. Raymond was to join the Weed political firm, a move that would help not only to make him one of the country's best-known editors but to lift him to political eminence. His membership caused ultimately the withdrawal of Greeley from the partnership, and this action, affecting American life for all time, altered the whole career of an Illinois lawyer and politician who in 1838 remained in rural obscurity. His name was Abraham Lincoln.

After busy, crowded, and eventful years, the three men who had first met in the *Evening Journal* office would come together for the last time on a hot June afternoon in 1869. Within the hushed solemnity of a New York City church, rivalries and enmities adjourned, Horace Greeley and Thurlow Weed would pay final honor to Henry J. Raymond before a procession carried his body to a green knoll in Brooklyn that looks out upon the bay and the ships going down to the sea.

2

The Boy Raymond

I

HENRY JARVIS RAYMOND was born on January 24, 1820, the year of the Missouri Compromise that startled Thomas Jefferson "like a firebell in the night" and warned the United States that its union was endangered by the conflict between free men and slave. The conflict that eventually was to seem "irrepressible" helped shape the lives of all Americans who grew to maturity in the years after 1820. For some, careers were made, for others, broken. Much of the conflict was reflected in the life of Henry Raymond; it brought him some of his greatest triumphs and some of his deepest disappointments.

His father was Jarvis Raymond, a young farmer in the Genesee country of western New York. Settlers in the ever-moving tide of American expansion had begun to seek out the Genesee, a region of lakes and rolling hills, of forest and meadowland, soon after the Revolution's end brought relative peace to the frontier, but there had been no certainty of life or possession until the end of the second war with England lifted the threat of sudden forays from the Canadian neighbor to the north. It was isolated country, rude roads stretching two hundred miles and more to the eastward before reaching Albany and the waters of the Hudson that lead to the sea. Not until the Erie Canal in 1825 linked those waters with the Great Lakes did the people of the Genesee have easy communication with the coastal regions from which many of them had come.

Jarvis Raymond's eighty acres lay a mile from the village of Lima, a tiny hamlet with post office, a few houses, a Presbyterian and a Methodist church. The first settlers had arrived from Connecticut in 1789 to lay the foundations for a community in country that nature seemed to have designed for the husbandman. Jarvis Raymond's ancestors had been Connecticut folk, though he was presumably born in New York State, possibly in Lima itself. In 1819 he had married Lavinia Brockway, daughter of Charles Brockway, another Lima farmer.

They were plain people, the Raymonds, hard-working, industrious, but poor and usually in debt. Religion was their chief satisfaction, as indeed it was for their neighbors and for most Americans in small towns and on lonely farmsteads. In Lima's First Presbyterian Church Jarvis Raymond was a ruling elder and also superintendent of the Sunday school. Unlettered though he was, he held minor public offices as he grew older, and neighbors remembered him after he was dead as a man of "sound sense, honesty of purpose and decision of character," as a "man possessed of a remarkably clear mind and a happy faculty of imparting ideas." Lavinia Raymond was also described as a "clear-headed person," but like her husband she remains a pale shadow in the life of Henry Jarvis Raymond, first of six children to be born on the Lima farm where the locust trees in summer cast thin shade and in winter raised their black branches against the sky. Three of the children died in infancy. Henry and his brothers, Samuel and James, grew to manhood.

It was a happy group in the snug little farmhouse. Family ties were strong, and when Henry Raymond was a man he recalled "the many happy hours" spent in the homestead and "the kind care of parents that had made it so blessed a place." Farm-born and a farmer's son, the boy Raymond did not escape the chores that come to farm boys, the driving of cattle home from pasture, the chopping of wood for stove and fireplace, the turning of a furrow at planting time, hoeing, haying, reaping. Nor did he fail to follow some of the pleasures of country lads, although when a man he said that hunting and fishing had held no attraction, and the recollections of them who knew him as a boy maintain that "chestnutting had no charms for him, bird's-nesting was a joy of which he never tasted, even the exhilarating pastime of coasting was but seldom indulged in."

Tradition has it that he could read when only three, and that when scarcely older he started to learn writing and arithmetic in the district school close by the Raymond farm. A serious-minded little pedant is the portrait drawn of the boy, and drawn perhaps unjustly, for those who remembered his "great natural quickness," "indomitable nervous energy," and "thirst for the acquisition of knowledge" may have been thinking more of the mature Raymond, the man of the world, than of the barefoot boy in homemade pantaloons. Yet his own record testifies to his being mentally alert, intelligent, and precocious beyond his years, a boy who read all that came his way and forgot little that was in his books.

District school was followed by an elementary school in the village, and then, when he was twelve, by the Genesee Wesleyan Seminary, whose stone building with its cupola had just given a new landmark to Lima. The Annual Conference of the Methodist Church had started in 1829 a movement to establish a seminary in western New York and, to attract subscriptions, had announced that the new institution would be established in the town that contributed most. Lima citizens, by banding together to raise $12,000 and to buy seventy-four acres of land, obtained the school for their town. Construction was begun, and in 1832 the seminary—though Methodist-controlled, it was nonsectarian—opened its doors to 341 pupils. Henry Raymond was among the 230 boys who that year started to write the educational history of what was to be a famous school and from which eventually came Syracuse University.

Of his three years at the seminary there is no record other than that he belonged to something called the Amphictyon Society and that one of his schoolmates was Alexander Mann, who was always to be a close friend. Raymond was only fifteen when he finished at the seminary, "too young," as he remarked afterward, "to go to college, for which I was better prepared than my father was to send me." He worked in a country store for a while—the owner paid him at the rate of $75 a year—and disliked the business heartily. Time hung heavy on his hands, yet with it all there was a chance to read and grow, to gather experience that before the year was over had included a winter's teaching in a district school at Wheatland, fifteen miles northwest of Lima.

He apparently liked the role of pedagogue, although it could not have been an easy part to fill, for he was after all only a boy and he must have faced sturdy farmers' sons who were seniors in age and superiors in strength. He boarded at farmhouses, taking his chances on the fare of good cooks and poor, sleeping in beds that many times were lumpy and damp and none too clean. Like the "brisk wielder of the birch and rule" in Whittier's "Snowbound," Raymond must have made happy the "snow-locked homes" by reciting classic legends:

Wherein the scenes of Greece and Rome
Had all the commonplace of home
Where Pindus-born Arachthus took
The guise of any grist-mill brook,
And dread Olympus at his will
Became a huckleberry hill.

All the while he was looking forward to college, and by September, 1836, he was ready to start eastward by canal boat on the tedious journey that ended at the busy Lake Champlain port of Burlington and the University of Vermont. The family farm had been mortgaged for $1,000 to make his college education possible, and he reached Burlington firmly resolved that opportunity purchased with such sacrifice would not be wasted.

II

The university, set upon a hilltop that looks east to Mount Mansfield, Camel's Hump, and the rolling ridges of the Green Mountains, west to island-studded Champlain and the distant Adirondacks, had known almost continuous hard times—its library was attached for university debts while Raymond was an undergraduate—and there had been periods after the first class was graduated in 1804 when the institution's very existence was threatened. In the Eighteen Twenties matters had looked up, and then was built the red brick row which for Raymond was always the university—a central hall, crowned by a great dome and cupola, and on either side, like outriggers, two dormitories, North and South College. Across the green, which when Raymond first saw it in 1836 had been fenced and formalized by ornamental gates, stood the plain, severe building where students listened to lectures on chemistry and anatomy. Down the university's hill to the lake-shore docks sloped the town, its unpaved, unlighted streets a checkerboard to which a few mansions, a few handsome churches, gave distinction. The place had a natural beauty at any time and most especially in late spring when the locust trees were white with bloom that laid heavy perfume upon the air.

Much of the university's vigor in the Eighteen Thirties stemmed from James Marsh, president from 1826 to 1833, and until his death in 1842 professor of moral and intellectual philosophy. Raymond got to know well this brilliant mind that ranged the fields of learning. Classic and modern literature, foreign languages, philosophy, all were grist for the Marsh intellectual mill, and from deep study of the European philosophers, particularly the teachings of Samuel Taylor Coleridge, he had evolved a philosophy of his own that breathed religious liberalism into an age stirring against the rigors of traditional Calvinism. In this mild-mannered, soft-spoken man, students found a sympathetic and inspiring teacher and friend. Raymond never forgot what he learned from Marsh and no man at the university influenced him more.

In 1836 the university had about 100 students and a faculty of seven. Alexander Mann, who had persuaded Raymond to come to Burlington, was already a junior, and another Lima boy, Alonzo Kimball, roomed with Raymond as a fellow freshman. Almost monastic in the simplicity of its life, the university nevertheless offered palatable intellectual fare through its lectures and courses. There was a library of 7,000 volumes, and the student literary societies provided 3,000 more. Raymond, who soon joined one of the societies, Phi Sigma Nu, found his keenest interest in writing and speaking, although the record shows him to have been guilty at times of failure in both, of absence and tardiness, of "indecorous conduct," "speaking without leave," "personalities." The College of Natural History, a student organization that was collecting geological and archaeological specimens and listening to lectures about them, had weekly gatherings—for a time Raymond was secretary—and in the slow misery of Vermont winters there was abundant opportunity for the wide reading that supplemented prescribed study.

The long winter vacation then customary in American colleges gave further opportunity, and what that meant a bit of reminiscence illustrates. It was Raymond's sophomore year. In class he had been reading Homer's *Odyssey*. "He had not read the *Iliad* in his preparatory course," a friend recalled, "and set about reading up. One book a day he assigned to himself as a task. But as these books were of unequal length, some days he had to overtask nature. . . . On one occasion he sat down to his task at 4 P.M.; the book was a large one, and he read away through the entire night, and did not complete his task until 4 P.M. of the next day." The ancient classics, of course, were not the only books to be read. There were English classics, modern English and American poetry, foreign and American literary periodicals; and periodicals were beginning to have a somewhat personal concern for Raymond.

Before coming to Burlington, he had discovered Horace Greeley's *New-Yorker*, had subscribed to it as "interesting and instructive," had continued to follow its literary and political departments. He submitted contributions to Greeley, and in the *New-Yorker* for September 30, 1837, was rewarded by seeing his verse, "The Flower-Girl's Song." Its pretensions to poetic elegance, Raymond admitted later, were not great, but at the moment he was proud of such lines as:

> I've been roaming—been roaming
> Far from the haunts of men,
> Where sylvan cascades foaming
> Awake the shaded glen.

He sent other verses to Greeley—"To Memory," which was printed, "Sonnet to the Rose," which was rejected because it was not a sonnet—and long, rather pedantic book reviews. A three-installment criticism of Richard H. Dana's *Poems and Prose Writings* was followed by a bristling exchange with a critic of his criticism. A two-installment review

of James Gilman's *The Life of S. T. Coleridge*, which showed the influence of the Marsh teaching; a shorter notice of the popular poems of
John G. C. Brainard; accounts of the university's commencements,
letters of comment—all these appeared above Raymond's initials or the
pen name of "Fantome" he had devised.

In Burlington, where he acted as the *New-Yorker*'s agent and did not
miss an opportunity to praise the paper, Raymond acquired reputation
as an orator as well as a writer. The Junior Exhibition at the 1839 commencement made the oratorical reputation seemingly secure. Henry
Clay, the Kentucky Senator who had already been twice a candidate for
the Presidency and would try again, was swinging through the country
on a political tour that brought him to Burlington. Fellow Whigs, out
in force to greet him, escorted him with great ceremony from the dock
to his hotel, and at night staged an illumination in his honor. The university got him to attend its commencement, a special attraction that
made more crowded the Burlington church where in summer heat the
exercises were held. Clay, dignified in black frock coat, white vest, and
brown pantaloons, kept awake only by repeated attention to his snuffbox
as the young orators delivered their interminable orations. Then came
Raymond's turn. His subject was "The Moral Influence of Reflection
upon the Past."

"A slender, boyish figure stepped gracefully out upon the stage," an
observer said thirty years later, "made his bow to the President, to the
Faculty and Mr. Clay, and then to the vast audience. His reputation for
ability was so well known that in an instant the buzz of conversation
ceased, and the first sentences of Raymond's oration broke upon the ear,
almost as clearly as if the church had been empty. . . . In a moment Mr.
Clay's manner changed. He was wide awake. As the young speaker grew
more animated, and recovered from the embarrassment, which he afterward confessed to me almost overpowered him at the thought of opening
his lips in the presence of that great master of oratory, the statesman
leaned forward in his chair in an attitude of intense interest, and so remained to the close. . . . Mr. Clay turned to one sitting next him to ask
who the speaker was. 'That young man,' said he, 'will make his mark.
Depend upon it, you will hear from him hereafter.' "

That night Raymond met the great Clay, leader of the Whig party, to
which the nineteen-year-old orator had already given his allegiance and
about which he was writing to the friends with whom he corresponded.
One of these was Rufus Wilmot Griswold, five years older than Raymond and somewhat precociously a man of the world. When only a boy
Griswold had started to work in an Albany newspaper office. He had
been an itinerant printer, possibly a sailor. He already knew some of the

literary men of the time and eventually would know many more, for as
a journalist, a licensed Baptist preacher, an editor of anthologies, he became one of the minor literary figures of the Eighteen Forties and
Fifties, though ultimately he was remembered chiefly as the slanderer of
Edgar Allan Poe. During 1838 and part of 1839 he was living in Vergennes, about twenty-five miles south of Burlington, editing the Vergennes *Vermonter*.

Somehow Raymond met Griswold and as early as December, 1837,
they were engaged in rather formal correspondence. Raymond as secretary of Phi Sigma Nu wrote to thank Griswold for an Irving autograph
given to the society's collections and to announce that the donor had
been admitted to honorary membership. Soon Raymond was writing
more personal letters filled with local political gossip, with requests for
loans from Griswold's library, with literary comment and personalities.
They saw each other when Griswold came to Burlington, and later Raymond visited in Vergennes. When Griswold in 1839 left his native Vermont to edit in New York a literary paper, *Brother Jonathan*, and then to
become Greeley's assistant on the *New-Yorker*, the correspondence continued, and following the 1839 commencement, Raymond with Alexander Mann went to the city to invade Griswold's leisure.

The Griswold friendship apparently heightened Raymond's interest
in literary journalism, although that interest had been considerable anyway, and possibly was partly responsible for a correspondence that
Raymond in the spring of 1840 began with Horace Greeley. The days
at the university were drawing to an end and the need for making a living
was close at hand. Journalism might point the way. "If I could obtain a
place in the *New-Yorker* under the shadow of your wing," Raymond
wrote Greeley, "I should be exceedingly well suited." Greeley had
counterproposals that proved embarrassing. He had no job to give, but
he would sell the *New-Yorker*, lock, stock, and barrel. Greeley was
thinking that politics was more his forte, and that he might leave the
fourth estate forever. Park Benjamin, editor of another literary journal,
the *New World*, and a former Greeley assistant, seconded the idea of
Raymond's buying the paper, but the dazed youth, lacking capital or
experience, ignorant of printing and publishing, had to confess "doubt"
and "self-distrust." To Greeley he replied halfheartedly that "the em-
ployment I think I should like, and with some experience I believe I
might make it go at some rate."

Before the idea was quite discarded, Greeley wrote Raymond some
advice and encouragement. "Your success in this as in any new undertaking," said the veteran, "would depend entirely on the advantages you
enjoyed, your own adaptation to the task you had undertaken. You are

a good writer on your own grounds; and I think would make an interesting paper with the help of a merely mechanical assistant to get up the commonplace occurrences and news of the day. . . . A newspaper ought to have some hobby, and some clique influence, some *esprit de corps* enlisted in its support. I believe I have erred in making my paper too catholic. The affectation of impartiality and independence answers a good purpose, but the practical thing repels."

With abundant advice from Greeley on journalism, with urging from his university teachers that he take up the scholar's life, Raymond reached commencement day and the exercises that brought him the ornate sheepskin of a bachelor's degree. Its wax seals still fresh, he went home to Lima. He was still short of twenty-one, delicate, intellectual-looking, dark-complexioned, blue-eyed, a man who would never stand more than five feet six, a man so filled with energy and enthusiasm, with curiosity and ambition, that the popular and contemporary biographer James Parton said of Raymond before he was much older that he regarded the world as "an oyster to be opened" and that he was "bent on opening it."

III

It was a Presidential year, and the Whigs, having shunted Henry Clay momentarily aside, to Raymond's keen disappointment, were out to elect William Henry Harrison, hero of Tippecanoe, and to drive Martin Van Buren from the White House. Harrison, no less an aristocrat than the squire of Kinderhook, had for the campaign's duration become the embodiment of democracy, a transformation made easier by a Democratic taunt that "Old Tip" would be content in a log cabin if he had enough cider to drink. Whigs took up the taunt, made the log cabin, as Thurlow Weed said, the "symbol of virtue that dwells in obscurity, of the hopes of the humble, of the privations of the poor, of toil and danger, of hospitality and charity and frugality." Political parades featured log-cabin floats. Whigs wore log-cabin badges. Greeley edited with enormous success a campaign paper, the *Log Cabin*, that Raymond in retrospect called "the best campaign paper ever published," the most powerful and effective of all the "immediate and direct agencies" in the ultimate Whig victory.

When New York Whigs held their convention at Utica, 25,000 people attended, staging such a parade as the town had never seen. Wagons, long lines of them, heading for other Whig rallies, raised dust clouds so great that it seemed an army must be on the march. From town to town huge balls were rolled to signify the swelling majority for Harrison, the crowds singing:

What has caused this great commotion, motion, motion,
Our country through?
—It is the ball a-rolling on, for
(Chorus)   TIPPECANOE and Tyler too:—
Tippecanoe and Tyler too.
And with them we'll beat little Van, Van, Van,
Oh! Van is a used-up man.

Raymond, whatever his disappointment that Clay was not the Whig candidate, was a loyal party man, a believer in the national bank, in a tariff, in internal improvements at government expense, and while he was too young to vote, he was old enough to campaign. Into the Whig enthusiasm he threw his own, and up and down the Genesee country, at Lima, at near-by Geneseo, the county seat, and at other towns and villages he appeared at log-cabin rallies to speak for Harrison. With all the skill, fluency, and confidence that had won him an oratorical reputation at the university he argued the cause of "Tippecanoe and Tyler too." He drew, says tradition, large audiences. Their applause quickly echoed away with their words of praise. One crusty Democrat who heard the boy-orator asked, and with a degree of bitterness, "what that little Raymond, with a face no bigger than a snuff-box, meant by coming round there to make political speeches."

Raymond belonged to a politically minded age and politics fascinated him, a fascination he was never able, except for brief periods, to overcome. Conflict between politics and his other interests warped his life. The Harrison campaign marked his apprenticeship, and on election day he and fellow Whigs saw "Old Tip" sweep to victory. He had carried New York State by 13,000 votes and the electoral college by 234 votes to Van Buren's 60.

With the campaign's end, Raymond turned to the serious business of finding work to do. He had decided that teaching might after all suit his talents best, and so he hunted, vainly, through the districts where he had but so recently listened to sweet Whig applause. No school was available even to a man with a degree from the University of Vermont, neither could opportunity for other work be found, and thereupon he decided to cast his lines in more distant waters. On one of late November's brief days he set out from Lima on a journey that by stage, canal boat, and Hudson River steamer brought him to New York City. A new world opened.

3

New York, 1840

I

THE NEW YORK to which Henry Raymond turned in late 1840 had already become the gaslit American metropolis, an island city of more than 300,000 people. He saw it with the curiosity of youth. There was the harbor, crowded with ships that had known many seas, ships that were laying down upon the docks the silks and spices of the Orient as well as the hardware and crockery of England. Along the busy waterfront, where the heavy drays clattered over the cobbles, ships planted a bristling forest of masts and stretched their bowsprits across the street until they thrust themselves almost into the warehouse windows. On the East River future queens of the American sailing fleet were building on the ways.

A maritime city, it was also a mercantile city, as Raymond quickly learned. Merchants might make fortunes from selling overseas, but they made fortunes also from selling to all America goods brought by the vessels that sailed up New York Bay. Finance was beginning to make its national headquarters in narrow Wall Street, where the Doric temple of the Custom House was nearing completion on the site of Washington's first inauguration. Business directories for the bustling city listed importers and jobbers, commission merchants, agents, brokers, storekeepers. There were cotton merchants, flour merchants, iron merchants, dealers in leather, in salt, in drugs, in dry goods. There were coffee roasters, booksellers, distillers, clothiers, fur dealers and coal sellers, cordage manufacturers. The list runs on indefinitely.

Approached from the waterside, where historic Castle Garden jutted its circumference toward the bay, the city seemed almost monotonously long, flat, straggling, the line of three-, four- and five-storied buildings of red brick and granite broken only occasionally by church spires. The dome of the classic-pillared new Merchants Exchange curved above the lower city, as did the cupola of City Hall, a gem of Federal architecture set amid the park that in the Eighteen Forties was a center of metropolitan life. Across Broadway, which citizens hailed as the world's finest street, stood brownstone St. Paul's, where Washington had worshiped, and, next door, the new Astor House, through whose columned portico passed in 1840, and for many years after, the bearers of great names in the Old World and the New.

Raymond quickly became part of the scene, came to know well the New York streets, dusty in summer and in winter deep with mud, streets crowded with high-wheeled omnibuses, gigs, hackney coaches, two-wheeled tilburies, phaetons. Pigs scavenged in alleys and even in the main thoroughfares, for the city-cleaning carts did poor service. Sandwichmen with their boards threaded through the heavy traffic, rubbing elbows with oystermen, who set up frail stands wherever custom might be attracted, with muffinmen crying their wares, with blackened chimney sweeps. New Yorkers—and foreigners thought them amazingly well-dressed—were familiar with the Negro women who in late summer sold corn on street corners, crying the song:

> Hot corn, hot corn, here's your nice hot corn,
> This corn is good and that I know,
> For on Long Island this corn grew.
> Hot corn, hot corn, here's your nice hot corn.

Sightseers always sought out the Tombs, the city prison—"a pile of bastard Egyptian," Charles Dickens called it. Its gray granite walls enclosing an entire city block were decorated with pseudo-Egyptian motifs that delighted contemporaries, who marveled at the prison's decoration and size. Round about the prison, and Broadway was not distant, lay a region of squalor and crime surpassed only by the notorious "Five Points," where vice lay "naked in all its deformity." Thieves and harlots and desperadoes frequented the gin mills and dance halls, the broken-down tenements and stinking cellars, or lounged upon sagging doorsteps that led down to narrow, crooked, and urchin-swarming streets.

New York knew poverty and crime; it knew also comfort, respectability, and wealth. Uptown, at Washington Square, along Fifth Avenue and its side streets, at newly opened Gramercy Park and elsewhere, stood row upon row of staid, red brick houses, green-shuttered, their high stoops leading to neat doorways on which brass or silver nameplates and bell knobs received a daily polishing. Some were simple homes. Others were mansions before which waited coachmen in livery.

The city claimed, and with considerable right, to be the intellectual leader of the nation, Boston not excepted. Horace Greeley asserted in 1839: "New York has become the metropolis in our country, not only of commerce, but of literature and the arts. . . . No man well acquainted with the history of Literature and Art in our country during the last ten years, can refuse to acknowledge that New York has towered above her sister cities." At the beginning of 1841 the periodicals published in New York were numbered in the scores. There were eleven newspapers. Book publishing was increasing. In the literary circle, aside from lesser names, were headliners like Washington Irving and William Cullen Bryant.

America's best writers contributed to the *Knickerbocker*, New York's leading literary monthly. The *New-York Review*, a scholarly quarterly, and the *New-York Mirror*, a weekly, stood high on the list of distinction. There were others, prominent among them for a time the *New World*, which Park Benjamin edited solely, it sometimes seemed, for the purpose of rushing out special supplements of cheap and pirated editions of English novels.

Among newspapers the *Sun*, a penny paper published for the poorer citizens, and the *Herald*, lively, scurrilous, fresh and vigorous, were Democratic in politics, although the *Sun* professed to be neutral. The dignified *Evening Post* and *Journal of Commerce* tended also to be Democratic, but were expensive and limited in circulation. Whig sentiments found expression in the *Courier and Enquirer*, the New York *American*, the *Express*, and the *Commercial Advertiser*. Except for the *Sun* and the *Herald*, which were setting a style for colorful, zestful journalism, these papers were dull and uninteresting—"undeniably sleepy," a working journalist once described them. They cared little whether news was lively and gave its presentation little thought. Some of them, the "blanket sheets," were so large—their pages might measure four feet in width—that to read them taxed ingenuity.

City and metropolis though New York might be, its surroundings remained rural. All upper Manhattan was a region of villages, country estates, woods, and open fields, while the Harlem River—great granite High Bridge was being finished to bring Croton water to the lower island—was a quiet waterway between wooded shores. Across the East River, Brooklyn, a city in its own right, had not expanded far enough to spoil the pastoral setting of the naval station on Wallabout Bay, and New Jersey, reached by chugging steam ferries, drew picnickers to its pleasant villages and groves upon the heights above the Hudson.

II

This was the New York in which Henry Raymond cast his lines. Except for his student visit, he had never seen the city and among its many thousands he knew well only Alexander Mann, who was now studying law in a Wall Street office. Yet Raymond had corresponded frequently enough with Horace Greeley for it to be natural that he should direct his steps toward Ann Street and climb the stairs to the cluttered garret where Greeley edited the *New-Yorker* and carried on a voluminous correspondence with friends and chance acquaintances, reformers, politicians, and unknowns. At the *New-Yorker* office Raymond found also his friend Griswold.

Raymond hoped that with Greeley and Griswold there might be a chance for work that would temporarily put money in his pocket. Greeley demurred, for he had just hired an assistant and had no need for another, but he did agree that Raymond might spend as much time in the office as he liked. It proved a happy arrangement. "I was at the *New-Yorker* every day," said Raymond, "and somehow or other a great deal of the work fell into my hands. I added up election returns, read the exchanges for news and discovered a good deal which others had overlooked; made brief notices of new books, read proof and made myself generally useful."

Then, without notice, Griswold packed off to Philadelphia to edit the *Daily Standard*, leaving Raymond alone on the job at a time when Greeley was absent. Griswold's departure brought a tart rebuke from his former chief. "I want to curse you," Greeley wrote him, "for going off so abruptly as you did, without leaving directions. It has ruined the *New-Yorker* for this week—dead as a hatchet. Raymond is a good fellow, but utterly destitute of experience or knowledge of where magazines, etc., are to be procured, as you well know. . . . He went to work as a novice would, shears in fist, and cut out the most infernal lot of newspaper trash ever seen. He got in type a column of *Lord Chatham*, which you published a month ago; three or four column articles of amazing antiquity and stupidity, and then gave out an original translation of a notorious story—which I fear we have once published—three columns and over of this, for a magazine week! Thus the *New-Yorker* is doomed for this week, and you are to blame for it."

It had been a bad start, but Greeley allowed Raymond to stay on, and when, shortly before Christmas, the younger man was offered a school in North Carolina, Greeley persuaded him to remain in New York, promising him a salary equivalent to the $600 he would have been paid as teacher. Raymond accepted. The decision was momentous for both

Greeley and Raymond, and though the elder man remarked of his assistant, "I can train him in the way he should go," he was not only to train him but to loose upon New York a young newspaperman to compete for the very audience Greeley himself sought.

At the moment, Raymond regarded the arrangement as temporary, and looking ahead to the decision that ultimately would have to be made about a profession, he turned to Dr. Marsh at Burlington for advice. "I have been considering with no little anxiety for a few weeks," he wrote him, "what profession I ought, in view of my circumstances, to study. Nearly all my wishes are in favor of Theology, and I am almost inclined to believe it my duty to prepare for the active ministry. And yet my pecuniary circumstances and those of my father are such as to make incumbent upon me to regard expediency somewhat; if I should decide upon studying Law I could enter my name in an office very soon, and enter upon the practice of my profession at least two years sooner, and with far better pecuniary prospects than I could in case I should study Theology.— Would you not favor me with some instruction upon this point?" And back from Burlington the famous philosopher, a consumptive invalid soon to die, sent instructions and advice, wise but not dogmatic, that left the choice to Raymond.

For the law Marsh had no enthusiasm, and while, as a minister of the Gospel himself, he could not but approve Raymond's interest in devoting his life to religion, he added a reservation. "I do not regard the ministry by any means," he said, "as the only sphere of action in which a disciple of Christ may promote effectively the interests of religion and the best good of his kind." Then came words for which Raymond may have been waiting: his former teacher pointed out the possibilities of a life in journalism.

"The press," said Marsh, "is used far less than it should be by public-spirited and enlightened men for dissipating the fogs of error which so often obscure the popular mind and for exciting a spirit of improvement. In a word, we need *public* men devoted to the *public* interest and capable of guiding the public mind in the right way to right ends."

Even before the Marsh letter helped to resolve some of Raymond's doubts—and the ministry henceforth was never mentioned—Horace Greeley's new man had settled into the routine of editorial work. He made the *New-Yorker*'s literary departments his chief concern. "We are getting along grandly," he wrote Griswold. "I am getting considerably naturalized." To a friend at Burlington he reported: "There's no great labor to be done, merely selecting literary matter and writing literary notices, foreign news, etc.—I am usually at liberty by Thursday evening."

New York life stimulated and excited him. He roomed with Alexander Mann in Vesey Street, not far from the Astor House, and only a few minutes' walk from the *New-Yorker* office, and the two men, though Mann was nine years older than Raymond, made much of all that the city offered. Raymond's editorial job admitted him free to exhibition halls, where panoramas and paintings were shown, and to lectures. At the Broadway Tabernacle—reserved on Sundays for Congregationalists —the best-known American and British lecturers periodically strode the platform. There were theaters to visit, among them the Olympic, the Bowery, and the large and elegant Park, Castle Garden, adjoining the fashionable promenade under the Battery's willows with a view that Raymond thought second only to that from Burlington's university hilltop, and Niblo's, where in warm weather amusement and refreshment were offered in the open air. There were libraries to use—the Mercantile, for example, and the New York Society with its 35,000 volumes and comfortable, carpeted reading rooms behind an Ionic façade. Though Raymond was ever serious-minded and a regular churchgoer, he knew of taverns to visit. "Come down here and we'll have a spree!" he urged his college friend Robert Hale. "New York is a glorious place."

As the winter waxed and waned, an improvement could be noted in the *New Yorker*'s literary department, and while all that improvement may not have been due to Raymond, outside the weekly's office he was given the credit for a large share of it. "Raymond is doing well in his critical labours," was the word a college friend sent to Burlington. "He has the air and confidence of a veteran in the art;—the *ability* of some veterans he certainly possesses." A regular book review section was created where there had been none. Notes about literary events were expanded. Selections from other periodicals, foreign as well as American, suggested more care than formerly. Dickens' *Barnaby Rudge* was being serialized—pirated. There were long reviews of Alexis de Tocqueville's *Democracy in the United States*, of the latest novel by Dumas, of Thiers great history of the French Revolution. From the Lowell *Offering* and *Dial* were taken reprints, though here the hand of Greeley is definitely apparent, for Raymond shared none of his editor's enthusiasm for New England transcendentalism.

Only a few of the literary notices Raymond wrote can be identified. He attacked William Cullen Bryant's *American Poets* for its absence of biographical sketches, notes, and comment, and challenged the poet's wisdom in selection. Another volume of verse—Fitz-Greene Halleck's *British Poets*—also earned his scorn, and Raymond asserted that Halleck's name had been placed on the title page only to sell the book. The selections, he argued, were poor and weighted in favor of the minor British poets. These attacks on contemporaries gave Greeley considerable pleasure, but his assistant's point of view on other matters did not always meet with approval. When Raymond, for instance, overpraised an article on Alexander Hamilton in the *New-York Review*, an outraged Greeley called it "ultra-Federalism" and liberally edited the copy before printing it.

Greeley's uncertainties about his new man did not end with political opinions. "Raymond is clever but careless," he complained. "He don't feel the grave importance of our vocation, and the necessity of throwing earnestness, power, into everything." Even when Raymond had been with the *New-Yorker* for several months Greeley was not wholly satisfied. To Griswold he poured out his feelings: "The most useless animal endowed with ratiocination, I will maintain, is a young man just out of college. Raymond is one of the best of the class, but that class is awful. . . . He can write rather better . . . (though slovenly English and often on uninteresting themes) but he knows (or did know) nothing of the details of Editorship, nothing about making up a paper in the head before it is transferred to type, and has no judgment with regard to selections. . . . He catches up a pair of shears and dives into a pile of exchanges like a rat in a scrap-book, making his selections on about the same principles. O, I have had a weary time of it! My other man, Darlington, is dull and heavy, and neither of them delights in working over-hours. But things are looking better now. Both are learning what is to be done and how to do it."

Raymond liked the work he was doing, said so, but the money Greeley paid him did not go far and he sought to increase his income. Quickly he learned that it was possible to write regular letters for out-of-town newspapers, letters, in an era before the telegraph, that reported events in and around New York. Some papers would take a daily letter; all would pay at a rate of one to three dollars for each. Griswold agreed to take a letter for the *Daily Standard*, and Raymond sent others to the Cincinnati *Chronicle*, the Bangor *Whig*, and the Buffalo *Commercial Advertiser*.

He also made money by writing patent-medicine advertisements. "I secured," he said, "what I deemed a first-class engagement to write a fancy advertisement of some Vegetable Pills which had just been invented, and which were to be commended to the public every morning in the daily journals by being ingeniously connected with some leading event of the day, for which service, which cost me perhaps ten minutes of daily labor, I received the sum of fifty cents." With the *New-Yorker*'s wages and outside earnings he felt that he was doing well. "I shall crowd myself into $1,000 a year before 1842," he told Hale.

III

It took Raymond but a short time to pick up the literary and journal-istic gossip of the city, to become familiar with the name, appearance, and reputation of the principal editors. In short, he soon felt quite at home in the world he had entered, for publishing was concentrated then, as for years to come, close to City Hall Park, and New York was small enough for men of any prominence to be known at least by sight by all who cared to take the trouble. What he learned about newspaper editor-ship he summed up in a single sentence: "The papers in the city all have two editors—one of whom does most of the work and the other writes a 'leader' occasionally and pockets all the glory." He was in the midst of the newspaper crusade against the sensationalism and vulgarity of the *Herald* and he believed much that was being said of James Gordon Bennett, the *Herald's* editor. "One of the slimiest scoundrels in exist-ence," he called him. When Raymond eventually became an editor in his own right, he crossed swords publicly with Bennett, but by then greater knowledge caused him to revise considerably this estimate of one of the really great forces in New York journalism.

Much of the talk that ran around the literary circuit echoed in Greeley's Ann Street garret. The *New-Yorker's* editor had become some-thing of a figure since the *Log-Cabin's* success in the Harrison campaign, and many men sought him out. Not all were politicians or literary men. Some were reformers who numbered Greeley among the sympathetic listeners for their causes, a listener sometimes, a supporter others. One of those who came to see Greeley was Albert Brisbane.[1]

In 1841, Brisbane, though still a young man, had already been promi-nent for several years as an advocate and propagandist for the utopian ideas of the French social philosopher Fourier. He had studied abroad, and in 1840 had published *Social Destiny of Man: or, Association and Reorganization of Industry*, in which he set forth the Fourier scheme for remaking society. The aim was simple: abundance of this world's goods for all. The method, on paper, was equally simple: organize society on a basis of communities in which four or five hundred families live together in a common household and in the common ownership and cultivation of a landed estate. In that way, it was argued, every member of society would eventually have adequate shelter, clothing, and food. Unemploy-ment, poverty, misery, and crime would disappear.

To Horace Greeley the ideas of Fourier came with peculiar timeliness and force, for he was deeply concerned with the miseries of society and

[1] Father of Arthur Brisbane, who in a later day became a national figure as an editorial writer for the Hearst newspaper chain.

their cause. During the panic winter of 1837–38, he had witnessed the sufferings of New York's poor and destitute and had been greatly moved. "Worst to bear of all," he said, "was the pitiful plea of stout, resolute, single young men and women: 'We do not want alms; we are not beggars; we hate to sit here day by day idle and useless; help us to work—we want no other help: why is it that we can have nothing to do?' " It set Greeley to thinking, and out of his thoughts came a series of *New-Yorker* articles that asked: "What shall be done for the laborer?" In such an inquiring mood he welcomed Brisbane and Brisbane's utopian answer.

The two men sat down together, discussed the problem, talked over Fourier and his scheme for associations. The immediate result was the publication in early 1841 of a magazine, the *Future*, dedicated to the propagation of Fourierism. Its life was brief, for the public failed to rally to its support and the New York press attacked bitterly, turning their guns also upon Greeley for his part in it. Raymond, as conservative as a young man could be, thought the *Future* a "stupendous humbug" and ridiculed the whole venture. With all the wisdom and intolerance of twenty-one he asserted: "Some delectable asses here (among whom I am sorry to say is Greeley) have started a plan for reorganizing society—elevating the social condition of the universal dogdom and allowing puppies to hold their proper rank in the scale of being. . . . Brisbane is at the head of it—a flippant, brainless jackanapes—ridden by this one idea of 'elevating folks.' I opine folks will 'elevate' the Old Harry with him. . . . I have had a long talk with him about it. He's a *case*."

Though Raymond described Greeley as a "glorious, jolly fellow in his inner man," he found it difficult to accept what seemed his unconventional philosophy of life. The uncouth figure of the man with his peculiar gait, his half-bald head, his untidy dress that marked him out among a crowd, none of that bothered Raymond. The ideas that flowered in the Greeley brain caused the uneasiness. "Mr. Greeley," Raymond told Marsh, and in a fashion that left no doubt as to the younger man's dissent, "inclines to materialism—and said that he believed the mind to be the *result* of the body! He is also an out-and-out utilitarian and in all his aims seeks only to make the outward condition of his fellows comfortable. He is strongly opposed to all classical studies and values science and, I presume, religion, only so far as they tend to some immediately beneficial result."

The new enthusiasm for Brisbane's Fourierism only bore further witness to the Greeley philosophy that Raymond so deplored and that he felt so damaging to Greeley himself. He is "an able and popular political writer," Raymond said, and again to Marsh, "but by this new alliance he will destroy the only commanding influence which he possesses. I think however his motives are unquestionably good."

While Greeley was interested in reforming society, he was also interested in the immediate changes that might be brought about by the more conventional methods of political parties. Particularly did he hope that the 1840 Whig victory at the polls would usher in a new national era. He had helped his party in the *New-Yorker*'s editorials, and had participated more directly in the struggle for power by editing campaign papers. Now he was prepared to launch a new and cheap Whig daily in New York in an effort to help the cause still further by appealing to the city's laboring classes.

Whig politicians in New York State urged Greeley to undertake the enterprise, and presumably it had the blessing of Thurlow Weed and Governor Seward. Some of these men promised financial aid, but only one actually came forward with a loan—of $1,000. The real burden fell upon Greeley, whose credit was good even if his purse was slender. He planned the paper that he would publish, thought out its policy. "My leading idea," he stated, "was the establishment of a journal removed alike from servile partisanship on the one hand and from gagged, mincing neutrality on the other. Party spirit is so fierce and intolerant in this country that the editor of a non-partisan sheet is restrained from saying what he thinks and feels on the most vital, imminent topics; while, on the other hand, a Democratic [or] Whig . . . journal is generally expected to praise or blame, like or dislike, eulogize or condemn, in precise accordance with the views and interests of its party. I believed there was a happy medium between these extremes—a position from which a journalist might openly and heartily advocate the principles and commend the measures of that party to which his convictions allied him, yet frankly dissent from its course on a particular question, and even denounce its candidates if they were shown to be deficient in capacity or (far worse) in integrity."

The *Tribune* was the name Greeley chose for his new paper. The first issue was scheduled for April 10, 1841, and its appearance was intended to be part of the general Whig triumph signalized by President Harrison's inauguration. Horace Greeley had just passed thirty. His chief assistant on the paper was to be Henry J. Raymond.

CHAPTER

4

The Tribune

I

APRIL 10, 1841, dawned gray and chill. Mingled sleet and snow fell in New York City, where a great funeral pageant was being staged for President William Henry Harrison, six days dead. Mourning crepe masked public buildings and billowed in the wind. Along the waterfront and in the harbor ships flew their flags at half-staff. At noon the city's bells tolled dolefully as a great procession set forth to wind through New York's streets, soldiers and citizens alike participating in a last, sad tribute to the man who had but so recently embodied the hopes of the Whig party. The first number of Horace Greeley's *Tribune* was published on that gloomy, inauspicious day, and the paper that had expected to celebrate Whig triumph joined instead in the general lamentation by turning column rules in the traditional newspaper token of mourning. Beneath the *Tribune*'s masthead appeared the last words of the one-month President: "I desire you to understand the true principles of the government. I wish them carried out. I ask nothing more."

Greeley printed about 5,000 copies of his first issue—approximately 600 subscriptions had been obtained—and remembered afterward that he succeeded in giving away nearly all he could not sell. A well-edited four-page paper, five columns wide, priced at one cent, it featured in this first number political news and literary notices. Advertising was slim. A few booksellers and dry goods merchants had inserted their cards. Pease's Horehound Candy, recommended by preachers for all public speakers and good also for whooping cough, Beal's Hair Restorative, Swan's Atmospheric Soda Fountain (patented)—these and a few others made up the bulk of Greeley's advertising support, paying fifty cents for each insertion of twelve lines or less.

The public bought the new paper, but not in numbers large enough to balance the books. "My current expenses for the first week," Greeley said, "were about five hundred and twenty-five dollars; my receipts ninety-two dollars." The paper had its own type, but no presses, and for outside presswork paid roundly. Greeley and Raymond helped to fold and mail copies to subscribers, thankful that out-of-town circulation was at first small. The beginning was the worst, and with the limited capital available—at no time did Greeley have more than $2,500 leeway—the wonder persists that the *Tribune* did not quickly founder.

Circulation was aided from an unexpected quarter, when the *Sun* sought to choke the rival upstart. *Tribune* distributors were intimidated. Sellers were assaulted, Moses Beach, the *Sun*'s publisher, himself participating in one of these blackguard episodes that came close to being a free-for-all between newsboys of the two papers. The public took up the quarrel, as did other New York journals, until Greeley's *Tribune* had been well advertised. Greeley made the most of the attack editorially. Maybe it did the new paper good, for at the end of seven weeks it could boast, probably with some exaggeration, that it was selling 10,000 copies daily. Advertising also rose; by the hundredth number the four columns of the first copy had become thirteen, and rates had been boosted two cents a line. The *Tribune* showed promise of profit, although Greeley described himself truthfully "as poor as a church mouse and not half as saucy."

The venture might still have failed, for Greeley was never much of a man of business, had it not been possible to announce on July 31, 1841, that henceforth the *Tribune* would be published by the partnership of Greeley and McElrath. Thomas McElrath—he paid $2,000 for a half interest in the paper—assumed "the entire business management of the concern." Greeley retained sole editorial responsibility. The new partner, a lawyer who had been a book publisher, a Whig who had sat in the Assembly, brought with him a sense of order and efficiency, a managerial ability, and a capacity for economy that were entirely foreign to Greeley. Thereafter the *Tribune* prospered, for the two men made an excellent team, so much so that a contemporary exclaimed: "Oh! that every Greeley could find his McElrath! and blessed is the McElrath that finds his Greeley!" Of his partner, Greeley, without full justice, wrote years later in his autobiography: "His business management of the concern, though never brilliant, nor especially energetic, was so safe and judicious that it gave me no trouble, and scarcely required of me a thought." In the business office for a few months McElrath employed a young man named George Jones, who had known Greeley when the two were Vermont boys together. Though nearly ten years older than Raymond, he became Raymond's close friend, a significant friendship that lasted so long as Raymond lived.

The paper that Greeley with Raymond's aid was editing in the clutter of the Ann Street office was a lively, fighting sheet, ready to take on all comers and yet anxious to present the news fairly, completely. It attacked the *Sun* as "slimy and venomous," as "jesuitical and deadly in politics and grovelling in morals." It boasted of scoops and flaunted its accuracy. It urged, demanded, reform of the city's government. It wore the Whig party's emblem on its sleeve the while it insisted on the right to think independently in politics as in all else.

On moral grounds Greeley always took strong stand. He assailed other papers, and here the *Herald* was a principal offender, for publishing the "loathsome details" of murder cases, and though the *Tribune* accepted theatrical advertising, its editor did not hesitate to assert that "each theatre contains within its walls a grog-shop and a place of assignation." When called to account for accepting advertisements of "heretical" books, Greeley retorted: "If any one should offer an advertisement of lewd, ribald, indecent, blasphemous or law-prohibited books, we should claim the right to reject it. But a work no otherwise objectionable than as controverting the Christian record and doctrine would not be objected to by us. True Christianity neither fears refutation nor dreads discussion —or, as Jefferson has forcibly said, 'Error of opinion may be tolerated where Reason is left free to combat it!' "

Greeley, a man of many enthusiasms, often used the *Tribune* as a pulpit from which to proclaim his conversions and to preach social reform. The *Tribune*'s editor advocated prohibition of intoxicating liquor. He opposed capital punishment. He told readers of his own belief in Fourierism, and after March 1, 1842, allowed Brisbane to use the paper's columns to sell utopian socialism. Greeley also espoused the doctrines of Sylvester Graham, who advocated the eating of whole wheat bread, more vegetables, coarse cereals, fruit; the *Tribune* gave considerable space to the Grahamites and the boardinghouses which sprang up as eating places for the believers in this dietary reform. Greeley's interest in these two movements alone caused the *Herald* to call the *Tribune* "the organ of the Fourierites and Squashites."

For all his idiosyncrasies, Greeley tolerated others' opinions and never tried to impose his own views on his assistants or to make them write to suit him. He was a good editor, a good teacher, and to Raymond he could teach much about drawing public attention to the paper and about making the paper interesting in itself. The very fact that many individuals thought the *Tribune* a radical sheet helped to make the paper more prominent, if only by carrying it into further controversy.

II

It was a year and more before the *Tribune* hit full stride, but even in its early months its pages showed the influence of an editor conscious of the need for presenting news ahead of rivals and for telling it with clarity and vigor. Financial and shipping reports were added. Foreign news was neglected, at least in comparison to the space it received in papers like the *Herald*, but domestic news was covered more and more completely as Greeley obtained correspondents in Washington and Albany and Boston. The literary department, which remained Raymond's special preserve, was gradually curtailed, though it continued to be conspicuous both for Raymond's book reviews and for selections from foreign books and periodicals. Carlyle was pirated. So were the poems of Thomas Moore, and the *Tribune* continued Dickens' *Barnaby Rudge*, which the *New-Yorker* had been serializing.

The editors were busy men. Greeley wrote an average of three columns a day, which meant about fifteen pages of foolscap, all in the painful penmanship that only experienced typesetters found legible. In the editorial round of preparing minor notices, reporting, proofreading, editing copy, choosing extracts to be published, rewriting contributions and soliciting others, Raymond was equally industrious. He worked hard and liked what he was doing. Of him Greeley said afterward: "I never found another person, barely of age and just from his studies, who evinced so signal and such versatile ability in journalism as he did. Abler and stronger men I have met; a cleverer, readier, more generally efficient journalist, I never saw. He . . . is the only assistant with whom I ever felt required to remonstrate for doing more work than any human brain and frame could be expected long to endure."

New York was hot and uncomfortable, the first summer of the *Tribune*, but for a few weeks the city tried to maintain its accustomed pace. Fannie Elssler, in temperature that registered ninety degrees, was dancing at the Park Theatre to a house "crowded to suffocation." The Chatham Theatre alleged that its patrons praised the pains it had taken to keep the "establishment cool and comfortable," and Corlis's Bowling Saloon boasted that its rooms were "lofty, cool." On the Fourth of July, steamers packed with passengers cast off for excursions down the bay or up the Hudson, but soon thereafter the weather proved too oppressive for any pretense. The "scorching season," it was called, and the *Herald* in a summing up of misery said, "More flies than rascals infest the city." One by one the theaters closed as New Yorkers sought relief at New Brighton and Rockaway, at boarding places along the Bloomingdale Road in upper Manhattan, in the Catskills, or at more distant Saratoga. Fannie Elssler fled to Coney Island for the "luxury of sea bathing."

It was a dull time for the newspapers, although Madame Restell, already building a reputation as an abortionist and as the "wickedest woman" in town, was convicted of a "flagrant misdemeanor committed in the prosecution of her infernal trade." The *Herald* sent a reporter to Jersey City to describe the steam frigate *Kamchatka* that was building for the Russian Czar. Greeley had the problem of a new press on his hands, a balky press that broke down when first installed, delayed his editions, and only gradually began to run off its regular 3,500 copies an hour in time for the carriers to start their rounds at six in the morning.

In mid-July Greeley sent Raymond by steamboat and steam cars to Utica for his first major independent reporting. The Supreme Court of the State was to hand down a decision in the case of Alexander McLeod, a Canadian who had boasted too loudly in an upstate saloon that in the Canadian rebellion of 1837 he had killed Amos Durfree, an American, during a shooting affray on the American side of Niagara. New York authorities had arrested McLeod and prepared to try him for murder. At that point the case developed international complications, for Great Britain, arguing that McLeod had shot Durfree, presumably a gunrunner, in "an act of public duty," demanded his release. On both sides of the Atlantic passions thereupon began to mount, for though the State Department at Washington may have wished to set McLeod free, the sovereign State of New York had sentiments quite otherwise.

In Utica that summer the United States District Attorney was seeking a writ of habeas corpus for McLeod. New York's Attorney General was resisting the petition, and to learn how the Supreme Court would rule Raymond had, as Greeley put it, "gone up the river." He represented both the *Tribune* and the *Courier and Enquirer*, and it was announced that he would "report the Opinions of the Judges" and "return with them to this City as fast as steam can bring him." Plans went awry, for the New York *American* had arranged for a special train from which Raymond with his dispatch was barred. Thus rivals reached New York first, and what could have been a scoop ended in failure and disappointment, although Raymond's careful extracts from the court's opinions—they ran to three columns—told *Tribune* readers belatedly that McLeod would have to stand trial, the wishes of the State Department and Whitehall to the contrary notwithstanding.

Soon thereafter Raymond slipped away from New York on vacation; his substitute Greeley described as "awful." "It gives me a tooth-ache to look at him, let alone anything further." But Raymond meantime was enjoying himself, for his holiday gave him the opportunity, by way of Saratoga, Lake George, and Lake Champlain, to return to Burlington for commencement. He spent several days in familiar surroundings, visited his former teachers, climbed Mount Mansfield, and then by boat and stage traveled westward across New York State to the farm at Lima. Of what he saw and did he told Greeley in long, stilted letters, letters that when published betrayed their author's study of the eighteenth century essayists and his own unformed style.

"Most Worthy Editor," he wrote from Burlington in one of them, "thoroughly sick of the heat, the excitement, and I must confess the labor of the great city during the season when the dog-star rages, I have sought and found relief in flight. . . . In the glorious summer-time, when all-embracing, life-awaking Nature had spread her mantle of beauty over all the earth, it is no time for man to cower in his closet, to shut his eyes to the delightful sounds that everywhere go up like an all-harmonious hymn, to the smiling, listening heavens above."

Three letters of this sort found place in the *Tribune*, and by the time the last had appeared Raymond was back in New York to aid, as he put it, at the "funeral ceremonies" of the *New-Yorker*. It was merged with the *Weekly Tribune*, that was destined to far greater circulation and influence than the daily editions ever knew, that was read across the country, in villages and small towns, by farmers and shopkeepers and workingmen. A century later a historian could say that "it was the *Weekly Tribune* which made the name of Horace Greeley a household word throughout the nation."

III

Raymond settled again into office routine, though the chances are he was somewhat restless, for the visit to Burlington had reawakened the old thoughts of a profession. Besides, Greeley was paying him only $15 weekly; to an ambitious young man pushing toward his twenty-second birthday that was not enough.

One stormy night that autumn, a night when the wind tossed fallen leaves and street debris about and drove the rain in sheets before it, Raymond climbed the stairs to the *Tribune*'s office to write a story for the morning edition. He was drenched, chilled, cold, but for a long while he sat in wet clothes while his pen moved rapidly across the pages. At last the final sheet had gone to the composing room. The night's work was done, but for Raymond the reward was a burning fever that for days kept him, almost unattended, in his bare room at the Vesey Street boardinghouse. Not even Greeley sought him out at first, and the *Tribune* halted his wages, an unhappy incident that rankled in Raymond's heart forever.

"Raymond is still down on his luck," Greeley wrote Rufus Griswold early in November. "I fear he will never be well. We apprehend he has bronchitis tending to consumption." But not long afterward Raymond was able to send Griswold the cheering message: "I'm getting well fast, and shall soon be able to take my seat in the office again." Before returning, he told Greeley bluntly that he would never work again for the *Tribune* at his former salary. Though Greeley gave Raymond $5.00 more a week, his assistant editor was now under pressure to turn his steps from journalism.

While Raymond had been ill, he had been visited by George Perkins Marsh, an erudite Burlington lawyer and student of Scandinavian tongues who was a cousin of Raymond's favorite university professor. Marsh, twice the younger man's age, urged upon him the wisdom of some other career, and what he urged in the sick room he reinforced soon after by letter. "I trust," Marsh wrote him, "you will not impute my addressing you again on the subject to an officious desire to offer advice where it is not needed." The subject Marsh stated clearly. "I fear," he wrote, "you are in a way to injure your constitution irreparably, and what is at your time of life an equally deplorable evil, that your present occupation is one which to say the least is unfavorable to intellectual improvement."

As an alternative to the *Tribune*, Marsh advocated teaching, and to make the alternative more attractive he sent Raymond a note of introduction to one of the Green sisters, who conducted an exclusive private school for girls on lower Fifth Avenue. The school was a severe, puritanical sort of place, its atmosphere made the more severe by the Quaker-like dress of the Misses Green, who were averse to jewelry and addicted to heel-less shoes. Men and women of some distinction served at one time or another on the faculty. At the moment the school needed a teacher of Latin, and Marsh pleaded with Raymond: "If the state of your health or any other reason induces you to entertain a proposal for engaging in instruction, I can assure you that this opportunity is well worth your attention. . . . I have reason to think that by spending a few hours a day in Miss Green's and other respectable schools, you may secure a very handsome income, without interfering with professional or other studies, and that the situation might lead to many valuable acquaintances, and to social advantages which otherwise are not easy of attainment to a stranger."

Raymond found the argument hard to answer, and was perhaps persuaded the easier by the additional income that part-time teaching promised. Without quitting the *Tribune,* he began teaching Latin conjugations and declensions to the young ladies at Miss Green's, and though it might have seemed that his time was filled, he still had some to spare. Before long he added the "professional studies" that his friend from Burlington had recommended. He began the study of law in a Wall Street office.

IV

The winter that year, as in many years before and after, filled the city with lecturers who attracted both followers of fashion and seekers of self-improvement. The New York Lyceum announced a program on which seventeen lecturers would appear. The Mercantile Library arranged for fourteen, the New York Historical Society listed ten, and this was but a beginning of lecture series that covered history, science, philosophy, religion, literature, phrenology, and many subjects more. It was a form of entertainment and instruction that appealed to Greeley. He praised the "System of Oral Lectures, which the distinguished and the learned men of our country are annually called to our city to deliver before the young and the old of both sexes, to audiences perhaps on the whole the most interesting and enlightened for their numbers ever addressed in any age or country." All New York papers reported lectures, but Greeley sought to give the *Tribune* preeminence in the field. He made the task Raymond's particular assignment.

Raymond, who knew no regular shorthand, devised a system of his own that, aided by keen memory, enabled him after a lecture to write with amazing accuracy a transcript of what had been said. His first important assignment was a lecture course delivered by Dr. Dionysius Lardner, Fellow of the Royal Society, former professor of natural philosophy and astronomy at London University. An Irishman, a brilliant popularizer of science, he had eloped in 1840 with the wife of a captain in the British Army, and while the husband was suing him for seduction, had crossed to the New World, where over a period of years his lectures earned him something like $200,000.

For the first Lardner lecture of the 1841 season New Yorkers crowded on a November evening into Clinton Hall, where in the small, poorly ventilated lecture room—its windows were always tightly shut—the air and heat often became so oppressive that "the fainting of one or more ladies was the result." Single tickets cost fifty cents, but for a dollar a gentleman could attend accompanied by two ladies, there to hear the learned doctor, who knew the art of dramatization, present scientific subjects in a manner laymen found fascinating. At his first lecture the model of a steam engine was exhibited to an audience that filled all seats, the aisles, and the galleries. Electricity, light, sound, navigation and, in particular, the solar system were among the wonders Dr. Lardner stood ready to explain until a high point was reached with the display of a primitive sort of planetarium, a moving panorama 150 feet long, 20 feet high, on which were shown 40,000 stars.

Two or three times a week for several weeks Dr. Lardner stepped forth upon the platform, and each time what he said was later laid in faithful fullness before the *Tribune*'s readers. Frequently Raymond's reports required an entire page. When Dr. Lardner had done, the *Tribune* reprinted the lectures in pamphlet form, prefacing them with the statement that Raymond had regularly reported them "with a fidelity and ability which elicited the warm commendation of the Lecturer as well as the Public."

There were other scientific lecturers, and geologists seemed the most numerous. Benjamin Silliman came down from New Haven to talk on the earth's structure, and Professor Edward Hitchcock of Amherst contributed of his geological knowledge. Greatest of them all was Sir Charles Lyell. His lectures, like the Lardner series, were reprinted as a pamphlet, and again Raymond was cited as the reporter whose accounts of "other Scientific Lectures have already been received with decided and merited approbation."

For Horace Greeley, with his philosophical sympathy for Massachusetts liberals and transcendentalists, probably the most important lectures of the winter were those delivered by Ralph Waldo Emerson, whom he now met for the first time. Greeley took Emerson to dinner at a Graham boardinghouse—and Brisbane went along, promising to explain the principles of Fourier. "*Il faut soumettre*," Emerson commented. He sent back to Concord a description of his editorial host: "Greeley is a young man with white soft hair . . . of sanguine temper and liberal mind, no scholar but such a one as journals and newspapers make, who listens after all new thoughts and things but with the indispensable New York condition that they be made available."

Raymond had little of Greeley's enthusiasm for Concord philosophy, and he wrote privately: "Emerson commences his Lectures here tomorrow evening [March 5, 1842] and it would not answer . . . for the 'Transcendental Organ' to neglect even the first syllable that may fall from his oracular lips." For six evenings Emerson spoke at the Society Library. "We had a pretty good company," Emerson said, "some few ardent hearers, a good many willing ones." It was an audience that listened sometimes with difficulty because the hall, like so many others, was overheated and smelly; one *Tribune* reader, irate at what he had endured, wrote Greeley: "I thought less of the lecture than I did of nitrogen, carbonic acid, cigars, snuff, onions and rotten teeth." In such an atmosphere

Raymond listened and took his notes, but his reports were sketchy and it was not one of his finest hours.

"Take good care of the Lectures and the Lecturers," Greeley once wrote Raymond when he left his assistant to run the paper, "and give an account of each so far as you can." But Raymond, despite his zeal for education, came to doubt the value of the lecture institution. He attacked the theatricality used to hold audiences. He asserted that lecture education gave the illusion of knowledge without the fact. Mental discipline, he charged, was ignored the while "vanity is fed, true worth disparaged and the relations of the highest intellectual culture to the wants of Society distorted and banished from the thought." Perhaps he agreed with Martin Chuzzlewit, who ridiculed the interest of New York women in lectures that ranged from "the philosophy of the soul" to "the philosophy of vegetables."

Most New Yorkers, of course, seldom fixed their full attention on the philosophy of anything, and even some who did were diverted in January, 1842, by a gruesome murder trial. The murder had occurred the previous September when the victim, a printer named Samuel Adams, had gone to the rooms of John C. Colt, a teacher of bookkeeping and brother of the inventor of the Colt revolver. There had been a quarrel over debts. Adams was never seen alive again, but his battered body, jammed into a packing box, was found later aboard a ship about to sail for New Orleans. Colt's arrest followed.

The case excited the public from the first, and it eventually provided the city with its most celebrated murder trial in several years. The *Herald* had made itself notorious, and famous too, in an earlier murder case, and the New York press had taken a leaf from Bennett's book on how to report a crime. Even Greeley, who had attacked the *Herald* many times for its concern with matters criminal, could not miss this opportunity to build circulation. He sent Raymond to report the trial.

On the opening day the prisoner was naturally the center of attraction. "He was without gloves," Raymond told *Tribune* readers, "was dressed in a frock coat of blue beaver cloth with a velvet collar, his hair was well brushed, his whiskers were neatly trimmed and he appears to have suffered scarcely at all either from his confinement or from the reflections his condition must naturally awake within his breast." The prisoner sat with his back to the spectators during the first long day while a jury was being chosen and, according to the *Herald*'s reporter, read the *Sun* and the *Herald*.

Not even the rigors of one of New York's coldest winter spells kept the crowds from City Hall Park and the courtroom. The rather callow Raymond, moralizing, explained the general interest. "The whole community," he said, "seems to have been suddenly aroused from a sleep of fancied security and repose, to a dread conviction that the security of human life is destroyed, the safety and even existence of social order and harmony put in fearful jeopardy and all the elements of discord and hate let loose to prey upon the vitals of the body politic."

The victim's widow, "dressed in deep mourning, with a small black bonnet and veil," was a constant court attendant, arriving usually on the protecting arm of her father. "An exceedingly interesting lady in her appearance," thought Raymond, while noting "a sad, mournful countenance, expressive of her deep affliction." Colt's mistress, a Miss Henshaw, was occasionally present, "dressed in a drab mantle." Raymond found her "good-looking but far from being beautiful." Samuel Colt, the inventor-brother, was usually in the courtroom to hear witness after witness tell of what he had seen, until it seemed that half New York had been peeking through Colt's keyhole on the fatal afternoon. Finally, as an exhibit the like of which had been seldom seen in a New York court, Adams' exhumed skull, "horribly mangled," was "placed upon the corner of the judgement seat." After ten days, Colt was found guilty, and sentenced to be hanged.

The New York press had missed little. Every day the *Tribune* had issued two extras with Raymond's practically verbatim account of the proceedings, prefaced always by a few paragraphs that described the courtroom atmosphere, the defendant's appearance, the chief witnesses. Column after column, sometimes six columns in a single day, the story was one that would have done credit to a court stenographer. Thomas McElrath, with an eye always on the business office, remembered a quarter century later how Raymond's reports had boosted *Tribune* circulation. The reports were not alone responsible, for other papers were doing their utmost to give readers a full, colorful account of the trial. The *Tribune*'s real strength lay in the speed with which it brought Raymond's stories to its readers.

Greeley, complaining that he had had "no rest day or night while that everlasting Colt trial was in progress," left Raymond in charge the final day when Ann Street before the *Tribune* office was packed with newsboys, clamoring for extras. Afterward, the *Tribune* boasted that time and again it had scooped the *Herald* and, what was even better, had left the *Sun* far behind.

V

By the time the *Tribune* reached its first anniversary, Greeley had got his paper well on its way. Meanwhile, the Whig victory, which the *Tribune*'s founding had symbolized, had turned to ashes in the party's mouth. The death of President Harrison had been tragedy enough. The accession of John Tyler as President made the tragedy doubly hard for Whigs to bear, for "His Accidency" had almost immediately abandoned the principles of the party that had brought him to the White House. He vetoed measures providing government funds for internal improvements. He opposed and vetoed bills that would have reestablished a Bank of the United States like the one President Jackson had destroyed. Veto of the bank bills—Henry Clay had been their chief author—ended Whig support of Tyler when he had been President only five months. His Cabinet, except for Secretary of State Daniel Webster, resigned, and Whigs, led by Clay, began to look to the next Presidential election.

The *Tribune* reflected the bitter Whig disappointment, although Greeley was slow to break completely with the President. "Don't be Tyler or anti-Tyler," he urged Raymond in February, 1842, when the latter was briefly directing the paper. Yet prolonged forbearance was not a Greeley trait, and before long the banner of Henry Clay was flying at the *Tribune*'s masthead. Greeley and Raymond alike did all they could to insure well in advance that 1844 would be a Clay year. Raymond wrote a brief sketch of Clay for Greeley's *Whig Almanac and Politicians' Register*, and then went to work expanding it into a full-length memoir. "It has been written in haste and 'to order,' " Raymond told Griswold when the book's 198 pages were finished, "but it has merits of impartiality, of better method, etc., which previous biographies have lacked." As a matter of fact, Raymond's life of Clay was undistinguished potboiling, but it had considerable circulation and certainly did not lessen the young editor's reputation.

Among Whigs Daniel Webster's persistence in remaining in the Tyler Cabinet was a source of constant concern and inquiry, the party waiting impatiently for the day the Massachusetts leader would explain himself. That day came on September 30, 1842, in the historic precincts of Boston's Faneuil Hall. The *Herald* had reporters on hand, and boasted in advance that it would publish the speech ahead of all other papers and in fuller form. The *Sun* was represented. Greeley sent Raymond for the *Tribune*, remarking that while it might not be the first to publish the great orator's speech, it hoped to have the best account.

A defiant Webster faced his audience that September morning. In a speech that had kind words for President Tyler, that appealed for "more moderation of party feeling," there were phrases in which Webster dared the Whigs to read him out of the party. "I will give no pledges, I make no intimations, one way or the other," he challenged. "I am a Whig. I have always been a Whig, and I always will be one."

The address set off an explosion among Whigs and a controversy between the *Tribune* and the *Herald*. Raymond's report of what Webster had said was on New York's streets by seven o'clock the morning after the Faneuil Hall meeting, hardly a half-hour after it had arrived on the Boston boat and fully two hours before the *Herald*'s account was laid before the city's readers. Tradition has it that Raymond wrote out his notes on shipboard, that on board also were printers and type cases, with the result that the words of Webster were in type and ready for the press when the Boston boat docked.

The *Herald*, unaccustomed to being scooped, perhaps indignant the more because it had scoffed that the *Tribune* lacked the intellect and talent "capable of doing justice to such an enterprise," could only charge that Raymond's report was "most shockingly garbled," and gibe that he lacked all knowledge of stenography. "Who after reading the miserable rubbish placed in the mouth of Mr. Webster," it asked, "would ever place any slightest dependence on any report that appeared in the *Tribune* again?" Raymond had his reply: that actually it was the *Herald*'s report that was garbled, that in addition its report had been filled with inaccurate Latin phrases which Webster would never have uttered.

The storm died away, for the public after all was chiefly concerned with getting the news and getting it quick. The *Tribune*, thanks to Raymond, had met that test and with Webster's speeches would do it again.

The next opportunity came in May, 1843, a few days after Webster had finally resigned as Secretary of State. A public dinner was being given for him at the Exchange Hotel in Baltimore, and it was known that he would speak. All the politically minded were anxious to learn his thoughts, for he was regarded by many as a political renegade confronted with the question: "Where am I to go?"

The *Tribune*, eager to publish "not only the *earliest* but the most *authentic* and *accurate* report of this Speech," sent Raymond, "long proved and well known to be the best Reporter in the State," to cover the dinner and arranged for "a special express run upon the railroad and exclusively for the New York *Tribune*." When Raymond reached Baltimore, he found that the *Herald*'s reporters, advertised as an "unequalled corps," were there ahead of him. That made the prospect dark. Besides, Webster at first was unwilling that the press should attend the dinner or listen to his speech. Afterward, the rival New York papers disputed the honor of breaking down Webster's unaccustomed reserve, but the *Tribune* always insisted that to Raymond's diplomacy and tact was due the ultimate invitation to attend.

It was a small dinner—about 100 were present—that began at six-thirty in the evening. A band played patriotic airs. There were suitable toasts, and at exactly nine twenty-two by Raymond's watch, Webster began to speak. He finished about eleven. Raymond wrote triumphantly at the close of his report: "Mr. Webster here sat down amid tremendous cheers: the band struck up a lively air and we left the room to start by Express, with our notes, for New York—leaving the 'unequalled corpse' of *Herald* reporters at the table, unable, for some reason to us unknown, to depart from the Monumental City till next morning."

The speech in itself was hardly notable, for Webster had left unsaid much that Whigs had wanted to hear, confining himself principally to the possibilities of reciprocal trade, notably with England. Such ideas outraged not only Greeley but the merchant Whigs of New York. For whatever it was worth, the speech was rushed to the public in a *Tribune* extra the following afternoon. The *Herald*'s account did not appear until fifteen hours later. Both reports ran about five columns and a half, but as on other occasions the *Herald* denounced the *Tribune* for what it called a "meagre outline" and described Raymond patronizingly as a "very decent lad."

Once more in 1843 Raymond did his utmost to give *Tribune* readers a detailed account of a Webster speech. In September the former Secretary of State left his beloved Marshfield to attend the New York State Agricultural Fair at Rochester, where a notable group of statesmen had come together. Present were former President Van Buren—at one of the exhibits he was given a newly patented claw hammer—and former Governor Seward. Governor Bouck of New York joined the group. Around the booths with their displays of tools, worsted work, paintings, and livestock milled 20,000 persons. There were plowing matches, and at one of them Webster was seen eating an "indifferent peach."

For his story Raymond traveled long, tedious miles. Low water and fog delayed the steamer to Albany so that he missed his train, and when he finally did set out, it was for thirty hours of railway torture, twelve hours more than the advertised time. "Many of the passengers walked part of the way," he said, "and easily kept pace with the cars." But he arrived in time for the chief events and particularly for a dinner given Webster in Smith's Dining Saloon, an affair postponed from afternoon to evening because Webster had been indisposed; indisposition, friends noted, was occurring more frequently than formerly, for he was drinking heavily. Though Webster that night of conviviality and at other times during the fair had little of real moment to say, his words were followed so closely by Whigs that Raymond thought them worth while to report in detail. The description of the fair and the digests of the speeches filled over seven of the *Tribune*'s columns one day and ran to another column and a half the next. The *Herald* did not compete.

VI

Raymond now had been with Greeley nearly three busy, eventful years. The *Tribune*, its Ann Street quarters outgrown, had moved to 160 Nassau Street, its address for so long as Raymond and Greeley lived, where the offices looked out upon City Hall Park and the magnificent new fountain made possible by the arrival of Croton water in lower Manhattan. Across the park on spring nights a band played on the balcony of Barnum's Museum and music reached even Greeley's top-floor office, where the dust gathered on his great desk, on his battered dictionary and the accumulating piles of correspondence. The *Tribune*'s assistant editor had begun as a journalistic stripling. Now he was an aggressive reporter with a reputation to defend; his editorial experience was swelling. He had traveled also, for vacations allowed him not only a chance to return to Burlington—in 1843 he had received a master's degree from the university—but to become better acquainted with the social life at Saratoga and as a tourist to push on to Montreal and Quebec.

As Raymond matured, Greeley spent more and more time away from New York, leaving his assistant to conduct the *Tribune*. He did not always approve of what happened in his absence. A notable instance had occurred in December, 1842, when the United States brig *Somers*, heavily guarded, put into the Navy Yard at Wallabout Bay. Its story was soon public, how an alleged mutiny led by Midshipman Philip Spencer, son of the Secretary of War, had threatened the vessel on the high seas, how the commander, Alexander Slidell Mackenzie, had executed Spencer and two other seamen. A sensational story, the more because of the political prominence of young Spencer's father, it filled many columns in the New York press, which made the most of the mutiny, the subsequent hearings, the court-martial, and Mackenzie's acquittal.

Raymond supported the unhappy commander of the *Somers*—many editors did not—and denounced those who "shed profuse and most pitying tears over the fate of every incarnate devil who suffers at the hand of Justice." So strong were the opinions he expressed that Greeley, when back at the office, felt called to explain that the stand was not his and that it did not indicate abandonment of his often proclaimed opposition to capital punishment. Greeley did not disown Raymond, declaring rather that the assistant editor had a right to set forth his own views whatever they might be. As for Greeley himself, this remained his position: "I would hold the criminal at large as one at war with Society, but I do not hold with killing or torturing prisoners of war."

Often when Greeley was out of town, he sent Raymond letters of instruction, rebuke, and advice. "Don't quarrel with anybody, nor entangle us in any way," he once warned. "If we are set upon, calmly state any facts needful to our justification." In the fall of 1842, when he was in Utica to report the verdict that acquitted McLeod and ended Anglo-American tension over the affair, he dispatched to Raymond warning and advice. "The infernal *Sun*," he said, "will probably get the verdict in time to send it through Express to Albany, and get it at New York on Tuesday night; if so, you must find out what it is that night *any how;* have a spy out and be careful that you are not cheated. If you don't get it then, have a man at the boat Wednesday, running your paper rather late, and some one to stick the verdict into the form five minutes after the boat lands.— We must be sensible."

"Don't think I won't growl at blunders in the paper, for I will," he wrote Raymond when listing mistakes and failings. "You make some errors because your heart is not in the business. No man can be an A-1 editor (or anything else) who does not regard that as the highest thing— to whom it is not a delight and a sceptre but a recourse. Here you come short. Curse Blackstone and fortune and office! What are they to 100,000 confiding readers! Then you are infernally Tory in your leanings, both in Church and State, and will cut me off, if you are not careful, from the sympathies of the true democracy . . . with whom I belong."

Letters like that helped to make Raymond cautious and careful, made him think more of editorial responsibility. He learned the need for initiative and alertness. He developed a sense of news value. He came to appreciate the power of simple, direct prose, and his own writing lost much of its roughness and imitative quality. He turned his back on Blackstone and the law. But Raymond never found it easy to accept Greeley's reformist zeal or the reforms which that zeal led the older man to adopt and propound. Tory, Raymond's leanings might be, but, so he believed, they were far safer, if the paper's welfare was concerned, than Greeley's radicalism.

Raymond had a more immediate complaint than philosophical disagreement. Greeley had never been willing to pay his assistant what the younger man thought he was worth, and that fact led to a crisis in their relations in October, 1843, when the *Courier and Enquirer* offered Raymond an editorship. Taken together, place and salary were not much superior to what he had on the *Tribune*, but the *Courier* would pay him $25 weekly to the *Tribune*'s $20. When Greeley refused him more, the two men parted. "It was a pity the *Tribune* let him go," a contemporary said a few years afterward. "It lost more than it had the slightest idea of."

Raymond and Greeley disagreed often and publicly as they grew older, but for the moment they remained friends, and on October 16, 1843, Greeley in the *Tribune* published a farewell paragraph of tribute:

Mr. Henry J. Raymond, who has, from its commencement, been connected with the *Tribune* as Assistant Editor, has relinquished his position, in view of entering upon another sphere of usefulness. We could not be satisfied to part without publicly testifying the esteem for him which our long intimacy has inspired, and acknowledging the obligation which his faithful and efficient services have imposed on us. As a reporter and Critic, he has hardly a superior in the Editorial ranks, while in the more general details of the profession his industry and tact are most creditable.—We hardly need add that our fervent wishes attend him on his future career.

5

The Courier and Enquirer

I

JAMES WATSON WEBB, editor and chief owner of the *Morning Courier and New York Enquirer,* had been for fourteen years, when Raymond joined his staff in 1843, one of the most colorful figures in New York newspaperdom. A tall, handsome, massive sort of man, a striking figure in any company, he had been called the "Apollo of the press." In his youth, he had fought Indians—his father had been an aide to Washington—and most of his life he answered to a military title, lieutenant, colonel, and ultimately general. Bennett, who had been his partner, described him as "a frank, manly blackguard, a fine-looking, burly, honest kind of savage," and admitted that in private life Webb was a gentleman. Webb characterized himself as "the best abused personage connected with the American press."

The abuse arose in part from Webb's ability to make himself a storm center. Toward rival editors he knew how to use vituperation, and with many of them, Horace Greeley in particular, he quarreled constantly. Webb was impulsive, excitable, and quick to challenge an affront, real or imaginary. Twice he caned Bennett on the street. On the steps of the United States Capitol he once threatened a Washington editor with both cane and pistol. When the Maine Congressman Jonathan Cilley attacked Webb's character on the floor of the House, the New York editor demanded personal satisfaction. It was refused, though Cilley did fight Webb's second and paid for his rashness with his life. In 1842, Webb, after being wounded in a duel with another Congressman, was arrested under New York's anti-dueling law, and only Governor Seward's pardon saved him from Sing Sing.

"Principles, not Men" was the *Courier and Enquirer*'s motto, and Webb followed it at the sacrifice of party regularity. He had begun his career as a Jacksonian Democrat, but turned Whig when Jackson warred upon the Bank of the United States, to which, so Bennett said, Webb was heavily indebted. As a Whig he adhered to the party's conservative wing while refusing on occasion to support the Whig ticket when it did not represent his views of sound policy. Yet among Whigs this "filibusterer general," as he was dubbed, attained a good deal of influence, exercising it usually from behind the arras, and his paper rose to leadership among the party's New York organs.

The *Morning Courier and New York Enquirer*, published in Wall Street, was a Wall Street paper. It catered to mercantile interests, to finance, and to shipping, and editorially it voiced the conservative views of the merchant class. On the tariff, for example, the *Courier* argued for duties that would protect but would not shut off the imports that were valued as the very lifeblood of downtown New York with its shipping and its trade.

At the *Courier*'s masthead appeared the legend, "By J. Watson Webb," and though the words were misleading, they told that the *Courier* was definitely Webb's paper. When eventually he disposed of the property after years of ownership, he asserted, with considerable exaggeration, to be sure, that he had always been "the sole and only responsible editor." Part owners and assistants helped briefly to shape the paper's course, yet Webb usually had the final word and seldom hesitated to speak it. Aggressive and combative by nature, he bestowed these qualities on his editorship, ever seeking to best rivals in the printing of fresh news and ever ready to spend money freely if it would redound to the *Courier*'s profit. When still young in his editorship, he owned three fast pilot boats that cruised sometimes a hundred miles to sea in order to pick up the European mails and papers from incoming packets. With the *Journal of Commerce* he organized one winter a pony express that daily brought to New York from Washington reports of the sessions of Congress. Such enterprise paid dividends, yet Webb, for all his efforts to obtain scoops, never succeeded in making the *Courier* a lively or human sheet, although his annual reprinting at Christmas of Clement Moore's "A Visit from St. Nicholas" half suggested that he wanted to lighten his paper's heaviness.

The rise of the penny press—the *Sun*, Bennett's *Herald*, Greeley's *Tribune*—made the *Courier* seem more dull and stodgy. Into their four-page issues the penny papers managed somehow to pack a quantity of interesting news, and while often, especially in the *Herald*, it was sordid stuff, many times it was the same news that the *Courier* published but was told better and with more attention to colorful and exciting detail. The *Herald* did more with foreign news than the *Courier*, just as the *Tribune* did more than the *Courier* in covering the news of the nation. The *Herald* had begun to illustrate with woodcuts, but the *Courier* long hesitated to follow the example.

Webb of course appealed to a far different readership than the penny papers, for his six-cent *Courier*, with its emphasis on commerce, did not sell widely among the masses, and he apparently long felt it unnecessary to alter the fixed style of the *Courier*, possibly arguing that its conservative merchant audience would not take kindly to innovation. At the time Raymond joined the *Courier* its circulation was estimated at about 7,000; the same estimate gave the *Sun* 20,000, the *Herald* 15,000, the *Tribune* 9,500. Circulation did not tell the whole story, for the *Courier* was an exceedingly profitable enterprise. Advertising supplied the profits. The paper's advertisements, extensive and diversified, served both as a business directory for the merchant and as a guide for the citizens seeking almost anything from a new dwelling to a new stove. To some extent, the *Courier*'s advertising supplemented for readers its columns of shipping news, of stock exchange and foreign market reports, or its listing of bank note values at a time when notes fluctuated in exchange and discount was common.

The *Courier*'s extreme size—Bennett had coined the term "blanket sheet"—gave abundant space for advertisements. In 1843 a *Courier* page measured twenty-three inches by twenty-eight and a half, and contained nine columns. In the same period a *Tribune* page, carrying six columns, measured eight inches less in both length and breadth. But the comparison does not end there. Of the *Courier*'s over-all total of thirty-six columns, as many as twenty-eight were often devoted to advertisements. The *Tribune* counted itself lucky if advertising filled fourteen of its shorter twenty-four columns.

II

Such was the prosperous *Courier and Enquirer* to which Raymond shifted his allegiance in October, 1843. Before beginning his new work in Wall Street among the banks, insurance companies, brokerage houses, and lawyers' offices that lined the narrow way from half-finished Trinity Church to the East River docks, he had to attend to some personal business in Vermont. It took him north to Burlington. The sentiment that had drawn him there annually since graduation from the university had not been wholly love of alma mater. In the near-by village of Winooski, he had visited often as a student the farmstead of John Warren Weaver, to whose daughter Juliette he had become betrothed. On a late October evening that fall of 1843 they were married. Ahead for them both lay happiness and sorrow and storm, until in the end they were almost strangers one to the other. All that was distant. At the moment they were youthful—Raymond was not yet twenty-four, his bride was more than two years younger—and they faced the future together filled with confidence and hope. Juliette Raymond, strong-willed, religious, and a good deal of the puritan, possessed both brilliance and beauty, and as she took up what was to be an extraordinarily long lifetime of New York residence she shared her husband's ambition to make the world his own.[1]

The young couple had only a brief honeymoon, and, back in New York, turned to a boardinghouse, perhaps such as that kept by Mrs. Pawkins with its "dreary waste of dining table," its "bewildering collection of cane-bottomed chairs," its guests who ate rapidly and well "as if a famine were expected to set in before breakfast time." Boardinghouse life was always a New York characteristic. It was natural for a young couple to accept it and to postpone the responsibilities of a household.

Raymond, taking his place in the *Courier* office, found the prevailing atmosphere much more worldly than that of the *Tribune,* meeting place for reformers and literary pretenders as well as politicians. There was not much room at the *Courier* for reformers of any sort, and however ready a welcome may have regularly awaited politicians, the paper's cavalier treatment of literary news testified to its lack of interest in those who dedicated themselves to the arts. On matters political Raymond was made to feel quite at home, for his first major assignment was reporting a Daniel Webster speech.

The *Courier* had been seeking to mend the rents in the Whig party fabric, and especially had it sought to reconcile Webster and Clay, something that no longer appeared difficult now that Webster had left the Tyler Cabinet and presumably repented his apostasy. An address that Webster was to make at Andover, Massachusetts, was expected to indicate where the elder statesman stood in regard to party principles. The *Courier* and the *Tribune* pooled their resources and sent Raymond north to Andover. He stayed overnight at the Tremont House in Boston, and then in the cold, bleak morning of a November day journeyed to the academic village where thousands of Whigs—Raymond put the total at 6,000—were gathering to listen to Webster's message. A natural amphitheater in a grove outside the village had been chosen for the rally. Surrounding pines and hemlocks sheltered listeners from a raw north wind

---

[1] She died in New York City on October 13, 1914, aged ninety-two.

as they stamped their feet in straw spread over partly frozen ground. Webster, half ill with a heavy cold, forgot his illness and his sixty years when the cheering sprang upon the air. Hatless, dressed in the famous blue coat with brass buttons, he stood forth to pledge allegiance to the principles of Whiggery and to defend himself against the critics of his service under President Tyler. "I am a Whig," he asserted in loud tones, and when his hour and a half of speaking was done, there was no question but that Daniel Webster had returned to his party and that his return was likely to mean much in the Presidential campaign looming ahead. Raymond, with his notes and his memory of the afternoon, took an express for Boston, caught another train for Norwich, Connecticut, and there boarded a steamer that brought him to New York in time for the *Courier*'s evening edition next day.

Following this out-of-town excursion, Raymond settled into the anonymity that usually surrounds editorial assistants. A daguerreotype shows him as still almost boyish in appearance, though carefully trimmed brown whiskers, shadowing his cheeks and chin, gave him a dignity to which a stock about his throat further contributed. This young man presumably had his hands full in the daily work of getting out a paper, of writing its brief local stories and selecting the extracts from out-of-town papers. He must also have aided in preparing stock exchange reports and shipping news. Possibly also he wrote occasional editorials, but it is impossible at this period to define his exact place in the *Courier* scheme of things. Equally difficult is it to define the influence he exerted, and it may have been only coincidence that soon after he joined the *Courier*'s staff the paper's contents and make-up began to change. The news seemed less hit-or-miss and was better presented. It was obvious that books, lectures and public meetings were receiving increased attention. When Colonel Webb sailed for Europe in the spring of 1844 to arrange for London and Paris correspondents, he probably left open the way for Raymond to have much more of a part in shaping the *Courier*, but again that part cannot be fixed.

III

Eighteen forty-four was a political year, and at Baltimore at the beginning of May the Whigs, confident again of victory, chose Henry Clay as their Presidential candidate, an event reported to Washington by the first news dispatch ever telegraphed, though Washington papers, rather than printing the telegram's contents, awaited the mails and the return of reporters. Whigs entered upon the campaign with assuredness made greater by the relative obscurity of the Democratic nominee, James K. Polk of Tennessee.

Polk and the Democrats were advocating eagerly and vigorously the annexation of Texas, which would enlarge both the Union and the territory open to slavery. Clay before his nomination had straddled the dangerous Texas issue, made the more dangerous because Northern Whigs were steadily resisting slavery's extension, and announced opposition to annexation "at the present time." He altered his position slightly when the campaign's progress demonstrated that the South wanted Texas and that party loyalty would not suffice to bring Whig votes to a candidate standing against annexation. But Clay, seeking to be all things to all men, failed to make himself wholly clear. The South remained suspicious of his intent. So did many of the anti-slavery voters of the North. Between these conflicting attitudes Henry Clay, assailed the while by constant Democratic attack, could find no effective compromise.

Raymond saw something of the campaign outside the city. While in Vermont in the late summer he sounded political sentiment, and had to admit that Vermonters took a dim view of both parties. Democrats accused Clay of favoring annexation. At the same time they asserted in protectionist Vermont that Polk favored a protective tariff, and though Raymond moralized about the political immorality such assertions indicated, he implied that Whigs found it hard to answer Democratic claims.

In September and October, he was back in the Genesee country ("the Garden of the World, as well as the Gibraltar of Whiggery," he described it) where four years earlier he had stumped for Harrison and Tyler. Once more he appeared at Whig meetings in Lima and the neighboring villages. "There is quite as much *excitement* as in 1840," he wrote the *Courier*, "and far more *cool*, though truth-seeking, discussion." He confessed that the Democrats were active, but he gave them little foundation for hope, and at the end of September reported: "I believe, from what I have seen, that if the election were to occur tomorrow, the State would give between 10,000 and 15,000 Whig majority; it should be doubled before November."

At Rochester he attended a great Whig rally that equaled anything staged for Harrison and Tyler. Special trains brought partisans from Buffalo and Albany, and long wagon trains drew in from the countryside. Rochester's hotels were so packed that private homes were thrown open for guests. Inscribed banners spanned the streets. The night before the meeting "the streets . . . resounded with the songs of exulting Whigs; ash-poles were raised on every corner of the streets; banners were flung to the winds to await the coming of the dawn; bonfires blazed from every square." In the morning a great procession formed—wagons and floats drawn by twenty to thirty-six horses or oxen, bands, mounted horsemen, marchers by the thousands. Raymond estimated that at least 100,000 persons had surged into Rochester for the speaking and the cheering and the fellowship of politics.

He returned to New York filled with confidence, but, still a political novice, he failed to understand the currents beneath the surface, or, if he did understand, kept the knowledge to himself. Several weeks before Raymond wrote his prophecy of Whig victory, Governor Seward had reported to Weed, "Everybody droops, despairs," and Weed admitted that "things look blue." By the end of October, though the *Courier* and other Whig journals were devoting their pages almost entirely to party pamphleteering, the Whig leaders knew in their hearts that all was lost. Election day only ratified their fears.

At the *Courier* office campaign trimmings were quickly packed away and the paper, after warning that Polk's election spelled disunion, resumed its customary paths. Raymond took up his routine, and now he had become virtually managing editor. In odd moments he wrote book reviews, found time to notice Rufus Griswold's new book, *The Poets and Poetry of England*, and to tell Griswold that he had liked it "with qualifications." He wrote also a series of learned articles on the lighting of the coasts that appeared later in the *American Review*.

IV

The winter was enlivened, for both Raymond and the readers of the *Courier*, by a personal controversy that gave Raymond a good deal of prominence around the city. The controversy stemmed from a scandal that in the late fall of 1844 had broken in the Protestant Episcopal Church.

Benjamin Tredwell Onderdonk, since 1830 Bishop of New York, had been charged with "immorality and impurity." A church court had heard the charges in what constituted the most sensational episode up to that time in the history of the American church, and on January 3, 1845, the bishop had been found guilty and suspended from office. Not all Episcopalians accepted the verdict. Some argued that the whole affair was a Low Church conspiracy against the High Church, which Bishop Onderdonk represented. Whatever the merits of the case and the attendant scandal, the aftermath found Raymond entangled with the distinguished Nathaniel Parker Willis, editor of the *Evening Mirror*.

Willis, then in his late thirties, handsome, a good deal of the dandy and a self-proclaimed man of the world, had written verse and had seen his own plays produced. He had lived long abroad, had written of what he had seen and of the social success he had attained. He had reputation, although he was steadily attacked as a snob. He had ability as an editor and his acquaintance among the literary men was wide. Poe wrote for the *Mirror*. So did Thackeray.

A few days after the suspension of Bishop Onderdonk, Willis wrote in the *Mirror* a long editorial casting doubt on the veracity of the women who had testified against the churchman. Without arguing guilt or innocence, he insisted that anyone who understood human behavior and the ways of men would appreciate that no "modest" woman could have taken the stand against the bishop, and that any who did should perhaps better have had her own life investigated. From such a thesis he proceeded to argue that no woman was ever molested by a man until she had indicated at least partial acquiescence, or, as Willis put it: "No woman is ever invaded until the enemy has given a signal from within." Such knowledge, he maintained, was common to all who had not immured themselves in closed, monastic lives, and Willis went on to say that he had heard the fact enunciated even from "libertines in their cups."

Colonel Webb was out of town, and Raymond, who was in charge of the *Courier*, saw a chance for fun. Recklessly he denounced with what Willis called an "indignation-hammer" the alleged assault upon feminine virtue. In a mild way the two papers exchanged remarks for several weeks, Willis ever seeking to explain away the apparent import of his words, while Raymond pursued him steadily. Never did Raymond fail to criticize what he called Willis's immoral attitude toward women and his apparent defense of Onderdonk's conduct. It might have ended there had not Willis lost his temper and loosed an insulting attack on the younger man. About a year earlier, said Willis, Greeley, out of charity, had hired Raymond, "a smartish country lad." He is still "green," and, "an innocent bumpkin," knows nothing of the world. "What is the worth of his judgement as to familiarities with *ladies!*" Now there was real trouble.

Greeley, entering the lists to set Willis aright, denied that he had ever hired anyone out of charity. "There are very few men connected with the New York Press," said he, "whose services we would prefer to Mr. R.'s." Webb, who was now back at the office, printed part of Greeley's tribute and opened the *Courier*'s columns to Raymond whenever he should wish to defend himself, and Raymond, after collecting the gossipy stories and accusations against his opponent, opened an offensive. He charged the fashionable Willis with having written the original editorial while in his cups. He declared the *Mirror*'s editor to be a "libertine," and insisted that his sketches about English society had caused that society to shut its doors to Nathaniel Parker Willis. In Rome, Raymond asserted, Americans had shunned Willis for his profligacy. As a strictly personal dig, he added that Willis owed his tailor money.

It was rough talk. Willis gave it back with good measure, describing the attacks upon him as coming from "the pen of a diminutive and busy little reporter." "This little viper," he said, "besides what is born under his tongue, has started up from the grass, as he crept toward me, the hidden slanders that were brooding unseen in the nests of prolific envy." Willis then denied all the charges against him, and to prove his case printed letters that gave the lie to his being barred from English society. Other letters further bolstered his position, until Willis reached his conclusion: "I declare myself a good citizen, a good husband and father, and a moral capable editor of the *Evening Mirror*, and *I challenge proof to the contrary.*"

Willis had proved his good name, yet in a sense he had been worsted, for Raymond, toward whom he had showed a good deal of contempt, had obliged him to bring forth his documents and fight. Raymond, kindness itself at heart, had not enjoyed the business overmuch. He wrote Griswold: "You were quite right in supposing that my quarrel with W. was not at all to my taste. I would have done a good deal to avoid it— but after the manner in which he treated me, what could I do? His position, compared to mine, gave him power to injure me very much, and it was not until I saw he was determined to use it, without stint or remorse, that I made up my mind to turn the tables and put him on the defensive. This, I believe, I did effectually enough, and yet I am heartily sorry for the whole affair, and would do a good deal even now to have it reconsidered, could it be done with propriety. But I think W. treated me very badly, and I do not think he had a right to expect anything else than I gave him." Willis never forgave Raymond, not even years later when mutual friends tried to bring them together.

V

The teapot tempest had lifted Raymond from obscurity. He was writing more and signing more, and in the summer of 1845, contributed to the *Courier* an extended series of reports based on a trip to Chicago by way of the Great Lakes. To a large extent, the reports were travel notes, and yet they contained also a good deal of observation on the state of the country and on the need for internal improvements.

There had been a five-day journey by boat from Buffalo to Chicago, a voyage that often was dull, except when Lake Michigan's waters whipped the little vessel and kept the passengers ill in the cabins. Chicago, a rising center of 12,000, a city built of wood and seeming to sit precariously on the flat prairie, struck Raymond as the boom town which it was, and he marveled, after the fashion of English travelers, at the speed with which men did things. He echoed Dickens when he wrote:

"Breakfast was dispatched, as all western business is transacted, in the most prompt and expeditious manner. Not a moment is wasted in waiting for waiters or for anything else. If the trout chance to be beyond man's reach, steak is forced to redeem the time, and the article nearest at hand is pressed into the service, until the service of servants can be commanded. In this way a meal is often finished before a single dish that was really wanted has been procured. This is all in the true spirit of that enterprise which has built the West. It may answer for fashionable idlers at the Astor to dawdle away an hour over a dinner . . . but men who have a city to create within a week, or an empire to establish 'before early candle light,' have no time to waste over egg shells and Mocha."

Not all his observations dealt with manners. He returned home filled with praise for the industry of the West, and he raised the timely political question as to whether the West would ever permit the separation of North and South in permanent national disunion. To tie the West more closely to the North he advocated the building of railroads that would bring the products of the West to Northern ports, more especially to New York. Once made the depot for Western products, New York's greatness would be guaranteed. His letters, with their enthusiasm for national growth and business advance, brought favorable comment from *Courier* readers, many of whom were investing in railroads and therefore had double reason to hope with Raymond that the Erie Railroad would soon be completed to link the Great Lakes with New York and that a railway would be pushed from the mouth of the Hudson north to Albany.

Raymond's reports confirmed his skill in handling colorful accounts of incidents and places. What he wrote also disclosed, more definitely than before, his ability to discuss broad issues with force and authority. It was an ability he demonstrated again some months later when arguing in the *American Review* for the purchase of California lest Great Britain seek that territory and the United States be forced to war against such British expansion. "The American System," Raymond declared on this occasion with all the certainty of a statesman, "has grown up, which claims a distinct existence, a perfect independence of all European control, and the right to shape its policy and its history, without interference, as it promises to do without the aid of any of the older nations of the Eastern world."

VI

The *Courier*, as Raymond matured and made himself felt more in editorial policy, seemed fresher and brighter. Its conception of news broadened, until an eight-page literary supplement was not uncommon.

Dramatic criticism appeared, and often as much as a column was devoted to a symphony concert. There was new emphasis on happenings abroad, and reports from around the country improved. Before the year was out Donald G. Mitchell began sending from Washington his light, colorful, and satirical "Capital Sketches," signing them "Ik Marvel," a name to become famous in American letters, but at the time a pseudonym which hid Mitchell's identity even from Colonel Webb. Debates with the *Herald* and the *Tribune* arose with regularity. There were letters on public questions from elder statesmen like Albert Gallatin, Jefferson's Secretary of the Treasury, and the "magnetic telegraph" began to bring reports from Philadelphia and Washington. Boldface headlines replaced the weak italic that had been customary, and the change was typographically for the better. Webb as usual boasted of the *Courier*'s size, and in April, 1846, asserted that a single issue might contain as many as 943,005 letters of hand-set type.

Compared with the *Herald* and its breeziness, the *Courier* still seemed dull, but Thomas Snowden, who had long been its printer and business manager, deplored the changes. "That little Raymond," he said, "will not rest contented till he has turned the *Courier and Enquirer* into a two-cent paper." But Webb did not agree, and was inclined to give his managing editor considerable rein. In July, 1846, he announced that Raymond would purchase a third of the *Courier*.[2] "This prospective interest in the paper," said Webb, "secures his connection with it, and we take pleasure in making this announcement from the estimation in which we hold Mr. R., and our appreciation of his services, and also from the interest which all our readers have in the continuance of his labors upon the *Courier and Enquirer*."

There was plenty of news, for that summer of 1846 the country was at war with Mexico, and General Zachary Taylor, with the victories of Palo Alto and Resaca de la Palma behind him, had driven the Mexicans across the Rio Grande and was preparing for a march into the arid plains of Nuevo Leon toward Monterrey. The *Courier*, which had accepted the annexation of Texas while attacking the maneuver of a Congressional joint resolution that made it possible, at first opposed the war, regarding it as "rashly provoked and undertaken by executive usurpation." There was something to be said for this view, but the *Courier*, unlike the *Tribune*, did not press it. Whigs generally, however unenthusiastic they might be about Mr. Polk's war, voted in Congress the money needed to support the armies, and the *Courier* took the ground that in time of war

[2] Apparently Raymond never was able to find the money to do so, and when he left the *Courier* five years later he gave Webb one dollar to cancel the purchase agreement.

there was no other stand than that of Stephen Decatur's "my country, right or wrong."

The war had got under way slowly. At a Fourth of July celebration in City Hall Park the name of Zachary Taylor had blazed in the fireworks that illuminated the night, but his greatest victory was still ahead and the heavy fighting waited while General Kearney moved toward Santa Fe and Frémont took California. So New Yorkers went about their business, complaining of the uncertainty of the gaslights and of the pigs that scavenged in the garbage-littered streets. The yacht club—and Webb was a great yachting enthusiast—held its regatta on a cool, beautiful day in July when the sails of seven vessels were spread across the harbor horizon, a regatta which the *Courier*, forgetting that it was the *Herald* that had introduced sports news, covered with detailed fullness. There was ballet at Niblo's Garden, soon to be destroyed by fire while firemen and police fought over liquor plundered from the cellars and grew drunk as they fought.

It was a state election year, but the *Courier* was out of sorts politically, for at Utica in September the Whigs had nominated for governor a prominent member of the Assembly, John Young, who belonged to the party's radical wing. Weed had left the convention in disgust rather than see Young chosen, for the Dictator had temporarily been pushed aside. The *Courier*, aligned with Seward and Weed and the conservatives, insisted that it was Whig to the core and insisted also upon its right to support the party's candidates or not as it chose. Election day brought the governorship to Young, who, "a comet for a season," served only one term, and even before the election many Whigs were thinking more about Presidential politics than the contest for the governorship. General Zachary Taylor—Whigs found it hard to forget their success in 1840 with a military hero—was being mentioned often as a candidate for the Presidency. In September his outnumbered forces had captured Monterrey after a three-day battle that General Winfield S. Scott called the "three glorious days," and the victory, marred though it had been in Polk's eyes by Taylor's generous terms to the defeated Mexicans, had made the American commander a national hero.

VII

After Monterrey the war tended to mark time. Politics also was temporarily adjourned, and Raymond now had the opportunity to engage Horace Greeley in a long-pending debate on socialism. Ever since the first days on the *New-Yorker*, when Raymond had privately ridiculed Greeley's alliance with Albert Brisbane, he had never failed to attack the principles of utopian socialism and the attempts to put those principles into practice. On the *Courier* Raymond's attacks were aided and abetted by Colonel Webb, who had no use for Fourierism.

In the early summer of 1846 the *Courier*, following its custom, attacked the socialism of Fourier on the grounds of irreligion, infidelity, and licentiousness. Brisbane in reply raised the whole subject of social reform. An editorial rejoinder loosed a series of communications between the *Courier* and the *Tribune*, until Greeley finally proposed that Fourierism be debated in a series of twelve articles by each side. The challenge was accepted, and late in November the *Tribune* led off with a half-column statement. The debate was to take six months to complete, and perhaps its slowness bears witness that public interest was too slight for any need to hurry. The New Bedford *Mercury*, one of the few papers anywhere to comment, called the discussion "flat, stale and unprofitable," and added—it was Thanksgiving time—"at this season of roast turkey and pumpkin pie we are thankful not to be under the necessity of reading all those questions of phalanxes, agrarianism, equal rights and licentiousness."

The debate nevertheless did hold a degree of drama. Some people were genuinely concerned over Fourierism and its possible threat to society. Many others were entertained by the spectacle of Horace Greeley, the liberal eccentric, an editor of increasing power and influence, in debate with the more conservative Henry Raymond, whom he had trained in the principles of newspapers and who was becoming a power in his own right. As the arguments unfolded, Greeley, though some thought him illogical at times, stood forth as thoroughly honest, burning with his convictions. Raymond, on the other hand, while perhaps equally earnest, was not above dragging in good red herring to serve his purpose. He capitalized public antipathy to free love by making much of the alleged threat to marriage and the family implied by the teachings of Fourier, though the threat, and Raymond knew it, was not borne out by association in practice. Greeley, charging him also with twisting evidence and citing biased sources, asked if there was not "a spice of roguery in the business." A contemporary summed up: "On one side we see earnestness and sincerity; on the other tact and skill. One strove to convince, the other to triumph."

Where the two men really stood on the subject of social reform they stated in their concluding articles. Greeley laid down as his fundamental beliefs that "man has a natural, God-given right to labor for his own subsistence" and that "in a true social state, the right of every individual to such labor as he is able to perform, and to the fair and equal recompense of his labor, will be guaranteed and provided for." Only through the sort of community organization or association described by Fourier could such rights be assured. "I believe," said Greeley, "that Christianity, social justice, intellectual and moral progress, universal well-being, imperatively require the adoption of such a reform as is here roughly sketched. . . . The principle of Association is one which has already done much for the improvement of the condition of our race; we see it now actively making its way into general adoption, through odd fellowship, protective unions, mutual fire, marine and life insurance. . . . In all these and many like them, I see the portents of 'a good time coming,' not for the destitute and hopeless only, but for the great mass of our fellowmen."

In contrast Raymond laid down the creed: "We regard it as our duty to do all in our power to benefit our fellowmen; but we are not of those who 'feel personally responsible for the turning of the earth upon its axis,' nor do we deem it our special 'mission' to reorganize society. . . . We should not differ with the *Tribune* as to the Christian duty of the rich towards the poor; but we cannot denounce them as the tyrants and robbers of those who have been less industrious and less fortunate. We would gladly see society free from suffering, and all its members virtuous and happy; but we believe social equality to be as undesirable, as it is impossible. . . . The Christian religion in its spiritual, life-giving, heart-redeeming principles, is the only power that can reform society; and it can accomplish this work only by first reforming the individuals of whom society is composed. Without God, and the plan of redemption which he has revealed, the world is also without Hope."

There was no vote on the merits of the discussion, and the verdict would probably have been decided in any event by the voters' prejudices. But the debate did about end Horace Greeley's public teaching of utopian socialism; thereafter the *Tribune*'s editor had less to say about the ideas of Fourier. Years later he said in his autobiography that the controversy with Raymond had helped to draw public attention to the principles of socialism and therefore had not been in vain, but to many observers it seemed rather that the public had learned too well what Fourierism might mean and that men had turned away from utopias in such guise. One contemporary said emphatically that the "discussion *finished* Fourierism in the United States." Both Raymond and the *Courier* emerged with enhanced reputation among the solid citizenry. So far as Raymond was concerned, he had completed the establishing of himself as an editor and writer, though, as it was said at the time, "of the varieties of composition, polished vituperation is not the most difficult."

He was already well established as a man of family. Soon after the birth of a son, Edward Henry, in the spring of 1845, the Raymonds had turned their backs on boardinghouses and set up homekeeping on West Thirteenth Street. There, in one of a row of high-stooped, red brick houses that stretched west from Sixth Avenue, Juliette Raymond arranged her furniture and treasured her white and gold wedding china with its monogram of gilt. Not far away loomed the heavy Doric portico of the Greenwich Presbyterian Church. Fifth Avenue with its mansions was a block and a half distant. There were shops and markets on Sixth Avenue, where every few minutes the omnibuses clattered by, carrying men like Raymond downtown to business. No. 110 West Thirteenth Street was the Raymond address for a good many years, but it was a home that Eddie, as his parents called him, never knew. Before his second birthday the baby died, and in the summer of 1847 Mrs. Raymond was awaiting her second child. He was born in September. They named him Henry Warren. In youth and early manhood he was to be his father's companion and to stand beside him in time of sorrow and great trial.

CHAPTER

6

Politics and the Press

I

IN JANUARY, 1848, Raymond for the first time visited Washington, where for more than a fortnight he frequented the halls of
Congress and the hotels along cobbled Pennsylvania Avenue. The
weather was mild, the skies clear, and winter's sun shone upon a
capital city sprinkled with veterans home from Mexico. The blue of
uniforms, the gilt of braid and epaulets, broke the gray monotony of
Washington's streets. Congress was in session, and in the plaza before
the Capitol with its stubby dome of wood, carriages wheeled and halted
in constant succession as legislators and those with business to attend
arrived before the building that Mrs. Frances Trollope once upon a
time had thought too beautiful and majestic to describe.

Mrs. Trollope's visit preceded Raymond's by almost two decades, but
Washington had not been altered very much since she compared it to
a fashionable English watering place and commented that "the total
absence of all sights, sounds, or smells of commerce, adds greatly to the
charm." Commerce was still absent, and the most notable changes were
marked by new government buildings, the Treasury, Patent Office, and
Post Office, all brave with classic pillars and pediments, that ornamented
Pennsylvania Avenue and near-by thoroughfares. In January, 1848, the
Norman towers of the Smithsonian Institution were in the future and
the cornerstone of the Washington Monument would not be laid for
another six months. The city, despite its 40,000 inhabitants, remained a
"rambling, scrambling village," a sleepy, half-Southern sort of place

that took on life only when the convening of Congress drew Senators and Representatives and hangers-on to the capital.

Washington was busy when Raymond arrived, and the hotels were registering a good many important guests along with the Congressmen who made hotels their homes. Henry Clay, still politically hopeful, was in town. Mutual friends were urging that he put aside 1844's bitter disappointment and pay his respects to President Polk, who was literally working himself to death over the papers that accumulated so rapidly on his White House desk. Ex-Governor Seward had come down from New York and had taken rooms at the National Hotel, close by the Capitol. Horace Greeley was circulating among the members of Congress; reports had it that he was seeing a good deal of Clay. At the Capitol there were some unfamiliar faces—a new Senator, Stephen A. Douglas, represented Illinois, and the Illinois delegation in the House contained a tall, rawboned member whose name was Lincoln—but it was the old faces, men like Webster and Calhoun and Thomas Hart Benton, that drew the attention of the visitors' galleries.

The Supreme Court was sitting, and one day Raymond went up to the Hill to hear Webster argue before the nine judges in their semicircular basement room that John Randolph once had likened to a cave. Before the judges, each in a velvet-covered mahogany armchair behind a mahogany desk, Webster was arguing the case docketed as Luther v. Borden. That barren legal label hid a chapter in the growth of political democracy, a chapter filled with controversy and bitterness and sorrow. It had begun several years earlier in Rhode Island.

Unlike other states, Rhode Island had clung to its colonial charter and had refused to adopt a constitution recognizing the principle of general male suffrage. The result had been a state controlled and ruled by a handful of voters. There had been stirrings against this oligarchic rule, and early in the Eighteen Forties Thomas W. Dorr had led a movement for reform. His People's party had organized a convention, drafted a constitution, which was ratified by popular vote. Under this constitution an election had been held, with Dorr the elected governor. When the existing state government had declined to recognize the Dorr regime, the two sides had clashed. Martial law had been proclaimed. Dorr, arrested, tried for high treason and sentenced to life imprisonment, had been released soon after his conviction, but out of the "Dorr Rebellion" had come the suit that Webster was now arguing before the Supreme Court.

There was a political tinge to it all, for the Democrats, making much of the people's right to change their own government, upheld Dorr. The Whigs threw their support to the conservatives. Party papers added fuel to the controversy, and though the Supreme Court's hearing had been postponed time and again, interest had not disappeared when the day of argument arrived. Raymond, seated on the cushioned sofa in the court chamber, was not just a listener that day. He was a reporter, taking rough notes rapidly as Webster spoke his well-formed sentences and developed the argument that ran on twelve, thirteen thousand words to a peroration glittering with Latin quotations.

The day after Webster's appearance, Raymond called upon him at his house in Louisiana Avenue, bringing the report with him, for Webster had no copy of his own, having spoken from notes that he later gave Raymond as a memento. "Mr. Webster," said Raymond of their meeting, "expressed great satisfaction at my report, and seemed especially anxious to have the argument clearly set forth. As I read over to him the successive points, to every one which seemed peculiarly clear, he would exclaim, 'Good,' 'That's true,' 'That's it,' . . . apparently forgetting that the argument was his own, and applauding the performance of some other person. After the report was finished, I expressed my great admiration of its iron logic." For about an hour the two men discussed the argument and other subjects, past politics among them.

Raymond recorded that Webster "talked very freely—with great dignity and deliberation, yet as socially and easily as if with an old friend. There was about him nothing of the hauteur usually ascribed to him; yet he never forgot, though he did not seem to remember, his character and fame. . . . I apologized for having trespassed so unwarrantably upon his time. He said he was very glad to see me, inviting me to call at pleasure, etc., etc."

Webster's argument—it filled four of the *Courier*'s columns—was only one of the dispatches Raymond sent to New York. He described Clay's appearance before the American Colonization Society one evening in the crowded hall of the House of Representatives. He sounded and reported sentiment in regard to the war with Mexico that was drawing to its close, and political opinion on the approaching Presidential campaign. He talked with Webster about these matters, and he found other members of Congress ready to discuss them, too.

The fact of the business was that Whigs were divided on the Presidency and apprehensive of the settlement with Mexico, fearing in particular that annexation of part or all of pre-war Mexico would reopen the debate over extending slave territory and so upset the sectional balance of power as to bring on the division of the Union that men feared and disliked to contemplate. Webster told Raymond that "the future was entirely overcast" but urged that "even if annexation of all Mexico should take place, and a dissolution of the Union should be the result, still . . . we of the North are on the safe side. We have the wealth, the numbers, the commerce, the enterprise. All the best elements of national power are on our side; we are the strongest, and in the event of dissolution we must still constitute the great nation of the continent." Some Southerners insisted, surprisingly, that they foresaw nothing but harm in annexation of Mexican territory. All these views reached *Courier* readers through Raymond's dispatches, along with his clear, striking reports on the state of political opinion.

"No person," he wrote, "can be long in Washington without hearing a great deal said of the Presidential Election." At the moment, though Webster had not put aside Presidential ambitions, Henry Clay and General Zachary Taylor were the principal contenders for the Whig nomination. Among Whigs Raymond found respect and affection for Clay, although many in the party felt he was out of tune with the times, and it was hard to forget his previous defeats. Almost equally hard was it to forget that the one great Whig victory had been won by a military hero. Taylor, although a Southerner and a slaveholder, thus seemed "available," but Raymond had to confess that not all Whigs in Washington were yet convinced. The *Herald*, approving some of his findings in regard to Taylor and Clay, remarked: "Mr. Raymond is an editor of the present age—not of the last. He belongs to that class of men who think out loud—not of those old drivellers of fifteen or twenty years ago, who never thought at all." It was praise from an unexpected quarter, although it had been inspired perhaps by Raymond's relatively kind words about Zachary Taylor's candidacy, for the usually Democratic *Herald* was whooping it up for Taylor along with as regular a Whig organ as the *Courier*.

II

Before the Washington trip Raymond, whose political activity had been growing, had attended a Whig caucus at the *Courier* office, where with Colonel Webb and several lawyers and bankers—the *Herald* called them the "Wall Street clique"—he had helped to plan a great Taylor mass meeting for Washington's Birthday. Although "Old Rough and Ready" had never voted in a Presidential election, and seemed so little like a Whig that the *Herald* had often urged that he be nominated on a nonpartisan basis, he had strong support among many New York Whigs. Thurlow Weed led these Taylor forces, though keeping out of sight and leaving apparent leadership to Seward, Webb, and others. It was an uphill fight, for there was an independent Taylor movement afoot that exponents of party regularity disliked, and the Clay forces, with an editorial spokesman in Horace Greeley, were very much alive.

Raymond took an active part in the developing contest. He wrote the address and resolutions for the Washington's Birthday meeting, and a caucus of leaders in the Astor House approved it with only slight changes. He also wrote the address for an independent Taylor meeting, excusing his apparent break with the party leaders by saying he had tried to give the proceedings "a Whig bias."

The Washington's Birthday rally, for all the planning, disappointed. An immense tent, expected to accommodate 15,000 people, had been raised among the ruins of Niblo's Garden. A great transparency bearing Taylor's famous command at Buena Vista, "A Little More Grape, Captain Bragg," had been stretched above the entrance, and above the platform another transparency hung. All was ready to insure that the Taylor rally would surpass in every respect a Clay meeting held with tremendous success the previous week at Castle Garden. But the weather was hostile. "It rained horribly," Raymond said afterward, "and was a doleful time." It was worse than that, for the rain, which later turned to sleet and snow, had soaked the tent until water trickled through every seam. The entrance was deep in mud, and the floor wet and slimy. Despite these woes, at least 5,000 Whigs did gather in the tent, where after the band had played "Hail, Columbia," the speeches began. Moses H. Grinnell, banker and former member of Congress, told his fellow Whigs, some of whom had sought refuge beneath the platform, that though the weather was "rough," they had shown that they were "ready." Raymond, chosen one of the secretaries, read his address, which after praising Taylor as the man "upon whom the Whigs in every portion of our common country can unite," developed and discussed the case against Mexican annexations. The speech was "very long," the *Tribune* remarked next morning. The *Herald* called it "inconsistent, absurd and incomprehensible."

Raymond had been mistaken, events quickly showed, in devoting so much of his address to territorial expansion, for the day following the Niblo's Garden meeting President Polk's private secretary carried from the White House to the Senate the peace treaty that had been signed at Guadalupe Hidalgo on the second of February. By its provisions the Rio Grande was made the border between the United States and Mexico, while California and New Mexico were ceded in return for $15,000,000 compensation. What had been almost an academic issue now stood before the Whig party as stark reality made more critical by the danger that should the treaty be rejected, popular demand for annexation of all Mexico might force territorial expansion far more dangerous to the preservation of the Union. Former fears had to be put aside. Party lines broke, and on March 10, President Polk wrote in his diary: "About ten o'clock P.M. Mr. Dickens, the Secretary of the Senate, brought me official notice that the Mexican Treaty had just been ratified."

III

Some Whigs remained unreconciled to the westward course of empire. Webster was one of these. In January he had told Raymond that he intended to speak against Mexican annexations and that he hoped the *Courier*'s managing editor would report his speech. Despite the peace treaty, he still intended to make his protest, and when a bill carrying a supplementary war appropriation gave the opportunity, he wrote Raymond of his plans. Raymond prepared for another trip to Washington.

The journey nearly ended in disaster, for the train on which he was traveling ran into an open drawbridge at Newark, and only the breaking of the coupling chains prevented the car in which he was seated from following others into the water. The accident—it cost two lives—turned Raymond back. He telegraphed Webster what had happened, and the Senator obligingly postponed his speech until March 23, when before a crowded Senate he denounced "all accessions of territory to form new states" and assailed the idea that New Mexico and California held anything of value to the Union. It was a long speech, two hours and a half, and out of keeping with the mood of most of the audience.

Raymond listened on the Senate floor, sitting at the desk of Senator Corwin of Ohio, which Webster had obtained for him as a special distinction. That night he wrote out part of his notes, and the next morning started for New York with the Senator and Mrs. Webster, who were hastening home to Boston to the deathbed of a daughter. "We took breakfast at Baltimore," Raymond said, "and went to Philadelphia, where we all stopped at Hartwell's. After dinner I completed my report, and in the evening read it over to Mr. Webster in the presence of Mrs. Webster and Senator Greene, of Rhode Island. All of them expressed frequent admiration of the accuracy and spirit of the report, and when I had finished Mrs. Webster said: 'You needn't give yourself any trouble, Daniel, about your speeches as long as Mr. Raymond reports them.' The effect of hearing her call him *Daniel* was curious." Webster, as he had done after the Dorr Rebellion argument, gave Raymond the notes of the speech.

Though not in full agreement with Webster's views, the *Courier* called the speech one of his ablest, and gloated a little because no other paper published a text with the Senator's imprimatur. The *Herald* quite rightly criticized it as a Northern man's views that would tend to alienate Southern and Western Whigs, and remarked rather sourly that from the *Courier*'s "self-puffing" articles "one would think . . . there was none but Mr. Webster able to make a speech in Congress, and none but themselves able to report it."

Webster's words were scarcely calculated to further his Presidential ambitions now that the tides were setting strong for General Taylor. In New York City, Taylor supporters opened headquarters in Lafayette Hall on Broadway, where early in April they held the first of a series of meetings to push the "Rough and Ready" candidacy. Raymond, the principal speaker, urged with "much energy, directness and spirit" Taylor's availability and extolled his military record. The meeting went off well, though Clay partisans were present as usual to cheer for "Harry of the West," who had, it was abundantly apparent, a good deal of popular support.

IV

The rival party managers busied themselves behind the scenes as the spring wore on. The death of John Jacob Astor drew public attention for a moment, and his will disposing of his vast estate attracted more attention and comment. There was Italian opera in town, and the company was losing money. Christy's minstrels had never known greater popularity. Political news contended with the exciting tidings from a revolution-swept Europe, and there were rumors that the dethroned Louis Philippe had arrived in town as Mr. Orleans. The rumors proved false, and were forgotten as the members of the press vied with one another in their extensive coverage of the Chartist movement in England, the new French republic, the upheavals in Italy, Austria, and Germany.

Pressure of foreign news and the prospect of added dispatches inspired by the Presidential campaign at home induced New York publishers to put aside some of their rivalries in news gathering, rivalries that in the past had led them to steal from each other the foreign papers that the pilot boats brought up the harbor. One day in May, 1848, representatives of six papers—the *Courier*, the *Journal of Commerce*, the *Express, Herald, Tribune*, and *Sun*—met in the *Sun*'s office to discuss the possibility of a cooperative venture in news gathering. David Hale of the *Journal of Commerce*, prime mover in the scheme, was present. Webb, though opposed to the idea, was also there along with Raymond.

Tradition has it that Raymond won Webb over to what was to grow eventually into the Associated Press, and in any event Raymond had an important part in the organization. The group bought a dispatch boat to intercept the ships from Europe as they approached Halifax, and from there to rush the European news to Boston, whence it might be telegraphed to New York. Raymond, with Frederic Hudson, managing editor of the *Herald*, negotiated with the telegraph company for "the use of all wires that may be in working order for the uninterrupted transmission of all the news we may wish to receive." Each paper sharing the expense would receive copies of these dispatches. Negotiations proved successful. It was a small beginning, but as the association expanded in the years ahead Raymond remained prominent in its growth and management.

In the midst of this extra activity, June arrived and the Democrats, meeting in Baltimore, chose Senator Lewis Cass of Michigan as their Presidential candidate. Delegates for the Whig convention assembled in Philadelphia, where on June 7 they began their deliberations in the narrow hall of the Chinese Museum. Spectators crowded the galleries, looking down upon the delegates and the flag-draped platform where a stuffed American eagle held in its beak a blue ribbon that bore in gold letters the motto "E Pluribus Unum." It was stifling in the crowded hall. The galleries were disorderly. Yet somehow the convention got to work. Taylor led the first ballot, pressed hard by Clay, with General Scott, Webster, and others trailing far behind. The party choice was not long delayed: on the fourth ballot Taylor was nominated. Millard Fillmore of New York, an anti-slavery Clay man, was named his running mate, to the disgust of Seward and Weed, who had little love for him.

There was no party platform—Taylor had never made himself clear on issues—and the ticket as a whole pleased no one. Clay supporters found it hard to accept the general. Many Northerners were unwilling to see a slaveholder the Whig candidate. Others, North and South, probably agreed with a Clay man who said resignedly: "We must mix up a little 'humbugging' with our glorious Whig creed, before we can expect a victory—and General Taylor's *military fame* is about the best we can make use of at present." The venerable and honored Philip Hone, ex-Mayor of New York and follower of Henry Clay, wrote in his diary: "I am disappointed, but I am satisfied . . . the question now is not whether Mr. Clay or General Taylor should be the nominee, but shall General Cass be the President of the United States."

Taylor's New York forces did the best they could, and late in June they staged a tremendous rally in Canal Street, where one mild, clear evening an estimated 30,000 citizens crowded around the hustings to listen to speeches and resolutions ratifying the Whig candidacy. Rowdies and ruffians made trouble, and even Philip Hone, chosen chairman, "as I usually am," he remarked, "when trouble is expected," could not completely restore order. The resolutions had been drafted by Raymond, and it fell to him to read them to the rally. In the summer twilight, he looked a tiny, almost boyish figure as he stepped out on the platform erected opposite National Hall. There were some cheers as he began to read the formal praise of Taylor and the pleas for Whig support and party unity. There were catcalls also, and boos, but his voice had power and resonance, so much that the next day the *Herald* reported: "During the reading of these resolutions, there was the usual quantity of disorderly and tumultuous conduct, but Mr. Raymond's lungs were strong enough to make him heard by the greater portion of those assembled."

He was to need both physical and vocal strength in the weeks ahead, for with the other *Courier* editors he was publishing a weekly campaign paper, the *Grapeshot*. He was in the thick of party organization and was in demand as a speaker at local rallies. Besides, political activity could not be allowed to interfere with the job of placing the *Courier* before its readers every day.

Foreign news that summer crowded even the columns of a blanket sheet like the *Courier*, which boasted a new type font and a fresh make-up that made it less stodgy than ever in its history. Each steamer from Europe brought new dispatches of the stirring events sweeping across the Continent. With some pride the paper remarked: "In the present condition of Europe the advantage of an extended and intelligent system of foreign correspondence cannot be overrated. That of the *Courier and Enquirer*, which has been organized with great labor and is maintained at a very heavy expense, will not suffer" from comparison with any other New York journal, a view that the *Herald* disputed, though neither needed to be apologetic. Ik Marvel, whose light and colorful letters from Washington, Saratoga, and elsewhere had been featured in the *Courier* in other seasons, was in Europe, and had begun at the end of June a distinguished series of reports from London and Paris.

His dispatches were often opinionated and so interpretative that Raymond must sometimes have felt that Marvel's ridicule of the English Chartists and the French republicans was giving the *Herald* grounds for the assertion that the *Courier's* foreign reports showed "want of sympathy with the liberty of the masses." Raymond, who regarded Marvel as a friend and had arranged his European tour, did not hesitate to express his disappointment over what he wrote. But it was not all disappointment. Marvel could be vivid when he chose, and his detailed description of the insurrectionary "June Days" that ended the radical phase of the revolution in France won the *Courier's* accolade for the "most connected and intelligible view we have seen of the causes, progress and incidents of the last bloody revolt in Paris." This special correspondent had considerable insight, and it led him as the summer advanced to assert that the "French are not fit for a republic" and to hint that an emperor might again rule in France. It was after all not without significance that Prince Louis Napoleon, the Bonapartist pretender, had been elected to the French Assembly and was restlessly awaiting the end of his English exile.

The news from France quieted, and Marvel left Paris for Germany. In New York, as the hot summer ended, politics again came into its own. The state situation was tangled by the nomination of Martin Van Buren, the former President, to lead the Free-Soil party. That split the Democrats, but how many free-soil Whigs would support Van Buren against Taylor none knew. Whigs appeared apathetic, Raymond reported after a visit upstate. There was none of the enthusiasm, at least in western New York, that he had witnessed in previous campaigns, and even at Taylor rallies in New York City loud shouts for Henry Clay were still being heard.

Raymond's campaigning for Taylor was interrupted by the news that the home of his Lima boyhood had been destroyed by fire. "I little thought when we were all there so snugly this summer that it would be for the last time," he wrote his father hastily. "It makes me sad to think that the old homestead has gone. . . . If you want anything of me, let me know it. I can let you have money, if you have need of it. . . . Come down and stay with us, and we'll try and make you glad the old house was burned." As soon as possible he set out for Lima, though his river boat was delayed by fog and his train ran off the track, to see for himself what had happened and to offer sympathy and aid in person. His parents cared for, he was soon back in New York. The city was under its regular late-summer siege by mosquitoes, and Raymond complained that they had nearly eaten up "little Henry," his baby son.

In the Taylor campaign's final weeks, Raymond was regularly on the hustings, and one night he spoke for two hours and a half in neighboring Paterson. Division in the Democratic ranks had after all made Whig victory sure in New York, and the state's vote made certain Taylor's choice. Philip Hone, the day after the polls closed, wrote in his diary: "The sun of Buena Vista set last night upon the most decided victory ever achieved in this city by the Whig forces—a perfect rout; everything is gained." Whigs celebrated generally what President Polk regarded as a national calamity. In New York a select 200 of them marked the party success with a great dinner at the new and fashionable Irving House, where after fifty courses had been served before the dessert, self-congratulatory speaking began among what Hone described as "as fine a set of Whigs as was ever assembled to 'hail the rising sun.' " Raymond, one of the speakers, proposed a toast for the press. Remarking that he was probably the youngest member of the fourth estate present—he was twenty-eight—he apologized as he praised his party because he had lost his voice through cheering for old Zach. The celebrants sat late at table, Hone confessing that he left "between the first and second of the morning hours." The *Tribune* thought Raymond had been able and eloquent.

In the Taylor campaign Raymond had won his political spurs. He had proved his ability as an orator and as a master in writing the formal phrases of political statements and resolutions. He had learned a good deal about the behind-the-scenes maneuvers that belong to party activity. Most of all he had become acquainted with the Whig leaders who shaped policy. Among them he had formed a lifetime friendship with William Henry Seward. The Seward friendship linked him with the Whig state machine, for Seward and Thurlow Weed through the recent victory at the polls had won dominance in New York and great influence at Washington, where the President-elect could hardly ignore Weed's share in his election. Raymond's work with the Whigs combined with his mounting success at the *Courier* to mark him as a man to watch.

V

The year 1849 opened with the news that France had found a President in the person of Louis Napoleon Bonaparte, who little more than a decade earlier had been an exile watching the sights of Broadway in the company of Colonel Webb. At Albany Hamilton Fish was inaugurated Governor in a simple ceremony described as "no less solemn and impressive" than the coronation of a king; after taking the oath he received well-wishers before the portrait of Lafayette that dominated his capitol office. The New York Legislature girded for a struggle between the Fillmore and the Seward Whigs, for Thurlow Weed was already planning the campaign that within a few weeks brought a United States senatorship to his friend the ex-Governor. There was excellent sleighing in New York City, its streets gay with smart turnouts and high-stepping horses, and the snow was damp enough for boys to wage snowball battles and to topple from dignified male heads the tall beavers fashion persistently decreed. The new year—it was the year of the gold fever, and the press was filled with lists of ships bound for California, with maps of the gold fields and the surrounding country—brought the season of public balls. Men and women were dancing the Hungarian polka, new and shocking and denounced by the *Herald* as "one of the most indecent and disreputable movements in dancing."

The March inauguration of President Taylor amid snow and cold seemed momentarily to cement Seward-Weed influence at Washington, though soon it became apparent that Vice-President Fillmore might have more weight with the Chief Executive than either the new Senator from New York or the state's Dictator. New York supporters of Taylor expected, however, to be remembered when the patronage was distributed, and with that thought in mind Colonel Webb went to the capital to seek a diplomatic post. He left Raymond in charge of the *Courier and Enquirer*, a responsibility that except for brief interruptions continued so long as he remained with the paper, for the Colonel found reasons to remain long away from the city, and his visits to the *Courier* office grew more brief and more rare.

New York, as winter gave way to spring, developed a rash of Shakespeare. Mrs. Kemble's readings of his plays had people "agog," and Philip Hone after attending one of her evenings declared she had "taken the city by storm." The American actor Edwin Forrest arrived in town with Shakespeare included in his repertory at the Broadway Theatre. His English rival, William C. Macready, was billed simultaneously for the Astor Place Opera House, opening with *Macbeth*. Raymond had a seat for Macready's opening night, May 7.

The flamboyant Forrest, idol of the galleries if not of the more critical in the boxes, had by the Eighteen Forties come to be regarded as the nation's leading actor. Macready, a celebrated English tragedian, had toured America with success, and as an actor was generally preferred over Forrest by what the *Herald* usually described as the "elite." In 1845, on a visit to England Forrest had played *Macbeth* in London, only to suffer the indignity of being hissed, treatment that he blamed on Macready, and apparently without cause. Soon afterward Forrest was in Edinburgh. Macready was also there, in *Hamlet*. His rival took a box for a performance and ostentatiously hissed him. Thereafter their quarrel would not down. Gradually their partisans took up what had been only a matter of professional jealousy and translated it into an issue of patriotism and class distinction. Among his supporters Forrest came to symbolize America and democracy ranged against Britain and aristocracy.

It was unfortunate, therefore, that the two actors had to play in New York at the same time and that each, as though to underline the rivalry, elected to appear in *Macbeth* the same night. It was doubly unfortunate that Forrest should be billed for the Broadway, a theater patronized by the masses, while Macready was to appear at the Opera House that the *Herald*, among others, had helped to link in the public mind to things aristocratic.

Threats of trouble had circulated before Macready's opening night, and when the curtain rose at the Opera House, police were scattered through the audience. It was a futile gesture, for when Macready walked on the stage rowdies in the gallery set up a tumult that could not be curbed. They hissed, they hooted and whistled. Before long the unruly audience got wholly out of hand. Macready reported in his diary: "Copper cents were thrown, some struck me, four or five eggs, a great many apples, nearly—if not quite—a peck of potatoes . . . a bottle of asafoetida which splashed my own dress, smelling, of course, most terribly." A chair plunged from the gallery to the stage, and by then the few women in the theater were hurriedly departing. Into the auditorium meanwhile leaked the shouts of a mob outside, pounding on the doors for admittance. After two hours of this sort of thing, the curtain was rung down and Macready fled the house by a back door.

Raymond wrote late that night to describe what had happened, and with greater indignation than discretion charged that Forrest had instigated the sorry business. "The only disgrace," he said editorially, "rests upon himself. . . . With his peculiar tastes he will probably enjoy the infamy." A good many New Yorkers probably agreed, but there was no proof, then or later, and Raymond, attacked by the *Herald* for his rash accusation, confessed that he could not support his charge. What must have been still more humiliating, he published in the *Courier* Colonel Webb's apology for his error. It was quickly forgotten, however, wiped out by events that piled one upon the other.

The city's sober minds generally deplored the Opera House affair, and, attempting to make amends, publicly urged Macready to play again. Washington Irving signed the statement, and with him appeared many men prominent in New York life; Raymond joined his signature to the rest. After such prompting Macready unwisely agreed to appear again in *Macbeth*.

Once more threats spread, and this time they were not only rumors. "Working Men, Shall American or English Rule in this City?" screamed handbills that denounced the "English Aristocratic Opera House." There was tension in New York. The more timid recalled Europe's revolutions and barricades, while others, at least among the city's leaders, were determined that order should and would be maintained. The *Herald* said ominously: "The rioters will be well licked tonight, or the city again disgraced."

Raymond that mild spring evening—it was May 10—reached Astor Place at about seven-thirty to find it "occupied by a dense crowd," a milling mass that filled not only Astor Place but spilled into Eighth Street and Broadway. Police guarded the Opera House; the doors were barred and the windows barricaded. Within the theater all seats were filled, though when the time came for the curtain to rise upon the witches' scene in *Macbeth* only seven women had joined the audience. Macready—he said afterward that he had gone "gaily" to the theater —dressed for the play, "nervous and ruffled" because his hairdresser arrived late. At last the performance began. This time the principal disorder was outside.

Unable to enter the Opera House, Raymond posted himself in Eighth Street to watch. In Broadway material for violence had been unwittingly provided, for a new sewer was under construction and the street was torn up; paving blocks, against the day when construction would be completed, stood neatly piled. A man caught up one. It thudded against a shuttered window. Another followed, and then another, until a steady tattoo beat upon windows and walls. Some, as time passed, shattered the shutters, broke into the auditorium, striking the great chandelier. Others smashed water pipes, flooding Macready's dressing room. The unhappy actor fled in disguise.

Police, unable to halt the rioting, stood by futilely until about nine o'clock a company of hussars, "mounted on white horses and riding two a-breast with drawn swords," clattered up Broadway and swung around through Eighth Street into Astor Place. A shower of stones greeted them. The hussars stood their ground and were soon joined by more cavalry and a battalion of infantry with "fixed bayonets gleaming above the heads of the surrounding crowd." There was more stoning, and the reading of the riot act was met with boos. Not even when the troops fired a volley above the heads of massed men did the stoning halt.

The soldiers reloaded, took aim. An officer barked the command to fire, and as smoke billowed in the night air, silence descended. The rioters, momentarily stunned, swayed back and forth and then broke in panicky retreat and flight. Nineteen men lay dead on the bloody stones of Astor Place.

Raymond, as he had done three nights earlier, hurried downtown to the *Courier* office to write of the untoward scenes. "We passed at different times," he said, "through every part of the crowd—which could not have numbered less than 25,000 persons; and yet among them all, we do not believe there were more than 500, if there were so many, who took an active part in the riot, and of these nearly or quite half were boys." He added further detail: "Those who took an active part in stoning the building were only fifty or sixty in number. . . . They took up stones from the streets, and men among them took large flag stones and broke them in pieces, distributing them among the mob, who hurled them at the windows. . . ." Terrible as the consequences had been, concluded Raymond, it had been necessary for the cause of law and order to urge Macready's appearance at the Opera House and to disperse the rioters drawn together by hatred of that unhappy actor. The strong medicine administered, Raymond averred, "must convince the world that we have Laws which protect personal and private rights, that we have Rulers who are disposed to enforce them."

There was a coroner's inquest. The press exchanged recriminations, the *Herald* attacking the signers of the card that had brought Macready's return engagement. Colonel Webb, suspecting probably that the attack was directed against Raymond in particular, answered that any right-thinking citizen would have done as he. The talk died away, and so far as possible the veil of forgetfulness was drawn across the Astor Place riot, though Forrest, whatever his responsibility, found his reputation permanently tarnished, and the Opera House never regained favor as a place of entertainment.

VI

Raymond was too busy to think long of what he had witnessed, for he had the *Courier* to manage and he was considering an offer to move to Albany to establish a new paper. His decision depended in part on the outcome of a prolonged argument with Colonel Webb over support of the Taylor Administration. Webb, conscious of his role in securing a Whig victory the previous year, had cooled his heels for many weeks in Washington in quest of a diplomatic appointment. Madrid was his goal, but hardly had President Taylor been inaugurated before the prospects looked poor for the *Courier*'s owner-editor to take up residence at the Bourbon court. "It is whispered," the *Herald* gossiped, "and pretty loudly, too, that he is terribly disappointed at the ungratefulness of republics in general, and this republic in particular." In the *Courier*'s columns the Colonel praised the new President and his Cabinet, but the fine words got him nowhere, and finally, about the time of the Astor Place riot, he came back to New York in great anger. He sold his town house as an expression of his disgust, rented his country place and prepared to attack the Administration in the *Courier* relentlessly and without quarter.

Fearful of what this could mean to the paper, Raymond protested, and with the aid of some of the Colonel's friends succeeded in pacifying the bitterly disappointed office-seeker, who as part of a cooling-off process decided to travel in the Middle West. Before his departure early in June, 1849, he agreed that the *Courier* need not oppose the Administration, but he also pledged Raymond not to support it either, a pledge from which Raymond quickly sought release. Though still unforgiving, Webb finally gave his managing editor the right to act as he thought best. The result was an editorial that on July 7 defended President Taylor's stand upon appointments and declared: "He has sought uniformly the promotion of the public good, and not the satisfaction of any personal interest. He . . . has acted always in strict conformity with what he believed to be his duty to the country."

Raymond justified himself as best he could with his absent superior, and his position brought dividends in the form of praise for Webb's magnanimity. If anything, the editorial had helped Webb's cause, although it was not wholly apparent at the moment, and the Colonel during his long summer tour wrote Raymond repeatedly requesting that the *Courier* set forth his position in his personal controversy with the President. But Raymond stood steadfast, seemingly convinced of the rightness of what he had done and certain that in the end he could win Webb to it.

New York underwent its usual torrid summer. There was cholera in town, and the death toll mounted while the press inveighed against the filthy streets that were blamed in part for the epidemic. On August 2 the *Courier* reported that 170 new cases and sixty deaths had occurred in the previous twenty-four hours. The Reverend John Wheeler, president of the University of Vermont, noted while in the city that the nostrums for cholera were "multitudinous." Raymond remained in his office, except for brief visits with his family, who were spending the hot months at Greenwich, where Mrs. Raymond was expecting another child. This time it was a daughter, Mary, who was born in early September. The *Courier* was showing great interest in the Hungarian revolution and its hero Louis Kossuth, and at a mass meeting in City Hall Park Raymond urged American recognition of Kossuth's republic and American support. A letter from Governor Fish approved such a position, and the meeting before it dispersed adopted a petition for American aid to the Hungarians in their struggle against reaction and tyranny.

With cooler weather Colonel Webb came back to the city and at last set his seal to Raymond's conduct of the *Courier*. Raymond himself put away thoughts of a paper in Albany, and that there might be no uncertainty of his conception of where direction of the *Courier*'s destiny lay, he wrote the Colonel: "You have a right to control the paper absolutely, and . . . I agree entirely with you that the *Courier and Enquirer* ought to be thoroughly independent—of *persons* as well as of parties. . . . I think I may safely appeal to the past to convince you of my readiness, so long as I may remain in the paper, to conduct it in conformity with your views and wishes. Whenever it should become no longer possible for me to do so, I should of course expect to leave it. But I anticipate no such case."

Webb now began once more to hope for a diplomatic mission. Raymond's editorial correctness had soothed any soreness that might have existed in Administration circles, and the Colonel's friends, Senator

Seward notably, were doing what they could to obtain the appointment so greatly desired. Rumors circulated that Webb's wish would be realized, and their truth grew so apparent that the *Herald* remarked sarcastically: "He makes a good appearance, dresses like a gentleman, talks well, rides well, eats well, drinks well, prays well, plays well and would make a capital minister or chargé to any court where there is nothing to do." At the end of November the Colonel was named American chargé at Vienna.

The *Courier* soon afterward announced that Colonel Webb had sailed for Europe and that henceforth Raymond would be in sole editorial control of the paper. The Colonel's departure—it had been unexpected and almost secret—caused a lot of comment in Washington, and men were now saying that he had hurried away to avoid what Raymond described as the "ordeal of the Senate's action." Senator Seward wrote Raymond that there was a "little restlessness" on Capitol Hill, and that "there is some little ground, not much, for the allegations that there are Whig Senators dissatisfied with appointments." It fell to Raymond to explain why Colonel Webb had sailed so abruptly.

Webb, a widower briefly, had secretly married early in November the daughter of Jacob Cram, a millionaire brewer, who did not learn of the elopement for more than a fortnight. When he did, he insisted, though approving the match, that the marriage be announced, something that Webb did not want to do until he had left the country, maintaining that his daughters might feel badly because the marriage followed so soon upon their mother's death the previous year. Cram remained adamant, and finally he and Webb agreed that the marriage should be announced within three days, the announcement to coincide with departure for Europe. Webb and his bride hurriedly packed their belongings and were on their way, leaving gossip and political rivalry to do their worst.

"These are the facts as I had them from Colonel Webb himself," Raymond told Seward, "and I should think they should obviate any injury he is likely to sustain from the supposition that he sought to anticipate the action of the Senate. I know that he would never have acted from such a motive, because with his usual sanguine disposition he did not allow himself to doubt for an instant that he would be confirmed by a very large majority." Presumably Seward in conversation with his colleagues in the Senate cloakroom passed along the explanation that Raymond had sent him, but he had to report in a few days that it did not suffice.

"It would evince a want of frankness," the Senator wrote, "if I should omit to say to you that there is a very great want of sound feeling among Whigs in regard to confirmation, and that the prejudice against Col. Webb has been too much aggravated by the circumstances to which you refer. Would it not be well to affirm in the *Courier* . . . that the suddenness of his departure arose from causes purely domestic and honorable to himself? Is there no esprit de corps in the Press? Have they no magnanimity? I wish you would try. How often has the Press had a diplomatic representative at all? If they could have met, the Editors, and selected one, whom would they have found that while distinguished by talent had a higher sense of the dignity of the Profession?"

However he may have felt about Webb's qualifications for diplomacy, Raymond had no intention of drawing the *Courier* into the controversy over the appointment, for had not he and the Colonel agreed that the paper should be independent of persons? But he was ready and willing to do what he could outside the *Courier's* columns, and so he drafted a statement of Webb's reasons for sudden departure, printed it, and sent a copy to every member of the United States Senate. It may have helped, but it was not enough. The Whig opponents of Colonel Webb had partners among Democratic members, and in the end Seward had to send Raymond the "unpleasant information" that Webb's name had been rejected.

VII

With Raymond's name at its masthead, the *Courier* went its way. From Boston came detailed description of Professor Webster's gruesome murder of Dr. Parkman. There were two Hawaiian princes in the city, their daily round providing copy for every paper. Niblo's was rebuilding. For the first time in years the *Courier* neglected to publish "A Visit From St. Nicholas" in its Christmas issue.

Over every editorial room, as over the nation, a growing shadow was being cast by the slavery issue and the impending Congressional debate over disposition of the territories acquired from Mexico. Talk of secession drifted up from the South, and the *Courier* one morning asserted prophetically that secession would leave the South the loser, since it would lift from the slave states the Constitutional protection of slavery and would turn the North wholeheartedly to abolition. Raymond would write many editorials on secession and slavery before the issue was settled once and for all. He would also participate directly in the political debates upon these issues. The start of that participation was now at hand.

CHAPTER

7

Albany Interlude

I

"AND NOW I find myself at Albany as member of Assembly," Raymond wrote in his journal on January 1, 1850. He lacked three weeks of being thirty, and his swelling political interest and activity had been rewarded the previous November by election as a Whig Assemblyman from New York City's Ninth Ward. Senator Seward regarded him as a political protégé, and while Raymond's relations with Thurlow Weed were less personal, the two had seen much of each other and were quickly to draw tight the bonds of political partnership. His former friendship with Horace Greeley, junior member of the political firm of Seward, Weed & Co., of course had cooled, but the very fact of his quarrels with the *Tribune*'s editor added something to his stature. Governor Fish had been told before the election that "Raymond is very friendly to you."

Yet most members of the New York Assembly knew little at first hand of Raymond's skills of oratory or leadership when he came up the river to register at Congress Hall, Albany's best hotel and for half a century a favorite with distinguished travelers, legislators, and lawyers come to attend court. From its high terrace the building looked out toward the park where the outlines of the Albany Academy, Philip Hooker's architectural masterpiece, balanced the brownstone State Capitol, which with its Ionic portico and its cupola crowned with a wooden figure of Justice dominated the well-planned city that climbed the hills from the Hudson's busy waterside, where the river steamers docked and the canal boats crowded their basin.

Architect Philip Hooker had found Albany a dingy country town reminiscent of old New Amsterdam and after a generation had left it a city of the American Renaissance. The classic façades of the Capitol and the Academy, the City Hall, and the central market recorded his taste. The city's chief churches, the Christopher Wren spires of some punctuating the sky, were his also, and after he had gone, the Greek revival gave the State offices across the street from the Capitol a solidly imposing temple of marble, one of the many striking buildings that caused a foreign visitor to remember Albany as a place "gay with some gilded domes, and many white marble columns."

A bustling city of 50,000 in which the old Dutch aristocracy still set a severe tone for social life, it became, particularly when winter's cold and the difficulties of travel marooned citizens and legislators alike, a provincial capital. There were plays to attend that winter of 1850, concerts and lectures, and Fanny Kemble came to town to read Shakespeare. There were parties and balls. The house on Elk Street that Governor Hamilton Fish had rented when he took office in 1849 saw brilliant receptions and dinners surpassing all others the capital could offer. For the legislators there were gay stag nights when wine and whiskey flowed long in the taproom at Congress Hall or at some lesser tavern. Sleighing, a popular sport, brought forth the simple pung as well as elaborate turnouts drawn by four or six horses, sleighs that to the jingling of bells dashed through the city streets frightening the pedestrian and endangering his life.

Raymond reached Albany at the moment of political crisis born of the struggle over slavery and the territorial legacy from the war with Mexico. The new lands to the west could not continue to remain unorganized and California already clamored for admission to the Union. On those rocks the nation threatened to split asunder, for just as Southerners insisted that slavery should not be excluded from the new lands, so many Northerners had made up their minds that the time had come to halt the further spread of an institution they abhorred morally, economically and politically. The Missouri Compromise that in the year of Raymond's birth had seemed to answer the slavery question finally had lost its finality, and at Washington the elder statesmen of the nation were striving to find an avenue that would lead away from secession and disunion.

The aging Henry Clay, the dying Calhoun, and Daniel Webster were leaders in the quest for compromise. William Henry Seward was not with them. However little brief he might hold for the violent abolitionism of men like William Lloyd Garrison, the Senator from New York was nevertheless outspoken in his insistence that further spread of slavery must be prevented and that slavery itself must be done away. He had stated his position often. At Cleveland in 1848 he had said boldly: "There are two antagonistic elements of society in America, freedom and slavery. . . . Freedom insists on the emancipation and elevation of labor. Slavery demands a soil moistened with tears and blood. . . . Slavery can be limited to its present bounds; it can be ameliorated; it can and must be abolished, and you and I can and must do it." Before 1850 was many months old Seward sounded even more resolutely the tocsin of freedom.

Whigs and Democrats alike were divided by the slavery issue—it could not be forgotten that it had been a Pennsylvania Democrat, David Wilmot, who in 1846 had precipitated the present crisis by offering in Congress the proviso to bar "slavery and involuntary servitude" from all territory won from Mexico—and the division extended to both national and state politics. Division appeared particularly in the North, where both parties contained elements that would compromise with the slave power, that would destroy it root and branch, or that would seek some middle ground such as Seward may have had in mind when he said that slavery could be "ameliorated."

When the Congress of the United States met at Washington in December, 1849, the issue of slavery in the territories promised to be the all-consuming business of the session. Many men believed the fate of the nation itself was at stake, and their concern, stirred by fire-eating talk of secession among Southerners, spread from the halls of Congress to state capitals, to cities and villages throughout the land. It was the dominating note of the New York Legislature of 1850. It was paramount in Raymond's mind as he unpacked at Congress Hall and prepared for his initiation into the hundred days of legislative routine prescribed by law.

II

The streets were icy and the snow lay deep when Raymond on the morning of January 1, 1850, walked to the Capitol for the Legislature's convening. The Senate was safely Whig, but the Democrats, thanks to their majority of one, organized the Assembly, electing officers and commanding committees. Then began the choice of seats in the lower house. It was a new phase of Raymond's political education, for he discovered, and to his amazement, that members, regardless of the seats assigned them by lot, were willing to buy seats more nearly in the Speaker's vision from those who had drawn better positions. Perhaps Raymond paid for his own seat, for it was a good one. In the semicircle before the Speaker he sat in No. 43, second from the aisle, second row, on the Speaker's left. Behind him was the visitors' gallery, supported by eight fluted Ionic columns characteristic of Philip Hooker's design; overhead stretched an elaborately decorated ceiling and the rich ornamentation of cornice and stuccoed frieze. None of the men in that hall with Raymond possessed his brilliance, although one of his colleagues, William A. Wheeler, a fellow Whig who had been a student with him at Burlington, almost a generation later took the oath of Vice-President of the United States.

Raymond was busy those first days at Albany. There were caucuses to attend, calls to make, conferences to hold. He paid his respects to Governor Fish. He talked committee assignments with the Speaker— ultimately he was placed upon the Committee for Banks and Insurance —talked finance, slavery, internal improvements, or the future of Texas with the fellow members who called on him at Congress Hall where the bedrooms were "commodious, capacious and elegant" and the parlors were "fitted up in the most desirable style, furnished with the richest carpets and the choicest furniture, elegant mirrors and everything that can conduce to the comfort of the guests." He saw something of George Jones, his old *Tribune* friend and associate, who was anxious about the possibility that new legislation might curb his profits as a buyer and seller of bank notes.

Raymond sought to become familiar with the historical background of the scene before his eyes. He read the annual messages of recent governors and the controllers' reports and turned to Hammond's *History of Political Parties in the State of New York*—he thought the style "worthless"—for more general knowledge of things past. He read Burke, probably with the eyes of an orator, current magazines—the *Literary World* was being sent to him from New York—current books, and managed also to send editorials to the *Courier and Enquirer* office. The program called for a long day, and time and again he was not in bed until midnight or later.

The spirit in which he faced his legislative duties he set down in his journal one day after he had read Whittier's tribute to William Leggett, who before Raymond had entered the New York newspaper circle had been an editor of the *Evening Post*, a writer of distinction, a defender of the laborer, and an active abolitionist to boot.

Leggett was certainly a brave and gifted man [wrote Raymond]. His abolitionism was a result of a noble impulse, but I cannot join with Whittier in wishing all young men to be like Leggett. The world needs discretion as much as zeal, and although the latter generally usurps all the honors and glories of heroism, the former does a great deal the most toward carrying on the daily affairs of society and states. If everybody were discreet and nobody zealous, things would certainly go on much better than if everybody were zealous and nobody discreet. This form of statement, however, misleads—as it makes extremes the standard of comparison and judgement, which is never safe. Zeal tempered and guided by discretion, or discretion warmed and energized by zeal, is the true temperament for safe and successful conduct.

It was a standard by which Raymond, increasingly as he grew older, measured his own conduct.

Governor Fish, also a moderate and a believer in discretion, a Whig who felt that Senator Seward and Horace Greeley had gone to extremes in their attitudes toward slavery, sounded the keynote for the Legislature of 1850 in his annual message, where he set forth the proposition that the people of the state were as one "in their fixed determination to resist the extension of slavery over territories now free." He denounced as unconstitutional any Congressional attempt to establish slavery in California, which, in company with New Mexico, President Taylor had invited to draft a constitution and ask admission as a state. He protested against the rising sectional antagonism with its threat of Southern secession. Yet to secessionists and slavery radicals he threw down the gage when he said: "New York loves the Union of the States. She will not contemplate the possibility of its dissolution; and sees no reason to calculate the enormity of such a calamity. She also loves the cause of Human Freedom; and sees no reason to abstain from an avowal of her attachment. While, therefore, she holds fast to the one, she will not forsake the other."

The Legislature was expected to put into words its own position on the critical issue, but it was not easy. Divided party control of the Assembly and Senate explained part of it; division within the parties compounded it. "Our Democratic Assembly," Fish told Seward, "finds difficulty in the expressions of its sentiments on the subject of the extension of slavery. I think it will find a voice, although it is late in attaining the power of articulation." But it was not only the Democrats. Fish might have added that the Assembly's Whig minority had not been of one mind, that there had been a good deal of caucusing and maneuvering before they decided where they stood, and even then their views were milder than those of their Senate brethren, who ultimately brought the Legislature to favor California's admission as a free state and to demand slavery's exclusion from all the rest of the territory won from Mexico.

Raymond, who had been more active in the framing of the slavery resolutions than might have been expected from a new member, had used the weeks of debate to clarify his own views on the subject. At first he had hoped to sidestep the whole business, and in the Whig caucus

had offered resolutions that would pledge loyalty to the Union but deprecate agitation of the slavery question for sectional purposes. Gradually he moved from the safety of so conservative an attitude toward the
exposed free-soil position of Seward, and finally, in his first major speech
as an Assemblyman, he put himself on record as a Seward man.

"Those whom I represent . . .," he said, "believe that slavery should
be prohibited from free territory by positive law." He argued that the
North opposed slavery both as an evil in itself and as contrary to the nation's best interests. The North, furthermore, wanted to end the unequal Congressional representation that slavery made possible and to
prevent the extension of slave territory in order to speed the extinction
of the South's "peculiar institution." "For my own part," he told the
galleries and the members seated in the semicircle around him, "I believe
that slavery's end must come. In this country, as in every other country
where it has had existence, its extinction must at some time, more or less
remote, be brought about." The Assembly's Whigs paid him the compliment of printing his speech and circulating it as a pamphlet.

Seward read it with "mingled pleasure and admiration." The new
member, he remarked, was "making himself a distinguished reputation."
To Raymond he sent welcome praise. "I have read and shall preserve as
an important part of the history of this critical period your speeches in
the Debates on the resolutions," was his message from Washington. "I
have many a time wished that we had you on the floor of the House here.
You however have been more truly occupied in sustaining the cause
of the Right at home." Such commendation might have turned stronger
heads than Raymond's, but he seems to have kept his balance.

Early in the session at Albany, Seward had told Raymond that "Mr.
Weed will explain anything to you which I am not at liberty, or at
leisure, to write." With Weed's guidance, the gentleman from New
York's Ninth Ward passed his apprenticeship. He sponsored private
bills, as did every member. He defended Seward, who at Washington
had proposed vainly that free lands be granted to exiles from Hungary's
revolution, and helped to push through the New York Legislature resolutions upholding Seward's proposal. Several times he presided over the
Assembly when it sat as a committee of the whole. He spoke eloquently
in the cause of free schools and higher education.

On one special issue before the Assembly Raymond expanded further
his growing reputation. Petitions had been offered for improvement of
the Racquette and Moose Rivers in northwestern New York, and at
the start of the legislative session the Speaker had asked Raymond to
act as chairman of a select committee to study the project. When the
offer was laid before him, he confessed ignorance of the subject, although

he favored developing the resources of the region—a wild, heavily wooded, unsettled part of the state. So he went to work. A month later the Assembly received his report, carefully documented and loaded with citations from previous official and private surveys. It attracted a great deal of attention for its careful research and investigation, and long after the relatively minor matter of opening the Racquette River country had been forgotten, the recollection of what Raymond's committee had done was talked about and cited in New York as evidence of the ability and ease with which he had taken to legislative duties.

The session was drawing to a close when on April 2 the flags at the Capitol were lowered to half-staff and a special message from Governor Fish brought word—it was hardly news—that in Washington John C. Calhoun, statesman of secession and nullification, had coughed his life away. A hush fell over the New York Legislature as the Governor's message was read, and before adjourning in tribute to the South Carolinian, both houses listened to their principal orators. Among them was Raymond, who rose in the spirit of *de mortuis nil nisi bonum* to say: "It has been said, and I think with justice, that in his public career, Mr. Calhoun was somewhat too sectional—but this peculiarity grew out of his devotion to his own State, which he regarded as his country, to whose interest and advancement he devoted his great energies and all his talents."

The Legislature hastened to complete its labors. In the early morning of April 11 the final gavel fell and the visitors, men and women alike, filed out from the crowded galleries into Albany's spring night. Only Raymond had stood out among the legislators. His almost precocious political sense, his rich voice and oratorical power had lifted him to heights that new members seldom attain; his relations with Seward and Weed made that position more secure, and when he boarded the boat to go downriver to New York and his office and his family in the house on West Thirteenth Street, he was already marked for higher place.

III

The session in Albany had been overshadowed by what was taking place in Washington, for events there were shaping that held deepest political meaning. At the end of January, a few days after Raymond had made his first major Assembly effort, Henry Clay had presented resolutions in the Senate designed to head off what he and elder statesmen like him feared was a grave threat to the Federal Union they loved. They were alarmed lest the bluff old soldier in the White House be obliged to carry out his warning that he would meet secession with armed force, possibly even with himself at the head of the troops. They found solace neither in this warning nor in the President's proposals in his annual message that California enter the Union as a free state and that, without mention of slavery, New Mexico and Utah be allowed to organize territorial governments.

Henry Clay, whose voice had lost its strength and vigor, came forward to avert catastrophe. He proposed to admit California as a free state, allow New Mexico and Utah to organize as territories, enact a strict law for the return of fugitive slaves, abolish the slave trade in the District of Columbia, and settle a Texas boundary dispute as well as have the Texan debt assumed by the national government. He spoke with all his accustomed eloquence for his compromise, heard it defended with classic brilliance by Webster in the famous Seventh of March address that brought scorn upon the great head of the Massachusetts Senator and the epithet "Ichabod" from Whittier, the abolitionist poet of Amesbury. For free-soil principles William Henry Seward was the advocate. Four days after Webster spoke, Seward delivered one of the momentous orations of his life.

There were not many of his colleagues on the floor when he began his speech in the little chamber with its crimson carpets and draperies. Nor were there many spectators in the gallery. He was not a popular figure in Washington, this New Yorker, for his views had more than once caused a "shudder" to run through the United States Senate. He had made known, however, that in essence he supported President Taylor in the present crisis, that he felt no compromise necessary in regard to slavery. In his March 11 speech, he went still farther.

To the South he spoke words of warning: "The question of dissolving the Union . . . embraces the fearful issue, whether the Union shall stand, and slavery . . . be removed by gradual, voluntary effort, and with compensation, or whether the Union shall be dissolved, and civil war ensue, bringing on violent, but complete and immediate emancipation." In words remembered long after the rest of what he said had been forgotten, Seward declared his belief in something above even the Constitution so far as slavery in territories was concerned. "There is a higher law," he asserted, and this invocation of the law of God resounded across the Potomac to the Southland and north to abolition country. It brought upon him greater praise and denunciation than he had ever known. More than 100,000 copies of the speech were sown across the land under the Seward frank, and the mail the speech inspired nearly overwhelmed him.

Raymond tended to go whole hog with Seward on the compromise issue, and editorials in the *Courier and Enquirer* had all along been far stronger than Democratic organs like the *Herald* could stomach. Throughout the winter and early spring the *Herald*, attacking the *Courier* as a "counting-room journal" and charging that it was "patronized by merchants and bankers," which it was, had been asking why it should take a stand on slavery that disturbed the country and therefore injured business. The *Herald* accused the *Courier* of catering to Seward and Weed, and on one occasion asked, with tongue in cheek, who might be responsible for its stand, since Colonel Webb was out of the country and Raymond was busy at Albany. That Raymond was writing most of the editorials and deciding policy was no man's mystery even during the legislative session, and after his return from the capital, the *Herald* needed to inquire no longer.

One slashing editorial followed another, keeping pace as it were with the events on Washington's Capitol Hill, where debate on the compromise resolutions continued day after day, month after month. The lilacs budded, bloomed, and faded, and as the hot days approached the Senate's red carpet was rolled up and the crimson draperies taken down so that the chamber might seem cooler than it was. In the *Courier* Seward's warning to the South was echoed. The doctrine of the "higher law" was defended. "The law of Nature," it was stated, "is superior to human law." And the time came when Webster was accused of being out of step with the North, and the whole compromise, which the *Courier* had once endorsed, was denounced in favor of President Taylor's plan for letting the territories decide their own destiny so far as slavery was an issue. "Northern Whigs and Northern people do not stand now, in reference to Slavery, where they stood ten years ago," the *Courier* declared.

But the compromise, whatever the arguments on either side, was obviously winning support, partly because men like Governor Fish began to agree that without some such arrangement the South might make real its secession threats. The country, moreover, tired of the endless debate, wanted to put slavery aside and get along with more profitable business, and so, after eight months of point and counterpoint, Clay's resolutions were adopted. "We look now for peace, for quiet, for the freedom from agitation and excitement," the *Courier* told its readers after the compromise had become law, but its blessing was not without reservation. The *Courier* had doubts of the deepest, and expressed them: "We believe the surest and safest way to *avert* danger is to *meet* it; that to compromise with rebellion is to encourage and foment it; and that every such compromise renders another inevitable."

Seward and his supporters meantime had received a blow that all but wrecked them and their party in New York, for on the morning of

July 9, with the words "I am prepared—I have endeavored to do my duty" on his lips, Zachary Taylor, President of the United States, had died unexpectedly in the midst of the capital's summer heat. There was mourning crepe on the public buildings, and flags, so recently lowered for Calhoun, again flew at half-staff. The new President was the color-less Millard Fillmore, who held William Henry Seward a dangerous rival to be struck down as quickly as possible. With misgivings and obvious hesitancy the *Courier* greeted the new Chief Executive, hoping for the best while recalling that Fillmore tended to lean upon those Whigs least hostile to slavery—the "cotton Whigs"—and suggesting that the President, like Webster, was probably out of tune with North-ern sentiments.

Raymond's misgivings about Fillmore's course as Chief Executive arose in part, of course, from fear of what it held in store for Seward, Weed & Co. As Vice-President, Fillmore had quarreled with Seward over the New York patronage. As President, he immediately began to remove from office both Seward and Weed appointees, including even the postmaster in Weed's home bailiwick of Albany. So direct a chal-lenge to the Senator and the Dictator could not go unanswered. In the end, it wrecked Fillmore's political career. More immediately, it split the Whig party of New York, for at the party convention in Utica that fall the Fillmore men seceded when the Seward-Weed delegates forced through a resolution approving their Senator's anti-slavery position. Both wings came together to send the Whig ticket to victory on elec-tion day, but the party was disastrously weakened, a symptom of the creeping paralysis soon to bring death to the Whig party in state and nation.

IV

Colonel Webb was still absent from the country—he did not return until autumn—and Raymond's activities were not confined to the *Courier* office, though his work there would have seemed to have been full-time. He was speaking often—at a banquet of the Associated Press, for example, and again at a public meeting to seek funds for a printers' library. In June the House of Harper had placed before the public a new monthly literary magazine. Raymond was its managing editor, a post that drew him closer to the Harper brothers and their sons in an association that had begun several years earlier when he started to read manuscripts for their publishing house.[1]

As the summer waxed, Raymond exchanged briefly both journalism and politics for one of the constant joys of his life, a visit to Burlington

[1] He remained managing editor of *Harper's Magazine* until 1856.

and the university on the green hilltop above the sparkling lake. In the ten years since he had received the parchment of his bachelor's degree, he had come to be regarded as one of U.V.M.'s distinguished sons, distinguished enough now to be elected to the board of trustees for a decade's service as a member of the corporation. He had been steadily active in the alumni association; in this August of 1850 he returned to Burlington to address that body on "the relation of the American scholar to his country and his times."

It was a learned speech, filled with citations from history, from the classics of ancient and English literature, and yet it was based partly, Raymond told his audience, on personal observation and experience gained "in the midst of the severe and incessant labors of active life." In a sense, therefore, he was stating his own philosophy when he deplored equally the conservatism that would halt all change and the radicalism that would overturn even the monuments of the past. He himself did not oppose change. He believed in it with all possible optimism. "The law of social growth," he said, "is . . . always from the lower to the higher—from that which is good to that which is better." Conservatism and radicalism he saw as necessary opposites for the equilibrium of society; each must counteract the other, and neither must be allowed to be in the ascendant. It was again zeal tempered with discretion, the Raymond tendency to keep the middle of the road, that underlay the remarks to the alumni at Burlington. "We must put our hands to the great work of social progress," he urged, "and give all the aid of our utmost strength to the enlightenment and the advancement of our fellow-man. Thus, and thus only, can we discharge the duties which every American Scholar owes to American Society."

V

That Raymond should be nominated again for a place in the Assembly was understood. His record justified it. He had the support of Seward and Weed, however much that support may have been disguised and however private may have been Seward's warm friendly letters in which he told him of his right to the "first and best trophies of victory." Nomination granted, election followed in sequence, and one night after the returns were counted, Whigs gathered in the new and luxurious Clarendon Hotel at Fourth Avenue and Eighteenth Street for a victory dinner.

Raymond was among the speakers after the cloth had been lifted. His theme was party unity, and he told his fellows that Whig unanimity on slavery was no necessity, that the guide should be "local sentiments on local subjects," that the constitutional guarantees of slavery should be respected, which presumably meant support for the new Fugitive

Courtesy of Mrs. George T. Lambert

The Young Raymond

His earliest known picture. This daguerreotype was presumably made when
he was first in New York City.

Horace Greeley

Thurlow Weed

William H. Seward

James Watson Webb

Slave Law. It was a conservative speech. It brought down a brief storm upon the reelected Assemblyman.

"Little Jesuit," the New York *Express* threw at him, charging that he preached radical doctrine in Albany and conservative in New York, accusing him of seeking to please both rural constituencies, with their free-soil tendencies, and urban voters, who disliked free-soil agitation for its upsetting effect on trade. Raymond defended himself as best he could, and made the telling point that he had pledged nothing to his constituents yet had been reelected by a larger majority than a year earlier when he was a political unknown. It was not the last time he would be called a demagogue and derided as a trimmer, as a striver to be all things to all men. It was the price he paid for failing to ally himself definitely with partisans, and in an age of party discipline, a man had to be either black or white. To be any shade of gray was to be suspect.

The *Express*'s attack passed harmlessly, and already the politically informed were whispering that Raymond would be the next Speaker of the Assembly. Greeley told him he was "the new Speaker presumptive," and William Wheeler wrote from upstate, "You are to be the man . . . so turn your attention to the Manual as soon as you please." The *Herald* informed its Democratic readers that Thurlow Weed's influence "will be used in favor of Mr. Raymond," whom the *Herald*'s managing editor described in his diary as "a man of considerable ability . . . little or no genius . . . short in stature and not very attractive in appearance . . . very amiable." The Seward-Weed candidate Raymond might be, but the choice would probably not have fallen upon him had it not been possible for all Whig factions to regard him as somewhat above their quarrels, as identified wholly with neither side. That was at least one reward of his being partially independent at a moment when the Fillmore and Seward Whigs were snarling fiercely at one another.

In his *Evening Journal* Thurlow Weed was vilifying President Fillmore and his works; a Fillmore organ, the *Register*, had been started in Albany in answer. The caterwaulings of the two papers so endangered party harmony that some of the influential Whig stalwarts, notably the New York City business group, sought to persuade the President to offer Weed a foreign mission. If accepted, the post would serve as a peace offering and would also remove the editor of the *Journal* from Albany and thus presumably end its assaults upon Fillmore. The scheme looked promising for a time, as did a companion piece for the purchase of the *Journal* by a group of Whigs and Weed's retirement from politics.

The second project was of direct concern to Raymond. It included him, in fact, for he was to take Thurlow Weed's editorial chair and possibly his political mantle. In the midst of the conversations looking to this end, he wrote to one of his elder advisers: "I stand perfectly still. I am, in truth, not attracted thither. I prefer New York. I *fear* the result of undertaking to steer so huge and so peculiar a craft as the Whig party of this state, and that is in fact the nature of the post in question. All this, however, will work up clearer bye and bye. Just now I stand and wait." In the end it all came to nothing. For more than a decade longer Thurlow Weed remained editor of the *Journal* and Dictator, and Raymond, who had already come up the river to Albany and settled again at Congress Hall, soon had another project afoot that would insure his remaining all the rest of his life on New York City's newspaper row.

VI

The Legislature—Washington Hunt was the new Governor—had convened on January 7, 1851, and the Whig-controlled Assembly promptly followed prophecy by electing Raymond to the speakership, where he made party harmony his objective but momentarily stirred the embers of strife by breaking the tradition that dictated the naming of a speaker's nearest rival to the chairmanship of the Ways and Means Committee. A Fillmore Whig had been the nearest contender. Raymond passed him over to select his friend William Wheeler. Ultimately it had to be explained in Washington, but the Administration did not allow the incident to disturb its current aim of peace among New York Whigs, and the Legislature pushed ahead with its work.

"I like my place very much," Raymond reported at the end of his first week. "Everything goes swimmingly . . . if not always *smoothly*." The *Courier*, from which he had taken leave of absence for the session's duration, sent him a sweet bouquet: "[The] Speaker, young as he is, presides with dignity and decision; and is altogether the most rapid and efficient that we have ever seen in that chair. A gentleman of very decided talent and familiar with the rules of order, his promptness and decision aid wonderfully in the dispatch of business; and it was frequently remarked to us, that the close of the second week of the session finds its business quite three weeks in advance of what it usually is." Even the *Herald* said agreeably: "The conduct of Mr. Speaker Raymond in the chair gives great satisfaction."

He had need for all his ability in the stormy weeks ahead. The first important business, and in this the Legislature bogged down, was the election of a United States Senator, a Senator whom the Whigs would name inasmuch as they controlled both houses. From the beginning it was obvious that Hamilton Fish led the field. His chief handicap arose from confusion over his views toward the Compromise of 1850, for how a man stood in that regard determined whether he was numbered with the Fillmore or the Seward faction. Actually, Fish felt he belonged to neither. None wanted party harmony more than he, and to achieve that end he was prepared to accept all the compromise save the Fugitive Slave Act. There he broke company with conservatives, although as he wrote the President, he was willing to await the opportune moment for the law's amendment. To neither side would he give pledges, a fact that caused it to be whispered in the Capitol lobbies that he was coquetting with the conservatives while wholly at Seward's command.

There were other candidates, few of them serious contenders, although Colonel Webb hoped that he might supplant the favorite and thus obtain some solace for his unhappy venture in diplomacy. He urged his cause with Raymond, and sought his help in furthering his candidacy, arguing "that it was of the utmost importance to the friends of Mr. Seward that he should have an abler associate to aid him in the Senate than Governor Fish would be." Because Raymond declined to mix business and political loyalties, Webb's candidacy got nowhere.

When the Whig caucus met in the Assembly's chamber in the early evening of January 31, Hamilton Fish had become the Seward-Weed candidate behind whom even some Fillmore Whigs were falling in line. Raymond, after the discussion had run out, moved that balloting begin, and when Fish received all but four of seventy votes cast, rose again to move that the nomination be unanimous. Nomination did not mean automatic election, for there were Fillmore Whigs temporarily allied with Democrats who were unwilling to see the former Governor move to Washington.

For weeks the upper house was deadlocked, a close party division making it impossible for a decision to be reached. Word came from Washington that the President favored the Fish candidacy, but that did not break the deadlock. Nor did Weed's influence prove any more successful, although the Dictator in his black cloak was seen day and night in the Capitol lobbies and offices. Not until March 18, when two Democratic Senators were absent from Albany, did the end come. Then abruptly an election was called, and at two in the morning, with the Assembly's galleries packed, the choice of Hamilton Fish as United States Senator was announced amid applause and hisses. "The exultant cannon of the victors startled the city from its slumbers."

The evening after the victory Raymond, whose health was reflecting the long hours he had spent in journalism and politics, was returning from the Normal School, where he had given one of the addresses that was building further his oratorical reputation. On State Street he encountered a band of carousing celebrators of the Fish election, a band that refused "no" for an answer when it insisted that the Speaker join their roistering. By main force he was escorted to Congress Hall and made to drink. "Bottle after bottle was called for," it was recalled, "and glass after glass was pushed up to the Speaker, who was compelled to drink 'supernaculum,' under the the fearful penalties of refusal which gleamed from the fiery eyes about him. The Speaker did his best, but that was nothing." Raymond escaped only because the entrance of a colleague distracted the attention of his tormentors, although his escape did not prevent a disorderly search of his bedroom and much tramping up and down the corridors before quiet at last fell upon Congress Hall.

The election of Senator Fish was but one episode in a session filled with argument about slavery, free schools, enlargement of the Erie Canal. Often Raymond left his Speaker's chair to enter in debate, and on the free-school issue he delivered what Thurlow Weed's *Evening Journal* called the "ablest speech of the session, a speech that 'elicited the most enthusiastic encomiums of all who heard it.' "

Raymond, a steady advocate of more and better education for all, had only to draw on what he had seen in his own boyhood when he told the Assembly: "There is no keener struggle anywhere in the world than that which often disturbs the heart of the fond father, between his desire to educate and fit for the highest stations of society and of life a promising and gifted son, and the poverty which shuts the college door against his entrance." The state therefore must come to the aid of such citizens, for "education is known and felt to be essential to the success of a republican government, the very first requirement of which is that every citizen shall be a ruler." He argued the need for better common schools, laid down the rule that "the property of any community should educate the children of that community" and insisted that in the school system there should be no distinction between the children of the rich and poor. "The child of the vilest drunkard on the face of the earth," Raymond insisted, "may justly claim from the state he is destined to serve, the education to fit him for that service." And finally, he spoke the "hope to see the day when there shall be, through the intelligent and well-directed bounty of the state, colleges, academies and universities, whose doors shall be wide open to the full and free education of every child." It was his greatest effort of the winter.

The cold almost isolated Albany those months, although there had been opera in town and "musical soirees" and Fanny Wallack had played *David Copperfield*. In March when the Hudson, its ice gone, flowed again untrammeled to the sea, a steamer-operator—apparently he had an axe to grind—invited the Legislature to New York. The invitation was quickly accepted. For several days Senate and Assembly stood adjourned while the members were officially received in the metropolis

and shown its public institutions. There was a cavalcade of forty carriages and omnibuses, the horses brave with plumes upon their heads.
There was a formal reception at City Hall ,where the Lieutenant Governor spoke almost inaudibly, and a great banquet at the Astor House—
Seward was present to speak and receive "three times three and a tiger"—
where Raymond, in responding to the toast to the Legislature, delivered
what was described as one of his most eloquent speeches. The *Herald* reported darkly that some legislators had frequented the notorious Five
Points where they had been seen dancing with Negroes; others had
been at gambling-houses and bordellos. When it was all over and the
visitors had steamed upriver, Bennett remarked that the legislators "have
had a good spree, and a considerable number of them have seen the
elephant."

VII

The session ended abruptly in confusion, its work unfinished. The
break came over the Governor's proposal for a $9,000,000 loan to en-
large the Erie Canal, a proposal that Raymond favored, although he
thought it had been brought forward inopportunely. There had been
debate over the measure's constitutionality, debate apparently resolved
when Daniel Webster and the great Whig lawyer Rufus Choate advised
that the loan could legally be made. Whigs foresaw, or thought they
did, that the canal issue might be a valuable campaign issue. In the face
of resolute Democratic opposition they pushed the measure through the
Assembly. The Whig-controlled Senate was certain to give its approval.
At that moment the Democrats staged a coup. Eleven of their Senators
resigned. A quorum was broken. In an atmosphere of excited recrimina-
tion the Legislature adjourned with a special session looming ahead.

Raymond was glad to have the session end, for he was tired and ailing.
Though he had laid aside during the session all work for the *Courier*,
he had continued to prepare copy for *Harper's Magazine,* adding to an
already heavy burden of correspondence the letters necessary to keep
in touch with the publishers in New York and the contributors around
the country. He prepared copy. He read manuscripts sent him from the
New York office, and selected extracts from foreign periodicals. His
regular summary of the month's events was one of the magazine's features. While he had no desire to halt this labor, he had decided, and his
physician had concurred, that a long vacation was immediately necessary if his strength was to be restored. It was with a European trip in
view that he left Albany after adjournment.

"We shall need you and miss you here," Weed wrote him, "but it is
a man's duty to take care of his health first. I am sure that you require

repose, and sincerely hope that you may return with restored health and strength. . . . If I can get away I will go to New York for a day before you leave. If not, prosperous winds and bright skies be around and above you in your out-goings and in-comings."

For a fortnight or so longer Raymond was at his old desk in the *Courier* office, but the days were troubled. The *Herald* had been charging that he was "devoted head, heels and brains to Seward, Weed & Co.," and it called him the paper's "writing anti-slavery editor," though neither accusation was wholly true. It found the *Courier* guilty of inconsistency toward slavery and thought it discovered the explanation in the conflict of Raymond's views with those of Colonel Webb. Bennett, ever the compleat angler in troubled waters, summed it up: "If the junior editor is to be at one end of the line and the senior editor at the other, heaven only knows where the float may be, under water, or above it."

Although under Raymond's direction the *Courier* had made handsome profits, equal to those of any other journal in the city, the *Herald* alone excepted, Colonel Webb now told Raymond that he disapproved of the paper's editorial position during his absence in Europe. He disapproved even more the stand Raymond was taking at the moment—"imbued with anti-slavery doctrines," Webb described it—and with his own hand he revised the last editorial Raymond wrote for the *Courier*. Raymond believed that his failure to further Webb's senatorial ambitions was not unrelated to the Colonel's attitude, but whatever the cause, the two men had reached the breaking point. A separation was in order anyway, for as all readers of the public press were aware, Raymond was preparing to shift his talents from the *Courier* to other journalistic fields. Under ordinary circumstances the separation might have been friendly, for Webb had often expressed high regard for Raymond's abilities. Instead, they parted in bitterness and anger and insult.

CHAPTER

8

Founding the *Times*

I

ON MAY 8, 1851, the Swallowtail packet *Constantine* dropped
down New York harbor from her East River dock on a
voyage for Liverpool that crew and passengers alike knew
would stretch three weeks or more before they reached the
Merseyside. Raymond was among the handful who had taken passage.

Sailing packets, once so fashionable, were losing to the popularity and
competition of steamships. They still made the eastward crossing at a
speed almost comparable to that of steamers, but the westward voyage
was a different matter, a packet often requiring a good deal better than
a month to sight Sandy Hook. Many travelers—and Raymond was one
of them—went to Europe by packet, returned by steamship, for the
packets were comfortable enough. They retained a reputation for superior food and wines, and eating was an important part of ship routine.
Between meals time might hang heavy. Yet there was shuffleboard on
deck. There were books to read, whist and poker and checkers to play.

Raymond had been looking forward to this Atlantic crossing that
would isolate him for the first time in the past decade from journalism
and politics. He needed the rest shipboard life would provide. He needed
to relax, for he had almost lost the art. But he had one final task to
complete before adding to the tonic of the sea the stimulation of travel
in foreign lands: the prospectus for a new paper, realization of long-
held hope.

Reports that Raymond was to edit a new journal had circulated in
New York for weeks before the *Constantine* dropped past Castle Wil-

liams and sailed out beyond the wooded heights of Staten Island and the bar off Sandy Hook. At the end of March the *Herald* had told of the reports, while expressing doubts of their truthfulness. If the paper ever appeared, the *Herald* commented, it would become the "leading organ of Sewardism in the North, including hostility to the Fugitive Slave bill, opposition to the compromise . . . to the administration of Mr. Fillmore and in favor of General Scott as the next Whig candidate for the Presidency, with Mr. Seward for the succession."

The Albany press picked up the story. The *Herald* repeated it, and the day after Raymond sailed for England, the *Courier* reprinted without comment at the head of its editorial column a gibe from the *Express:* "Mr. Raymond, we are told, has it in contemplation to edit a small paper in this city, with abolitionist tendencies, upon his return from Europe—to establish which, the little rich *coterie* in this city, *well known without naming*, have promised a large and lavish fund." Raymond would edit a new paper, but the rest was distortion, and no account hinted that for years he had been pointing toward the day when he would have his own journal.

II

There is a legend that when the *Tribune* was very young, and Raymond was in its office, he used to talk with George Jones about the paper the two might sometime own. The legend may be faulty, but certainly the two did discuss such a project seriously soon after Raymond left Greeley to work with Colonel Webb. Early in 1846 their schemes had gone so far that a rough draft for a paper was prepared. Jones, who had a good many valuable business relationships in and around Albany, sought to see what he could do about raising the money for a new journal, and Fletcher Harper, one of the publishing brothers, agreed to put $5,000 into the enterprise if plans matured. "In your ability to make the paper acceptable to the class we should look to for support," Jones wrote Raymond, "I have no sort of fear and have even faith enough to believe that we should not close the first year with a loss of any of our original investment. . . . I do believe I could manage the working part of an office as well as any of them are managed in New York and in some parts of their arrangements . . . I think improvements could be made. . . ."

Both men based much of their optimism on the histories of the *Herald* and the *Tribune*. Bennett had only $500 when in 1835 he founded his immediately successful paper. Greeley, of course, had been almost equally devoid of capital, yet within a few months after publishing the *Tribune*'s first issue had been making money. Those facts impressed

Raymond and Jones, and they were still more impressed after Jones had reviewed the *Tribune*'s history with Thomas McElrath, Greeley's business genius. What others had done so successfully, they felt they too could do.

Raymond proposed a paper of wide coverage. He wanted city news emphasized—public meetings and dinners, sermons, religious gatherings, ship news, market and stock news. "The *law* courts," he said, "should be carefully, accurately and more fully reported than is usual—as they relate to the business, and thus enlist the attention and interest of a very large class of people." He wanted two correspondents in Washington during the sessions of Congress. He foresaw the need of a regular correspondent in Albany during the Legislature's sitting. He also proposed that the paper have correspondents in Boston, Philadelphia, Baltimore, Charleston, New Orleans, and Montreal. Summaries of European news would be handled by a regular correspondent in Paris, but English news could be picked up from the English press itself. His own job he defined as follows: "The editor should see and examine *everything* that goes into the paper—in every department, and should besides write such editorials upon matters of news as might be needed. This would serve to *fill up* and give life to the editorial department. The editor should also take care that nothing immoral should get into *any part* of the paper and would of course see that all employed as writers, reporters or correspondents worked in such a way as to promote the interest and build up the character of the paper."

For some reason, most probably because the capital was not forthcoming, the plan had to be put aside. It was not forgotten, and in 1851, the scheme was revived. This time the long-dormant seed sprouted and bore fruit.

How it all came about has been often told. Raymond's membership in the Legislature made possible constant association with Jones in Albany; close friendship was drawn closer. It was not long, Jones recalled many years later, before they revived "a long talked of project of starting a new daily paper in New York." Of one thing they soon became certain. The days of starting a paper without considerable capital belonged to the past.

Presses and paper and labor demanded that any new enterprise have a large backlog before attempting the delicate business of publishing. Jones thought $40,000 would be enough, but Raymond declared that $100,000 would be nearer right, and Thurlow Weed warned that even that sum might be insufficient. The long discussions between Jones and Raymond in Albany's Congress Hall were soon shared by a third person: Edward B. Wesley, like Jones a bank-note broker in the capital.

He became an active participant in all the negotiations, a second also to Raymond's demand that if a paper was to be started it have adequate capital.

It was Wesley, in fact, who began the quest for money. Armed with letters of introduction from Raymond, he went to New York and beat a path from door to door in a fruitless bid for investors. Then the triumvirate descended upon the city. Again calls on likely stock subscribers proved unsuccessful and even the Harper brother, who had seemed so willing five years earlier to put some money on Raymond and Jones, had only encouraging words. Wesley was undaunted. "We have talked so much about this newspaper business," he said, "that I feel quite unwilling to give it up."

Yet it was still touch and go as to whether the three men would ever launch a paper. One day they sat down together at the Astor House to review prospects, and at that talk Wesley resolved the problem of capital. He proposed that Jones and he invest $20,000 apiece, and that with the $40,000 capital Jones in the first place had thought would be enough, they attempt the risky business. Before Raymond rode uptown to West Thirteenth Street that day, Wesley's arrangement had been accepted, and Raymond himself had agreed to write a prospectus for the new paper, and to send it to his partners from Europe while they pushed ahead with the problems of the new daily.

III

The tiresome, often disappointing preliminaries were behind when Raymond boarded the *Constantine*. The prospectus was ready for mailing to America when he landed at Liverpool. "My health is better than it was last Winter," he wrote his brother Samuel from London, "but I do not gain strength as rapidly as I hoped. I presume I shall never be as celebrated as Samson was for strength!" He had joined forces with several Americans and with them traveled slowly across England, stopping at places that held interest for a man from the New World.

In Derbyshire he visited Chatsworth, the historic estate of the Duke of Devonshire, with its great house—the "most magnificent private mansion in England." Its conservatory, covering an acre and a half, was filled with tropical plants and exotic birds, and the fountains in the gardens were hardly surpassed by those of Versailles. Chatsworth had a famous library and an art gallery in which Titian, Murillo, Holbein, Dürer, and Leonardo were represented. To Raymond it represented a way of life wholly new, and he described what he saw with almost boyish naïveté when he told his brother that the Duke of Devonshire "has a house as large as the Seminary in Lima, in the midst of a park containing two thousand acres, and presenting the most beautiful variety of surface you ever saw. The Duke is *well off*, having a yearly income from his estates of one million five hundred thousand dollars."

He went on to London, a wonderful year to be there, for in Hyde Park the Crystal Palace, inspired by the great conservatory at Chatsworth, was drawing British and foreign visitors by the thousands. "The articles exhibited," Raymond reported, wide-eyed, "surpass, in elegance and splendor, anything I ever dreamed of." With the eye of a scholar who knew English history and literature he looked for the landmarks of Queen Victoria's capital, the Abbey with its monuments, the houses of Parliament, and the palaces. "In London I have visited all the principal places," he boasted, and then, after three weeks or so, he tossed across the Channel and went up to Paris, where the Prince-President was plotting the *coup d'état* that would bring back the imperial "N" and the golden eagles of his famous uncle. Raymond, slightly homesick at times for his wife and two children,[1] covered a lot of ground and quickly. After France came Switzerland and before he went down to Southampton to sail for home he had included Scotland in his itinerary. With August he was home again, ready to enter upon the most important business of his life.

IV

In Raymond's absence Jones and Wesley had not been idle. His prospectus had reached them on the third of July, and the following day they had gone to West Point, taking the document with them. They climbed to the ruins of old Fort Putnam on the hill that looks down upon the academy and the Hudson where it cuts through the mountains, and there in one of the most beautiful settings in America they read together what Raymond had written. At dinner they read it again to one of the officers at the Point. "The oftener we read it," Wesley remembered, "the more we were charmed with it." Soon afterward they had the prospectus printed; it circulated among prospective readers as a dignified handbill on blue-tinted paper.

New-York Daily Times was the name Raymond had chosen for the paper, a journal that proposed to cover all the news of the day with special attention to "legal, criminal, commercial and financial transactions in the City of New York, to political and personal movements in all parts of the United States, and to the early publication of reliable intelligence from both continents." Special correspondence from all over the world was promised, along with reports of activities in Congress

---

[1] A third child and second daughter, Lucy Margaret, was to be born on December 26, 1851.

and the Legislature, in learned societies, in religious groups. The new paper, it was stated, would include "literary reviews and intelligence, prepared by competent persons, and giving a clear, impartial, and satisfactory view of the current literature of the day; criticisms of music, the drama, painting, and of whatever in any department of art may merit or engage attention."

The prospectus pointed the political direction of the *Times*. Raymond gave assurance that while Whig in fundamental principles, the *Times* would be "free from bigoted devotion to narrow interests." In a long paragraph that set forth succinctly his moderation, he stated:

> In its political and social discussions the *Times* will seek to be conservative in such a way as shall best promote needful reform. It will endeavor to perpetuate the good, and to avoid the evil, which the past has developed, while it will strive to check all rash innovations and to defeat all schemes for destroying established and beneficent institutions, its best sympathies and cooperation will be given to every just effort to reform society, to infuse higher elements of well-being into our political and social organizations, and to improve the condition and character of our fellowmen. . . . It will inculcate devotion to the Union and to the Constitution, obedience to law and a jealous love of that personal and civil liberty which constitutions and laws are made to preserve. While it will assert and exercise the right freely to discuss every subject of public interest, it will not countenance any improper interference on the part of the people of any locality, with the institutions, or even the prejudices of any other. It will seek to allay, rather than excite, agitation—to extend industry, temperance, and virtue—to encourage and advance education; to promote economy, concord, and justice in every section of our country; to elevate and enlighten public sentiment; and to substitute reason for prejudice, a cool and intelligent judgement for passion, in all public action and in all discussions of public affairs.

Whatever enemies might say, this was no abolitionist manifesto. It spoke rather in tones of compromise. Yet it was obvious Raymond had no intention of being tarred with the brush of the cotton Whigs. He made it clear that he thought the Union could be preserved, and on its existing basis, but only if North and South alike agreed to be tolerant of each other's peculiarities. In short, sectionalism was to be subordinated to nationalism. On other matters the *Times* intended to be enlightened and decent—"the best and the cheapest daily family newspaper in the United States." Charles A. Dana summed it up when he said that Raymond "aimed at a middle line between the mental eccentricity of the *Tribune* and the moral eccentricity of the *Herald*."

Six days after Raymond landed in New York, he signed with his partners the articles of association for Raymond, Jones & Company. These gave him control of the editorial department. He could decide policy, hire assistants and reporters, and, with the approval of his partners, fix salaries. His own salary—he had been paid $40 a week on the *Courier*—was to be $2,500 annually, payable quarterly. Although he had put in no money, he was allotted twenty shares of the new company's one hundred. "I contributed all that I owed, and that was a good deal," he said afterward—but the stock was his as the "equivalent of his editorial ability." The business department was given to Jones and Wesley. Each held forty shares of stock.

The articles made certain that control would remain with the partners, for though each had the right to sell his shares, purchase would give new owners no voice in the conduct of the editorial or business departments. Both Jones and Wesley did soon dispose of some of their stock—at $1,000 a share—to increase the capital of the *Times*, but the "rich coterie" of New Yorkers that the *Herald* had said was behind the venture could not be found among the stockholders. Francis B. Ruggles, an upstate lawyer, and E. B. Morgan of Aurora, a businessman and one of the founders of the Wells-Fargo Express Co., bought a few shares. Three others from upstate subscribed for small amounts. Not a resident of New York City was among them. Not one, with the exception of Raymond, was politically prominent, whatever their partisan sympathies or however much they might have been drawn to a paper sure to have the support of Seward and Weed.

A half-finished brownstone building at 113 Nassau Street was found for the *Times*, and workmen were hastily set to preparing it for printers and pressmen and reporters, a business office being opened temporarily in a vacant shop across the street. A Hoe steam press was bought and installed in the basement, although the installation was slow, finally delaying for two days publication of the first issue. Raymond meanwhile busily recruited a force for his editorial department. He chose young men like himself, but men who had been gathering experience for a decade in the newspaper offices of New York.

For first assistant he turned to the *Courier*, selecting Alexander C. Wilson, a cultured, well-read journalist who had stocked his mind with encyclopedic information. From the *Courier* also was brought husky, bearded James W. Simonton, with whom Raymond had worked both in the *Courier*'s Wall Street office and on assignments in Washington. Simonton, later to head the Associated Press, took the night editor's post. James B. Swain became city editor. In the days when he had had a printing shop, he had published Raymond's life of Clay; later he had been with Greeley on the *Tribune*. In the close circles of New York journalism, Raymond of course knew these lieutenants well, knew that what they lacked in years they made up in full information of the city in which the new paper was about to be born.

V

New York was a fast-growing city of over a half million in 1851, though business was still massed near Manhattan's tip and residential sections were only beginning to push against Forty-second Street. Thackeray had described the city's bustling, ever-changing quality: "Houses are always being torn down and built up again. . . . There are barricades and scaffoldings everywhere." He found in Broadway "a rush of life such as I never have seen." The rush was understandable, for New York had 589 omnibuses, usually overcrowded, 4,200 licensed carters, not to mention the hundreds of private carriages that raised dust from the cobbled streets. The city had 250 public schools, 260 churches, 16 first-class hotels. It had garden-surrounded mansions and slums. Immigrants torn loose by the Irish famine and 1848 revolutions were pouring across the Battery docks from the packet ships. It was a city of fashion and filth, of poverty and crime, of wealth and show. Raymond hoped to tell about this lusty metropolis in the *Times*.

His scope was wider, of course. There were state and national affairs to record, political maneuvers at Albany as well as more significant developments in Washington, where quiet had descended after the compromise debates had died away. The telegraph—there were about 11,000 miles of line in the United States—would flash the most important bulletins, and the mail, brought by steamcars, coach, or stage, would supply fuller, more detailed accounts. Raymond hoped also to inform his readers about the Europe of Queen Victoria and Louis Napoleon Bonaparte and the young Francis Joseph of Austria. Steamers would bring to New York special correspondence and the foreign papers, touching first at Halifax in most instances and thus allowing telegraphic summaries of important news to be tapped out for the Associated Press and the waiting offices in New York.

"Upon all topics," Raymond announced, "Political, Social, Moral and Religious, we intend that the paper shall speak for itself; and we only ask that it may be judged accordingly. We shall be *Conservative*, in all cases where we think Conservatism essential to the public good; and we shall be *Radical* in everything which may seem to us to require radical treatment, and radical reform. . . . We do not mean to write as if we were in a passion, unless that shall really be the case; and we shall make it a point to get into a passion as rarely as possible."

By September 17, 1851, the *Times* was ready to appear, even though its Nassau Street quarters were still littered with the debris of construction. "All was raw and dismal," one of the staff remembered; floors were only "open lofts, destitute of windows, gas, speaking-tubes, dumbwaiters." But the staff had been recruited. Editors and reporters were on hand to write the first issue's copy that boys would rush to the eighteen printers waiting to set type for the city's newest paper. That first night, as edition time neared, Augustus Maverick, later to be Raymond's biographer, watched Wilson writing "at a rickety table at the end of the barren garret, his only light a flaring candle held upright by three nails in a block of wood; . . . the city editor and the newsmen and the reporters, all eagerly scratching pens over paper, their countenances half-lighted, half-shaded by other guttering candles; . . . Raymond, writing rapidly and calmly, as he always wrote, but under similar disadvantages; and all the night the soft summery air blew where it listed, and sometimes blew out the feeble lights; and grimy little 'devils' came down at intervals from the printing-room, and cried for copy; and every man in the company, from the chief to the police reporter, gave his whole mind to the preparation of the initial sheet." It was probably the happiest night of Raymond's life.

In the morning carriers delivered to New Yorkers the four-page *New York Daily Times*, price one cent. Hoe's "Lightning Press" was not yet in perfect order, and Raymond apologized for printing that was less clear and distinct than it should have been. Yet the *Times* was a neat, well-written, dignified paper, its six-column pages presenting the grist of the world's news. Queen Victoria "had been very enthusiastically received" in Scotland. There was unrest in Austria, and France looked forward uneasily to a Presidential election. President Fillmore was traveling triumphantly in New England. The New York State Fair at Rochester was awaiting Jenny Lind's arrival, and during the "Swedish Nightingale's" absence, Catherine Hayes, the "Swan of Erin," was singing her way toward being New York City's toast. There had been a fugitive slave riot in Lancaster, Pennsylvania. An ice cart had run over a young man in Spring Street. Six ships had brought in 1,282 immigrants. On the stock exchange securities were firm, but Erie Railroad stock was moving up; cotton was off a cent a pound. James Fenimore Cooper had just died, as had the Reverend Sylvester Graham, founder of the Grahamites, who left his name attached to a flour and a cracker while he himself was forgotten.

The *Times* in its variety reflected the society of which it told. Its news was relatively unexciting, for the world at the moment was experiencing placidity. But the debut had been made, and Raymond had told his readers that the paper could be expected to appear "every morning (Sundays excepted) for an indefinite number of years to come." Public reaction to the *Times* had to be awaited; circulation figures would tell that story as the weeks and months passed. Meanwhile, other papers, except for the

Tribune, which was openly hostile, were fraternal in their greetings to the new members of the fourth estate, and the *Courier and Enquirer* put aside momentarily old enmities to salute the *Times* and to praise Raymond as a "gentleman of . . . high abilities and wide influence." "Seldom," said the *Courier,* "has a public journal been started in our midst with higher promise of usefulness and brighter auspices of success."

Raymond was more reserved. "I must work hard for five years," he said, "to put this bantling on a solid footing."

CHAPTER

9

The Year One

I

TYPESETTERS at the *Times* busied themselves at their cases as usual on the night of September 16, 1852. Under the title "The Year One!" they were sticking into type a long editorial that reviewed the progress of the *Times*. A printer's devil had just brought it from Raymond's office to the composing room, where the acrid odor of printer's ink never lifted. It gave the lie to a *Tribune* stockholder who a year earlier had scoffed at the *Times* and said, "It cannot succeed."

The year that was ending had not been easy, and Raymond felt that he had reason to boast of what he and his associates had accomplished. "More successful in all respects than any new paper of a similar character ever before published in the United States"—such was his accolade for his *Times*. "Not one of the established and powerful journals by which it is now surrounded . . . closed the first year of its existence with an experience at all comparable to that of the *Daily Times*. In circulation, in income, in influence, in everything which goes to make up the aggregate of a successful journal, it challenges a comparison with any other paper ever published."

The *Times* had had to compete with both the *Herald* and the *Tribune*, each of which had long since found its audience, and each of which usually printed eight-page issues that allowed not only room for more news than the four-page *Times* could cover but room also for far more advertising. Despite these handicaps, Raymond had been confident at the start that he could build circulation on what a contemporary described as the "class of quiet, domestic, fireside, conservative readers" who "liked neither the *Tribune* nor the *Herald*." He reported the news as fully as space permitted. He gave the reformist enthusiasms of the *Tribune* as wide a berth as he did the sensational and vulgar that leered from the *Herald*'s columns.

From the beginning Raymond had known that he could count among his readers the Whigs who followed Seward's leadership and who, even if they did not agree wholly with Seward on slavery, were ready to halt further compromise with the South. The Senator, a subscriber from the first, wrote Raymond from Washington when the paper was still new: "Mrs. Seward is now separated from me and writes that 'home' at Auburn is lonesome without the *Times*, which of course I cannot live without here." Many other Whigs felt similarly, but Raymond did not regard his paper as a partisan organ. Rather did he attribute much of its success to "attention to matters of general instead of special interest," and effort "to allow moderation, impartiality and common sense a share at least of that influence too often sought by spasmodic and fanatical violence."

He developed that thought more specifically in one of his editorials. The *Times*, he said, "has endeavored in all respects to pursue such a course upon all subjects as should commend it to the sober judgement and common sense of the community, even where it might not echo hasty opinions or disappoint partisan prejudices and expectations." He underlined his position when, alluding to slavery and its controversy, he stated that while the *Times* "shuns all fantastic schemes of reform—the offspring of fanaticism rather than reason—it gives its hearty cooperation to all judicious plans for removing existing evils." The *Times*, he promised, "will respect Constitutional rights of every section of the country, while it will assert the duty of all sections to abide by restrictions, and their right to exercise the powers which the Constitution confers."

Such professions did not protect the *Times* from being attacked day after day, week after week, month after month as an organ "devoted to the interests of the anti-slavery crusade," and while Raymond in rejoinder could cite chapter and verse in his editorial columns, his Seward friendship provided foes with ready ammunition whenever they desired to open fire. It was James Gordon Bennett who assailed and ridiculed the *Times* most often and whose barbs stung. "Penny abolition paper," "nigger penny organ," he called it, and such epithets aroused Raymond more than the personal abuse Bennett loosed against him. "Raymond," said the *Herald*, "may be likened to a monkey, prying into everything, continually chattering over small discoveries, and always very busy about very insignificant trifles. In fact, he is the monkey editor, chattering and skipping about, and playing the very mischief among the crockery."

Personal abuse every editor anticipated, and Raymond was no stranger to it. He understood from his years on the *Tribune* and the *Courier and Enquirer* that the strong language used by one editor toward another was designed in part to draw public attention and to sell copies, and while words might hurt momentarily, their effect was important only as they influenced circulation. The *Herald's* attacks may have given the *Times* free advertising, but the results were impossible to weigh, and of more consequence at the start was a different sort of attack by Greeley's *Tribune*.

A decade earlier Moses Beach of the *Sun* had set plug-uglies upon Greeley's newsboys in an attempt to end the *Tribune's* threatened rivalry at its start. The *Tribune* now aimed to administer somewhat similar medicine to the *Times* by forbidding carriers to handle the new paper under penalty of losing their *Tribune* routes. The effort failed. The *Times* was sold just the same. Boasting that its ninth number had over 10,000 circulation, it reprinted with pleasure a comment from the Buffalo *Express:* "It certainly speaks well for a newspaper that it is pretty uniformly stolen before it reaches its destination. That has been the fate of the copy of the *Times* directed to us."

There were various ways of building circulation. Carriers left the *Times* for a week at house doors "for the perusal of the family and to enable them, if they desire it, to receive it regularly." A week's subscription cost six cents. A good many families did begin to take the *Times*, and it found its way also into business houses and professional offices, into banks and brokerage rooms. Ragged newsboys cried morning and afternoon editions on the streets. News vendors sold the *Times* at railroad depots and at the ferries that crossed the East and North Rivers or steamed to Staten Island. To build out-of-town circulation the *Times* joined with the American Art Union—a cooperative organization designed to stimulate interest in the work of American artists. The Art Union, seeking membership, printed a circular that was reproduced in daily and weekly editions of the *Times*, copies of which were then sent to former Art Union members. The Art Union paid only for the paper required, and the *Times* obtained easily a list of potential readers, though this stroke of business later proved embarrassing when a court investigation of the Art Union's affairs laid bare the relationship.

As the year 1851 gave place to 1852 the *Times* claimed a daily circulation of 23,720 copies, and it was still rising. It fluctuated, of course, and soon tended to halt at about 25,000, a total larger than the *Tribune's* and only 15,000 below the *Herald*'s. Raymond asserted that Bennett's hatred for his paper stemmed from the *Herald*'s loss of 5,000 subscribers to the *Times*, though when Bennett challenged him to prove it, Raymond's enthusiasm for such a test soon ran out. There was a weekly *Times*, and after a while a *California Times* was published fortnightly when ships sailed out past Sandy Hook for the gold fields. It was the *Daily Times* that mattered. In the "Year One," according to a register on the Hoe press, 7,550,000 copies had been printed for the 312 daily issues.

II

When the *Times* was started, Raymond told the public that he had "abundance of means" to guarantee success, and when the first year was over, he declared that neither labor nor expense had been spared in the twelve-month effort. It had been an expensive effort indeed, so far as the *Times* treasury was concerned. More than $100,000 had been spent on the various departments, $40,000 for newsprint alone. Such expenditures could not be long maintained without the counterbalance of revenue from subscriptions and advertising.

Subscriptions were doing nicely, but without advertising the paper could not live, and, admitting the fact, it stated during the first week of its existence: "The very expensive scale on which the *Times* is made up, and our intentions to spend upon it all the money requisite to make it a complete and acceptable newspaper, renders it necessary of course that we should have a good deal of advertising. But we design to make it the *interest* of advertisers to come to us; and until they feel it to be so, we shall not annoy them with solicitations."

So bold and independent a course was scarcely calculated to attract advertisers to a paper that had yet to prove itself more than a temporary addition to New York's journalistic world. Yet when there was complaint that the *Times* had set its advertising rates too high, the reply only reiterated the declaration of independence: If any advertiser "desires to advertise at our prices for *his own interest,* let him do so—if not, he need not grieve on our account. . . . We understand very distinctly that no paper can be sustained by advertising given to it as a *favor.*"

High rates, which the limited space in the four-page *Times* dictated, independence of attitude, newness, all combined to keep advertising much less than it might otherwise have been. The paper's first issue contained six columns of advertising. By the spring of 1852 eight or nine columns was a common average, but by then the *Times* was openly in the market for advertising support. It promised that insertions would be printed in clear, conspicuous type, well-displayed and arranged "under proper heads so as to make reference perfectly easy." No longer cavalier toward prospective advertisers, it made much of the size of its circulation and the quality of its readership, and pointed to the diversity of advertising in its columns—importers, brokers, jobbers, dry goods merchants, ship companies, booksellers, places of entertainment, houses to sell and to let, situations wanted. Patent-medicine makers inserted their cards; in one of them Colonel Webb endorsed "Dr. Rogers' Syrup of Liverwort, Tar and Conchalagua." Advertisements, maintained the *Times*, present "a daguerreotype of the social life of the people."

All types of advertisements save one were welcomed at the *Times* business office. The line was drawn against abortionists, against medicines that would induce abortion, against books on birth control, venereal disease, sex relations. The *Times*, always a family paper, warned austerely: "Advertisements of certain classes of Medicines, Doctors, Books, etc., etc., will not be inserted in the *Daily Times* at any price."

Despite its circulation and its growing advertising, the *Times* had operated during its first year at a loss. The early weeks, naturally critical, had been complicated unexpectedly when George Jones fell ill. Without his guidance in the business office a bad period became worse, and disaster threatened as expenses mounted and revenues seemed unlikely ever to catch up to them. Confusion, uncertainty, worry, ruled the publication office. At that dark moment E. B. Wesley, who had had so large a part in the paper's founding, came down from Albany to see how things were going. He visited Jones and heard the sorry report.

Alarmed, he hurried from Jones's Brooklyn home to the *Times*. "I went to the publication office and looked through the building, and became still more discouraged," Wesley said. "I met Mr. Raymond at the office; we looked the situation all over, and I said to him that there must be a change of business management, or we had better shut up at once and go no further." Neither Wesley nor Raymond wanted to admit failure, but lacking newspaper experience, Wesley hesitated to take over the publication office himself. There was no alternative. He disposed of his Albany brokerage office, took the business reins of the *Times*. Jones relinquished his stock, withdrew from the partnership and for nearly five years remained outside the paper. Under Wesley's shrewd and able direction prospects grew brighter, and later, when the crisis had wholly passed and the future was assured, it was to his "brains and pluck and money" that credit had to be given for the *Times*'s sound foundation.

III

Raymond, busy with the many tasks of editorship, still had time to correspond regularly with Seward. Both were intensely interested in Louis Kossuth, the Hungarian revolutionary whose defiance of the

Habsburgs had made him in America a symbol of European liberty. Kossuth had lost his fight when Russia intervened to put down the Hungarian revolution, and he had been living in Turkey, a restless exile. Now he was about to arrive in the United States as a guest of the nation.

Seward and Raymond saw political significance in his visit. Raymond's editorial sense told him also that Kossuth would be big news, and he intended that the *Times* should profit from it. Raymond was not alone in appreciating Kossuth's news value, for no foreigner since Lafayette had returned to America a quarter century before had produced so much popular excitement. New York was planning a great official dinner. With Raymond as committee chairman, the press was planning another. Among the city's papers only the *Courier and Enquirer* took a wry view of the approaching visit.

The firing of cannon from the Narrows to Quarantine on December 5, 1851, told that the S.S. *Humboldt* with Kossuth aboard had reached America. It was a winter day, clear and cold, and when he stepped ashore on Staten Island to be received in a tent erected for the occasion, he shivered miserably in the "Esquimaux wrapper" provided for him, and in reply to the formal address, spoke feelingly of the "bracing wind of your northern climate." "The illustrious champion of popular rights is among us at last," the *Times* exulted.

Two days later, December 7, Kossuth landed on Manhattan. Harbor shipping had been decorated. The city's bells pealed, and cannon boomed from Governors Island, Bedloe's Island, the Navy Yard, and Brooklyn Heights. He came ashore at Castle Garden—the Battery's trees were black with cheering boys—reviewed the troops drawn up and then, dressed in a black velvet frock coat with belt and sword, rode through applauding crowds to City Hall. Torchlight processions serenaded him that night at his lodgings.

At the Irving House more than 400 prominent New Yorkers and distinguished guests gathered for the municipal dinner for Kossuth. In the banqueting hall, where evergreens masked the salon's columns and the Stars and Stripes was linked with the Hungarian Tricolor, the dinner moved slowly through its many courses and the wine was passed and repassed. The evening's guest of honor spoke for more than an hour. Toasts followed. That to the press belonged to Raymond, and as he prepared to respond, his figure dwarfed in the gay assemblage, James Watson Webb challenged his right to speak. Cries of "Raymond!" "Webb!" echoed through the banquet hall, and when quiet was momentarily restored, Raymond tried to explain that he was only performing a duty assigned him. Webb once more challenged his right. There were cheers, hisses, and boos, and as confusion mounted, the police were called.

Raymond at last had an orderly audience to which amid applause he praised Kossuth and urged: "The First Minister Plenipotentiary from the Independent Republic of Hungary—May he hasten to receive the welcome which awaits him on these shores." The toast was the signal for Webb again to take the floor, and again to be greeted with hoots and howls, with "Sit down!" "Hear him!" "Order!" "Order!" Mayor Kingsland announced that Kossuth wished Webb to be heard. Raymond also pleaded that his former employer be allowed his say, and Webb did speak briefly, though only to assert that the audience's hostility left him no choice but to withhold the address he had prepared. It was printed in the *Courier* the next day, in the *Times* the day following, and in these printed columns New Yorkers learned of Webb's outright opposition to Kossuth and his cause, opposition that, strangely similar to that of President Fillmore, was based on the argument that public concern with what was held to be solely a European matter endangered American neutrality and held the threat of war.

The *Herald*—it called Webb "General Bootblack"—deplored the Irving House proceedings, and especially the choice of Raymond as representative of the press. "Little Master Raymond," said the *Herald*, "is nothing but a flibbertigibbet, who is continually making a noise, and, like the fly on a cart wheel, exclaiming 'what a tremendous dust I kick up!' . . . He is the youngest, the vainest, the silliest member [of the press]."

Not all newspapermen agreed with the *Herald*, and when, a few nights later, the press gave its Astor House dinner for Kossuth, Raymond was a principal speaker. It was a distinguished company. William Cullen Bryant presided. Henry Ward Beecher asked the grace. Horace Greeley was present, and so were George Bancroft, the historian, President Charles King of Columbia, the Governor of Rhode Island, New York's Mayor, and many others. The *Herald* assailed the dinner as arranged primarily by abolitionists to glorify the *Times* and *Tribune*, and voiced its suspicion of Seward's relationship with the Whig editors Greeley and Raymond—"the kitchen maids of all work—both somewhat colored in complexion."

Raymond's speech was naturally devoted to praise of Kossuth and Hungary's struggle for independence. He compared the Hungarian struggle with the American against Britain. He called for an Anglo-American partnership to bolster the cause of Hungarian and European liberty. As for American neutrality, he turned for support to Daniel Webster, knowing full well that in this instance Webster did not agree and quoted the Secretary of State's words on an earlier occasion: "Our neutral policy not only justifies, but requires, our anxious attention to the political events which take place in the world, a skillful perception of their relations to our concerns, our relations to their consequences, and a firm, timely assertion of what we hold to be our own rights and interests." There was almost an ovation when Raymond finished with the toast: "Our Neutral Policy, as defined by Daniel Webster— A policy that *protects* neutrality, that *defends* neutrality, that *takes up arms*, if need be, for neutrality." Raymond's address had been shrewdly devised, for he had attributed to the Secretary of State most of the controversial remarks, and had thus seemed to associate the Fillmore Administration with the Kossuth demonstration.

The dinner, though it led to the founding of the Press Club, which every Saturday for years dined at the Astor House, was soon forgotten, but the political aspects of the Kossuth business expanded. "It is pretty evident that the abolitionists have completely got hold of Kossuth for the present," the *Herald* remarked, and if Seward was to be regarded as an abolitionist, then there was no doubt that the Seward Whigs were striving to make Kossuth their own.

A Congressional resolution of welcome was pending on Washington's Capitol Hill—the New York Senator had sponsored it—but it was meeting opposition. "I had only time the other day," Seward wrote Raymond, "to say a word of hope about the Kossuth resolution. The truth is that the conservatives succeeded in forging an effective weapon out of his speeches, and played off very adroitly upon the Senate his expression of discontent. Their strength is exhausted. We are growing strong. Let him be *patient*. Let us pass *this* resolution. When that has been done, and he comes here we shall have the power to do something else bold and generous enough to atone for the lukewarmness of the past." The resolution was eventually adopted, but Seward men began to have increasing doubts that Kossuth would win Congress and the Administration to anything more than sympathy for the cause of Hungary.

Slaveholders found it hard to listen to Kossuth's brave words about liberty, and conservatives, Whig and Democratic, hearkened little to the talk of European revolutions. Kossuth would "feast on disappointment" in Washington, Seward prophesied when the visitor started a triumphant journey from New York to Philadelphia, Baltimore, and the capital city, where Webster warned that "if he should speak to me of the policy of 'intervention,' I shall 'have ears more deaf than adders.' " Yet Washington gave him a hearty welcome after all. Senator Seward took him to the White House, where President Fillmore dined him. He was invited, the first foreigner since Lafayette, to address Congress, and

Congressmen feted him at a banquet at the National Hotel, where Webster, whom Seward had persuaded to attend, offered somewhat indis-
creetly a toast to Hungarian independence that made Kossuth momentarily happy.

"The Hungarian question has settled down into the old worn channel of politics," Senator Seward soon confessed, and the fact was well
borne out by the attitudes of the New York press. Raymond had made
the *Times* a Kossuth paper, and was deeply engaged in controversy with
the conservative *Courier*, now generally dubbed "the Austrian organ in
Wall Street." The anti-Seward *Herald* attacked Raymond's activity
in the raising of funds for the Hungarian cause, though the *Herald*'s
managing editor had ultimately to admit that "on this excitement the
Times gained laurels and subscribers, and the Hungarians dollars and
sympathy." It could not go on forever, and while Seward worked in
vain for a Senatorial resolution protesting against the Hungarian Republic's fate, and Kossuth toured the country, Raymond turned his paper to other matters.

IV

The *Times* had marked the start of 1852, with a special eight-page
issue containing Longfellow's "Mass for the Dying Year" and also an
elaborate chronology and necrology of the twelve months past. Over-
sized issues, the extra pages largely a literary supplement, were soon to
appear frequently. There was news from France of a *coup d'état* by the
Prince-President on the anniversary of Austerlitz, and now France was
an empire in all but name. In Brooklyn "a daughter of the 'green isle' "
had been fined five dollars for "reeling intoxication." The Stuyvesant
Institute near Astor Place exhibited Leutze's painting, "Washington
Crossing the Delaware." Ole Bull, the Norwegian violinist, returned to
America, and Lola Montez, mistress of royalty, had trouble with her
Waverly Place landlord. The scandalous divorce suit of the actor Edwin
Forrest and his wife filled columns of the *Times* and most other papers,
and was discussed, the *Herald* said, "among all kinds of society, from
the literary coterie and the codfish aristocracy down to the merest
jabberers on the Five Points."

It was a severe winter. River ice often halted the ferries, and the cold
caused great suffering. Raymond noted that the streets seemed filled with
beggars, some of them women with babes in arms, and he pleaded editorially for public relief. The beggars were not alone upon the crowded
and ill-maintained thoroughfares. "A friend who attempted to cross
Broadway, a day or two since," said Raymond, "fared rather badly. He
barely succeeded in escaping the pole of one omnibus by dodging under

the wheels of another, and reached the sidewalk in time to save his neck, but not a pair of new inexpressibles, which were utterly ruined by a ragged urchin, who gave him the benefit of a broom full of mud and water, at the same time soliciting 'a penny for keeping the pass clean.' "

The *Times* reported local gossip—"Strakosch the pianist and Patti the warbler" had been married. It recorded vital statistics—12,000 Irish immigrants had arrived in a single day. Francis A. Ruggles, one of the paper's stockholders and a member of the editorial staff, resigned to become head of a gold-mining company, and Raymond one morning took time to set forth his ideas of an editor's qualifications.

"Enough of the past is always with him," he wrote, "to throw some light upon the future. What he loses in profundity he gains in surface. The deficit of power is compensated by augmented velocity. What he has is ready for instant use. . . . His politics are what occasion, or bias, or fanaticism dictate. . . . Upon all subjects, whether polemical, parliamentary, public or private, pacific or pugilistic, he is sure to have opinions ready made. . . . We doubt whether, in the average of a year's results, they will not be found as near the truth as we are at all likely to get, short of another stage of existence. To these mental preparations and a constitution like the Wandering Jew's, [add] a patience as inexhaustible as his frame; and a physical endurance equal to that of a victim of the Inquisition or of Sing Sing Prison discipline and you have a disembodied conception of an editor. Whether there be any such in the flesh, we are not prepared to say."

V

The pressing problems of the day were too much at hand to permit journalistic introspection often, and in the spring of 1852 the chief of these problems was political. The Whig party was showing definite signs of dissolution, though the leaders remained hopeful that another election could be weathered. Northern Whigs found it increasingly hard to work with their brethren in the South. President Fillmore, leaning more and more on the South for support, was warring on the Seward Whigs, and Raymond in a long editorial on the state of politics asserted that the President was seeking to drive Sewardites from the party. In this situation Raymond pleaded for a "candidate with national views and national strength" and hoped for a Whig convention in which there would be mutual concession and mutual forbearance.

The Seward Whigs, and it was no secret, were grooming General Winfield Scott, the Mexican war hero, as their man, and were rounding up delegates who would vote for his nomination. Scott (he was sixty-six, a Virginian, and knew more of soldiering than of politics) had never expressed himself, so far as anyone knew, on slavery, the only issue in the country that mattered. His supporters hoped to keep him uncommitted. Seward wrote Raymond: "Faithfully believing that General Scott's vantage ground is his silence on the question, I pray you turn our friends to the duty of standing on that ground in the Convention. I sincerely believe that all would be lost by any compromise resolution." Many letters of that sort passed between the Senator and Raymond, who was acting in many matters almost as his lieutenant in New York, whether the subject was pre-convention politics or the need to explain privately to colored delegations the Senator's views on emancipation and African colonization.

Raymond went down to Baltimore at the middle of June to report for the *Times* the proceedings of the Whig convention that was meeting in the same bunting-draped hall where a fortnight earlier the Democrats had chosen as their nominee General Franklin Pierce of New Hampshire. The city was hot with the heat of June. Every street corner seemed to buzz with the talk of politicians, and at night delegations and their bands paraded with banners. There were Webster men, Fillmore men, Scott men, and over all fell the shadow of sectional rivalries. "There is . . . prevalent and dominant here," wrote Raymond, "an exceedingly bitter feeling between the North and South—or, rather, between the National Whigs North and South who do not wish the Slavery question introduced into the canvass at all, and the ultra men, who insist upon a full endorsement of the Compromise measures as a condition precedent to the nomination of a candidate."

Circumstances pushed Raymond forward as a spokesman for the Seward and Scott men, who suddenly realized they lacked a vigorous debater. It was arranged that one of the New York delegates should withdraw, pleading illness, and that Raymond should thereupon take his place, an extraordinary procedure, but one approved by the committee on credentials and by the convention itself. He might have sat there almost unnoticed had he not drawn the lightning by a dispatch to the *Times* following the adoption of the Whig platform. In its framing Southerners had had their way. Not only had the planks been adopted before a candidate was chosen, but these approved the Compromise of 1850 and "acquiesced" in the Fugitive Slave Law that already had set the North afire. That the Seward Whigs could accept such a platform might have seemed impossible, but they had their eyes on Scott's candidacy, and they feared open opposition might wreck both Scott's chances and the party's. Raymond described the situation in his dispatch. "Tomorrow," he said, "it is believed that Kentucky, Tennessee,

Virginia and one or two others will give Scott the nomination on the third or fourth ballot. The Northern Whigs gave way on the platform, with this understanding. If Scott is not nominated, they will charge breach of faith on the South."

The *Courier,* a Webster organ, picked up the dispatch, and telegraphed a paraphrase to Webb at the convention, where its reading caused almost a riot. Southerners exploded. They denied that there had ever been any "understanding"; they charged that their honor had been insulted, and moved to oust Raymond from the convention, alleging that he had accused "its members of corruption and foul play." Raymond called it all a "ridiculous tempest," but it was a tempest he rode with courage and distinction as he defended himself and sought to explain away the obvious meaning of his dispatch. In the end he threw down the glove to his Southern tormentors, and in particular to Edward C. Cabell, member of Congress from Florida. Cabell, a fire-eater, had insisted before the convention that Scott make himself clear on the Compromise of 1850, and Raymond, prompted by Seward, had assailed him in the *Times* as an enemy of Whig unity. Now the two met head-on.

A Louisianian who attended the Baltimore convention said afterward that Raymond, "a Yankee, of rather small stature, college-bred, and of a high intellectual character," had displayed "the first . . . real, genuine courage" he had ever witnessed. Describing the attempt to oust Raymond from the convention, this Southerner said:

Cabell of Florida, a veteran debater, distinguished for his reckless physical courage and sharp tongue, had volunteered to make a speech against "the Abolitionist," and he opened with a degree of bitterness that was unparalleled in any body governed by parliamentary rules, and he was in the meantime supported and cheered on by apparently a large majority of the house. The gentleman assailed, who had an almost boyish appearance, kept his feet (for Cabell spoke against his having the privilege of a personal defense), and with fixed eye watched the Floridian as he went on with his unqualified denunciations. . . . Two or three times Cabell stopped, perfectly infuriated at the unexpected coolness and self-possession of his supposed victim, but the moment he commenced his defense, Cabell would begin again. . . . This struggle continued for nearly three long hours, but when it did end, the assailed had the attention of the convention. . . .

At last . . . Raymond commenced a defense of his position, and satisfied, in a few moments, every logical mind within his hearing of the propriety of his right to the seat. . . . Had he stopped here his political status would have been secured; but he demanded more than this. Changing his voice, and turning upon Cabell, he opened upon that gentleman with a speech that was full of argument, wit, and burning sarcasm. He denounced what he called the fashion of certain Southern men to bully Northern representatives in Congress and in national conventions, carrying their points by overbearing insolence and threats of personal injury. He shook his finger at Cabell, and said that he defied this cowardly and unmanly practice, and that he had determined for all time to yield everything to courtesy, reason, and brotherhood, but nothing to threats of intimidation.

The convention completed its labors on June 21, and in New York the cannon at Battery Park saluted the nomination of General Winfield Scott, "Old Fuss and Feathers," as Whig candidate for the Presidency of the United States in 1852. There was a great ratification rally in New York, preceded by a torchlight procession with transparencies and rockets and Roman candles. There was praise for Raymond, of whom a fellow delegate said: "He stood up firmly before Southern chivalry, and the Northern blade did not break." There was still warmer praise from Seward: "I am glad to have an occasion for writing a word which I must do in haste to sympathize with you in the trial through which you passed at Baltimore, and to congratulate you on your brilliant triumph which has made you known to the Nation as you were before known to the State. Onward Dear Raymond and Upward."

Yet for all attempt at celebration, a good many Whigs were sick at heart. The Baltimore platform was hard to swallow. Seward called it "wretched," and privately anticipated "defeat and desertion." Greeley "spat" upon it, renouncing it editorially and writing one for himself and the *Tribune*. Southern Whigs, however much they liked the platform, disliked Scott, fearing that he would be dominated by Seward, and even Seward's public avowal that he would take no office under Scott if the latter were elected did not allay these fears. Webster, his health failing fast, bitterly disappointed that the Whig convention had not chosen him, refused to support the party candidate, and as if to make the prospect wholly dark, the free-soil men who might have been expected to vote for a Seward nominee chose a Presidential candidate of their own, thus splitting the radical elements in the Whig party. At this moment, and almost as an omen of party disaster, Henry Clay, the great Whig hero and for so long the great Whig leader, died in his rooms at the National Hotel in Washington.

10

Building and Growth

I

HUNDREDS of Whigs gathered around the Chambers Street depot in New York on October 18, 1852, to greet General Scott, who was arriving at the end of a tour that had carried him through part of the Middle West and across New York State. Taking advantage of a law permitting the head of the army to travel about the country to fix the location of soldiers' hospitals, he had journeyed to Kentucky and then swung north and eastward, allowing himself to be seen and to be persuaded to speak. He had visited Seward at Auburn. He had dined with Weed, who found him looking forward "buoyantly to an easy and triumphant victory." It was a stumping tour without precedent, and had laid Scott open to criticism and ridicule, but there had been cheers enough, though party leaders did not fail to note that the recent September elections had shown less popular enthusiasm for Winfield Scott than for Franklin Pierce, who had been one of his officers at Puebla and Churubusco.

New York City Whigs did what they could with their cheers to sustain the candidate's buoyant mood. They crowded around his carriage as he drove through the October afternoon to the Astor House, where he rested and dined before spending the evening with party leaders at Senator Fish's home, but no public meeting had been planned and the general, complaining that fatigue would not allow his speaking, declined to address the supporters massed at his hotel. The campaign was nearly over. Many Democrats professed fears as to the outcome. Others showed supreme confidence, and for weeks the New York *Herald* had prophesied Whig defeat, applying to the party its dictum: "Parties—political, religious and social—like codfish and cabbages—have their day."

Raymond had begun a weekly *Campaign Times* on the eve of the Baltimore convention. It was his chief contribution, for like Seward, Weed, Greeley, and many others, he had lost all heart in the contest. He spoke at a few rallies, attended meetings in his Ninth Ward, but all the artificial enthusiasm whipped up by the marching and parading of the Lundy's Lane clubs left him unmoved. There were rumors that he wanted to be Governor, and Greeley told Weed that Raymond had such ambitions, but there could have been little truth behind the talk, and when his district toward the end of September nominated him for Congress, he asked that his name be withdrawn. "Acceptance," he said, "would involve personal sacrifices which my judgement tells me I ought not to make."

Across the campaign's final days fell the shadow of death, for on October 24 Daniel Webster died at Marshfield. The nation exchanged party banners for mourning, and General Pierce forgot partisan animosities long enough to attend the funeral, held out of doors while the sun of Indian summer beat down and the breeze blew in from the sea. Newspapers, regardless of party, appeared with mourning borders, and gave their pages over to accounts of the statesman's last hours and to the long days of his years.

Raymond wrote the *Times* obituary. For hours the Sunday that Webster died, Raymond's pen covered rapidly page after page while printer's devils rushed the copy to compositors. Two assistants helped, but the task was essentially Raymond's. The obituary filled twenty-six of the *Times*'s forty-eight columns, and Raymond had written sixteen of them, a feat reported throughout the city's news rooms, and recalled whenever Raymond's achievements as an editor and writer were listed.

Four days after Webster's funeral the nation went to the polls to demonstrate that his party, like himself, belonged to history. In New York City it was a wet and dreary election day, and interest was so limited that the customary fights at voting places were few and spiritless. When all the votes were in, Franklin Pierce had carried every state but four; his party had elected Horatio Seymour Governor of New York and would control the State Assembly also. "Was there ever such a deluge since Noah's time!" Raymond wrote Seward, confessing that he saw no future for the Whigs. Yet he was not downcast. "We are not among those," he said in the *Times*, "who consider the welfare of the country for all time irretrievably bound up in the result of any one election. . . . In the long run, we believe . . . that it is not in the power of any administration greatly to check our advancement in the career of social prosperity and of national greatness upon which we have entered." Such views did not fit the ordinary pattern of partisanship to which editors cut their cloth, but Seward approved, and his approval always pleased Raymond.

"I am surprised, but gratified," he wrote the Senator, "to hear you say that you like anything in the *Times* since the election, because I greatly feared that my conviction of the actual state of facts might not jump with either the judgement or wishes of my friends. I shall seek now to navigate the *Times* into a position of independent thought and speech, being moderate and conservative, but making progress always, as I hope, toward beneficent ends. I think it quite likely I shall often need the charitable constructions of my friends, and therefore, bespeak yours in advance."

Raymond thought he was making his valedictory to political life and turning his full energies to editorship, something George Jones had urged him to do from the moment they planned the *Times*. It had seemed difficult two years earlier. Now the difficulty was less, for Raymond believed not only that the Whig party had spent itself, but that the anti-slavery crusade was ended, and that the country was entering upon an era of good feeling like that which had characterized the Administrations of James Monroe. Seward remonstrated, though the two men were in essential agreement on the wisdom of adjourning politics until some new issue reawakened the sentiments of party.

"I see," said the Senator, "how difficult a channel you have to take to ride in safety over the dead swell of the sea now that the storm is passed. I have learned charity to Editors and Publishers, and so I am not likely to be grieved by the course the *Times* may have to pursue, although I shall compassionate you. But I trust that you mistake in supposing that the Whig party will not come up as such. The Whig party cannot indeed come up again *now*, nor could any other come up now, nor at any time until occasion calls for one to rise. Can't we sleep in the meantime with our old flag wrapped around us as well as if we should tear it in pieces? It will be easier to recall the scattered to its folds than to another. Pray think of this. Malcontents will divide. Some will be for taking and dipping the flag into the ink; others for casting it away altogether. . . . While I agree then with you on the advantage of moderation, nay almost of silence, indifference, sleep or at least inactivity, I would not favor the idea of removing the flag and name. We shall be wanted again sometime."

Ultimately Raymond came around to this view of party revival, and some months later forecast Whig return to the political stage. "This

Mrs. Raymond and Children

Left to right, Mrs. Raymond, Mary, Lucy and Henry; *front row*, Aimee and Walter. A picture taken in Switzerland in 1858.

The Times Building and Printing House Square, looking toward the City Hall

venerable body," he said, "now so stiff and cold, is not dead but only laid by for a season." During that season he abjured partisanship. "General Pierce," the *Times* had declared after the 1852 election, "will enter upon his high office with a more general degree of kindly feeling from all sections and parties than has been usual for some years past," and it was in that spirit of kindly feeling that Raymond greeted the new President at his inauguration on a wet, snowy, blustery March day in 1853. The inaugural message was hailed for its manly tone, sincerity, and earnestness, and Raymond commended in particular Pierce's suggestion of a vigorous foreign policy that would not balk at territorial expansion or brook foreign interference in the hemisphere's affairs. The message hinted also that the Administration would not be slow in furthering republican principles throughout the world. It was just what Raymond wanted to hear, for he was still ardent in his belief that the United States should press vigorously in Europe the cause of republicanism. Despite the failure of Kossuth's mission, it was a belief shared by many Americans, though obviously most preferred to express it in words rather than in action.

The *Times* kept watch as Pierce, weighed down with sorrow, for his only child had been killed in a railroad accident shortly before the inauguration, fumbled with the business of government. Office-seekers almost overwhelmed the new President, who struggled with the patronage, making appointments that pleased neither politicians nor public, while seeking to shape policies that would unite party and nation. Yet the Democrats gained further at Whig expense in the spring elections, and the Administration remained confident that its aims would be attained. It needed above all the support of New York Democrats, and in part to woo them Pierce came to New York in July, 1853, for the opening of the Crystal Palace Exhibition that in imitation of London's great fair was ready for inspection at Sixth Avenue and Forty-second Street.

The trip was disappointing. Plans called for visiting Baltimore and Philadelphia—Pennsylvania Democrats were lukewarm to the Administration—as well as other cities along the route, and preparations were made carefully. Pierce was to speak briefly at the several stops. Major addresses would be left to members of the Cabinet, and particularly to Jefferson Davis, Secretary of War. But Pierce caught cold in Baltimore, and felt miserable throughout the tour. The crowds were out, he tried his best not to disappoint, and Davis outdid himself, but somehow nothing went quite as smoothly as intended.

The *Times* had complained before the President's arrival that New York had done little to prepare his reception. At least, the paper urged, the city's streets could be cleaned and the "immense heaps of garbage" removed. Hurriedly a banquet was arranged, a reception committee named, and when the time came the guns fired the proper salute as Pierce landed at the Battery. Flags and bunting were flying. The troops were drawn up for Presidential review, and Pierce, the *Times* remarked, "looked right well" as he rode between their ranks on a great black charger. It was a hot day, and a sudden shower, drenching the crowd and the President alike as the procession reached City Hall Park, left Pierce bedraggled for the slow ride uptown. There were cheers. Handkerchiefs were waved from windows, and the friendly *Times* thought Pierce pleased the public. He changed to dry clothes before entering the Crystal Palace, but the change caused him to arrive late to face an audience impatient over the delay. Pierce was so hoarse he could be hardly heard, yet when it was all over the *Times* felt the honors belonged to the President. The eventual political compensations were few.

The *Times*—its cordialities toward the President led the *Herald* to say facetiously that it was to become the Administration's New York organ—tried to find good in Pierce's foreign appointments. Raymond liked especially the choice of George N. Sanders as consul in London, not so much for Sanders himself as for what his selection might signify. Sanders, a Kentuckian, had made himself leader of the Democrats who called themselves "Young Americans" and who argued that vigorous foreign policy was the best means of ending sectional issues. They sought American aid for liberal regimes and revolutions in Europe, and in this advocacy had Raymond's support. He voiced it publicly at an Astor House dinner for Sanders, urging that the "influence of this country upon the current of European affairs should be made thoroughly and vigorously American." It was another echo of the Kossuth visit, and perhaps Raymond foresaw that Sanders' home in London would become a center for Kossuth and Garibaldi and others whom the revolutionary failures of 1848 had sent into exile.

What little applause the Pierce Administration received was stirred by its conduct of foreign affairs, particularly by its indication that the United States intended to be heard in foreign capitals. Raymond was in tune. Yet the American public as a whole was largely indifferent at the moment to party politics and matters political. The colorless phrases and uninspired statements in Pierce's first annual message epitomized the calm that had descended. "It strikes us, indeed," the *Times* concluded, "as the least partisan message which has been sent to Congress for many years. This feature of it furnishes additional evidence of the fact we have often noted, that the lines of division between political parties are just at present not easy to be traced."

II

During this period of political stagnation Raymond made the *Times* financially sound and well-riveted in popular demand. On the first anniversary he had enlarged the paper to eight pages in order to make room for more news and more advertising. Increased size forced up the price, and the *Times* now cost two cents instead of one, a change that reduced by perhaps a third the paper's 25,000 circulation. More than a year and a half passed before the lost ground was regained.

Fall in circulation did not affect advertising. The *Times* had carried twelve columns of advertisements on September 30, 1852, when the eight-page edition was just getting under way. Two months later the total had risen to fifteen. By April, 1853, the figure was twenty. But there was still plenty of room for news. "It has never been our intention or wish," readers were assured, "to make the *Daily Times* mainly an advertising sheet. . . . We shall never permit advertisements so far to encroach upon its space as essentially to diminish the amount and impair the variety of its reading matter."

Because of advertising Raymond got into another row with Greeley. It came about in this fashion. At the 1853 session of the Legislature, a law was passed requiring banks to publish in a designated newspaper weekly statements of their condition, and to pay for publication at the paper's regular advertising rates. The State Superintendent of the Banking Department had power to name the paper in which the statements would appear. Here was a real plum, since the statements ran to better than three columns. In New York City it came to the *Times*, quite naturally, perhaps, since D. B. St. John, a former *Times* stockholder, headed the Banking Department. That other New York papers should feel injured should have caused no surprise, and the sense of outrage was doubled because the statements in themselves constituted news which had to be published by any journal pretending to adequate coverage of the financial markets. It fell to Greeley to assail what he described as abuse of public place to serve a private interest.

He had asked St. John at the beginning if proofs of the bank statements would be furnished other papers by the *Times*, and St. John had requested that such be done. When the *Tribune* one day failed to obtain a complete set of proofs, Greeley boiled over. "I feel deeply wronged in this matter," he wrote St. John indignantly, "and even if you are a partner in the *Times*, and share in the profits of this operation, I think you may live to repent of it. . . . Heap public money on your partners or favorites as you can, but it is not right to use the power of your office to supply them with public legal information to my damage." When

St. John quickly replied that he was no longer a *Times* stockholder, Greeley retorted that at least he had been when the law was "concocted." St. John denied that he had ever had anything to do with the law, but Greeley refused to believe him and charged recklessly in a letter to Weed that the whole affair had been engineered by Raymond—a charge that Greeley could sustain only by twisting facts. While these exchanges were progressing, Raymond wrote Greeley what the latter called a "scoundrelly letter" telling him that he would furnish proofs of the bank statements at his own convenience. That letter completed Greeley's case. He denounced the letter, its author and St. John. "All this insolence of this little villain," he told the Banking Superintendent, "is founded on your injustice." Greeley's protests moved neither St. John nor Weed, and the bank statements continued to appear in the *Times* every Tuesday morning, but the *Tribune*'s editor had pinned "little villain" on Raymond, and long after the correspondence with St. John had become public property and been forgotten, "little villain" was remembered and used by many who had no knowledge of its origin.

The Greeley quarrel did not harm the *Times*, which was beginning to see the promise of prosperity. Greater advertising meant greater revenues, and while expenses in the second year had more than doubled those of the Year One, revenues were catching up.

With an eight-page edition every morning, the *Times* was a busy place in the hours that editors and reporters, printers, and pressmen were getting out the paper. Half the paper was made up by ten o'clock in the evening, and these forms were then sent from the composing room on the top floor to the pressroom in the basement. The remaining four pages were held for late news, but by three in the morning these also had been closed and the daily run had started. It was ended by six o'clock. Printing was not the sole operation, for by the time the run was completed, between five and six thousand copies had been mailed at the post office while packages and bundles of papers had been delivered to the railway stations for out-of-town circulation. All had to be folded, and folded by hand—a laborious operation, though some boys boasted that they could fold as many as 1,400 copies in sixty-two minutes. At six in the morning newsboys, ragged and dirty and pinched with poverty, and the regular carriers were massed outside the pressroom, yelling, pushing, eager to begin the day's business. With tickets bought the previous evening they bought in turn their papers, and the *Times* was out.

The paper, its quarters cramped and overcrowded, began to look around for a building that would accommodate its expanding operations. Such a building was found at the corner of Nassau and Beekman Streets, and into it the *Times* moved in the spring of 1854.[1] Circulation by then surpassed 28,000, a figure that had taxed facilities and had made new quarters and new presses essential.

III

There were many reasons for the growth of the *Times*. The *Herald* might attack it for its "gentlemanly silliness" and charge that it was "bereft of all virility and strength," yet the *Times* was giving readers what they wanted. James Parton said it succeeded because it "was conducted with tact, industry and prudence." The Buffalo *Commercial Advertiser* described the *Times* as "the best written paper in the country, and in point of intellectual labor, copiousness of information etc., best in the country." It might not be all that, but Raymond was striving to win for the *Times* the widest possible news coverage from the greatest variety of contributors. In reporting lecturers—Thackeray was the most distinguished of them in the winter of 1852–53, and the *Times* thought him inferior to Dickens—the paper fell into the traditional patterns, as it did with its weekly accounts of Sunday sermons. The *Times*'s reports of meetings and conventions were apt to omit the illuminating details readers found in the *Herald*, and its local news seemed often matter-of-fact, but in special correspondence from Europe and from the United States and in special features the paper had distinction.

In May, 1853, Raymond had sailed for England on the *Arabia* to arrange for special correspondence. It was a hurried trip, and how much was actually accomplished is unknown. Raymond must have had an opportunity to see John Walter of the London *Times*, whom he had got to know on his first visit to England, and one evening he drove out to the "Star and Garter" in Richmond for a great dinner the American banker George Peabody gave for the American Minister. Ex-President Van Buren attended, there were toasts, a musical program, and the long drive back in a procession of carriages. Kossuth was in London, and Raymond managed to persuade him to write for the *Times* a series of special articles on European politics and American foreign policy. They began to appear early in June, 1853, as "Democratic Letters on European Matters and American Policy." Long before the twelve unsigned numbers had been printed, the public guessed that the author was Kossuth, a fact the *Times* often hinted without admitting. The series put a feather in

[1] On May 15, 1854, Hudson of the *Herald* wrote in his diary: "Among my visitors today [was] Mr. Henry J. Raymond . . . Mr. R. called to obtain a few ideas in regard to the arrangement of a newspaper office as he is fitting up a new establishment. Being benevolently inclined I gave him all the information he desired and sent him on his way rejoicing."

Raymond's cap, for whatever might be one's feelings about Kossuth, there could be no question that to list him as an editorial contributor was something of a coup.

Raymond had been on less certain ground when he sent Frederick Law Olmsted into the South to report on economic and social conditions in the cotton kingdom. Although Olmsted had done some writing and had been briefly an editor, he was no trained observer; but needing work, he applied for the assignment. It was quickly settled. Raymond, Olmsted said afterward, "did not ask my sentiments on slavery or any other subject; and the only intimation I received of his expectations as to the matter that I should write was a request that it should be confined to personal observations, and the expression of a wish that I would not feel myself at all restricted or constrained by regard to consistency with the general position of the paper or anything else." Olmsted's first letter —he used the pen name "Yeoman"—was published on February 16, 1853, and letters appeared thereafter at irregular intervals for a year. During that period he received no word from Raymond as to whether the letters were good or bad. Not until the last had been printed did Raymond signal well done by stating publicly that Olmsted had written the "best report that has ever been made of the industrial condition and prospects of the Southern section of the Union." With that opinion there has been general agreement down the years.[2]

Other contributors wrote features less distinguished but closer, perhaps, to the average reader's interests. Charles Loring Brace, who had toured Europe with Olmsted and as an alleged Kossuth sympathizer had seen the inside of a Hungarian prison—a fact that could only recommend him to Raymond—contributed "Walks Among the New York Poor," in which with detail and color and a good deal of emotion the founder of the Children's Aid Society drew attention to the misery in the metropolis. J. Ross Browne, a popular writer and famous traveler, told of what he saw in distant lands. Fitz-James O'Brien sent to the *Times* sparkling, witty, and sophisticated essays. He brought to the paper a clever versatility that for the next decade made him, as a contemporary said, "one of the most brilliant of all the brilliant brotherhood of the Bohemians of New York." Of quite a different sort were the sentimental papers by Minnie Myrtle (Nancy Johnson), one of the few newspaper-women of the Eighteen Fifties. Her themes often were such homely ones as "Our Baby," but in summer she traveled afield, usually to Saratoga, and from the vantage point of the Congress Hotel reported the social life of the watering place.

[2] Olmsted's reports were brought together in book form as *A Journey in the Seaboard Slave States.*

To further the *Times* Raymond capitalized his friendships and acquaintances among men in public life. He made himself *persona grata*, for example, to the popular orator, Edward Everett, one-time president of Harvard, Secretary of State in the last months of the Fillmore Administration, and briefly United States Senator from Massachusetts. Everett was always careful to send Raymond copies of his speeches and lectures in advance of their delivery, and Raymond sought also to persuade him, with small success, to contribute to the *Times*. Though Everett did send a few brief articles, he was under too great pressure for any regular arrangement.

"I have noticed with admiration," he wrote Raymond in the summer of 1853, "the amount of talent, labor and editorial skill developed in your paper. It can not fail, if persevered in, to place the New York *Times* in the front rank of the Journalism, not only of the United States, but of the world. You have powerful neighbors, but have no reason to be discontented with your relative position. . . . I will now and then try to furnish you part of a column, when I think I can do so to any good purpose; and what after all is the great thing for the Journalist, I will furnish you at all times an appreciative reader.

"In the meantime let me thank you for the friendly allusions so often made to me in your volumes, rendered doubly acceptable by contrast with the unvarying ill-nature of your neighbor the *Tribune*, which, indeed *Gov. Seward told me* (as this was in private conversation it is of course *entre nous*) is to be accounted for by the indication of a friendly feeling on your part!"

Seward knew at first hand of Greeley's ill will toward Raymond and the *Times* and of the jealousy that underlay it. Though the Senator tried to give all Whig papers his speeches in advance, accidents sometimes did occur, accidents which Greeley quickly interpreted as direct discrimination. Thus, early in 1853 James W. Simonton, who had become the *Times* correspondent in Washington, and James S. Pike, the *Tribune*'s man, learned the nature of a speech the Senator was to make. Simonton wired an account of it to the *Times*, and other papers picked up the story, but Pike not only failed to wire, but never obtained a copy of the speech, though Seward had been ready to give him one. For what was obviously Pike's fault, Greeley blamed Seward, complaining bitterly in what Seward called an "ugly" letter.

"My former note was ugly," Greeley admitted, "but I don't like to have news snatched from me. . . . I only ask such treatment as you would cheerfully accord to your bitterest enemy; and I protest against others imposing on your good nature and getting permission to print your speeches before you make them. Simonton's telegraphic outline is copied into the Albany *Journal* and other papers ahead of your Speech, giving the impression that *The Times* is your special organ and its filibustering editorials and general negation of principle generally agreeable to you. I do not dispute your right to *make* it your organ—I would just as soon that were the case as not—but unless you intend that, I object to whatever gives a false appearance of it."

IV

Much of Greeley's bad temper was reserved for private correspondence, but occasionally it broke loose in public. There was such an instance in the late winter of 1853, when Greeley and Raymond aired their differences over the international copyright treaty then pending in the United States Senate. As the *Herald* noted: "The philosopher of the *Tribune* and the doughty little blue stocking of the *Times* have got into a very pretty quarrel." The background could be found in the practice common in both the United States and Britain to pirate books and magazines published on the other side of the Atlantic, a profitable business to which Greeley was no stranger.

Gradually the sentiment had spread that authors had property rights in what they wrote, and that these rights could not be destroyed by the miles of heaving ocean. There had long been copyright protection within an author's own country; now the urge was to extend that protection, and for that purpose Webster while Secretary of State had negotiated a treaty, which the press of New York, except for the *Times,* was supporting. Raymond asserted that he did not believe the treaty's supporters had fully considered what ratification would mean "to the people, to the intelligence, to the education and all the best interests of this country." "Cheap books," he said, "have done quite as much as republican institutions . . . to make us the most universally educated people on the face of the earth." International copyright, he felt, would end cheap reprints of British books. He went farther: "Thousands and hundreds of thousands of printers, pressmen, paper-makers, stereotypers, folders, binders, etc., etc., obtain a living by work furnished upon the reprints of English books. Confirm the treaty now before the Senate and . . . English books will not be reprinted here . . . thousands of our citizens will be thrown out of work."

That was the practical aspect. Raymond argued there was a legal side also. "The author," he said, "is entitled to fair reward for his labor. . . . His right to that every nation acknowledges and has enacted laws to secure. . . . The law of each country defines and limits his right, by giving him a defined and limited monopoly in the sale of his books. The man who plants an acorn owns the oak that may grow from it, provided it was planted upon his own soil; but if the wind should waft its acorns upon his neighbor's ground, he would scarcely be sustained in asserting a natural right to their products."

As a proponent of international copyright, Greeley immediately attacked this position, alleging that Raymond's opposition to the treaty was shared only by "a few extensive and wealthy publishers." Every reader knew that Greeley meant the great publishing house of Harper Brothers, a house that *Punch* once said was "built of the skulls of English authors," and with which Raymond had so long been closely associated. Although *Harper's Magazine* had depended for much of its early success on the pirating of British authors, the Harpers had begun to buy American rights to British works—they had done so in 1852 with Dickens' *Bleak House*—and they had apparently made no effort to shape or defeat the copyright treaty. When Greeley attacked the Harpers he was not being wholly just, nor did he have proof at hand when he said Raymond's stand had been determined by his friendship with the firm. Raymond probably appreciated that appearances were against him, and his position was not made the easier by the fact that Fletcher Harper, Jr., son of one of the brothers, had just bought into the *Times* and entered its business department.

The dispute flared. Asserting that Greeley was not a good one to talk about financial influences on editorial positions, Raymond alleged that the *Tribune*'s editor had boosted in his columns stocks in which he had a financial interest and that he had been paid for recommending to *Tribune* readers Dr. Watts's Nervous Antidote. Greeley called such charges lies. In the heat of debate, each attacked the other's record in politics. Each sought to clear himself. The debate proved nothing so far as copyright was concerned, and the treaty itself was destined to languish in the Senate and ultimately to die. But if nothing else, the exchange had widened the gulf separating Greeley and Raymond, a gulf that now assumed political significance.

To their philosophical differences Raymond and Greeley had added a professional rivalry that extended to politics. Greeley, ever the crusader, wanted to rush in, to advocate reform without regard for its practical or political implications. Although his socialism was pretty much in the past, he had added new enthusiasms, among them great interest in spiritualism. He had been and remained a strong proponent of temperance and he agitated for a law to make temperance more or less compulsory. Because the editor of the *Times* had no sympathy for such attitudes, there was cause for a man with Greeley's strong views to accuse Raymond of "general negation of principle."

The *Tribune*'s editor had additional complaints. He was disturbed, exceedingly so and he felt with reason, by the treatment he received from Seward and Weed. Each passing month, so it seemed to him, saw evidence accumulate that his services went unappreciated. Raymond was the favored one, Raymond whom he had trained as a newspaperman and who had not only set up the *Times* to compete with the *Tribune* but had won for it more esteem among New York Whigs than the *Tribune* had ever enjoyed. Seward showed a steady friendship for the *Times*. Weed, Greeley suspected, had high regard not only for the *Times* but for its editor, although Greeley had been a laborer in the Whig vineyard while Raymond was studying Latin verbs at the university. It was not pleasant to contemplate. It made Greeley uneasy about the value of his partnership. Personal slights, though hard to bear, could be borne. But it was insupportable that his partners could find merit in the "little villain" and in the *Times*.

CHAPTER

—11—

Partners in Politics

I

THE UNITED STATES at the opening of 1854 had entered a period of unparalleled prosperity for the banker, the merchant, the farmer, the planter. The whole nation felt the impact of improved transportation that developed a great free-trade area for the exchange of manufactured goods and the products of the farm. As railway networks spread across the land the roar of passing steam cars heralded a new day. In the North manufacturing was booming, and investors were finding that factories as well as railroads afforded opportunities for gain unsurpassed in American history. *De Bow's Review* said that in the West humanity was moving across the prairies "to enter into possession of 'Time's noblest empire.' " With a world demanding cotton the South felt that cotton was indeed king, and while railroad building, as Raymond had noted at the time of his Chicago visit in 1845, was binding the West to the North and breaking the traditional north-south routes of trade, the significance was lost upon most men when they discussed slavery's threat to national unity.

The Compromise of 1850, most Americans hoped, had settled the slavery issue, and the national prosperity seemed to testify to its beneficial effects on trade. President Pierce had praised domestic tranquillity in the annual message that the *Times* had liked so much, and he had promised "that this repose is to suffer no shock during my official term if I have power to avert it." His promise was scarcely a month old when Senator Douglas of Illinois laid before the United States Senate on January 4, 1854, a report from the Committee on Territories approving a bill for the organization of Nebraska Territory. The bill proclaimed the doctrine of "popular sovereignty"; its application would repeal the Missouri Compromise of 1820 that forbade slavery north of 36°30′, for Nebraska was above that line. By Douglas's reckless action slavery had once more become the dominating issue in American politics, for in the North men of all parties held to the belief that the Missouri Compromise was almost as sacred as the Constitution.

The *Times* said nothing as Douglas and his colleagues polished the bill and maneuvered for Pierce's support. Not until January 18 were *Times* readers warned of impending controversy. "The Independent Democrats in Congress," Simonton wired from Washington, "will issue an address to the country, setting forth their objection to Gen. Douglas's Nebraska bill, and appealing for help to defeat it." Five days later the revised bill—it specifically repealed the Missouri Compromise—was laid before the Senate, and Douglas said privately, "It will raise a hell of a storm." In the *Times* the storm broke with hardly a preliminary rumble.

"Passage of this Nebraska bill," Raymond thundered, ". . . will root out from the Northern mind the last vestige of confidence in the good faith of the advocates of slavery, and create a deep-seated, intense and ineradicable hatred of the institution which will crush its political power, at all hazards, and at any cost." President Pierce he denounced: "His Administration has taken the first step toward plunging the country into a renewed agitation of the question of slavery, which will prove more formidable and fatal to the public peace, than any similar contest through which the country has thus far passed."

Alarm bells rang throughout the North to summon men to the cause of free soil. The New York Assembly had before it resolutions condemning the Nebraska bill, and similar resolutions became commonplace in the legislatures of the North. In New York City a call was quickly circulated for a great mass meeting at the Broadway Tabernacle, where Henry Ward Beecher and Horace Greeley and Lucy Stone—in Bloomer costume—had been drawing capacity audiences to the Anti-Slavery Society's lectures. The *Herald* attacked the Tabernacle meeting, which some of the city's prominent merchants had organized, as an affair got up by Seward's friends as a move toward forming an anti-slavery party, of which he would be the leader. The *Herald* exaggerated, and yet from the first, opposition to the Nebraska bill had partisan overtones. The bill—it was amended so that Nebraska Territory could be divided into two states, Nebraska and Kansas—split the Democratic party, for many Northern Democrats now broke with the Pierce Administration. A divided Democracy could be only pleasing to the Whigs, who were making common cause with Free-Soilers and abolitionists in protesting abrogation of the Missouri Compromise. Out of these elements, diverse though they were, might be built a party Northern in sentiment and one that in Raymond's words could crush slavery's political power.

Five months after introduction of the Nebraska bill, cannon at the Washington Navy Yard announced its passage by the Congress. During those months the North had been swept by agitation. The *Times* had told of mass meetings that rallied the bill's opponents in cities and towns, of the great Tabernacle meeting in February at which Beecher, near the peak of his oratorical powers, lifted an audience to so high a pitch that men and women wept, and were unashamed. The *Times* sent its own man to report a mass meeting in Boston's Faneuil Hall, and printed a full account along with the text of a speech Seward had delivered the same day in the United States Senate. "The voice of New England," said Raymond, "rings along seven columns of this morning's *Times*, and New York's sentiments, from the mouth of her distinguished Senator, cover another page." There were texts of many anti-Nebraska speeches to print, Senator Sumner's, for example, and Senator Everett's, and letters to publish from readers across the state, across the country. Reports of anti-Nebraska resolutions adopted by legislatures flooded in, and as public temper mounted, there began to be accounts of the burning of Douglas effigies. The *Times* thought this form of protest "feeble, foolish," but the burnings continued until Douglas said later: "I could travel from Boston to Chicago by the light of my own effigy."

Raymond had stated his position at the start. He opposed slavery as a "moral, social and political evil," but insisted that its abolition was a matter for the South, not the North, to decide. "We have scrupulously abstained," he said editorially, "from meddling with slavery." Abstention did not mean neutrality, and Raymond put the *Times* squarely against repeal of the Missouri Compromise—repeal would be "a flagrant violation of good faith," "a needless and wanton insult to Northern sentiment." The slave power wanted repeal, he asserted, in order that the South might count the votes in Congress needed to control the tariff, to decide appropriations for public works, and to push measures favorable to the slaveholding section but unfavorable to the North. He looked ahead, and shortly before the Nebraska bill became law, warned readers that "the Slaveholding Power is preparing for a disruption of the Union, by making the Union while it lasts an instrument of extending and consolidating the Slave Empire."

Throughout the months of debate Raymond confined himself to the editorial page. He signed no calls for mass meetings, made no appearances on the platform, and only once, in a letter declining to address an anti-Nebraska meeting, ever stated his position publicly outside the *Times*. Perhaps he believed he exerted more influence through editorials, though in the past he had not always felt that way, and remembering his love of public speaking it is easy to imagine that the restraint did not rest lightly.

The *Times* in any case demanded all his attention. The move into new quarters in May, 1854, had been expensive and there had been new presses to be bought to accommodate the paper's swelling circulation. He was expanding his own stock holdings. This was no time to dissipate energies, and besides on the success of the *Times* depended his ability to meet the debts he had accumulated. In April he had turned to Weed for financial assistance. "I want help," Raymond had written Weed, "and I know you will at all events excuse my coming to you for it. . . . I have been buying Ruggles' part of the *Times*—six shares. And I want to borrow money to pay him and also to pay up instalments that will be needed for new presses, etc. I want $5,000 or better still $7,000, for one, two or three years: for which I can give *one quarter* of the *Times* establishment as security. I should like it at 7 per cent, but if needful will pay some bonus."

Weed came to Raymond's aid, for the Whig Dictator was always ready to be generous with his friends and associates, but his aid put Raymond under obligation to him. Perhaps it was just as well that the readers of the *Times*, and its enemies also, remained unaware of the financial ties that thus bound the editor to the Seward-Weed machine.

II

Despite the Nebraska controversy, the *Times* did not ignore what was happening elsewhere. In Europe there was war between Russia and Turkey, and the steamers with their regular reports from London and Paris brought warnings that Britain and France were likely to be drawn into the conflict. There was smallpox among New York's poor. There were fires and explosions that brought down denunciation of the carelessness of those responsible. There was temperance agitation. At the Broadway Tabernacle temperance lectures competed with those against slavery, and Horace Greeley found it hard to determine whether his anti-liquor or his anti-slavery sentiments had the upper hand.

New York reformers were seeking to follow the example set by Maine in 1851 by the adoption of a prohibition law. They had spoken and written for temperance, had emphasized the evils of drink, and had done their best to capitalize on an obviously growing public sentiment for curbing the liquor traffic. Greeley had worked for temperance, but it was Myron H. Clark of Canandaigua, a State Senator and leader of the temperance

movement in upstate New York, whose name was most directly associated with prohibitory legislation. He had sponsored a bill in 1852 to
suppress "drinking houses and tippling shops," and though it failed, he
continued the fight. In 1854 he again introduced a temperance measure
and this time the signs were more favorable. A Whig, his party controlled
the Legislature. Governor Seymour, though a Democrat, appeared
likely to approve even a Whig-sponsored temperance bill, for in his
annual message he had recommended action. Public opinion was on
Clark's side, and when at the end of March, 1854, his bill "for the suppression of intemperance" was passed by both Senate and Assembly,
the *Times* felt forced to say: "We are glad. . . . If judiciously administered the law will do great good."

When Governor Seymour vetoed the bill in a resounding message that
held it to be both unconstitutional and "calculated to injure the cause of
temperance and impair the welfare of the state," the *Times* quickly re-
versed itself. The law was too extreme, the *Times* now held, and could
not be enforced. "It is not politic," asserted the paper, "to erect a des-
potism in our midst, even for the sake of escaping evils which personal
and social freedom of necessity involve." Governor Seymour had given
the impending state campaign an issue as significant as that created by
the Nebraska bill, for temperance advocates redoubled their efforts,
aware now that success depended on control not only of the Legislature
but of the governorship as well.

Temperance was to be a campaign issue. So was condemnation of the
Nebraska legislation. Such issues could be fought out in the traditional
pattern of party, but would they be? Widespread and growing demand
for a new party both Northern and anti-slavery in principle threatened
political habits. Yet Raymond, and he was expressing not only his own
views but those of Seward and Weed, contended in the *Times* that "no
party could be found or formed which would represent a firmer and
more unmistakable hostility to the aggressions of the slaveholding interest than does the Whig party of the Free States." To arguments for
a new party he replied: "The policy in question is very much like that
of disbanding a strong, disciplined and well organized army, on the eve
of an engagement, in the hope of raising a better one by calling for volunteers." He had scarcely masked the fear of Whig leaders that a new
party in New York State would insure Democratic victory on election
day, a victory doubly costly since it would guarantee Seward's defeat
for reelection to the United States Senate in 1855. Such defeat, whatever
its burden for the Seward-Weed machine, would be generally regarded
in the nation as a rebuke for the anti-slavery cause of which the New
York Senator was being more and more generally recognized the leader,

Aware that somehow the new party demand must be diverted, Seward men joined a call for a nonpartisan anti-Nebraska convention to meet in Saratoga in the middle of August. Raymond was a signer. Apparently a new political organization was about to be born, just as under the oaks at Jackson, Michigan, a new party calling itself Republican had recently come into being. Sewardites had other plans.

III

On the eve of the convention call, Raymond journeyed upstate, to "this dear soil of my early home," to spend the Fourth of July at Lima, and to deliver a patriotic and anti-slavery address at Geneseo on the national holiday. A few days later he spoke to the literary societies at the University of Rochester commencement. It was pleasant to visit Rochester. His brother Samuel, an insurance broker, lived there, and his old roommate, Alexander Mann, edited the Rochester *Daily American*. Raymond always enjoyed the atmosphere of any university, and he must have felt thoroughly at home when he rose to discuss the theme of a state system of education, carrying on his speech to the New York Assembly more than three years earlier. He pleaded for a state-supported system from the elementary school through the university. "It is the duty of our great state," said he, "to make just as full and complete provision for the education of her children in the higher departments of science and of general culture as she has already made for their instruction in the elements of knowledge." He outstripped custom and practice in enunciating such a doctrine, and he was even farther in front when he announced: "The only limit that can be fixed to education is the capacity of the citizen to receive and profit by it." It was a noble address, and one that did him credit and honor, for New York State not only lacked a publicly supported university but still depended to some extent on private support for its school system.

The summer was a busy one for Raymond. Presumably he had returned to the city by the time of the birth of his son Walter on July 19, but he was soon away again for the annual visit to Burlington and U.V.M., and scarcely had the commencement activities ended before he was in Saratoga as a delegate to the Anti-Nebraska Convention.

IV

The anti-Nebraska men arrived at the height of the Saratoga season. Hotels were crowded, and ex-President Tyler, a bit out of place in the convention atmosphere of Whiggery and anti-slavery, was among the distinguished guests who appeared on the promenades and drank the waters of the spa. Senator Seward and Thurlow Weed were in town.

So was Horace Greeley, who had been attending a convention of the Sons of Temperance which vacated St. Nicholas Hall just in time for the 400 anti-Nebraska delegates to move in.

What the *Herald* called the "Saratoga Holy Alliance" of Raymond, Greeley and other Seward "instruments" controlled the convention from the start. The alliance, though Greeley had no heart in it, had small thought of naming a ticket for the state campaign; to a platform there was no objection. Amid almost continuous disorder and confusion Raymond carried the burden of the struggle, for Greeley, though chairman of the committee on resolutions, succumbed to fatigue, leaving the task to Raymond, who shared none of his desire for plowing a fresh furrow. The resolutions, carefully framed, denounced the Kansas-Nebraska Act, condemned popular sovereignty, approved the colonization movement that had started emigrant trains moving into Kansas. They ignored the question of a state ticket, selection of which would have automatically called for a new party.

Reading of the resolutions loosed protest through the hall, but the *Herald's* correspondent noted that the opposition, lacking organization, got nowhere because every attempt to speak was met by the shouting, hissing and stamping of "Greeley's and Raymond's rioters." Ultimately Raymond offered an amendment shrewdly designed to weaken still further the new-party men. It proposed that selection of a ticket be postponed until after the major parties—only the Whig party was really concerned—had made their nominations in September. An adjourned Anti-Nebraska Convention could then decide whether to accept these nominations or to make its own. Proposal of this amendment and Raymond's plea for it signaled further uproar and excitement, but the amendment along with the other resolutions was adopted before the convention adjourned to meet at Auburn on September 26.

V

The Saratoga hurdle successfully passed, Whigs looked forward to the naming of a ticket that would attract anti-Nebraska and temperance men as well as old-line party members. Greeley wanted very much to be the Whig candidate for governor. He had labored long for Seward and Weed, and he regarded nomination for the governorship as a reward overdue and certainly well-deserved. His work in the cause of temperance, he believed, made him a strong candidate, while his part in the anti-Nebraska agitation made him all the more acceptable. So in the late summer Greeley called on Weed at his New York headquarters, Room No. 11 in the Astor House.

At the moment, Weed was not as sure of his political position as he would have liked. To a situation already complicated by temperance and anti-slavery had been added a new and untried element, the Native American or Know-Nothing movement. Organized in secret lodges, appealing to popular liking for things mysterious and to general sentiment for Americanism and Protestantism as opposed to foreigners and Catholicism, the Know-Nothings in New York, and in other states too, were upsetting party allegiance and destroying party organization. Many of New York's anti-Seward Whigs hoped to use the Know-Nothings to defeat the Senator's influence in the party, and he was a promising target. Since his period as Governor nearly two decades earlier, Seward had been a friend of the Irish immigrant in America and of the Roman Catholic Church. Not every Know-Nothing was anti-Seward, nor was every anti-Seward Whig a Know-Nothing, but exactly where the line was to be drawn not even so astute a leader as Thurlow Weed could be certain. But Weed did understand that the Know-Nothings hoped to gain control of the Whig convention. If they succeeded, the way would be difficult for the Sewardites, who had as their goal control of the next Legislature, on which depended Seward's senatorship.

Of Greeley's availability as a candidate Weed probably had grave doubts in any case, and the complex political situation argued further against it. Weed recalled in his autobiography how Greeley asked him if he did not "think the time and circumstances were favorable to his nomination." "I replied," said Weed, "that I did not think the time and circumstances favorable to his election, if nominated, but that my friends had lost control of the state convention. This answer perplexed him, but a few words of explanation made it quite clear. Admitting that he had brought the people up to the point of accepting a temperance candidate for Governor, I remarked that another aspirant had 'stolen his thunder.' In other words, while he had shaken the temperance bush, Myron H. Clark would catch the bird. I informed Mr. Greeley that Know-Nothing or 'Chocktaw' lodges had been secretly organized throughout the State, by means of which many delegates for Mr. Clark had been secured. Mr. Greeley saw that the 'slate' had been broken, and cheerfully relinquished the idea of being nominated."

Greeley, for whom public office always seemed a greener field than journalism, was keenly disappointed, and a few days later called again on the Whig boss. "Is there any objection to my running for Lieutenant Governor?" he asked. Once more Weed had to oppose Greeley's ambition, explaining to him that one temperance man on the ticket would be sufficient. "Mr. Greeley . . . left me in good spirits," Weed recalled, but he deceived himself, for Greeley had been deeply hurt,

VI

The Whigs met at Syracuse on September 20, "the same old Whigs," the *Herald* described them, "with their sleek, well shaven faces, neat apparel and grave deportment—the same brisk young Whigs, with very high shirt collars, very new hats, very stiff linen, very well dyed whiskers, very large bowed cravats and very shiny black clothes." Weed and his aides worked behind the scenes, seeking to gain control of the convention, and succeeding, by informal caucuses at which there were free wine and cigars in abundance. Greeley was present; so was Raymond. "The editor of the junior Seward organ," the *Herald* remarked, "was lobbying partly for Weed, partly for Patterson [George W. Patterson, a prominent Seward Whig], partly for several other people and a great deal for himself."

Rumors circulated that Raymond was to be nominated for Lieutenant Governor as part of a bargain to win Weed's support for Clark as head of the ticket. Probably there was a bargain, for on the convention's second day Raymond was nominated for Lieutenant Governor by acclamation. Whether Weed told the truth or not is questionable, but he explained it this way: "I went to the convention prepared to acquiesce in the nomination of Mr. Clark for governor; and caring only that the other nominees should be so selected as to strengthen the ticket. No candidate for lieutenant governor had been designated. Many delegates were anxious to ballast the ticket by the nomination of a candidate for lieutenant governor who was not committed in favor of prohibitory or Maine law legislation, and yet who would not be obnoxious to temperance men. Several names were canvassed, but none seemed to unite all interests until that of Mr. Raymond was suggested. . . . Mr. Greeley not only held me responsible for that nomination, but supposed that in my conversation with him the intention to urge it had been concealed. In that supposition, however, he erred, for I had not thought of Mr. Raymond in that connection until his name was suggested to me at Syracuse." Raymond, who had apparently been unaware of Weed's talks with Greeley, seems to have gone to the convention believing Weed favored the *Tribune*'s editor for second place on the Whig ticket.

Why should Raymond, who only a few months earlier had shunned political activity, have now emerged as a candidate for office? He may have been under considerable pressure from Seward and Weed to stand for the lieutenant governorship, for as president of the State Senate he would hold a post of great importance when the time came for Seward's reelection. His financial obligation to Weed may have made it difficult for him to resist the pressure. Yet what seems most likely is that Ray-

mond found it impossible to forego the prospect of office; his good resolutions to devote himself wholly to the *Times* faded, and he allowed
himself to be drawn again into the arena.

For Raymond the cheers of fellow Whigs must have been pleasant,
a pleasure made double when at Auburn the Anti-Nebraska Convention
gave him its nomination also and applauded without restraint his promise of full allegiance to the principles so recently adopted at Saratoga.
There was debate over Raymond at the Temperance Convention, and
his nomination was accepted only because he pledged support of Maine
legislation. "I am decidedly in favor of a prohibitory law," he wrote.
He was openly and frequently accused of turning his coat for political
purposes, but the temperance men for the moment regarded him as one
of their own.

The campaign proved anything but straightforward. The Whigs in
convention had pushed Nativism aside, had ignored the issue in their
platform, but the Know-Nothings did not take defeat quietly. They put
up a ticket of their own that threatened to split the Whig vote and insure victory for the Democratic candidate, Governor Seymour. The
threat was very real, since the Know-Nothing vote defied analysis.
Clark, who had been sympathetic toward Nativism, attracted some
Know-Nothings. Raymond had never been an outright foe. Could the
Clark-Raymond ticket therefore draw Know-Nothing support, or would
the Know-Nothings with the anti-Sewardites insure its defeat?

The Whig press reflected the confusion. In the weeks before election
the *Times*, while supporting the Whig party as the defender of the
Missouri Compromise and emphasizing the anti-Nebraska issue, ignored Raymond's candidacy and the Whig ticket. Greeley sank his own
sentiments in wholehearted advocacy of Clark and Raymond. The candidate for Lieutenant Governor, said he, is "a young man of decided talent,
remarkable assiduity," who possesses "a legislative experience which
will prove valuable in the chair of the Senate." Other editors were less
certain. "Of Raymond we know too much," commented the New York
Mirror. "He is a man of more ability than stability. Like the Irishman's
flea, you put your finger on him and he isn't there." Alexander Mann
in the Rochester *Daily American* rallied to his friend. If he had been
"selected for the first office," Mann asserted, "it could not then be said,
as it is now, that the strength of the ticket was on its tail."

Raymond participated little in the campaign. He made few speeches,
but in his major address on the eve of the election, he called for a halt to
the extension of slavery. "We must prohibit slavery in Kansas and Nebraska," he said. "We must refuse the assent of Congress . . . for the
formation of new Slave States. And we must refuse assent to the admis-

sion of such States into the Union when the application shall be made." He had taken a position with the vanguard of free-soil men, however much he might fall behind abolitionists like Garrison and Gerrit Smith, and his words were broadcast across the state.

Whig headquarters in New York City were at the Broadway House, and there, amid flags and banners, party workers gathered on election day to await results. Returns came in slowly, so slowly that at first it seemed the Democrats had won. Days passed. First Raymond's election as Lieutenant Governor was conceded and then Clark finally squeaked through by 153 votes, 600 fewer than Raymond. By this narrow margin the Seward-Weed machine regained state control, but the Know-Nothing candidate, while running third, had piled up a big vote and it must have been obvious to Weed and his circle that the old parties were nearing the end of their tether, that not for much longer could the popular urge for new party alignments be denied.

VII

A few days after the election an embittered Greeley sat down to write a long letter to Seward. "It seems to me a fitting time," he said, "to announce to you the dissolution of the political firm of Seward, Weed & Greeley by the withdrawal of the junior partner." There followed an extended review of Greeley's association with the firm and a denunciation of the treatment he had received from its senior members and of their failure to give him political office and political support. He attacked in particular the favors shown Raymond in the campaign just past. "No other name," he complained, "could have been put on the ticket so bitterly humbling to me as that which was selected. The nomination was given to Raymond, the fight left to me. And Gov. Seward *I have made it*, though it be conceited in me to say so. What little fight there has been, I have stored up. Even Weed has not been (I speak of his paper) hearty in this contest while the journal of the Whig Lieut. Governor has taken care of its own interests and let the canvass take care of itself."

The letter, with its revelation of Greeley's thirst for public office, worried Seward. "Has Greeley written to you, or do you see him now-a-days?" he asked Weed. "Today I have a long letter from him, full of sharp, pricking thorns. . . . Raymond's nomination and election is hard for him to bear." The Senator tried to soothe Greeley's feelings, but the *Tribune*'s editor had made up his mind. "My political life is ended," he wrote, rejecting Seward's olive branch. "If you will understand that what I have desired from you—what I think you have unwisely withheld—is some sort of public recognition that I was esteemed a faithful and useful coadjutor—I need say no more."

The political firm had been dissolved, although the public did not know it. Greeley continued on many occasions to support Seward and his cause. Yet the rift, for which Raymond had been in part responsible, grew ever wider, its extent unmeasured until the great crisis in Seward's political life in 1860.

CHAPTER

12

Birth of a Party

I

GOOD OMENS attended the Whig inauguration at Albany on January 1, 1855. The day was bright, bracing, and the crowds gathered in the snowy streets could parade in best bonnets and beavers. Ceremonies had been scheduled for ten in the morning, and long before the hour the Capitol had filled with spectators. There was delay, but restlessness and impatience dissolved before the advancing acclaim that announced the arrival in the Assembly chamber of Governor Clark and Horatio Seymour, arm in arm, Lieutenant Governor Raymond, and the Governor's military staff in uniforms of blue.

Clark and Seymour spoke briefly. There was polite applause, there were cheers also, and then loud calls for Raymond. Raymond refused to speak, for this was Clark's day and he had no wish to subtract from its satisfactions. He sought to remain in the background both at the formal ceremonies and at the reception when long lines of well-wishers greeted the state's new Chief Executive and its Lieutenant Governor.

Raymond had come to Albany a few days earlier to aid Clark with his message, and had taken lodgings again in Congress Hall. In some circles talk had it that Raymond hoped to be the next Governor, and Greeley gossiped that his political rival was "quietly and industriously laying pipe for the next step," although the evidence was hard to discover, and Raymond probably could not have defined the limits of his political ambition. His legislative colleagues liked him as a congenial companion, as a just and fair presiding officer, though all must have been aware that he had been charged frequently with trimming and that his apparent shift on the Maine law had been attributed to desire for office. There was appreciation of his oratorical power, of his skill in debate, of his broad knowledge and understanding, and it was recognized that as editor of the *Times* and as part of the Seward-Weed machine he possessed power far greater than that customarily associated with the lieutenant governorship.

The job of Lieutenant Governor was neither arduous nor exacting. Ordinarily it amounted to little more than presiding over the Senate and serving on state bodies like the Canal Board and the Board of Regents. There was some patronage to distribute, and there were favors to bestow, although in most instances the final word rested with the Governor and the best that Raymond could do was to assure applicants for place that he would speak to Clark in their behalf. Behind the legislative arras, however, a Lieutenant Governor could exert considerable political influence, and Raymond was prepared so to do.

Seward's reelection as Senator was the immediate and dominating business. Since the Whigs controlled the Legislature, it would have been only routine had the party been united. But many Whigs, including some with Know-Nothing views, disliked Seward, and he had been in public office too long not to have gained other enemies. His opponents sought to block any election until the Legislature united on a Know-Nothing. Seward men had to forestall the maneuver. Weed assumed direction, but his promises of patronage and legislative measures were unrecorded, and so far as the public knew, his efforts were exerted chiefly through lavish dinners and entertainments at his Albany house. Refusing all engagements, Raymond remained in Albany for the weeks of the contest, and soon was deep in the trading and lobbying. By the end of January, he could write Hamilton Fish: "We are confident of our ability to reelect Gov. Seward."

The work of Weed and Raymond and their lieutenants began to tell. Know-Nothings found themselves unable to agree on a candidate, and some of them rallied around Seward's standard. Anti-slavery Democrats turned to him as party lines broke. When the Whigs in early February prepared to caucus, Seward said cautiously: "Our friends are in good spirits and reasonably confident." His seat was safe, and the Whig caucus made the fact certain. In the caucus Raymond was cheered repeatedly when he praised New York's senior Senator and said: "The champions of slavery fear him as the friends of freedom love him. They fear him—not as an enemy of the Union—but because they know that he will never cease to war against the unjust and unconstitutional encroachments of slavery."

The victory had only to be ratified, and on a bitter winter's day the New York Senate and Assembly met in joint session to hear Raymond announce that William H. Seward had been "duly elected Senator of the United States for six years from the fourth of March, 1855." Shouts shook the frosted panes in the classic hall, and the handkerchiefs of ladies fluttered in the crowded galleries. The brief Capitol ceremony ended, a 300-gun salute broke Albany's icy quiet, and as the booming died, "masses of the victorious party repaired to the public houses and poured down their parched throats streams of liquor." "Intoxication," said the *Herald* correspondent, "ruled the remaining part of the day and night." Bonfires burned in the streets when darkness fell, and torchlight processions accompanied the bands that wound up Albany's hill to serenade Weed at his home and Raymond at Congress Hall.

Seward was in Washington when the news came. Friends hurried to congratulate him, and in the Senate chamber even political foes like Douglas were among the colleagues who pressed around to wish him well. From an overflowing heart Seward wrote Raymond: "Accept most sincere and grateful acknowledgements . . . for the manliness and boldness as well as firmness with which you in common with so many and such noble friends carried me through the most perilous crisis of my public life. May God bless you and all of them, and enable you to perform better services and attain higher than those which have filled up my life."

II

After the excitement of the senatorial contest any other legislative business seemed anticlimactic, but one item on the calendar could not be ignored: the bill to ban the liquor traffic. In the session's closing days it was passed, a harsh bill with sweeping provisions that not only struck down the traffic but denied the right of jury trial in case of violation and provided strict regulations for search and seizure. Temperance men were pleased, but a good many moderates were alarmed, and many a lawyer prophesied that the law would be held unconstitutional, as indeed ultimately it was.

Raymond's place in this fight was not wholly clear. At Auburn he had professed belief in temperance and prohibition. Now, it was commonly said, he had done his utmost to shape prohibitory legislation in a form so extreme that the courts would throw it out. Moreover, the *Times* was critical of the new law. The *Tribune* was not alone in accusing Raymond of double-dealing, and his part assuredly had not been straightforward.

Always a master of the plausible statement, Raymond showed once again his mastery. To the *Tribune* he retorted that while he believed in temperance and a temperance law, he knew of no requirement to support a law just because it suited the *Tribune*. He confessed that he had always doubted the "ability of legal prohibition to destroy intemperance." The process was not so easy, and he laid down the propositions that the "public mind could be won to prohibition more easily than it could be driven," that too harsh a law would create more evil than it could cure. "Too lax a law," insisted Raymond, "would be better, far better, to begin with than one too stringent."

Raymond's answer did not turn away the *Tribune*'s wrath, and although New York's saloonkeepers, some of them, blamed the temperance law on Raymond and boycotted the *Times*, the *Tribune* returned to the contest and got down to personalities. By way of muddying the stream, it accused Raymond of intemperance, although in a hard-drinking age he was notably restrained. Raymond, said the *Tribune*, had downed three glasses of champagne before speaking at an Astor House banquet during the Legislature's drunken visit to New York City in the late winter of 1855. He was known, it added, to like brandy and water. Worst of all, at a large party he had given in Albany for Senators and Assemblymen, absence of alcoholic refreshment had been more apparent than real: in a private room there had been plenty to drink for those who wanted it. The *Tribune* later admitted it lacked complete evidence, and Raymond defied the *Tribune* and temperance men alike by insisting that a glass of wine or a mug of beer did not make a man a drunkard.

Despite the editorial clamor, temperance was about worn out so far as New York politics was concerned. The liquor traffic balked enforcement, and in New York City local officials looked the other way. The reforming spirit was being diverted because slavery, not the grog shop, stirred men's minds, and temperance leaders like Greeley soon accepted the fact that temperance as a political issue had to be postponed. The issue now was Kansas.

Southerners insisted that Kansas should be slave; Northerners were equally insistent that it be free. It could not be both, and from that impasse stemmed crisis. The pattern had been set in November, 1854, when a band of Missourians crossed into Kansas to insure election of a Southerner as territorial delegate to Washington. In the following March the maneuver was repeated when armed Missourians—the "Border Ruffians"—again invaded Kansas to seize the polls in the election of a territorial legislature that by this act of violence and fraud was made secure for slavery. Free-soil men in Kansas at the time were so greatly outnumbered by Southerners that an honest election would probably have returned a pro-slavery legislature anyhow. Whether the North would have accepted such a demonstration of popular sovereignty is doubtful, but the situation was wholly altered when the Border Ruffians convinced the North that the South had no interest in popular sovereignty and had no intention of allowing Kansas to work out its destiny.

Andrew H. Reeder, Governor of the territory, a well-meaning but weak man who had intended to be impartial in his administration, described in detail during a visit in Pennsylvania what had happened, and the *Times* on May 1, 1855, published his report. With its publication the North took fire. The *Times* said it flatly: there could be no more slave states; Kansas could enter the Union only under the banner of freedom; men pledged to oppose further extension of slave territory must be elected to Congress. Raymond was only reiterating what he had said and written during the previous autumn's state campaign, but behind the reiteration now lay a situation, not a theory.

III

Kansas often seemed unreal even to the editors of the *Times*, boasting of their burgeoning circulation—almost 40,000 daily—and of their full and accurate livestock market reports. Besides, the Crimean War, and notably the siege of Sebastopol that was nearing its climax, sometimes overshadowed guerrilla exchanges on the Kansas prairie, and the profitable pressure of advertising called for constant care in selecting the news. Often the unspectacular routine of everyday living took precedence over all else. In the *Times* hoop skirts were ridiculed. The ailanthus tree, which flourished in New York back yards and which, as Henry James recalled long afterward, lent a "peculiar fragrance" to Washington Square, was denounced editorially as a "filthy, worthless foreigner," and went on flourishing just the same. The great French actress Rachel delighted discriminating playgoers, although her audiences wished she were more familiar with spoken English. In defense of seekers after knowledge, the *Times* rebuked for rudeness an attendant within the Byzantine precincts of the new Astor Library.

In late spring Raymond took off on a junket by boat and horseback through the North Country to trace the route for a proposed railroad between Saratoga and Sackett's Harbor, and while the fortnight's adventure in the woods had compensation in the guise of male fellowship, the weather often turned bad and he returned suffering from a cold sufficiently severe to dampen recollections of comradely campfires. With summer Minnie Myrtle renewed her gleaning from life in the watering places, and lesser contributors submitted accounts of mountain and seaside resorts. Superficially everything fitted the traditional pattern; yet change seethed beneath the surface. It was most manifest in politics.

In June the Know-Nothings had split over slavery. Only the Democrats could now so much as pretend to being a national party, but the
Democrats had long lacked unity in the North, and in New York the
party's wings were so far apart that agreement on a common ticket was
difficult. The new Republican party in state after state above the Mason-
Dixon line was pulling together remnants of older organizations—Whigs
who had no place to go, Know-Nothings who opposed slavery's extension, Democrats with free-soil principles, abolitionists, temperance advocates, a strange aggregation held together by common hostility toward
further expansion of slave territory. New York was now ready to join.

IV

The *Times* in July, 1855, published calls for Whigs to meet in convention at Syracuse in September, and for Republicans (anti-Nebraska men
had adopted that name a year earlier) to meet in the same city on the
same day. Fusion had begun, and Weed busied himself to make it reality.
Raymond lent editorial support. "Party lines are not permanent," he said,
and he argued that the common sense of outrage over events in Kansas
had already dictated political realignment: "Party leaders, by following
that sentiment, may seem to lead it; but they cannot stifle it nor suppress its development."

When the conventions assembled at Syracuse the die had been cast.
Greeley, who had been foremost in advocating a new party and had
proposed the name Republican, was present. So were Raymond and
Edwin D. Morgan, a relatively new figure in the political tent. It was
quickly settled. The two conventions met separately, then jointly, ful-
filling Seward's prophecy to a delegate: "You will go in by two doors,
but you will all come out through one."

During the ensuing off-year campaign Raymond did all he could to
sell the new party. He spoke in his own ward and elsewhere in the city.
Upstate he appeared on the same platform with the Lieutenant Governor
of Ohio to assert: "The Republican Party has no sectional aim: it claims
only the reaffirmation of a principle of compromise." In the *Times* he
went farther. Republicanism, he said, did not mean abolitionism; the
party "has nothing to do with Slavery per se, with its morality, its policy
or its existence as a form of society. It regards it simply in its political
aspect, as an interest in the nation, entitled to its share of legislative favor,
though not content with that, but insidiously usurping power and supremacy over all other interests, and making them subservient to its
ambition." Repeatedly he argued that extension of slave territory was
the issue, opposition to it the basis for the Republican party and for its
appeal to labor as well as capital. This was no radical movement, he

contended; it was essentially conservative. Only its failure would bring radicalism. "Unless there is to be some limit to this steady march of Slavery," he warned, "all conservatism would disappear and the Whole Free States would be driven to the open ground of Abolition."

The fall elections did not go well, although Seward, speaking magnificently in Albany a month before the polling, had filled his listeners with crusading zeal as he called them to stand with him beneath a banner "untorn in former battles and unsullied in past errors." The cause could not die so long as Kansas bled. "The question of slavery domination," said Raymond, "must be fought out on the plains of Kansas," and so apparently it would be unless a compromise could be devised to lull the passions arising in Congress, the press and wherever men gathered to discuss the state of the Union. The Presidential election of 1856 would provide new opportunity to thrash out the issue.

In preparation therefor 400 Republicans from twenty-three states gathered at Pittsburgh on February 22, 1856, to form a national organization in the atmosphere of a religious revival. "Enthusiasm is abundant, confidence and unanimity remarkable," reported the *Times* correspondent. "If the Republican pear is not ripe, it has a tempting look." Before adjournment the Republicans set June 17 as a date for their first national convention, and adopted an address to the people. Raymond wrote it.

He had not gone to Pittsburgh, but hurriedly in the midst of the legislative session had put together the rough draft of an address for the New York delegation. The convention liked it, adopted it unanimously. Raymond had written a sober statement of the chapters of history preceding formation of the Republican party. It was logical; it was comprehensive, and it contained material for Republican orators whenever they wished to cite history in attacks upon the slave power. Only in the concluding statement of principles did he set forth a program: repeal of the Kansas-Nebraska Act; resistance by "constitutional means" to slavery in any territory; support for "our brethren in Kansas"; immediate admission of Kansas as a free state; overthrow of Democratic control in Washington.

The Pittsburgh address was long, and Greeley wrote his managing editor: "Have we got to surrender a page of next *Weekly* to Raymond's bore of an address? The man who could inflict six columns on a long-suffering public, on such an occasion, cannot possibly know how to write an address." Yet publicly Greeley called it "able" and the *Weekly Tribune* carried the full text. From many other Republicans Raymond had more friendly comment.

Such a one was Charles Sumner, Senator and Massachusetts bluestocking, who sent effusive praise while not hesitating to point out a couple of minor historical errors. "I adopt it as a practical exposition of the true aims of the Republican party," he said. "Your address carries the reader along satisfied to the end. It is strong and yet moderate, conservative and yet progressive, with clearness and eloquence . . . the arguments seem to move with a firmness of tread, which has the promise of victory."

"Everything promises this time victory to the right," Raymond assured Sumner in reply. "If the Republicans are prudent in their nominations, they will carry the election, and then the current will be turned in regard to Slavery. . . . The Day dawns!"

V

Seward believed that he was the man to lead the Republicans in their first national election, but Weed, who was pursuing a policy designed, he hoped, to cement the variety of factions and opinions composing the new party, was not so certain. He had made it a cardinal principle that candidates for office should not alienate any significant group. Better yet, they should be men who could win support from some faction that might otherwise have been reluctant to join wholeheartedly in the campaign. Availability, always the greatest political asset, thus became a primary test, and for all his loyalty to Seward, Weed questioned that his long-time political partner could pass the test. In addition, the New York Dictator understood full well that the Republicans were unlikely to win the Presidency in 1856; Seward might better be saved for 1860, when the elements in the party would be fused and victory more assured.

That Raymond was privy to Weed's point of view he demonstrated in a surprising *Times* editorial on April 18, 1856. Seward's "nomination," he said, "would be as a matter of course, but for the fact, that in the western and New England States, the Republican Party owes its strength in a very great degree to its alliance with Americanism [Know-Nothingism]: and Mr. Seward took the precaution at a very early day, to reiterate his fixed hostility to the principles and policies of the American Party. . . . It is not at all unlikely that the Republicans will find it necessary to do, as all other parties have been compelled to do—take up a *new name*, one not identified with the political struggles and animosities of the past." Such a pronouncement in a paper so wholly identified with Seward and his principles served emphatic warning that Weed had jettisoned the Senator.

There were dissenters. Of Seward an upstate Republican wrote Weed: "Is it not possible that we are mistaken in supposing that he is not our best candidate?" And Seward himself did not take kindly to Weed's decision. "It is a delicate thing," he complained, "to go through the present ordeal, but I am endeavoring to do so without giving any one just cause to complain of indifference on my part to the success of the cause." On the eve of the Philadelphia Convention he wrote to his wife: "From all I hear 'availability' is to be indulged next week and my own friends are to make the sacrifice."

For all his assertion in mid-April of Seward's unavailability, Raymond had changed his mind by the end of May, and he called upon the New York Republican delegation to "present William H. Seward as their favorite and only candidate for the Presidential nomination." Seward, he said, was the "strongest," the "most fitting" candidate. There should be no compromise. Outwardly it might have seemed that Raymond was seeking to play with both Seward and Weed, but events had convinced him that the Republican party was more united and more potent than he had at first believed. He had been discouraged by the outlook when the Legislature adjourned in April after a session characterized by corruption and incapacity. "Tadpoles and poliwogs were mainly the burden of the Senate proceedings," the *Times* had reported. Because Know-Nothings had controlled the Assembly, legislation had been impossible, and even the annual supply bills had failed of enactment. Though party affairs had seemed to stagnate, actually the political current was setting fast.

In late April a great Republican rally in the Broadway Tabernacle had brought out 3,000 New Yorkers to demonstrate for a free Kansas and to cheer the new national crusade for exclusion of slavery from the territories. Raymond and William Cullen Bryant and Charles A. Dana had been among the vice-presidents, and while the evening's orators often failed to make themselves heard in the farthest gallery, the enthusiasm of this first great Republican rally in the city ratified political change. In Congress the debates over Kansas permitted no flagging of enthusiasm. Seward had delivered one of the most powerful speeches for the immediate admission of Kansas, and as copies circulated through the North by thousands, his political stock rose rapidly. A visitor to Cincinnati reported: "Seward has grown immensely popular in this section. He is allowed to be the great man of Congress and the great power at Washington, second only to the power of slavery." Then in May Charles Sumner rose in the Senate to deliver his "grand and terrible philippic," "The Crime Against Kansas."

As the *Times* rushed the speech into type, printing 60,000 copies in a special supplement, an event in Washington made Sumner the first Republican martyr. In his philippic he had abused slaveowners and South Carolina; he had been downright insulting to South Carolina's Senator Andrew P. Butler. Representative Preston S. Brooks, a kinsman of Butler's, sought satisfaction. Confronting Sumner in the Senate chamber, he caned him, striking him again and again until he fell bleeding in the aisle. Brooks's assault touched off new Northern excitement. Said Raymond in the *Times:* "The revolver, the club and the bowie knife are to be the weapons by which the champions of Slavery propose hereafter to silence their opponents. . . . The success of Ruffianism in Kansas has emboldened the champions of Slavery to introduce it to the Federal Capitol. . . . Northern men must . . . meet the Pro-Slavery bullies with their own weapons and upon their own ground." "Bully" Brooks's attack, asserted Raymond, had vastly strengthened the Republican party, and certainly Republicans sought to make the best political capital out of it.

Sensation had piled upon sensation during May, for the Kansas troubles had reached a momentary climax in the sack by Border Ruffians of the free-state town of Lawrence and in John Brown's Potawatomie massacre. All were Republican grist. Small wonder that Raymond believed party prospects loomed bright, and that in his optimism he turned to Seward as the real Republican leader and the new party's logical candidate. It was too late.

Weed had already fixed on the explorer-adventurer John C. Frémont, a man without political record, as the "available" candidate. "In May," he wrote, "the way opened too bright and clear to mislead any political pathfinder. I then became assured that Frémont was the best man to put in nomination." When the hosts gathered at Philadelphia, Seward got the cheers, but he refused to allow his name to be presented and the nomination went to Frémont on the first ballot. Though the choice disappointed many Republicans, it gave the party a slogan, "Free Men, Free Soil, Frémont," and in the summer months before the campaign got actively under way, editorial writers across the North began to discover the Republican candidate and to publicize his real or imaginary qualifications for the Presidency.

VI

It was not a happy summer for Raymond's own political aspirations. The Weed policy of selecting candidates who would solidify the party barred Raymond from immediate advancement. He was too closely identified with the Seward wing to make an acceptable coalition candidate. He had alienated temperance forces. He was sure to be opposed by the Greeley camp. Besides, he had no significant political following of his own. Though he was part of the machine, a very useful part thanks to the *Times* and his own writing and speaking abilities, he lacked political strength to command preferment, and he knew it. Presumably

Weed, if he had so desired, could have brought about Raymond's nomination for Governor in 1856, but as a political strategist he had other plans.

If he had not done so before, he probably made them clear when Raymond stopped in Albany at the end of July on the way to Burlington for the annual meeting of the university trustees. Perhaps Raymond already understood them well, but he made public what they meant in his political life when, shortly before the meeting of the State Republican Convention at Syracuse, he declined in a public letter a proposal that he stand for Governor. Said he:

I shall not affect any distaste for the honors, the associations, and the duties of public life, nor deprecate the opportunities it affords for promoting cherished principles and advancing measures deemed essential for the public good. . . . The prospect, moreover, of renewing for another year the acquaintances and associations in the Senate, which I found so agreeable last winter, would of itself be for me a strong inducement for desiring re-election to my present office. But other considerations—personal, domestic, and professional—outweigh even this, and constrain me to decline being a candidate, under any circumstances, for any official position whatever in the coming canvass. Even if I had no other reason for this determination, I should find a sufficient motive in the desire to remove whatever obstacle even my name might offer to the perfect harmony of the movement against the aggressions and usurpations of slavery.

The *Herald* charged later that Raymond withdrew on condition that he be elected United States Senator on the expiration of Hamilton Fish's term in 1857, but there was no truth to it. Weed had picked Preston King, a former Democrat, to succeed Fish, and Raymond had no desire to dispute the decision. In fact, when talk that he would stand for the Senate became embarrassing, he asked Weed to publish in the Albany *Evening Journal* a denial of his candidacy. As he said later: "I never expected, sought, or desired to be elected United States Senator. . . . I cannot afford to hold any office which diverts my time and attention from my private and professional pursuits." He may not have been wholly candid in his explanation, and it may have been with considerable regret that he put aside the hope of public place, but he accepted with outward grace Weed's political strategy, and without rancor threw himself into the Republican crusade.

In the late summer of 1856, when foes raised the cry that Frémont was a Catholic, a cry raised to divert supporters with Know-Nothing sentiments, Raymond was thrust forward with a formal denial. He reviewed Frémont's religious background and religious life for the Cincinnati *Gazette*, and when the unconvinced charged him with being vague, set forth unequivocally in the Rochester *American* the report of a conversation he had had with Frémont on the religious issue. Frémont had declared himself a Protestant, and a committee of Protestant pastors later sustained this declaration.

To writing for Frémont, Raymond added speaking. With Henry Wilson, who had been elected to the United States Senate as a Know-Nothing and who was to die a Republican and a Vice-President of the United States, he addressed a jubilant Frémont rally in the Broadway Tabernacle. Later, in the same hall, he debated the campaign's issues with Lucien B. Chase, a Congressman from Tennessee. Never before had he had such an audience as on that night, for Republicans and Democrats alike packed the hall—hundreds stood outside—to hear spokesmen for the North and South. Raymond summoned all his oratorical powers, his knowledge of history, his ability at verbal jousting, and in the course of his hours upon the platform traced not only the history of the slave power from the time of Washington to Pierce, but loosed a terrific indictment of slavery as a threat to free labor, free speech, and a free press. He carried his listeners with him, won their applause, their cheers, and when the audience piled out into the October night, it carried away the vivid recollection of a powerful little man striking resounding blows for Republicanism.

On the *Times*'s editorial page he discussed day after day the issues of the campaign, urged voters to identify Frémont with human freedom. On election day New York was safely Republican. The state gave its vote to Frémont, chose its first Republican Governor. Republicans won the Legislature. But the new party fell short of national victory. Frémont lagged nearly 500,000 votes behind James Buchanan.

Raymond, who on election eve had declared, "The Presidential chair is the last entrenchment of Freedom; the election of Frémont is its last hope," put the best face possible on party defeat and hoped that Buchanan might not cut too sorry a figure. Said he: "The *Times* is tired of politics and wants rest. . . . It prefers for a little to stand back, and look on. . . . We are to have a Democratic Administration for the next four years. . . . We don't see any very strong warrant for believing that its policy will be more just, more national, more conservative than that of its predecessor. . . . We shall not declare war upon it in advance. . . . Good has come out of Nazareth before, and may again."

——————13——————

Portrait of an Editor

I

THE TIMES had prospered,[1] and when Raymond at the end of 1856 temporarily put politics aside, the paper had already become a New York institution. His bantling had grown to full stature, its editorial influence and reputation assured, its financial problems solved. In the new building the *Times* was planning, the fast-growing city would gain a landmark as familiar to New Yorkers eventually as the City Hall itself.

Raymond had learned too well in his days with Greeley in the Ann Street garret that tradition dictated dark, dirty, ratty newspaper offices in back streets, offices reached by narrow, rickety stairs, and furnished with chairs and tables that, if they collapsed, were cast into an obscure corner with other journalistic refuse. The *Times* intended to break with that tradition. Conscious that, with the heavy investment required to keep pace with the mechanical improvements in printing, newspaper publishing had become a major business enterprise, it wanted a building that would serve efficiently the needs of such a business while advertising its success and prosperity. A site nicely fitting such a plan was available.

For generations the Brick Church had occupied the triangle where Nassau Street and Park Row meet, but with the city's march uptown the Presbyterian parishioners had kept step, and the time had come for the church to follow its congregation. Not in years had so valuable a property come onto the New York real estate market, and E. B. Wes-

[1] The first *Times* dividend—20 per cent—was paid on July 2, 1855.

ley, who remained the real business director of the *Times*, formed a syndicate to buy. He planned to sell the prize lot, the apex, to the paper, to dispose of the remainder as profitably as he could. The scheme proved difficult to consummate. There was litigation over title. There were charges, spurred by the *Herald*, that the *Times* was speculating. But in March, 1857, after a private sale had been blocked, the property was put up at auction, and for $100,000 the paper bid in the coveted lot. Two months later the cornerstone was laid for what the *Times* immodestly but truthfully described as "the largest, most imposing and most elegant newspaper establishment in the United States."

Late that summer, while freestone for the walls was being lowered into place and the new building was taking form, a convulsion in near-by Wall Street set off a chain reaction that slowed construction. A speculative bubble in real estate and railroading had burst, and what at first seemed a disaster only to the Stock Exchange and to Wall Street's private banks soon grew to nationwide panic. Banks failed, business houses collapsed, and unemployment grew. There were jobless demonstrations in New York that autumn and winter, and the shivering hungry begged for bread before Fifth Avenue's mansions. But the panic was short-lived, and by spring business burgeoned again. In dazzling testimony to the recovery, as well as to its own prosperity, the *Times* completed its building. Visitors called it "palatial."

Five stories it rose above Park Row to a pediment where great gilt letters spelled "The N. Y. Times." It dominated Printing House Square and City Hall Park, and looked unobstructed across the park to Broadway and the Astor House. The gaslit and steam-heated building was fireproof, or so regarded. It was light, clean. The first-floor publication office provided the show, and when afternoon sun cut through the plate glass windows onto frescoed walls and ceiling and tessellated marble, there could no longer be doubt that the *Times* had set a new style for newspaper establishments.

A broad iron staircase swept from the main entrance on Park Row to the fourth-floor editorial offices. There were private offices for editors —Raymond's looked toward the Astor House and, across town, to the shimmering Hudson and the New Jersey shore. There was a reference library unequaled in any newspaper shop. On this floor also were the news room and a general writing room for reporters to tell about their city.

II

Raymond, the clink of boot heel on marble announcing his arrival, customarily reached the *Times* at eleven o'clock in the morning, paused briefly to talk with Wesley in the publication office, and then, surrounded by his books and papers and the engravings he had chosen for his walls, got down to work at his slant-top mahogany desk. There were letters to answer, editorials to write, articles to solicit. In the job of getting out the paper, nothing was too unimportant for his attention. Thus, in May, 1858, following receipt of an article from an officer aboard the frigate *Niagara* that was to lay the first Atlantic cable, Raymond took time to send him both rebuke and instructions. "Please," he said, "write only on *one side* of the sheet. Your letters hitherto have been upon both sides and it has been impossible to get them ready for the press until a day after they are received. . . . In your report of the proceedings during the laying of the Cable, be as minute & detailed as possible as a good deal of the interest of such accounts depends upon the fulness with which incidents are given."

In his office Raymond received callers, discussed policy and problems with the men who made the *Times,* and often gave cause for wonder that he could do so much so readily. The famous churchman and editor Lyman Abbott, when a young man on the *Times,* had watched Raymond at work, and recalled in his autobiography: "He could attend to two or three things at once, and apparently give his mind to all of them. He worked in an office open to his subordinates, received their reports, answered their questions, and gave them their instructions without taking his eye from his paper or stopping his rapidly moving pen."

Raymond worked hard, too hard for a frail body, and often he ended his day half blinded by headache, yet he drove himself always to greater endeavor. He expected every man on the *Times* to work hard also, according to the commandments he had set down: "Get all the news; never indulge in personalities; treat all men civilly; put all your strength into your work, and remember that a daily newspaper should be an accurate reflection of the world as it is." Demanding Raymond might be, yet his editors knew that he was no "ignorant pretender, destitute of practical acquaintance with the requirements of editorial labor." They understood that he had done all that he asked of them to do, and they respected him accordingly. They respected him also for his tact and consideration. When things went wrong, when men made mistakes, he did not rant or scold or lose his temper. Criticism and correction he gave in private. "All men," he often said, "have their sharp points. What's the use of running against them?"

Raymond once summed up his theory of organization in a rebuke to an insubordinate member of the staff: "There is but one editor of the *Times.*" Yet he was no autocrat. He was always available for suggestion or complaint. He exacted discipline and obedience from the top to the bottom of the *Times*, and as part of the discipline delegated responsibility. An assistant like the city editor enjoyed full authority in his field so long as it was used wisely; if it were not, it could be withdrawn, but until such time Raymond would, and did, support the assistant in decisions made and orders given. These men recognized Raymond as the final arbiter, and on him, of course, rested the ultimate responsibility, a concomitant that he gladly accepted, shielding writers and reporters when necessary, assuming public blame. Outside his office he was so wholly identified with the paper that to him the unthinking attributed both the good and the bad in the *Times*. Raymond was not sorry to have it so.

Early in 1857, there was a celebrated instance of Raymond's acceptance of responsibility. As Washington correspondent, James Simonton had been following closely the lobbying attendant upon enactment of a bill to aid railroad construction across the northern prairies. Supporters were seeking extensive land grants—4,000 acres for each mile built—and Simonton became convinced that to win votes money was changing hands. He had no direct evidence, but he had the word of witnesses on whom he could rely. He talked it all over with Raymond, and the two agreed that, even though secondhand, the evidence of corruption was overwhelming, that the story should be told, that the source of the evidence should be protected. Simonton wrote his story, pulling no punches.

"The scheme," said he, "is one of the most enormous efforts that log-rolling corruption ever conceived. . . . The proportion of honest men who have anything to do with it would have been scarcely sufficient to save Sodom and Gomorrah from destruction, while there is hardly an individual hanging about the capital, living upon ill-gotten gains, and whose hands reek with the slime of Congressional corruption, who does not look to the Minnesota land bill as the present Mecca of his hopes." A *Times* editorial, seconding Simonton's sensation, set the price for a vote at $1,000.

Hardly had the *Times* arrived in Washington before a great roar was loosed on Capitol Hill. A move was begun to bar Simonton from the House; but it was halted after two members had acknowledged that attempts had been made to bribe them. The sorry business was referred to a select committee for investigation. Almost its first act was to summon Raymond. He readily admitted his authorship of the editorial, but declined to reveal the source of information, a position he defended against all critics, and, goaded by rival editors, there were many. "Whenever," said Raymond, "any person communicates to the Editor of the

Times information touching public affairs which it is important for the public to know, and whenever the Editor is satisfied that it is done in good faith and for proper motives, the confidence of his informant will be kept under all circumstances, and at any hazard."

For Simonton this policy stored hazards indeed. Because he abided by it, the committee held him in contempt, placed him in custody of the sergeant-at-arms; ultimately he was barred from the House of Representatives as a correspondent. Since the House eventually expelled four of its members for corruption, such treatment approached persecution, and the *Times* with a good deal of rightness asserted that the treatment of Simonton looked "like an attempt to *punish him* for having publicly denounced the corruption which he knew to exist." Though Simonton's usefulness as a Washington correspondent was ended, Raymond had use for him elsewhere, and soon packed him overland to Utah, where war threatened between the Mormons and the United States Army. The war failed to explode, but the roving Simonton sent back stirring, revealing reports of the Western frontier and the Mormons, and he had a chance to talk with Brigham Young, greatest Mormon of them all, before moving on to California and the gold fields.

Raymond knew a good news story when he saw one, and while sympathizing with Simonton in his joust with the House committee, he had not failed to make the most of the Congressional scandal as news. Nor did he allow readers to forget that it was the *Times* that had brought the corruption to light. He claimed, and rightly, that the *Times* had served the public good, a claim less easily established in the Burdell murder case, which for months in 1857 filled the paper's pages.

Dr. Harvey Burdell, a well-known New York dentist, had been found one winter morning stretched stiff across the blood-soaked carpet of his office. He had been strangled, mutilated, and the gruesome murder had quickly developed overtones of sex. The doctor, it appeared, had been secretly married to his housekeeper, a Mrs. Cunningham, who neither as wife nor housekeeper had been bound by the Seventh Commandment. Not a salacious detail was neglected by the New York press. Not since the Colt murder case when Raymond was a cub, had the city reveled so morbidly in crime. For days the *Times* gave ten, eleven, twelve columns to the story as the lives of Burdell, Mrs. Cunningham, their friends, and family were laid bare. To the surprise of all, Mrs. Cunningham when brought to trial was acquitted. But if she had not killed Burdell, then who had, asked the *Times*, and why did not the New York police find out? To spur them on, as well as to keep the story alive, the paper offered $5,000 reward for information leading to an arrest and conviction. In the end, the *Times's* reward went unclaimed, and Burdell's murderer remained forever free, but it had all made for interest and excitement and had fitted Raymond's formula for news as an "accurate reflection of the world as it is."

For some views and comments on that world Raymond turned to outside contributors. Thus on one occasion, in a letter that revealed a good deal about his conception of what made a good editorial, he asked George Perkins Marsh, the same Marsh who had once urged upon him the folly of a career in journalism, to write for the *Times*. "What I want," said Raymond, "is *strong, clear, able editorials upon topics of current interest*—political, social, economical, legal etc., etc., and I should be very glad to make an arrangement to receive three, four, or more a week from you. You are so thoroughly furnished with all needed knowledge upon all topics of discussion, and you write with such fluency, that an hour a day would probably be all the time you would need to give it—for half the strength of an editorial lies in its being *off-hand* and extempore in its style, even though it embodies the result of considerable reflection. I should want nothing better for my purposes than an exact transcript of such remarks upon any topic as you would make *in conversation*. . . . They ought to be about a column in length and the more sharply and strongly worded the better. . . ."

Marsh, scholar, politician and diplomat, was of course only one of many from whom Raymond solicited contributions. Any man of wit and reputation was fair game so long as he could contribute to the making of the *Times*, and such a one was the brilliant and popular Boston critic Edwin P. Whipple, who had lectured in half the lyceums of the North and was almost as well known in St. Louis as in his boyhood Salem. From Whipple Raymond asked for "a sharp & telling letter about men & things in Boston . . . political movements—political men." He was in the market for editorials also. "I want," said Raymond, "more life, vigor and interest in the paper & should like exceedingly to have you help me to it if possible. I will pay ten dollars each, for letters or articles that may suit our columns. You may write as often as you can find material & inclination: only let them be *sharp* and *telling*. I want something to make the public talk—*sensational* in the better sense of that very questionable word."

Rufus Griswold, the friend of Raymond's youth, had been asked occasionally to write book reviews and literary notes, but Griswold, harassed by domestic sorrow and scandal, broken by the tuberculosis that in the summer of 1857 closed his life, could no longer be depended upon to meet deadlines. So Raymond, whatever his personal regard for Griswold, had called upon others, and more and more frequently he sought out Evert A. Duyckinck, critic, one-time editor of the *Literary World* that Raymond had liked to read his first winter in Albany. The requests were varied: two columns on Dr. Elisha Kent Kane's account of his Arctic explorations; a "careful, judicious and reliable notice" of the American sculptor Erastus Dow Palmer; an article on property qualifications for voting; two columns or so on Mrs. Browning's *Aurora Leigh*, with the admonition, "If you can spice it with a personal notice of Mrs. B. it may make it more popularly readable." Duyckinck spiced it for three columns and a half, and was paid fifteen dollars.

There were many unsolicited contributions and many contributions that could not be accepted. A young reporter for German-American papers—his name was Henry Villard, and he was to become a great financier after being a good reporter—called at the *Times*. "Mr. Raymond," he said, "received me kindly, but gave me no encouragement at all, and declined to receive and examine one of my English productions. He intimated that the *Times* had more editorial contributions than it could print, and that it was always ready to pay liberally for what it published, and for valuable news. He was perfectly polite, but brief and decided. His whole manner, indeed, revealed the vigorous, resolute mind that characterized his career as a journalist."

III

Lyman Abbott said that Raymond lacked the "power of passion" that would have made him a great editorial writer. He lacked the power of partisanship, too, despite his place in politics, and it got him often into trouble. At election time Raymond found it easy to pipe the party tune, but between campaigns he regularly asserted his independence. Thus the *Times* in May, 1857, announced that it was to be "hereafter in its political conduct, entirely independent of all Political Parties—judging all events and all men *upon their merits*, and giving praise and censure, support and opposition, where either may be deserved, by a strict and impartial regard to the public welfare." From an editor who as author of the Pittsburgh Address had been hailed as godfather of the Republican party, and whose close alliance with Senator Seward had always been apparent, such a pronouncement might have seemed nothing less than astounding had it not been for earlier refusal to hew to the party line.

Even so, Republicans and Democrats alike jumped on the *Times*, accused it of backsliding. Raymond was not fazed. "Whatever may be done," he said, "which shall tend to the promotion of the public good shall have our support, no matter what political party may be entitled to the credit of doing it." Neither he nor the *Times* had changed positions on fundamental issues like the ending of slavery's dominance in Washington, the admission of a free Kansas, the halting of slavery's extension. Those issues, Raymond argued, were not party property—as indeed the break between Buchanan and Douglas soon dramatized—but for party men such talk came close to treason, and it was compounded by the *Times*'s sympathy for Douglas in his quarrel with Buchanan over Kansas.

When the abolitionist preacher Wendell Phillips attacked the *Times* for seeming to be Republican one day, Democratic the next, Raymond retorted with a statement of basic policy. "A daily journal," said he, "ought not to be a mere electioneering pamphlet, nor should it make itself the mere tool and slave of any party. . . . The *Times* . . . is Republican . . . whenever it can justly commend the action and the position of the Republican Party; whenever it sees reason to applaud the conduct of the opponents of that party, as tending to promote the public welfare, it will not hesitate to do so, even at the risk of being considered Democratic; and whenever any one is in doubt as to its position on any particular day, the best possible way to resolve such doubts is to buy and read it."

To Phillips, Raymond's rejoinder seemed muddled, wrong-headed, as it did to the staunch Republican partisan, who held that no Democrat could do anything but wrong. Raymond, men said, lacked stability and reliability. "I have been surprised," said a member of the Weed machine, "to find how common is the distrust of him." It was for his want of partisanship that partisans distrusted him. In his tolerance and moderation, the intolerant and immoderate took cold comfort. Raymond understood.

He set forth his understanding when he wrote to the president of the University of Rochester that "the great mass of men belong to one or other of the political parties—and each is more or less incredulous as to the existence of evils in its own ranks. I have learned, however, not to look for absolute & unmixed good—or evil—in any one organization and I believe it to be a good & patriotic service to *criticize both & all parties*, in the light of common sense and exclusive regard for the public good. Such a course I find offends *all* by turns & secures the warm attachment of none. While this does not in the least diminish my conviction of the necessity and utility of precisely such service, I confess it does sometimes dishearten and depress me in its performance." In a still broader sense, Raymond characterized himself: "If those of my friends who call me a waverer could only know how impossible it is for me to see but one aspect of a question or to espouse but one side of a cause, they would pity me rather than condemn me; and however much I may wish myself differently constituted, yet I cannot unmake the original structure of my mind."

It was the intellectual's explanation, and Raymond remained always a good deal of the bluestocking that Bennett liked to call him. It was not only that he was bookish and that the literary department of the *Times* interested him as much as the political, but that in matters other than political he frequently allowed logic and reason to overbalance hard, unpleasant facts, and that he remained in adult life the cold, logical debater of the university. He was inconsistent—most men are—and he scrapped on many occasions the aloof view of the scholar—but he retained it sufficiently to impress those who did not know him well as a complex personality whose devious ways could be best set down as those of a trimmer.

Like most men, Raymond had few intimates who penetrated his inner mind, who got beneath his polite reserve and outward placidity. But the young college graduate who had discussed German philosophy with Charles Dana in the *Tribune* garret could, given the proper occasion, talk just as easily in full manhood on a host of subjects. Said Theodore Tilton, editor of the *Independent:* "We knew him well—as well as one comes to know another in the companionship of travel, or in the late-at-night converse which pours itself out in self-revelation. Not to know him thus intimately was not to know him at all. . . . When . . . he chose to impart himself to one or more companions, he became a flowing fountain of anecdote, reminiscence, and gentle satire." It was out of a store of knowledge that spanned the fields of science and philosophy, of literature, of history, out of a store of experience drawn from politics and political association, that he drew the reminiscence and anecdote which made him good company at small private dinners and at public entertainments. Intellectual curiosity kept the flowing fountain well supplied.

In the early Fifties, for example, Raymond had been fascinated with Captain John Ericsson's invention of an engine designed to propel ships by hot air instead of by the steam that blew up ships and crews with startling regularity. He got to know Ericsson, traveled on trial runs of an experimental vessel propelled by a caloric engine, wrote about it for the *Times,* lectured on it widely. Out of it all grew a familiarity with mechanics that set him apart from most of his contemporaries who were still hardly accustomed to the fact of the steam engine.

IV

In the fast-growing city that the Census of 1860 would show just short of 900,000 population, Raymond's bewhiskered face, his large, shapely head, and trim, well-dressed figure were quickly recognized. Politicians saw him, a man who despite his approach to middle age managed to appear youthful, in Weed's famous Room No. 11 at the Astor

House. He dined at August Belmont's house in Fifth Avenue. Often he dropped in at the Athenaeum Club, a favorite with journalists, and joined in the wit and conviviality that made it famous. Fellow editors like William Cullen Bryant and Manton Marble of the *Evening Post* were members. Young lawyers with political ambitions—Chester A. Arthur, William M. Evarts, and Joseph H. Choate—sat down with them. Once a month the Press Club met at the Astor House, sometimes to listen to some celebrated visitor in the city, more often for clever talk among the members, talk to which Raymond contributed his own wisdom and personal charm.

Raymond liked the theater, and attended often. And there was good theater in the late Fifties. Edwin Booth was not alone in making the stage brilliant. It was the time of Laura Keene and Charlotte Cushman. Fanny Kemble read Shakespeare. Dion Boucicault dominated as a playwright even before he opened the sensational and controversial *The Octoroon* in late 1859.

The New York Associated Press, which by 1856 was firmly established, drew steadily on Raymond's talents. On more than one occasion he had been its spokesman in efforts to wring favorable rates from the telegraph companies and to maintain contracts which would assure the association a monopolistic control over news distribution. It meant that he debated long with Cyrus W. Field and others concerned with telegraph business in prolonged night sessions at the Astor, in private rooms at Delmonico's in William Street, or at Peter Cooper's brick and brownstone house off Gramercy Park. Always Raymond worked for compromise. Usually he won, although stockholders in the telegraph companies and out-of-town editors denounced the Associated Press for its power to win privilege and maintain monopoly over news, foreign news especially, sent by wire.

Municipal politics interested Raymond hardly at all, but now and then he joined with civic leaders and businessmen in the cause of good local government. He regularly opposed the braves of Tammany. He helped draft resolutions that launched movements against the chronic corruption in city government, and he signed calls for rallies to sponsor the candidacies of men pledged to honest administration. But the task was not much more than any man of prominence would undertake. Except as he exerted influence through the pages of the *Times*, Raymond's role remained perfunctory, for reform, political or social, was not in his blood.

Yet he had a deep and sincere concern for the unfortunate, and did what he could do to aid them. "In secret benefactions," said a friend, "[he] was profuse to prodigality." Raymond had visited the festering dens of the Five Points; he had talked with the broken and battered who lived in that blighted area. He had eyes to see the poor and homeless who haunted the city's streets, and he wanted to relieve some of this stalking misery. His heart bled at what he saw regularly as he rode downtown to Park Row: homeless boys and girls—there were thousands of them in New York—who roamed the streets, existing as best they could by petty thievery, by collecting rags and bones to sell, by peddling apples or matches, and then, when day was done, seeking out a packing box for bed and shelter. The sweeper at crosswalks, a girl clothed in rags and often coughing with consumption, seemed fixed in the New York scene. All this Raymond wanted to end.

In the *Times* he argued for the need to give the city's waifs proper shelter and protection as well as training in a trade that would make them ultimately self-supporting. So far as he could, he helped organizations with such aims, and his friend and editorial contributor, Charles Loring Brace, probably stimulated Raymond's concern for industrial schools that Brace and others were establishing to help the homeless. Raymond spoke for these organizations; he served on their boards of trustees, and he contributed to them even as he did to the Association for Improving the Condition of the Poor.

From charity, Raymond's social philosophy carried him to other philanthropic projects. When a library for working women was proposed, he gave it editorial support, helped further by joining in a campaign for funds, and as president of the board of trustees watched the library open quarters in New York University's building on Washington Square.

Raymond aided Dr. Elizabeth Blackwell, the first woman in America to hold a medical degree, when in the early Fifties she organized the New York Infirmary for Indigent Women and Children. He accepted a place on the board of trustees, and remained on it so long as he lived, long enough to see the infirmary grow, prosper, and add ultimately a medical college for women.[2] Similarly Raymond assisted the organization and advance of the New York Woman's Hospital, of which Mrs. Raymond had been among the founders. He did much to secure its charter and served on its board of governors. His own part in the furthering of these institutions Raymond minimized, rightfully giving the whole credit to the women who had been their inspiration. It made him conscious of woman's role in the world's shaping. Said he, somewhat loftily: "If the moral and social influence of women were taken away from the world, the governments left would degenerate into mere force, and would tend rather to curse than to bless mankind."

[2] From this college Raymond's youngest daughter was graduated in 1889.

V

Life was busy, yet not too busy for Raymond to be a devoted father to the children growing up in the house on Thirteenth Street. He found time somehow to be with them, to watch over them, and when he was absent to write them the simple letters a parent writes his child. There were summer excursions, usually to Coney Island. There were drives through newly opened Central Park, and sometimes on quiet autumn afternoons he walked with them about the neighborhood, the same neighborhood where Mr. James's little boys, William and Henry, had scuffed through fallen leaves on the sidewalks and in the gutters.

Minnie Myrtle, who sometimes lived with the Raymonds, thought it a comfortable, informal home, and with the saccharin that pleased so many readers of the *Times*, she described the family living room:

There is a bright fire in the grate, and by the windows there is a bookcase and a bird, and though everything is neat, the chairs and tables do not sit up so prim and stately, forbidding you to sit in them. . . . The children, too, belong to the family room, and here they are hopping, and skipping and jumping—Henry and Mary and Lucy. . . . On the table is the great family basket . . . with its stacks of linen and stockings and frocks and pinafores, fresh from the laundry, all ready to be mended. . . . On a little table·in the corner is the family Bible, not bound in gilt and placed there for ornament, but in a stout, hardy dress that will bear use; and morning and evening I know it is taken by the youthful father, while all are gathered round to hear, and opened at some portion which they can understand, and read with a few impressive comments.

Though "not very pious," as the *Herald* once rightfully observed, Raymond adhered to the forms prescribed by a churchgoing age, and often on Sunday rode over to Brooklyn, crossing the East River on a Beecher-boat, as the Sunday ferries were called, to hear Henry Ward Beecher preach the Word from his nationally known pulpit in Plymouth Church.

Raymond brought his friends into this family circle. There were little parties for the men from the paper. There were relatives coming and going, Raymond's father and mother or his brothers, Mrs. Raymond's parents from Burlington, cousins, nephews, and nieces. Sometimes the clatter of horses on the pavement, the rhythmic rattle of a carriage, announced the arrival of some man in public life, as it had Daniel Webster in his latter days.

This pleasant routine of family and home was broken, irreparably as it turned out, when Mrs. Raymond and the children sailed for Europe in 1857 to be abroad for more than two years. She wanted to educate the children in foreign schools, and presumably had persuaded their father of the wisdom of her course. He spent part of the summer with them, and before parting saw them comfortably settled outside the resort town of Vevey on Lake Geneva, but it was a hurried trip and Raymond was back in New York before his third and last daughter, Aimee, was born in Switzerland at the end of August.

The following summer he joined them again, and this time his trip was more extended. He landed in Liverpool in July, and on the way up to London visited Chatsworth, which had so overawed him eight years before, Stratford, Oxford, Kenilworth. In London there was another of George Peabody's elaborate dinners at the Star and Garter, with speeches and toasts and music, and an eloquent speech by Raymond on how the American press could better Anglo-American relations. He called at the United States legation, and Benjamin Moran, the assistant secretary, wrote in his journal: "During the morning Henry J. Raymond, the editor of the New York *Times*, an active good looking young man, came to see me. Mr. Raymond is about 5 feet 6 inches high, has hazel eyes, black hair, a brown complexion, a fine expression. . . . He talks well & is talented."

From London Raymond ran down to Yorkshire to see the Brontë country in which Mrs. Gaskell's recent *Life of Charlotte Brontë* had stirred his interest. He put up at the Black Bull in Haworth, walked over the moors which the sisters had so loved, and called at the parsonage to talk with their father and Charlotte's husband. Before leaving he drank a glass of wine with them. "When night came on . . . I ate my chops and drank my ale in the plain little parlor of the Black Bull Inn," he recalled, and until long past midnight sat listening to the landlord and his wife reminisce about the Brontës.

It had been very pleasant, this literary pilgrimage, but Mrs. Raymond and the children and the baby he had never seen were awaiting him in Switzerland, and so after a few weeks he crossed to the Continent that was teeming that summer with Americans. He ran into Hamilton Fish. In Paris he just missed being a guest at a dinner to celebrate the laying of the Atlantic cable; the *Times* correspondent substituted for him in response to a toast to the press. Just how much he saw of his family is questionable, for he moved about a great deal. After some Swiss mountain climbing, he traveled into southern Germany to visit Heidelberg and Stuttgart, and in September he was in Brussels for an international copyright conference at which he heard reiterated all the arguments that had been set forth in the copyright debate in America only a few years before.

Raymond returned to America in late October, but a lonesome homecoming it was. No one had calculated what his family's residence in

Europe might mean to him. He missed his children. He missed the affection that he craved, the inspiration, the self-confidence, the sense of balance, that stem from happy marriage. Summer holidays together were not enough, and gradually the months' long separation loosened the marriage ties. Often lonesome, discouraged, heartsick, he could not turn to his wife, because she was absent, and to compensate he sought companionship elsewhere. Before long he found it.

—14—

Solferino

I

AT THE Tuileries on New Year's Day in 1859, Napoleon III held his annual reception to the diplomatic corps. Shortly after noon the diplomats in their gilt braid and decorations were greeted by the enigmatic Emperor, who spoke first to the Papal Nuncio, then passed on to Count Joseph Huebner, the Austrian Ambassador. To the startled Huebner the Emperor remarked in a tone that some thought not unfriendly: "I regret exceedingly that the relations between France and Austria are not this year all that I could desire."

The unexpected remark loosed a war scare on the Continent. Foreign chancelleries took alarm, aware that Napoleon III had given notice that he might intervene to lift the Austrian yoke from the shoulders of the Italian provinces and duchies, that France might stand beside Sardinia in the cause of Italian unification. Rulers and their ministers conferred uneasily. In most minds remained only the questions of when the French would march and what pretext would loose the war Europe had long expected.

It was nearly three weeks before the English papers brought the news to New York, but readers of the *Times* were not unprepared. They had already been told of the "general uneasiness" on the Continent. Even before the war scare, an editorial reviewing relations between France and Austria had suggested that the two powers might clash. Malakoff,[1]

[1] Dr. William E. Johnston, *Times* correspondent in Paris.

whose regular dispatches on things French were generally more concerned with cultural and social subjects than with politics, did not regard the New Year's incident seriously, but the *Times*, once it had digested the English papers, prophesied: "The prospect of a tremendous movement to oust Austria from Italy, and reconstruct the map of Southern Europe, is neither dim nor distant."

Far from New York's newspaper row the diplomats busied themselves with their dispatch boxes. The social season opened in Paris and the Imperial Court turned to preparations for the political marriage of the Emperor's cousin, the notorious and dissolute Prince Victor Napoleon, to the child princess Clotilde of Savoy. In America the *Times* seldom missed an opportunity to attack President Buchanan. There was a new quarrel with the *Herald*, but business after the recent panic was much better and the *Times* told how pressure on space had forced the omission of four columns of advertising. Late in March an insignificant note reported that Republicans in Rockford, Illinois, thought that the Honorable Abraham Lincoln might make a proper Vice-Presidential candidate for the Republican party, that "some of 'Old Abe's' friends look still higher for him."

New Yorkers, however, were never allowed to forget the clouds gathering across the Atlantic. In one *Times* editorial after another the position of the powers was discussed, military might analyzed. The probable effect of European war on American business was set forth—the *Times* never faltered in the belief that France and Austria were bound toward war—and more and more space was given to the European situation as England sought to mediate and Russia suggested a congress of the powers. When Malakoff, who had never thought war would come, told of the massing of troops near Paris, of soldiers setting off for the south shouting *"Vive l'Italie! Vive l'Empereur!"* there was no surprise. At the end of April it was war.

Pro-French from the start, the *Times* followed the war as carefully as distance permitted while the French moved into northern Italy and the Austrians under the youthful Emperor Francis Joseph brought up their forces. Napoleon soon set out for the front, taking with him the iron camp bed and the silver table service that his famous uncle had once used in northern Italy. They fitted nicely into the Napoleonic tradition that the Emperor never allowed himself to forget. That *Times* readers might follow better the movements of the opposing armies, a front-page map of the war zone, the first of many such maps to appear in the *Times*, was published on May 21, accompanying a variety of war stories from the European capitals. Raymond was setting a pattern that the *Times* was never to forget.

II

Raymond wanted to be in Europe if events momentous to the world of 1859 were shaping. Besides, a European trip might restore his health, which again had been poor, and would reunite him with his family, which was now settled in Paris. At the end of May he booked passage on the *Arago*, a new steamer of the United States Mail Line that was winning popularity, and persuaded Judge James Forsyth of Troy, a friend since student days at Burlington, to make the journey with him. He left his associate William Henry Hurlbert, a brilliant eccentric and Bohemian whom a contemporary described as "the only artist among American journalists," in charge at the *Times*. There was a gay sailing party, and gifts of fruit and food were brought aboard before the *Arago* steamed down the harbor on its thirteen-day crossing to Havre.

Raymond lay abed mornings in his little seven-by-nine cabin, and when finally up and about spent most of the day on deck, for the sea was calm and the weather clear. Much of the time was given to eating and drinking; at night there was whist in the main saloon, or abundant talk before cabin lights were extinguished at eleven-thirty. But it was an uneventful voyage that made welcome the sighting in the bright June sun of the cliffs of England. There was a stop at Southampton, then at Havre, where Raymond went ashore. "I am stouter, blacker and heartier by half than when I left home," he wrote to George Jones after the train had brought him across the pleasant fields of Normandy to Paris.

The French capital was again crowded with Americans that year. Charles Sumner was there, recuperating from Brooks's caning, still weak, yet able to turn his quarters in the Rue de la Paix into a meeting place for his countrymen. At Sumner's Raymond saw John Bigelow of the *Evening Post*. John Lothrop Motley was also there, and the Reverend Theodore Parker, soon to die of consumption, although Raymond thought he appeared less the invalid than might have been anticipated. Governor Fish and his family were again in Paris, and Senator Seward was momentarily expected. Raymond had not crossed the Atlantic only to see Americans. He had other plans, and directly he set about carrying them out.

Four years earlier the London *Times* had raised its prestige to new heights through publication of William H. Russell's dispatches from the Crimean battlefronts. Stirring, graphic descriptions of the fighting, ruthlessly frank exposures of the blunders of command and of the appalling ill-treatment of the sick and wounded, the dispatches had made both the *Times* and Russell famous. The exposures had helped to bring down the Aberdeen Ministry. They had stirred Florence Nightingale to undertake her great mission of mercy. What Russell had done for the London *Times*, Raymond might do in Italy for the New York *Times*, though he expressed it more modestly when he wrote Jones that he hoped to "have a look at the armies."

While Malakoff went about obtaining permission for Raymond, Forsyth and himself to visit the front, Raymond started sounding French opinion, flushed and excited by the great Franco-Sardinian victory at Magenta on the fourth of June. "The war itself is popular," he found, "and the splendid victories with which it has opened have raised the feeling of the people into absolute enthusiasm. . . . All declare that *independence* is what the Italians need first of all, and that so far as Austria is concerned her domination in the peninsula is certain to be terminated by this war." Royalists, for whom it was hard to cheer the victories of a Bonaparte, were cool toward the conflict, and some uncertainty was stirring in informed quarters over Prussia's attitude, uncertainty not yet tinged with enough worry to damp enthusiasm, for Frenchmen did not doubt that final victory would crown the imperial eagles in Italy just as sixty years before it had the eagles of the first Napoleon.

III

The necessary arrangements made, Raymond with Forsyth and Malakoff headed southward by railroad, first to Lyons, then to Saint Jean de Maurienne. As they traveled through the peaceful valleys of Savoy, the signs of war swelled around them. Artillery companies rode on their train, and when they transferred to the diligence that bore them across the Mont Cenis Pass, they kept company with long processions of mule carts carrying biscuits, flour, oats, tools, of trains of artillery, of wagons loaded with munitions. For the sixty miles across the pass there was "an almost unbroken line of the sinews of war." From Susa, on the Italian side of the Alps, to Turin they were constantly among singing, shouting soldiers, and every railway station had become a depot for war matériel.

The trio were in Turin by June 19, and they took the opportunity to drive out to the two-week-old battlefield of Magenta, where among orchards, vineyards, and wheat fields the French and Sardinians had overwhelmed the Austrians and opened the way for the invasion of Lombardy and the capture of Milan. Raymond wrote a long description of the field, his fine, legible writing covering forty-two pages before he was done. The account, like another but shorter one from Turin, was never published. Perhaps Hurlbert found no space available in the *Times*. Perhaps neither was ever sent, but Raymond kept the dispatches among his papers long after the war had receded in memory.

At Milan, where French and Sardinian flags were flying from every window and an enormous tricolor crowned the cathedral's spire, the *Times* party ran into difficulties. The authorities refused to allow Raymond and his friends to follow the victorious armies that were believed to be maneuvering for another battle. Blocked, fuming with impatience, unable to obtain any news, they settled down to wait.

Raymond made the best of a bad situation. He watched the troops in the streets and the dashing officers, who hurried about. "As I stood this afternoon in the door of my hotel, the Albergo del San Marino," he wrote the *Times* on June 21, "a common coupe hack drove by, with two officers inside, and followed by a crowd of people. It stopped at the City Hall, which is close at hand—and while one of the officers got out, the other, who remained inside, was saluted with loud cries of '*Viva Garibaldi!*' . . . There is nothing very marked in his appearance—though he has a good face and wears a look of resolution. He wore the uniform of a Sardinian officer, a green coat, a small cap with a projecting front, and silver epaulettes." Not so long before, the officer in the green coat had been an exile on Staten Island.

Raymond visited the military hospital, and he thought the wounded well cared for. He went to the military encampment in the Place d'Armes, where the bivouac fires blazed in the summer night, casting shadows on the tents and parked cannon, and he walked among the soldiers "making themselves agreeable to the black-eyed but not overly clean females for whom camp life seemed to have a resistless temptation." But he was only killing time and was anxious to move on.

The delay in Milan was less prolonged than had been feared, and the twenty-third of June found the three men "in pursuit of the Grand Army," as Raymond put it—traveling eastward by diligence the sixty miles from Milan to Brescia. The highroad was packed with marching soldiers and carts that rumbled slowly through a powdering dust that covered Raymond and his companions as for eighteen hours they drove onward. The clear, warm day gave way to night and it was one o'clock in the morning when their carriage reached Brescia, where officers and soldiers filled inns and lodging houses. After writing a dispatch for the *Times*, Raymond slept on a bench that night, but he was beginning to accept the discomforts of war, the absence of beds and the scarcity of food, even as he accepted the fleas of Italy. An "eager and mordant race," he called them.

The front was close now. Only seventeen miles away, at Castiglione, the Emperor Napoleon had his headquarters. The Austrians, too, were near, but when Raymond settled down on his bench in Brescia, he was unaware that they were already moving forward to precipitate the decisive battle of the war and the bloodiest. History has called it the Battle of Solferino.

IV

The American journalists—the only representatives of the American press to witness the battle—first learned that fighting had been joined when, after starting out in a rented carriage, they began to meet oxcarts loaded with freshly wounded men. A few miles outside Castiglione they could see through glasses the smoke of battle, and as they pushed the horses harder the sound of cannon reached them. The road grew more and more crowded with artillery, with soldiers and pack trains, and when, under cover of a dust cloud, the Americans rode into Castiglione, they entered a village filled with "carts, carriages, horses, donkeys, oxen, soldiers, sutlers."

The battle had begun at dawn. On one side were the French and Sardinians, 135,000 men under the command of Napoleon III, on the other 160,000 Austrians led by the Emperor Francis Joseph. The Austrians had picked the place of battle and chosen well, for they had the advantage of fortifications and of strong natural positions that if held would bar the way to Venetia and the fortress city of Mantua. Castiglione, where the French had encamped, stood on a small height, but eastward spread a level plain that stopped short before a smooth but steep ridge and a series of isolated hills. These heights the Austrians had fortified. To storm them French and Sardinians crossed the plain in full view of the Austrian batteries.

The battle was a quarter done when Raymond began to watch it from "a steep, sharp-backed ridge, which commands a magnificent view of the entire circuit of the plain." Earlier the French Emperor, smoking his endless cigarettes, had followed the fighting from this same hilltop, but as men charged through the mulberry groves and grain fields and died under the broiling Italian sun, he had moved elsewhere to follow the course of conflict. The hill gave the Americans every advantage. Below them they saw "the enormous masses of MacMahon's infantry deployed," saw the troops move toward "the front, where the artillery was posted, as their services were required." Austrian guns blazed. Smoke enveloped the armies. To Raymond "it looked as if the thunder clouds of heaven had descended to the earth and were pouring their lightnings into each other's breasts."

Through the long day the battle continued. Three times the French took and retook strategic Solferino on the hill across the plain. Time and again Allied and Austrian soldiers charged, bayonets flashing. Cavalry dashed forward. Slowly the Austrians were pushed back. As they began to abandon their fortified positions, dark clouds came across the sky, the sun disappeared, and a brief, violent storm broke. The wind and downpour halted the fighting long enough for the Austrian Emperor and his army to begin a retreat eastward beyond the Mincio that flows from Lake Garda to the Po.

The storm sent Raymond and his fellow watchers to shelter in a French divisional headquarters, where until the rain halted and the sun once more shone down they helped those caring for the wounded.

Raymond described the battle's final hours: "From about seven o'clock until after nightfall an incessant and most terrible combat was . . . kept up. The batteries of the two armies were apparently about half a mile apart—and at the outset they were served with nearly equal and effective vigor. But the Austrians gradually slackened their fire and several times took up new positions—while the Sardinians poured a rapid and uninterrupted shower of balls upon them, suspending only for a few minutes, and then renewing it again with redoubled fury. The wind had now gone down, the air was still, and the sound of musketry, as well as of cannon, were distinctly heard. The former was continuous, sharp and incessant, sounding like the constant and irregular pattering of hail upon a roof. . . . Over the Sardinian park rose a dense white cloud of smoke, directly upwards, its sides perfectly upright and well-defined, and spreading outward both ways at the top like an enormous sheaf of wheat. The sun was making a glorious setting in the West, and as his light gradually departed, the vivid flashes of each discharge of the cannon gleamed through the smoke. . . ."

About nine in the evening—Raymond had been on the field for twelve hours—the battle ended. There had been more than 30,000 casualties, but the carnage was over. Castiglione that night was a confused camp of victory. Soldiers slept in the streets for want of other quarters. The wounded filled the houses and the public buildings, while lines of suffering men pushed down the great road toward other villages where they might find care. For Raymond there was to be but little sleep. He had a story to write, a story of the fighting and of the thousands, dead or wounded, who lay "this bright, starry night upon the bloody field."

V

In rooms at a dirty little inn Raymond and his companions sat down in candlelight to tell of what had happened. He did the writing, but each contributed what he had seen and learned. As Malakoff told of it afterward: "Our information was gathered partly by the eye and partly from the wounded men and officers as they came from the field. Each one could relate what his regiment did or was doing, at what point of the field it was engaged, and whether it was suffering much or little. By putting all the facts together we arrived at a nearly accurate *ensemble*." All night the task went forward. Toward morning the battle report was finished.

Now remained only the problem of hurrying the dispatch to America as quickly as possible. All three hoped that this account of Solferino would reach New York ahead of any other, certainly before copies of the London papers—the London *Times* particularly—could bring eyewitness descriptions by fast steamer. "If I can only beat the *Thunderer* into New York," said Raymond, "the *Times* is made."

Because of foresight in obtaining from the American Minister in Paris a passport describing him as a "Bearer of Dispatches," Malakoff had prevented the French military authorities from seizing the carriage that he and Raymond had rented, and in this carriage Malakoff set forth at dawn to ride the dusty miles to Brescia. There, thanks to friendship with French officers, he placed the precious story in the hands of an imperial courier setting out for Paris. Three days later in the French capital what had been written at Castiglione was delivered to Mrs. Raymond, together with instructions to rush the manuscript to the first and fastest steamer leaving for New York. The need for haste she fully understood, and without delay she rode down to Havre where the *Arago* was about to sail.

The plan succeeded, for although bulletins announcing the battle appeared in New York papers before Raymond's dispatch, his account, published on July 12, eighteen days after Solferino, was the first full description to be printed in any American paper. *Harper's Weekly*, which in map and engraving had been following the war from its first shot, gladly reprinted much of what Raymond had written, and in journalistic circles the fame of his achievement lived long.

VI

Raymond did not know until weeks later of the coup that he had scored, and meantime he had more to see and more to write. The horrible suffering of the wounded almost overwhelmed him. He had seen men, while the battle was still in progress, who "walked along, their faces completely covered with blood from sabre cuts upon their heads. Many had their arms shattered—hundreds had their hands tied up—and some carried most ghastly wounds upon their faces. Some had tied up their wounds—and others had stripped away the clothing which chafed and made them worse. . . . Those who were more severely injured rode upon donkeys or in carts, and a few were carried upon mattresses on men's shoulders." The battle's end did not halt this sorry spectacle, for the French had made almost no provision for caring for casualties. A Swiss observer of the intense suffering—his name was Henri Dunant—was so moved that he was spurred to found what became the International Red Cross. Writing out of deep indignation and disgust, Raymond challenged that "nothing can excuse the barbarous cruelty which attended the removal of tens of thousands who were taken from the bloody field of Solferino."

The French requisitioned the rude, heavy oxcarts of the Italian peasantry to serve as primitive ambulances on which sorely injured men were piled, exposed to the sun, and in heat and dust trundled from the battlefield. In near-by villages, public buildings and churches became emergency hospitals, but still more room was needed. Thousands of the wounded were stretched on pallets in the open air. All, in the absence of proper nurses, were tended by the villagers, who did what they could, and that was little. Raymond, watching the tragic processions, saw that "as the carts came into town, many of the poor wretches stretched out their hands, piteously crying for water, or for wine, as they were perishing of thirst."

Once he went into a church that had been converted into a hospital. The furniture had been removed from the nave, the chapels and the altar, "and upon rows of mattresses extended lengthwise on the stone floor, as closely as they could lie, the wounded were placed. . . . Men and women charged with the care of them were passing to and fro—not to soothe or comfort the dying, for there was no time for that—but looking for those who might still be saved. And over the altar, looking down upon the horrid scene, was an immense, well-painted, life-like picture illustrating the Sermon on the Mount, and representing the Redeemer saying to those about him—'Blessed are the peacemakers, for they shall be called the children of God.'"

The wounded that crowded Castiglione only added to the confusion caused by the presence of army stragglers and Austrian prisoners and by the absence of command, for the Emperor of the French had moved his headquarters six miles distant to the village of Volte and with him had gone military authority. This demoralization was responsible for "the race of Castiglione."

It was described at the time. Forsyth described it afterward, recalling that he and Raymond had just finished their luncheon when "an alarm was heard coming down the street from the direction of the battlefield, and, increasing in its progress, developed into a full-fledged panic as it came to us, bearing along the narrow streets crowds of all sorts of people, frantic with fear, and running for their lives, and exclaiming: 'The Austrians are coming to kill the wounded soldiers and liberate the prisoners.' . . .

"Mr. Raymond and myself both joined that procession and for the first mile kept up with the best of them, all making good time. When outside of the village, we turned off from the military road, which was thronged, and took a country road leading circuitously to the village of Montechiaro, five or six miles back from the same military road. Being somewhat exhausted at the end of the first mile, and beginning to collect our wits, and venturing to look over our shoulders for the Austrians in pursuit, and seeing none, we slowed down to a walk and made our way into Montechiaro in about two hours."

The false alarm, for such it was, had been started by some teamsters who had glimpsed an Austrian cavalry detachment that was coming into Castiglione to surrender. "Thus was the 'Race' got up and run," Forsyth added. "Probably few prudent men could be found, who, under the circumstances, would have failed to take part in it." He and Raymond thereafter made its anniversary an occasion for reunion and reminiscence.

The heat grew worse on the Lombardy plain, and food, scarce from the start, became increasingly dear. Discomfort was beginning to wear, but Raymond and Forsyth, rejoined by Malakoff, stayed on another day at Castiglione, driving out over the battlefield where the mulberry trees had been shattered by cannon balls and the wheat had been trampled. The debris of battle lay around—broken wagons, abandoned muskets, tattered uniforms, cartridge cases, and spent shells. Dead horses were bloating. Unburied French and Sardinians and Austrians were half hidden in the golden wheat. The stench was overpowering, though Raymond tarried long enough to pick up a bayonet and a cannon ball as souvenirs before riding down the white road to French headquarters with the intention of presenting credentials for an audience with the Emperor. Napoleon was lunching when they arrived. A long wait seemed probable, and they decided to forego the privilege of meeting the head of the victorious armies; instead, they spent their time in the French camp, where the troops were resting after their ordeal and army bands were filling the air with martial music.

At Castiglione that night they found quarters at another wretched inn, but they were too tired to complain of poor accommodations. Raymond wrote home of how they had been able to get but "one room with an enormous bed which three of us shared with the infinitely more numerous occupants who had the right of prior possession, and who labored zealously to enforce their claims throughout the night. Italian floors," he added, "are never washed; and next morning we found where four large pools of blood from wounded officers had left in our chamber marks of the battle. . . . But we slept as soundly as if a groan had never been uttered, nor a pang endured, within a hundred miles of us."

VII

Suspecting that the Austrians would avoid another Solferino, suspecting also that an armistice was likely, Raymond now decided to return to Paris by way of the Italian lakes. With Forsyth—Malakoff stayed with the armies—he journeyed from Bergamo to Como, leaving war and the signs of war behind. "For a long part of the way," he reported to the *Times*, "we had Monte Rosa and the great chain of snowy Alps to which it belongs in full view, and for the whole distance the broad, rolling plains of Upper Lombardy were spread out beneath us." Como held them briefly. They crossed Lake Maggiore and by the Simplon Pass entered Switzerland, reaching Paris in time to hear the cannon at the Invalides announce the peace that on July 11 had been signed at Villafranca.

Paris was illuminated in celebration, though Raymond thought the celebration "had a perfunctory look." Frenchmen had not expected the war, which had seemed but a succession of victories, to end so suddenly. Their disappointment almost equaled that of the Sardinians, who raged at the settlement that stopped short of unifying Italy and allowed Austria to remain master of Venetia. While Raymond tried to argue that the victories of Magenta and Solferino and the magnanimous peace had strengthened the Emperor's position in both France and Europe, he had soon to report that "the peace does not grow in favor," and to note that the Emperor remained in seclusion at St. Cloud rather than face the resentment of Parisians.

For the *Times* Raymond undertook to explain why the war had so suddenly spluttered to a close. "I presume the simple explanation of the peace is to be found," he said, "in the fact that Napoleon *knew* that Prussia intended to join Austria the moment the war should have reached German soil." That had been important among the reasons for the Villafranca meeting between Napoleon III and Francis Joseph, but there had been others. French clericals had been loud in criticizing the revolutions the war unleashed in Italy with consequent threat to the Papacy's temporal power; such criticism threatened political repercussions in France. Greatly moved by the slaughter at Solferino, the Emperor had no heart to risk repetition, perhaps even to risk defeat, against the Venetian fortresses, particularly as defeat might be hard for a nephew of the great Napoleon to explain at home.

Now that the war had ended, Raymond settled down with his family for a brief holiday before returning to America. His stay gave him a chance to read on July 29 in the semi-official *Constitutionel* pleasing commendation of his dispatches as "narratives of irreproachable exactness, written in a lively and picturesque style." He was called an impartial journalist, and his account of Solferino was singled out for special mention. "It is easy to recognize in it the scrupulous fidelity of an eyewitness," the *Constitutionel* commented. "It is a piece of testimony in favor of our army, not surprising certainly to us here, but of special value nevertheless, because it comes from an observer who is a foreigner, and who writes in a journal of the New World, without suspecting, probably, that it would ever be seen by a European reader." The *Constitutionel* might have been less extravagant had it seen Raymond's account of the Solferino wounded, but it would be almost a fortnight before that dispatch, printed in the *Times* of July 22, reached Paris.

There was another newspaper item that Raymond read, and one less pleasing. Whenever away from New York, he wanted to see the *Times* regularly, but the Italian trip had prevented it, and a surprise awaited him. He soon learned of it. While walking across the Place de la Bourse he met a friend who asked if he had read the *Times* editorial that, under the title of "The Defensive Square of Austrian Italy," discussed the strong positions of the fortresses of Venetia. Raymond had not. Immediately he went to one of the public reading rooms to discover an article that had convulsed New York.

The temperamental Hurlbert had written the editorial after returning from a gay sailing party at which he had drunk a lot of champagne. Unhappily, he had previously ordered that proofreaders should never change his copy. They followed orders. The result was disastrous, for the discussion of the Austrian quadrilateral, a subject difficult enough at best, made no sense.

In the column of type appeared sentences like these: "Austria has neglected nothing which might assure her dominion over the waters of the Danube. She has done all in her power to favor the development of Europe, which is the pacific development of England. . . . If we follow the windings of the Mincio, we shall find countless elbows formed in the elbows of the regular army, at places like Salianza, Molini and Borghetto. . . . If we follow up the course of the Mincio, we shall find innumerable elbows formed by the sympathy of youth. . . . Notwithstanding the toil spent by Austria on the spot, we should have learned that we are protected by a foreign fleet suddenly coming up on our question of citizenship. A canal cuts Mantua in two; but we may rely on the most cordial Cabinet Minister of the new power in England."

There was more gibberish of this sort, and though an apology to readers and a corrected text of what Hurlbert had meant to say were printed in the *Times*'s evening edition, the damage had been done.

Raymond was furious. To Forsyth, he denounced the article in strongest terms, but he never disavowed it. His friends knew, of course, that he had had nothing to do with it, but in an era of personal journalism, when a paper was closely identified with the responsible editor, the incident was hard to live down, and for many months after Raymond had gathered up his family and brought them home in the late summer of 1859, he heard himself called the "elbowed hero of the Mincio."

——15——

Disunion

I

THE DEEPENING shadow of disunion lay upon the land, striking fear in the hearts of men like Raymond who did not believe with Seward in the "irrepressible conflict." [1] Yet events supported Seward. For nearly a decade, resolution of each sectional crisis had served only as an interlude between crises, and extremists on both sides had used the accompanying political disturbance to insure against final peace. Moderates and conservatives found themselves regularly disadvantaged, often misunderstood, and obliged to pursue arguments that made sense only if one believed that the nation could live half slave and half free. Raymond was such a believer, for however much he detested slavery and opposed its power at Washington, he insisted that the Federal Union could be, must be, preserved.

That was why he had always refused to consort with extremists and why he had so deplored the Dred Scott decision that in 1857 swept away the long-established right of Congress to bar slavery from the territories. "The Supreme Court," the *Times* had said, ". . . has laid the only solid foundation which has ever yet existed for an Abolition party; and it will do more to stimulate the growth, to build up the power and consolidate the action of such a party, than has been done by any other event since the Declaration of Independence." The prospect was alarming, for existence of a powerful abolition party might drive the South into secession or make inevitable the horrors of civil war.

[1] A phrase in Seward's Rochester, New York, speech of October, 1858. By making him seem more radical than he was, it did him great political damage.

In October, 1859—it was a Sunday night, and in New York the *Times* was going to press with an optimistic editorial that "the talk about disunion at the South is nearly over"—a new crisis, more alarming than any that had preceded it, was precipitated by the abolitionist fanatic John Brown. With a band of men he seized the United States arsenal at Harpers Ferry as the first move in a crack-brained scheme for a slave revolt. Colonel Robert E. Lee and a few marines quickly snuffed out John Brown's raid, the act of a madman, Lee called it. That was Raymond's view too, and he set it down in an editorial denouncing attempts to seek political significance or partisan advantage in Brown's wild plan. "The great mass of the people North," said Raymond, "whatever may be their political sentiments or party relations, regard every such attempt to emancipate Southern slaves with horror and execration."

It was not easy to convince Southerners. To them the raid seemed part and parcel of the Seward doctrine, of the abolitionist preaching heard for many years in Northern halls and pulpits. The very existence of the Republican party, sectional and anti-slavery, bore further witness to a hostility to the South and its institutions that Virginia's Governor Wise warned "inevitably drives to disunion." Southern hotheads were glad of the chance to raise the alarm, and Northern abolitionists helped not at all by outspoken sympathy for John Brown in great mass meetings like those addressed by Wendell Phillips in Brooklyn and New York.

While fully reporting events at Harpers Ferry, and John Brown's quick trial and hanging, the *Times* mirrored the nation's mood as it told of disunion talk in the South, of abolitionist meetings and sermons in the North, and got itself into a brisk controversy with the Reverend George Barrell Cheever, the abolitionist crusader at the Church of the Puritans in Union Square. Public attention was diverted briefly by news of the annual agricultural fairs, by sports contests, by accounts of the *Great Eastern*, the largest vessel yet built and one so cranky that her transatlantic crossing was repeatedly delayed. But accounts of the *Great Eastern* and woodcut illustrations of her hull and engines obscured only momentarily the continuing crisis that worsened when Congress met in December to provide for disunionists both a rostrum and a sounding board.

Raymond appealed again and again for a halt to the strong talk that was raising temperatures the country over. "Let the North speak," he urged in the *Times*, "but let it speak honestly and fully. . . . The only durable and decisive good which can be done by Northern speaking now, must be done by an explicit assertion of the unquestionable though madly questioned fact, that not only the Conservative and Pro-Slavery North, but the whole Northern people, including the masses of the so-

called Republican and Anti-Slavery Parties, are earnestly and sincerely
bent on preserving the fabric of the existing Union, and on doing justice
to the rights, privileges, and the prejudices even, of the Southern members of our confederated Republic."

The North soon found its voice through mass meetings that pledged
loyalty to the Union in strongest terms and denounced all men and
every act tending to alienate the sections. At Boston there was a tremendous demonstration at which the former Whig Edward Everett
spoke from the same platform as Caleb Cushing, who had been Attorney
General in the Administration of Franklin Pierce. From retirement
Pierce sent a letter applauding. Philadelphia had its Union meeting, and
as the movement gathered momentum, setting off manifestations in
many a Northern village and town, New York staged its own at the
Academy of Music on Fourteenth Street. Cannon summoned the dem-
onstrators, 10,000 strong, and rockets broke overhead as Democrat and
old-line Whig cheered for the Union.

Not many Republicans attended, giving substance to Southern sneers
that Union meetings held little meaning since radical elements stayed
away. The *Tribune* was critical, the *Herald* also, and the *Times* warned
that only representation of every faction would give the demonstrations
proper weight. Yet to Raymond there seemed point to making clear, if
only for the record, that a large and significant part of the North held no
abiding hostility for the South. It was in such a spirit that he gave the
movement his voice.

At the end of December he went north to Troy for a Union meeting
that dissidents threatened to disrupt until police brought order and
allowed him to proceed. He tried to explain the Southern point of view;
he approved the hanging of Brown, and he stated emphatically his position that "both sections have duties to perform in the common effort
to restore peace and harmony to our common country." "The Union,"
said Raymond, "was made for all sections alike. Each must tolerate many
things which it may not be able to approve in the opinions and prejudices
and conduct of the other. Each must be prepared to concede the rights
of the other. Each should be ready to come forward in the proper spirit,
waive some of its extreme demands or claims, and even something of its
rights in order to preserve this Union as a whole."

A few nights after the Troy meeting, he spoke in Albany to similar
purpose. Once more he pleaded for sectional understanding, for con-
cessions both North and South. He went further to urge that the North
had no intention to molest slavery where it already existed, and that,
whatever the result of the impending Presidential election, the North
should strive to convince the South that the power of the Federal Union

would be used to protect the South and its institutions and to punish those who might seek to injure.

There were times when Raymond's scalpel-sharp mind cut quickly to the core of an issue, laying bare the fundamentals previously hidden by the proud flesh of partisanship or moral fervor. The Albany speech was such an occasion. What is the mainspring of the sectional controversy, he asked in effect, and then gave his answer: a struggle for power. "I believe I state only what is generally conceded to be a fact," said he, "when I say that the growth of the Northern States in population, in wealth, in all the elements of political influence and control, has been out of proportion to their political influence in the Federal Councils. While the Southern States have less than a third of the aggregate population of the Union, their interests have influenced the policy of the government far more than the interests of the Northern States. . . . A general knowledge of the action of the government for the past ten or fifteen years, the decisions and composition of the Supreme Court, the organization of the committees in the Federal Senate, the rule that obtains in the distribution of Federal office etc., are quite sufficient to show its general truth. Now the North . . . claims a proportionate share of influence and power in the affairs of the Confederacy. It is inevitable that this claim should be put forward, and it is also inevitable that it should be conceded. No party can long resist it. . . . It is quite as strong today in the heart of the Democratic party of the North as in the Republican ranks; and any party which ignores it will lose its hold on the public mind."

Other men were thinking along similar lines and giving their thoughts public expression, but Raymond was unique in the extent that he put his analysis above party. He tried as always to look at both sides; his aim was better understanding, but the approach was too intellectual to make many converts in a period of partisan and sectional passion. Said the *Times* in commenting on the Albany speech, and Raymond may have dictated the editorial himself: "We are quite aware that, in these days of partisan excitement, it will be very difficult to convince any men of either section that the other is not wholly and exclusively at fault."

II

Raymond understood that the Presidential campaign and election of 1860 would serve only to exacerbate the differences between North and South, and he made public confession that he feared the "peril of the feverish mood in which the nation now chafes and frets toward the crisis of a new Presidential contest." Perhaps he had hoped that out of the Union meetings would come a Union party that would bring together moderates both North and South, an alignment of Republicans and Democrats that would leave extremists of both parties irritating but unimportant splinters. The idea of uniting for the common good was not new to him.

He had been friendly to Stephen A. Douglas because for a time he felt that the Illinois Senator might provide truly national leadership, and with Greeley and other Easterners he had urged a fusion of Illinois Republicans and Democrats to further Douglas' senatorial candidacy in 1858. It had come to nothing, but for Douglas, a middle-of-the-road man, the *Times*'s friendship died slowly. His speeches and articles got special treatment, and Douglas late in 1859 found excuse to thank Raymond for the "courtesy and kindness" shown him by the *Times*.[2]

Raymond's friendliness for Douglas underscored his tendency to drift from the Republican party that he had helped to form. He had not abandoned it, but he had become critical of its policies and its place in American politics. He recognized its sectional character, and understood what that meant in terms of sectional strife and disunion. He suspected that many Republicans did not want permanent peace with the South lest it remove their party's cause for being, and at Albany he asserted bluntly: "I think I scarcely exaggerate the facts of the case when I say that the Republicans rely with substantial confidence upon the South for political issues and popular excitement in every recurring canvass." Such bluntness was hardly calculated to increase Raymond's popularity among Republican radicals. Yet he was not always so critical. He praised the Republican National Committee when in its call for the 1860 convention it promised to maintain "inviolate the rights of the States" and to defend "the soil of every State and Territory from lawless invasion." More talk of that nature and less talk of abolition might yet convince the South that the Republicans were not hellbent on destroying Southern rights and institutions.

Many Republicans, as the campaign year opened and moved ahead, agreed with Raymond, for it was increasingly apparent that too radical a position would alienate much of the party's Northern support, that whatever the mood of the Republican rank and file, it was not abolitionist. A conservative tide was setting. In the *Tribune*, Greeley was pushing the Presidential candidacy of Edward Bates of Missouri, former Whig and one-time slaveholder, a conservative whom Greeley called the "only Republican whose election would not suffice as a pretext for civil war." At Cooper Union in February, Abraham Lincoln, Illinois' favorite son,

---

[2] The 7,100-word text of a speech delivered by Douglas at Columbus, Ohio, in September, 1859, was telegraphed to the *Times* at a cost of $497, an instance of journalistic enterprise unusual in that day.

spoke conciliatingly. "Wrong as we think slavery is," he said, "we can yet afford to let it alone where it is." And Seward had receded from the high-water mark of his "irrepressible conflict." His words in Congress no longer echoed the higher law and no longer demanded the end of slavery. In March he promised the South that "if your sovereignty shall be assailed, no matter what the pretext or who the foe, we shall defend it as the equivalent of our own." The *Times* applauded the new tone, and Raymond gradually found it easier, since abolitionists were apparently not going to dominate the party, to call himself a Republican. After all, he had no other political home.

He had had a chance to satisfy himself as to the conservative mood of the North, for in February, 1860, he made a lecture swing across the Middle West. He stopped in Ohio, went on to Detroit, and then to St. Louis, where he had a long talk with Edward Bates before dining with him at the Planters Hotel. It could not have been a very productive interview, for neither man wanted to commit himself, and Raymond probably learned much more from others with whom he talked during his tour. Bates wrote in his diary that Raymond was "doubtless a most intelligent man, but he seemed reserved, and rather watching me than displaying himself. . . . I took care to say nothing that I had not said and published often before." That Bates was Greeley's man might have been enough to keep Raymond at a distance, and Raymond must have suspected that Greeley was doing all in his power not only to advance Bates but to use him to block Seward's Presidential ambitions. One could read that between the lines of *Tribune* editorials.

As for Raymond, whatever his questionings about the Republican party, its leaders and its policies, he remained always a Seward advocate. He did not approve all that Seward had said and done, and yet in his mind there was only one logical Republican candidate in 1860, his friend and sometime patron, William Henry Seward.

III

Chicago Republicans in preparation for their party's convention threw up in great haste a vast wooden auditorium, "The Wigwam," [3] that was barely finished when the 466 delegates and some 40,000 camp followers rolled into town. While contractors nailed up the last strips of bunting and moved plaster busts of American heroes into place, the convention vanguard got down to politicking and fun. Greeley, who had come as a delegate from Oregon, shuffled about, "looking innocent as ever," and drawing crowds wherever he went, for the *Tribune*'s editor had made himself a national figure through his *Weekly*, and he was

[3] So called, said the New York *Herald*, because it did not look like one.

about to prove that his political influence was not inconsiderable. Of all the state groups, New York's was the largest and most conspicuous, and as it settled into headquarters at the Richmond House, delegates and hangers-on alike were supremely confident that they would win the nomination for Seward.

Raymond, though not a delegate and of recent years a very silent partner in Seward, Weed & Raymond, attended as one of Weed's lieutenants. There had been a jolly journey westward in a special car supplied by the Southern Lake Shore Railway, and in foretaste of the conviviality ahead an abundance of food and drink and good cigars at the road's expense. At station stops crowds cheered the traveling Republicans, bands serenaded, and cannon roared salutes. With companions in the special car Raymond had opportunity to rehearse the convention outlook and Seward strategy. At the Richmond House he found familiars: William M. Evarts, his fellow clubman at the Athenaeum who was to place Seward in nomination, George William Curtis of *Harper's Magazine*, General Webb, with whom he was again on friendly terms.

Pro-Seward men from other delegations called at the Richmond House. One of them, Carl Schurz of Wisconsin, was disappointed not to "find there any of the distinguished members . . . we most wished to see—William M. Evarts, George William Curtis, Henry J. Raymond, Governor [Edwin D.] Morgan and others. We found," he recalled later, "only the chief manager of the Seward interest, Mr. Thurlow Weed, and around him a crowd of men, some of whom did not strike me as desirable companions. . . . They had marched in street parades with brass bands and Seward banners to produce the impression that the whole country was ablaze with enthusiasm for Seward. They had treated members of other delegations with no end of champagne and cigars to win them for Seward. . . . They had spent money freely and let everyone understand that there was a great deal more to spend. Among these men moved Thurlow Weed as the great captain, with ceaseless activity and noiseless step, receiving their reports and giving new instructions in his peculiar whisper, now and then taking one into a corner for a secret talk, or disappearing with another through a side door for transactions still more secret."

Exactly where Raymond fitted into the transactions is now unknown, but as he moved about among the delegates in their suits of black, with a cane or cotton umbrella essential to the costume, he had abundant opportunity to counter the argument, which Greeley and William Cullen Bryant assiduously circulated, that Seward's radicalism made him an unsafe candidate. Raymond's very presence in Chicago offered proof that he no longer feared that Seward and the party pointed toward disunion. For more than a decade Raymond had known Seward, had trusted him, and now at the climax of Seward's political career it was as much a privilege to work for him as it had been when pushing anti-slavery resolutions in the New York Legislature in 1850.

Raymond must have recognized early that Seward victory was not sure. Greeley seemed to be everywhere, working for Bates, talking down Seward, whispering that the New Yorker, while a great man, could not be elected. There were delegates from many states who doubted that Seward with his past anti-slavery record could win votes, who feared that as the nominee he would handicap local slates. They listened to Greeley as well as to supporters of Seward's rivals. Seward's alliance with Weed hurt him, and reports of vast corruption in New York politics were cited as reason enough to keep Weed's power from Washington. Among anti-Seward men and the uncertain, Illinois Republicans sought in the pre-nomination caucusing to make capital for Abraham Lincoln, maintaining that, as a man who had no long record of leadership against the slave power for enemies to attack, he lacked Seward's vulnerability. This argument carried weight. Republicans had no intention of waging their 1860 campaign on slavery alone; the platform with its emphasis on the tariff, a homestead act, and internal improvements proved that.

Joseph Howard, Jr., the crack *Times* correspondent at the convention, reported at the start that Sewardites faced tremendous opposition, and he was presumably reflecting Raymond's opinion when he wired the *Times* that Seward men "stand firm, but they are compelled to acknowledge to themselves that the speck has become a cloud, and may yet become a storm." Whatever Raymond's uncertainties, whatever the worries of other Seward managers, they were not shared by the rank and file which Weed had brought to Chicago. "The New Yorkers were exultant," wrote the Cincinnati *Commercial's* reporter in describing the eve of balloting. "Their bands were playing, and the champagne flowing at their headquarters as after a victory." Even Greeley thought that Seward would win.

In the final night of caucusing, Seward lost ground, and when the convention on May 18 met to ballot, his strength was ebbing fast. He led on the first ballot, but on the second he was pressed hard by Lincoln. Bates and the others no longer counted. The third ballot would be decisive, and while pulses quickened and palms perspired, the roll call began. Steadily, as each delegation cast its vote, the Lincoln total rose until it stood one and a half short of the 233 necessary for a choice. Then Ohio switched to Lincoln, and "there was a noise in the Wigwam like the rush of a great wind, in the van of a storm—and in another breath, the storm was there. There were thousands cheering with the energy of insanity." Only the New York delegation, many a member in tears, sat silent—like "marble statues," the *Herald*'s correspondent thought—until Evarts could gain the floor to eulogize the defeated Seward and then in melancholy tones to move that Lincoln's nomination be made unanimous. In distant Auburn, townspeople who had come to celebrate with Seward furled their flags and sadly turned back to their homes.

Raymond, hiding his disappointment as best he could, next day rode down to Springfield with the committee of notification to salute the rising sun. There were bands and bonfires when they reached the Illinois capital, and countless rockets. Before Lincoln's plain, two-story house tar barrels blazed as the committee and some threescore guests turned up the front walk, where Raymond noted a wide-eyed young Lincoln perched on either gatepost. The candidate, tall, gaunt, and homely, met his callers at the back of the double parlors. He listened to the committee chairman's brief speech, replied with similar brevity, and then talked informally with the guests who crowded the simple parlor with its haircloth chairs and sofa. Carl Schurz said he did not "present the appearance of a statesman," but Raymond, while regretting Lincoln's lack of the "practical experience of men and factions, which the passing crisis will render indispensable in a Republican candidate," thought he made a "highly favorable" impression. "No one," added Raymond, "doubts he has the intellectual ability, the honesty of purpose and the fixedness of political principle essential to the high position for which he is in nomination."

Yet Raymond was not yet ready to declare himself. He wired the *Times* not to plump for Lincoln, and while Seward quickly promised Lincoln his support and Webb came out for him, Raymond demonstrated again the political independence that made partisans despair. "When all parties to the Presidential contest shall be fairly in the field," he said, "we shall be better able to decide what course it becomes independent citizens to pursue."

IV

On the way home, Raymond stopped in Auburn to visit Seward who, half sick with disappointment, was striving to distract himself by work about his estate. Webb was there, and the three men talked over what had happened at Chicago and the reasons therefor. Greeley's part could not be ignored. After the balloting, many New Yorkers had accused the *Tribune*'s editor of betrayal, but Raymond, who earlier at a delegation dinner had defended Greeley's right to act as he thought the best interests of the party required, had been unconvinced. Seward, he now discovered, subscribed to the betrayal theory, and what was more, had a document to support his belief. The document was Greeley's bristling letter written in November, 1854, to dissolve the firm of Seward, Weed & Greeley.

In political gossip the general contents had long been reported, although Weed said afterward that he had never read the letter and Raymond had never seen its text. Now he had a chance to read this unhappy protest against failure to gain public place; it convinced him quickly that Seward had good basis for questioning Greeley's fine talk about availability, and he decided that it was time to tell what he knew.

Surely with Seward's knowledge, presumably with his approval, Raymond sent the *Times* from Auburn a letter accusing Greeley not only of responsibility for Seward's defeat but of treachery in posing before the delegates as a friend of the man whose candidacy he fought. Greeley's "voice was potential," wrote Raymond, "precisely where Governor Seward was strongest—because it was supposed to be that of a friend, strong in his personal attachment and devotion, and driven into opposition on this occasion solely by the despairing conviction that the welfare of the country and the triumph of the Republican cause demanded the sacrifice." But Greeley was no friend, had not been for nearly six years, and the proof was a letter he had written Seward in 1854.

Webb said afterward that Seward had not intended that Raymond should reveal existence of the letter, but reveal it he did, and the effect of it was as of charges of grape and canister. Greeley "had privately, but distinctly," Raymond wrote, "repudiated further political friendship . . . with Governor Seward, and menaced him with hostility whenever it could be most effective, for the avowed reason that Governor Seward had never aided or advised his elevation to office. . . . No use was made of this knowledge in quarters where it would have disarmed the deadly effect of his pretended friendship for the man upon whom he was thus deliberately wreaking the long hoarded revenge of a disappointed office-seeker. . . . Stimulated by a hatred he has secretly cherished for years, protected by the forbearance of those whom he assailed, and strong in the confidence of those upon whom he sought to operate, it is not strange that Mr. Greeley's efforts should have been crowned with success."

The attack, a combination of truth, surmise and loose interpretation— far from menacing Seward with "hostility," Greeley had said specifically in 1854, "I trust I shall never be found in opposition to you"—bespoke years of personal and professional rivalry embittered by the gall of political defeat. It set New Yorkers by the ears. The *Herald*, which had already likened Greeley to Brutus, now compared Raymond to Mark Antony, and *Vanity Fair* thought well enough of the idea to cartoon it. Greeley, stung, quickly hit back, although the stoutness of his defense depended on one's prejudices. He denied that he had posed as Seward's friend at Chicago. He accused Raymond of distortion, and there was some truth to the charge, and in a pun that delighted political regulars characterized Raymond as a man with "constitutional addiction to crooked ways." Finally, he called for publication of the 1854 letter —he had no copy—so that people could judge for themselves.

Partisans took sides—Democrats were delighted by the Republican row—and the mails brought to Raymond and Greeley praise and blame alike. "Greeley's affair with Raymond diverts attention from the candidates temporarily," remarked the *Herald,* and so it seemed until in mid-June, Weed gave the letter to Greeley, who published it in the *Tribune* on June 14. The *Times* printed it a day later, as did most of the New York press. An amazing revelation of office hunger, it did Greeley no good, but neither did it make the case for betrayal watertight. It still depended in which camp one stood. Raymond had said his say. Weed asserted publicly that the letter explained Greeley's ill will, and Seward, if Greeley's own recollections were correct, never saw his one-time partner again. As a footnote to the controversy, the Democratic editors of *Vanity Fair* summed up their own and not unshared views:

Brutus Greeley

I have nipped him at Chicago,
I have made my Seward wail,
I've ordained that Uncle Abram
Shall be ridden on the rail.

Did he think that I forgave him?
Did he think I was an ass?
Did he think I'd love my enemies,
And let occasion pass?

If he did he was mistaken,
And I guess he knows it now,
For I nipped him at Chicago
And I made a precious row. . . .

V

When Greeley had said after the Chicago convention, "The past is dead. Let the dead past bury it, and let its mourners, if they will, go about the streets," he had spoken more truly than he and his critics knew. Weed himself had helped to bury the past by calling on Lincoln at Springfield. The Weed machine would support Lincoln, and one of Weed's lieutenants, Governor Morgan, was ready to set up headquarters in the Astor House as chairman of the Republican National Committee. At Cooper Union on June 7 there was a monster meeting to ratify the Lincoln ticket, with the traditional rockets and Roman candles cutting the night sky, and bonfires blazing at the street corners. There were cheers for "Old Abe," but there were cheers also for Seward and for Greeley, who kept strange company that night with Raymond and Webb among the rally's vice-presidents.

Republicans were optimistic, for the opposition was badly divided. At Charleston in April the historic party of Jefferson and Jackson had split, and the result had been ratified at Baltimore and Richmond in June by the nomination of two Democratic tickets. Douglas headed the one representing Northern Democrats and conservative, Union sentiments. Southern Democrats, sparked by such ardent disunionists as William L. Yancey of Alabama, made John C. Breckinridge, Buchanan's Vice-President, their candidate. A new party, the Constitutional Union, put up John Bell of Tennessee and Edward Everett of Massachusetts, and sought to combat the sectionalism that had divided the Democrats and brought the Republicans into the field. For the first time in the country's history no truly national party existed, a fact that in itself contributed further to the waxing sectionalism and the sentiment of disunion.

The campaign got quickly under way, yet there was much to distract from politics. A Japanese delegation, the first from the recently opened nation to visit the United States, toured the East in Oriental robes and afforded with their fans and swords all the interest and excitement of a circus. The visitors came to New York in June to parade before the curious who jammed Manhattan's downtown streets. There was a military review, a dazzling display of Japanese flags, and then an elaborate ball that developed into a grand drunk.

The youthful Prince of Wales, the future Edward VII, landed in Canada on a tour that included the United States, and to report the royal progress for democratic readers, the *Times* sent Joseph Howard, Jr., to travel with the Prince. In distant Sicily, Garibaldi was leading the insurrection that would rid Naples of its last Bourbon king. New Yorkers followed the fighting with personal concern, for many had contributed to the cause, and the *Times* office had been a center for Garibaldi contributions. In the midst of it all, the long-awaited *Great Eastern* arrived at Sandy Hook bar, passed it with hesitation and sailed up New York harbor, her giant hull and towering masts magnets for sightseers who thronged the waterside.

It was to be the last summer of peace, and almost as though they understood, Americans crowded lesser resorts as well as fashionable watering places. Saratoga was jaunty with ladies in crinoline, and at Newport as many as 200 carriages turned out to raise dust in the daily drives. There were fewer Southerners, who had always made gayer the life of Saratoga and Newport, but Northerners took their places on hotel verandahs and at the bathing beaches. In July, Raymond went to Burlington as usual for the university commencement, but for his family it was a quiet summer as Mrs. Raymond was expecting her seventh and last child.[4]

After their return from Europe the Raymonds had moved into a larger, more imposing house in West Ninth Street, a house better suited to their increasing prosperity. The *Times* was making money. Raymond's salary had been increased, and in the summer of 1860, following Wesley's withdrawal from the partnership, he and George Jones bought the Wesley shares. He had felt that the *Times* lost prestige to the *Tribune* when Greeley triumphed at Chicago, but it did not seem to be reflected in circulation, and at the end of summer as the campaign gathered momentum, every New York paper found itself hard-pressed to meet demand. The *Times* had been belated in all-out support of Lincoln, arousing false hopes among Douglasites that it might swing to them, and there had even been a project among them to buy the paper, but by the time party orators were in full voice, the *Times* was firmly in the Republican camp.

Never had there been such a campaign to report as this one in which the fate of the Republic was at stake. Night after night Republican "Wide-Awakes" with their torches and oilskin capes marched and sang for Lincoln in towns and cities of the North. There were giant rallies and barbecues. There were banners and buttons, and always the presses of the nation turned out the special supplements and fliers that took to voters distorted arguments characteristic of American campaign years. Never had so many orators stumped the states. Never had so many spoken with such fear behind their words, for up from the South rolled constantly the threat of secession and disunion should Black Republicans elect Abraham Lincoln President of the United States.

"We regard the struggle as one for political power," said Raymond, "and slavery as playing merely a secondary and subordinate part on either side." He had said the same thing in January at the Union meeting in Albany, and he reiterated it now in speeches and editorials. The North was ready to use in politics the economic strength developed over the years, to take from the South the political power that blocked at Washington policies desired by Northern industry and agriculture and labor. In such a contest for power, the moral issue of slavery had, as Raymond rightly understood, but secondary place.

4 Arthur William, born January 20, 1861; died November 20, 1864.

He appreciated that change in the balance of power could cause "local excitement and temporary disturbance," but the possibility left him unalarmed. Certainly it was no cause for Northern surrender. "The efforts of Southern politicians to coerce the judgement of Northern men by threats of dissolving the Union," he boldly stated, ". . . must certainly be based on very false and degrading estimates of the manhood and morals which have control of action in the Free States . . . There are points at which concession becomes disgrace; and sad as will be the alternative of offending our brethren of the South, it would be a less evil than the voluntary surrender of our rights under the coercion of Southern alarmists."

At mass meetings in New York and Brooklyn he had talked himself hoarse in the cause of Lincoln and the Republican party, and in the campaign's last days he drew heavily on his strength to speak many times in the upstate counties. Seldom did he stop short of an hour and a half, and at Rochester before a wildly enthusiastic rally he spoke two hours without interruption. Audiences had been filled with fervor, their cheers had been tonic, and he returned home for the election brimming with a sense of victory. "My own opinion is that Lincoln's majority in the State at large will not be less than 40,000," he said. It turned out to be more than 50,000.

It was in the confidence of victory that the *Times* printed its final campaign editorial, seeking to lay the last lingering fear of what victory might mean: "Mr. Lincoln's position is eminently conservative. His election will by no means involve a triumph of the ultra anti-slavery element of the Northern and Eastern States. . . . The attitude of the Republican party is eminently national and conservative. . . . Its candidate is an eminently just, upright and conservative statesman—pledged by his opinions, his declarations and his life against any invasion of Southern rights and any denial of Southern justice. The whole country has confidence in his honor and fidelity to the Constitution and that confidence will not be misplaced or betrayed."

Election day in New York City dawned dank and drizzly, but as the day wore on, the sun broke through the clouds. Voters, the campaign's heat forgotten, went orderly to the polls. There were few fights, fewer drunks than customary on an election day, but it was not for want of interest. Every bus that rattled over the cobbles was a political battleground as passengers refought the campaign. Before every newspaper office in Printing House Square crowds milled awaiting the returns. At the *Times*, men packed close against the plate glass windows as though to discover from the activity within some clue to the history being made. "Until the night had grown old and morning was born, the clamorous crowd demanded more news and latest intelligence. They demanded to know the fate of the Union before daybreak, and many of them learnt it before they went home." The *Times* headline told the story: "Astounding Victory of Republicanism." Abraham Lincoln would be the next President of the United States.

VI

Rumblings of disunion heard during the campaign grew louder now as secession came up for supreme test. The danger could no longer be ignored, but there was still time for Northerners to warn Southern fire-eaters of the full meaning of secession, to offer just concession and compromise within the framework of the Constitution, and to make doubly clear that Southern failure to accept Lincoln's election would explode the hideous powder mine of civil war.

Each dispatch from the South, each mail, brought news of movement toward secession. In South Carolina a call was out for a convention to consider the "value of the Union," and the rolls of applause that greeted spokesmen for disunion made it easy to anticipate the final vote. An old firebrand named Edmund Ruffin was touring the state, agitating against the low, vulgar tyranny of Black Republicanism, and wherever he went South Carolinians met him with bands, the salute of cannon, and secessionist oratory. Reports of agitation elsewhere might be less spectacular, but unrest was gathering momentum, and Northerners, skeptical hitherto that Southern radicals meant business, watched with growing anxiety. "The whole public mind," said the *Times*, "is feverish —apprehensive, alarmed."

At this critical moment, Raymond in one of the great intellectual efforts of his life addressed a series of open letters to William L. Yancey, a propagandist of secession and exponent of Southern nationalism, who had come North during the campaign to expound the extreme Southern view on slavery and its constitutional position. Raymond in refuting Yancey on constitutional grounds sought also to state what he held to be good Northern and Republican doctrine of the nature of the Union. The result was an exercise in political philosophy, an assertion of political thought. "We have reached a point in our political history," wrote Raymond, "when the welfare of both North and South requires that we should understand distinctly the basis on which our government rests; the spirit which is to guide its administration; the *relations it is to hold to the institution of slavery*. The election of Mr. Lincoln marks an era in the political history of the country; and his administration is to decide the issue and bring the conflict to a close."

Raymond knew that Yancey and other Southern radicals would not be deterred by anything he said. The best he could hope was that he might strengthen Southern moderates in their resistance to secession, and if not in the Deep South, then in Virginia and the border states. South Carolina he knew could not be stayed, and even before he had finished his final letter South Carolina had seceded, "pitched her alien tent, and raised her hostile flag." If all else failed, he would give the North a statement of principles and a stirring assertion of faith.

He was at his best when he asserted the final authority of the Constitution over the dispute between the sections. It allowed him to reject the Southern theory that the Union was only a compact between sovereign states. It sanctioned his insistence that the Federal Government could coerce a state that seceded, and, fundamental to the whole debate, it supported him in his vigorous denial of secession. He based his position on Article VI of the Constitution: "This Constitution, and the laws of the United States which shall be made in pursuance thereof . . . shall be the supreme law of the land; and the judges in every State shall be bound thereby, anything in the constitution or laws of any State to the contrary notwithstanding." "That," said Raymond, "is the whole case."

"South Carolina may declare herself out of the Union twice a year, if she pleases . . . but she cannot impair in the slightest degree the duty of every individual within her borders to obey the laws of Congress. . . . The Federal Government . . . deals with individuals and requires *them* to obey its laws. If they refuse, it may compel obedience. If the State interposes, and resists such attempted compulsion, then *the State 'makes war' upon the Federal Government* . . . a war of rebellion—a war of revolution. And the only question that remains is, whether the Federal Government has a right to put down rebellion—to suppress insurrection against its authority. And that question seems to me equivalent to asking whether it is a government at all, or only a sham."

His argument brought Raymond to an ominous conclusion: "Disunion means war." He did not flinch, driving home his understanding of impending tragedy with specific warning: "South Carolina must not expect . . . to be recognized by the Federal Government as an independent state *without a war*. Any such recognition . . . as a mere legislative act, would be treason to the Constitution, and would justify a revolution. It can only be done through an amendment of the Constitution; by a formal amendment of the nation, and the creation of another upon its ruins. To that, people who constitute the nation will never consent. You must win your independence, if you win it at all, just as every other nation has done—by the sword." In short, force would be used if necessary to combat secession; there would be none of Greeley's acceptance of peaceable secession which the *Tribune*'s editor had announced in his famous editorial urging that the Southern sisters be allowed to depart in peace.

Why did South Carolina wish to secede? Why did other states talk secession? Raymond's answer echoed the speeches he had made for months: the struggle for power. "The election of Lincoln is regarded [by the South] as conclusive proof that Northern supremacy is a fixed fact. . . . All the sectional excitements and political paroxysms of the last twenty years have been but the strenuous resistance of the South to what she has felt to be the inevitable tendency of events." The present crisis was the latest, the greatest, chapter in this history of resistance, for the South was making its final stand.

The four letters, spread over a month, were not concerned wholly with political philosophy. They expressed Northern sentiments in regard to slavery and secession. They were filled with the desire to explain the causes for conflict, and by understanding them, to remove them. Raymond was critical of the growing tyranny of the slaveholding oligarchy in the South itself, and yet he was just as critical of Northern failure to abide by the rules of neighborliness and the laws of the land. Essentially, he was conservative, seeking to assure the South that a Republican administration would not overturn Southern institutions, that Lincoln would uphold the Constitution that would guide his every act. But if assurance and concession could not halt the South, then, he reiterated, there would be war.

"We shall stand . . . upon the Constitution which our fathers made," he wrote as an eloquent conclusion to his last letter. "We shall not make a new one, nor shall we permit any human power to destroy the old one. Long before that day shall come the people of the Northern States will stand together as one man—forgetful of all past differences and divisions—to preserve the American Union, and crush any revolution which may menace it with destruction. We seek no war—we shall wage no war except in defense of the Constitution and against its foes. But we have a country and a Constitutional Government. We know its worth to us and to mankind, and in case of necessity we are ready to test its strength."

VII

If logic and reason could have prevailed against the forces shaping the nation's destiny, letters like Raymond's to Yancey might have had more than momentary significance. But logic and reason were out the window, and the time for compromise was slipping by. In Congress, a special Senate committee of thirteen, including such leaders as Seward and Douglas, Davis and Toombs, failed to find a road to compromise and quickly announced the fact. A House committee labored longer, but hardly more successfully, and even before its work began a group of Southerners in the House had issued a call for a "Southern Confederacy."

President Buchanan had denounced secession in his annual message, had pleaded for "peaceful constitutional remedies" to avert war and disruption of the Union, but he provided no great leadership, and his discredited Administration was obviously falling apart. Like many another Republican, Raymond believed that the President was deliberately aiding disunion. He wrote Lincoln: "Buchanan, it is clear, means to do all the harm he can, and unfortunately he has the power to do a great deal. He will leave things in a very bad shape evidently for his successor."

To allay the fears of the South and to still the gathering storm, Raymond called upon the President-elect to make some reassuring statement, and, rather presumptuously, he sent Lincoln some notes for the sort of statement he believed necessary. He was not at all convinced when Lincoln replied that anything he might say would be so twisted and distorted by extremists on both sides that it would do more harm than good. That, thought Raymond, was only allowing matters to drift, and certainly such a view helped not at all the Union men at the South who in the end might be the ones to force compromise on the fire-eating Yanceys. "The Union men at the South *stand in need of backing*," Raymond told Lincoln. "It is not worth while to attempt in any way to satisfy either the Disunionists there, or the party malignants here. But the Union men of the South must belong to our party—and it seems to me important that we should open the door for them as wide as the hinges will let it swing."

In letters to Raymond and to many other men North and South, Lincoln indicated that he would compromise—except on the extension of slave territory—and he tossed aside as the words of madmen charges that he was "pledged to the ultimate extinction of slavery," and that he held "the black man to be the equal of the white." He said none of this publicly, perhaps because the Republican party was so loose an alliance of conservatives and radicals, one-time Democrats and unregenerate Whigs, that he dared not do anything to dissolve his support. This unwillingness to speak out gave radicals in his party an advantage. Simultaneously it strengthened the hand of extremists in the South.

Editors like Raymond, Senators like Seward, political bosses like Weed, could offer the hand of fellowship, could warn of disaster unless the extended hand were clasped, but so long as Lincoln remained silent, so long was it possible for Southern radicals to reject compromise and to urge that the incoming Administration would trample Southern civilization in the dust. Already the issue had become one of saving the border states, for the Deep South was rapidly setting up a house of its own. Mississippi had seceded on January 9, Florida on the 10th, Alabama on the 11th. Before the month closed, Georgia, Louisiana, and Texas were out of the Union.

"God save the Republic," the *Times* had cried on New Year's Day, and to many readers the cry must have seemed one of despair. But Raymond was seldom without hope, and he remained confident as one blow followed another that the Union would somehow still be saved short of war. To Judge Forsyth, his companion at Solferino, he wrote that "if we can only hold things *still* for three months all will come right. The compromises talked of are not needed. They are either too much or too little. If the Union is saved, it must be because it is *worth* saving, and the South will find that out as soon as anybody if we only give them to understand that they have *got to make the discovery* or else take the consequences." He was not for surrender—he had made that clear in the Yancey letters—but he was for forbearance and patience, and he reiterated his view not only in correspondence with a friend like Forsyth, but also in editorials.

"The Southern States have taken into their own hands the decision of their fate," said the *Times*, following Georgia's secession. "There is no necessity for civil war, unless the Southern States see fit to begin it. Not a gun need be fired, unless they choose to fire it, and even then we can well afford, as we have done hitherto, to meet violence with forbearance, and passion with calm appeals to reason and experience, until the South makes a conflict unavoidable, and then the consequences must be upon their own heads."

A gun had already been fired, and South Carolinians had chosen to fire it. On January 9, the unarmed steamer *Star of the West*, carrying reinforcements for Major Anderson at Fort Sumter in Charleston Harbor, had been fired upon as it sought to cross the bar, and had turned back rather than bring on war. The echo of the cannonade died away, and the smoke from the Charleston batteries drifted out on the sea breeze. It was as though the curtain had fallen on the dress rehearsal for a tragic drama in which the actors now knew their places and for which the stage was set.

CHAPTER
—16—

War

I

IN THE pre-dawn darkness of April 12, 1861, a shell burst over beleaguered Fort Sumter in Charleston Harbor. The men and women massed on Charleston's housetops and quays cheered as the shell's crimson arc died away, and old Edmund Ruffin, who had fired the first shot, became a hero. Hours earlier Jasper, the *Times* correspondent in Charleston, had wired the paper the single word "War." [1]

It was late afternoon before New York learned the details of the attack, but the *Times*, drawing on Jasper's one-word dispatch, had already warned readers of what was ahead, and that very morning had printed a map of Charleston Harbor to pinpoint the spot where fighting would begin. Yet like death, sure and long anticipated, the war shocked and surprised when it came. In the first moments of their shock, New Yorkers surged almost instinctively toward Printing House Square, where the newspaper offices were quickly surrounded by a multitude that snatched up the extras as they came damp from the *Times* and *Tribune* presses. In his gaslit office above the throbbing crowds that spring night, Raymond began the next day's leader: "The Disunion conspiracy, which has for the last twenty years been gnawing at the heart-strings of the great

[1] Jasper, whose real name was Dr. George H. C. Salter, said several years later: "On the 10th [he meant the 11th] of April, 1861, at 8 o'clock in the evening, I sent the New York *Times* from Charleston, S.C., the most startling telegram that was ever flashed across the wires, the simple word 'War.' My Press colleagues at the Palmetto City laughed at my assertion that Fort Sumter would be bombarded at 4:30 A.M. the following morning, but as I had exclusive information from Gen. Beauregard's headquarters, the New York *Times* had the benefit of it."

American Republic, has at last culminated in open war upon its glittering and resplendent flag."

To Raymond, after so long in the shadow of disunion, it was as though "a heavy burden of anxiety had been lifted." All his labors toward averting the conflict, toward finding some compromise, had failed —as he must long have known they would. At least twice during the gloom of the secession winter, he had been in Washington, but nothing he learned there had given him any hope, whether he sought the counsel of Seward or of his fellow moderate Charles Francis Adams, whose secretary-son Henry admired Raymond as a "man of the world" and took to him "most kindly." Nor had Raymond's experience at meetings of New York Republicans caused him to misread for a moment the fact that the party's spirit was warlike, that any compromise was most unlikely even if desired by the South, which having set up its Confederacy appeared quite content outside the Union.

What had ultimately caused Raymond to despair was not so much the fact of disunion as the apparent inability of the Lincoln Administration to do anything about it. He had deplored Lincoln's refusal to state his policy before inauguration, arguing that all attempts to save even the border states were foredoomed until the new President had set a course, and while Raymond had liked Lincoln's inaugural message immensely, his pleasure had worn off as weeks passed and Lincoln seemed more concerned with handing out jobs than with saving the Union.[2] The President had told him that he felt "like a man so busy letting rooms at one end of the house that he can't stop to put out the fire that is burning at the other," and while Raymond understood he had not approved. Finally, on April 3, he had spoken his mind in a sensational two-column editorial, "Wanted—A Policy." It hammered the Administration with all the vigor at Raymond's command:

"Our government has done absolutely nothing towards carrying the country through the tremendous crisis which is so rapidly and so steadily settling down upon us. It allows everything to drift, to float along without guidance or impulse to do anything. . . . The Administration *must have a policy of action*—clear and definite. The country looks eagerly to President Lincoln. . . . The people want *something* to be decided on— some standard raised, some policy put forward, which shall serve as a rallying point for the abundant but discouraged loyalty of the American heart. In a great crisis like this, there is no policy so fatal as that of having no policy at all."

[2] Raymond, though he denied it, was popularly believed to have wanted a plum for himself. Through his influence his old friend George Perkins Marsh got the mission to Italy—and held it for twenty years.

Now, less than a fortnight after the writing of that editorial, the fall of Sumter had dictated that the policy should be war. In a proclamation that set the North aflame, Lincoln called for 75,000 troops to put down the rebellion. Raymond had not wanted war, but if it had to be, then he was for pushing ahead with all energies in the unhappy task of deciding the issue of disunion forever. To him the firing on Sumter meant "the beginning of the end." During the next four years, so far as his independent spirit allowed, he would make the *Times* a New York mouthpiece for Lincoln. More consistently than any other New York editor he would support the Administration's conduct of the war as it unwound from battlefield to battlefield—Bull Run, Shiloh, Antietam, Fredericksburg, Gettysburg, Lookout Mountain—and to final victory at Appomattox.

II

"Unfurl the banner of the Union" was the watchword in New York, and the *Times* put out a huge flag measuring twenty by thirty feet. The *Herald*, long sympathetic toward secession, failed to show the colors, and a mob, hooting and jeering, threatened to sack the place until old Bennett in a fright sent hurriedly for a flag, displayed it, and saved his shop. Such incidents did not subtract much from the overwhelming show of patriotism. "The great body of our people," said the *Times*, "have but one heart and one purpose in this great crisis of our history." It found proof on every New York corner, "in every car, on board every ferry-boat, in every hotel, in the vestibule of every church."

Men jammed recruiting offices, and streets resounded to the tunes of "The Girl I Left Behind Me." Soon the troops were marching away. Within a week of the firing on Sumter, New York's famous Seventh Regiment had gone. A small boy—his name was Edward Mitchell and he grew up to edit the *Sun*—remembered afterward how he watched "through the morning mists the stacked muskets and bivouac fires along the cobblestones of Forty-second Street and the Belgian blocks of Fifth Avenue, where the tall fellows of the New England regiments . . . were heating coffee and warming doughnuts before marching downtown." Plans were rushed for barracks in City Hall Park across the street from the *Times*, and at least one of the city's better-clothing makers got ready to profit from shoddy uniforms.

Major Anderson, the commander at Sumter, reached New York with some of his men to be hailed at a great mass meeting in Union Square as the first Northern heroes of the war. Crowds with banners great and small jammed the square and overflowed into near-by streets, and while Major Anderson got most of the cheers, the rally's orators were not forgotten. There were many. One was the Democratic Mayor Fernando Wood, who had but recently suggested that New York secede too, and set up shop as a free city. Republicans like Hamilton Fish spoke from the same platform as Raymond, whose power as an orator made him as popular at patriotic meetings in the city as in the villages of Staten Island.

In Raymond's view of things, the rallies were essential for organizing the home front to support and aid the men who shortly would be dying for the Union. He knew something of what the British had done during the Crimean War; what they had done, Americans could do, and so he threw his strength behind the collection of a National Patriotic Fund that, on the British pattern, would aid the wives and dependents of soldiers in uniform. Like most Americans he was familiar with the great work of Florence Nightingale in the tragic hospitals at Scutari and Balaklava, and he had not forgot the horrid cries of the wounded at Solferino, where there had been no hospital corps. In America he hoped that there would be no scenes like those he had witnessed at Castiglione.

He inserted in the *Times* on April 22 a call for women to meet with Mrs. Raymond at the house on Ninth Street to form an organization "for the purpose of preparing bandages, lint and other articles of indispensable necessity for the wounded." The women came, several hundred of them, to crowd the Raymond parlors with their billowing hoopskirts and to make the air heavy with eau de cologne. Before they were through, they had an organization—Raymond was made treasurer, Mrs. Raymond secretary—and they had found in the brownstone building of the Society Library on near-by University Place a workroom where they could roll bandages, sew on hospital garments, and enroll volunteers for nursing. They urged that women elsewhere in the city follow their example, and Mrs. Raymond suggested that a central committee be established. The idea caught on. Within a week it had spurred a great mass meeting in Cooper Institute at which the Women's Central Association for Relief was formed. It was the beginning of the famed United States Sanitary Commission.

Steadily in the *Times* Raymond gave editorial aid to the war work of the women, and when he could he helped with time and money the organizing of their associations and their nursing corps. The war put on him extraordinary burdens as an editor. Recruiting had sapped his staff. Many men had marched away, among them the brilliant Fitz-James O'Brien, who would never return. Demand for news had led to a Sunday edition, and meanwhile circulation soared beyond what the presses could handle and meet the publication deadline.

Correspondents were a problem. Jasper, who had been arrested by the South Carolinians as a spy, had been released, but at Harpers Ferry another *Times* man was picked up and spent a week talking himself free from the Virginians. The fact that he had been in Wheeling to report the Unionist convention that aimed to set up West Virginia as a Union state made him suspect from any Confederate's point of view. Then in Washington, the indispensable Simonton had been wounded accidentally by a militiaman; it put him to bed for a long while.

Raymond himself itched to be a correspondent. He wanted to exchange the confinement of an editor's office for the freedom of a roving reporter. It had not been easy to remain in New York while the full tide of secession and war swirled around Washington, but he had restrained himself, learning at second hand from Weed and many another who had been in the capital something of what was going on. By the end of June he had reached the bursting point. He wanted to find out for himself what was happening and what was likely to happen, and if in the course of his inquiry he chanced to meet up with a battle, he might be able to send the *Times* reporting as vivid as that he had sent in 1859 from the plains of Lombardy. He cleared his desk, put together the essentials for several weeks from home, and set out.

III

The weeks after Sumter had been weeks of preparation that brought raw, ill-equipped troops to Washington and to the camps and garrisons along the line dividing North and South. They were not only untrained and badly equipped. They were badly led. None was ready to fight, nor did responsible commanders want to risk a battle. Yet in the North, the public wanted action, and with the cries of "On to Richmond" in his ears, General Winfield S. Scott, the aging commander of the armies, reluctantly put aside his anaconda plan for crushing the South in a great encircling movement and ordered new plans, less ambitious, that would send the armies into Virginia.

Scott described his anaconda strategy to Raymond one night when they dined together at the general's quarters in Washington, and he told how the pressure of editors like Greeley and Dana, spokesmen of the "On to Richmond" school, had forced him to scrap the broad plan. It had not required one of Scott's famous dinners—his table was one of the best in Washington and the old general was a connoisseur of claret and terrapin—to convince Raymond that an immediate move might be dangerous. During a fortnight with the armed forces, Raymond had seen quite enough to know that the army was not ready.

After leaving New York at the end of June, he had passed through Baltimore, where the chief of police had just been arrested for traffic with secessionists and the memory of the April attack on the Sixth Massachusetts Regiment lived on, and had taken a steamer down the Chesapeake to Fortress Monroe, where with Weed and Senator Wilson of Massachusetts he was a guest of General Ben Butler. The general —Raymond noted that he was bald and cross-eyed—tried to put on a good show and to be the gracious host, but rain spoiled a grand review that he had planned at Newport News and his social graces did nothing to conceal his incapacity as a commander. The troops had been looting private homes in the neighborhood, which Raymond explained by the fact that "their discipline has been excessively lax." They had not been "drilled effectively" either, he reported, and their "camps do not present a creditable appearance." He noted the "hang-dog" look of many a soldier, the "dirty, worn, ragged clothes," the "broken-out shoes."

It was all quite discouraging, and his observations a few days later in the region around Harpers Ferry gave him no higher opinion of the three-month volunteers. Reports that Pennsylvania troops under General Robert Patterson were going to attack the Confederates led by General Joseph E. Johnston had drawn Raymond to western Maryland in hope of witnessing the battle. He had gone by train as far as possible, then had hired a wagon with a tipsy driver to take him the weary miles to Martinsburg, where Patterson had his headquarters. But there was no battle. The Union forces had advanced so slowly that Johnston had withdrawn into the Shenandoah Valley without a fight, and in Patterson's camp there was now only routine business. After looking over the Pennsylvanians and talking with their commander, soon to be mustered out in disgrace, Raymond hurried back to Washington, where rumors insisted that the hour for the march to Richmond was at hand.

He put up at the National Hotel and in the cruel summer heat set about surveying the city. Soldiers in every sort of garish uniform— Zouaves in baggy pants, the Garibaldi Guard in red blouses, militiamen in blue—were everywhere, and often they were drunk. Their white tents canopied open fields; their heavy wagons lumbering through the streets raised dust curtains that hung long in the muggy air. Mountains of supplies were piled along the wharves. Great warehouses and stables were rising for the army, and fortifications of a sort had been thrown up around the city. As he moved around the wartime capital, interviewing army men or talking with Senators and Representatives in town for a special session, Raymond came to appreciate full well that General Irvin McDowell, commander of the forces at Washington, spoke truth when he complained, "This is not an army." Raymond understood that it took time to organize and equip an effective force, and he warned in the *Times* against haste in mounting an offensive. Those who were demanding that the army move would be the first, he said, to attack the Administration should the advance fail.

But relentless public and political pressure forbade further delay, and the decision had been taken. Wagon trains were steadily moving across the Potomac and troops had their marching orders. On the evening of July 16, Raymond rode out to the pillared Lee mansion on the heights at Arlington, where McDowell had his headquarters, to learn from the general himself when the advance would begin. He could not find McDowell, but the hustle and bustle at headquarters told him plainly enough that the army was under way. That was all he needed. He drove hastily back to Washington to complete preparations for traveling with the troops.

IV

Early next morning, and before daylight, Raymond passed over the Long Bridge onto the soil of Virginia. With him in the carriage he had hired were the *Times* Washington correspondent, Lorenzo L. Crounse, and Charles Loring Brace, who was now in Washington with the Sanitary Commission. Crounse's wife had packed a hamper of food, and it was almost like a picnic as they drove through the wooded country and between the yellowing fields of grain until, by taking a side road, they caught up with the army and saw in the fresh morning light the bayonets glittering among the trees.

For a time they rode alongside McDowell and his staff. Occasionally they halted until trees felled to block the road had been cleared away; it gave opportunity to eat the blackberries ripening in the July sun. Horsemen galloped past. Wagons and caissons sometimes got tangled in the military traffic. At an abandoned rebel camp, Raymond cut from a sandbag the label "The Confederate States" and planned to keep it as a souvenir. Brace thought everything "beautiful and picturesque."

The advance halted at Fairfax Courthouse, and Raymond was distressed to note that soldiers looted the deserted homes of Virginians who had fled before McDowell's army. When he described the encampment for the *Times*, he tried to defend the action of the soldiers, attributing some of it to high spirits, and their conduct was not without its funny side. "After we were fully in town today," he wrote, "two of the troops dressed themselves in women's clothes and promenaded the town amid the shouts and not over-delicate attentions of the surrounding troops." As darkness fell, campfires flared in the hollows and on the ridges. Sentries called, and an occasional courier dashed on horseback along the roads. "The troops," Raymond wrote, "are bivouacked tonight in the fields and under the open sky. The General and Staff, like the men, sleep on the ground rolled in their blankets." Raymond, no soldier, found shelter in a small hotel, where he slept late the following morning, and it was eleven o'clock—he had been separated from his companions and the carriage—when he finally reached Centreville, toward which the army was moving. The Confederates under Beauregard were just ahead.

"I began the tour of Centreville," Raymond reported, "in search of food, as I had had no breakfast, and was nearly famished. While swallowing a cup of very poor coffee, which I persuaded the servants of a deserted mansion to sell me, I heard the sound of cannon in the direction of Manassas. I immediately pushed forward on foot, under a blazing sun, and after a brisk walk of three miles—during which the only refreshment I could procure was a little vinegar and water—I came to a wood . . . where guns were posted and skirmishers were out."

Troops under Colonel Daniel Tyler had been ordered to make a reconnaissance of the swampy terrain around Bull Run. They had been caught in heavy fire, as Raymond, watching through glasses and listening to the muskets crackle among the trees, realized long before the Unionists began to fall back in considerable disorder. For a while he was in real danger, for he had stood near enough a Northern battery to be part of the target when Southern guns opened fire. Shells burst around him, one dug up the ground only twenty feet away, but he kept his position until the fighting halted and it was time to write a dispatch that would inform but not discourage. He was disappointed that Northern men had not done better, but he blamed Tyler more than the troops, and he wrote confidently that the setback would not affect the battle's outcome.

McDowell had fixed Sunday the 21st for the decisive stroke, and at an early hour that summer morning he rode forward with his staff— Raymond accompanied them—for the opening attack. The general felt miserable, for he had been poisoned by canned peaches, and besides he was not too optimistic of what lay ahead. Raymond had earlier reported that the Confederates were as strong as the Federal forces, that they were well entrenched; actually, at the time he wrote, the Southern strength was a good deal less than the Northern, but presumably he reflected the mood and opinion of McDowell's headquarters. Neither Raymond nor McDowell as the guns began to speak knew that Johnston had moved rapidly from the Shenandoah to reinforce Beauregard. The weak, incompetent Patterson, so recently Raymond's host at Martinsburg, had allowed Johnston to slip away, and the Union paid dearly for Patterson's blunder.

About a mile from the rebel lines, Raymond found a spot from which to watch McDowell's columns move to the assault, although there was not much to see, for heavy woods hid most of the fighting and what the trees did not mask was effectively curtained by smoke that billowed from the guns and by dust raised by the marching men. Like other newspapermen—and at one time or another during the morning hours Raymond had the company not only of Crounse and Brace but of Henry Villard of the *Herald* and E. C. Stedman of the *World* [3]—he could learn from staff officers what was happening. He could not have missed the essential drama of the battle even if he had been so inclined. Much of what he saw and heard and felt he included in a dispatch that he took into Centreville from the field at two in the afternoon. McDowell had already claimed victory, but Raymond, aware that no battle is won until it is ended, reported cautiously to the *Times* that "the result is not certain."

His caution had been wise, for before he got back to the field the tide had turned. Beauregard, strengthened by Johnston's force, struck at McDowell's left, struck hard, and the Union soldiers, short of provisions, exhausted after long hours on foot, caved in. Soon their sole purpose was to escape, and what might have been an orderly withdrawal became a rout in which foot soldiers and cavalrymen, gun carriages and supply wagons, were tumbled together with the spectators, many a Congressmen among them, who had driven out from Washington to watch the Union win the war.

Raymond on his way back to the field had gone scarcely a quarter of a mile from Centreville when he met a great number of fugitives. "Our carriage," he said afterward, "soon became entangled in a mass of baggage-wagons, the officer in charge of which told me it was useless to go in that direction as all our troops were retreating." Raymond went to a high point of ground and saw, by the dense clouds of dust which arose over each of the three roads by which McDowell had advanced, that the army was indeed in retreat. What was more, the cannon flashing in the rear told him that the Confederates were pursuing. Without investigating further, he turned about for the twenty-six-mile drive to Washington.

"After I had driven something over a mile," Raymond wrote in his final dispatch on the battle, ". . . the crowd in the rear became absolutely frenzied with fear, and an immense mass of wagons, horses, men on foot, and flying soldiers, came dashing down the hill at a rate which threatened destruction, instant and complete, to everything in their way. The panic spread as they proceeded and gathering strength by its

[3] Stedman wrote his wife: "Mr. Raymond was with me in the hottest cannonade, and was as cool as a cucumber."

progress, became absolutely terrific. The horses caught the frenzy of the moment, and became as wild as their masters. My driver, attempting to check the speed of our carriage, found it suddenly crushed under the weight of an enormous Pennsylvania army wagon. . . . The opportune arrival of another carriage containing a couple of Congressmen, relieved me from the dilemma, and took me to Washington."

It was midnight when a battle-soiled Raymond, sunburned, hardly recognizable beneath the dust that lay white upon his whiskers, rode across the Long Bridge into a city where rumors of disaster were spreading gloom. He quickly got to work, writing with the speed that had made him famous as a reporter a detailed, vivid account of what he had seen and of what had happened. For the debacle, he blamed the officers in particular; better leadership would have halted the disintegration of the regiments before it had well begun. Better officers would have meant better discipline from the start. Yet it was hard to defend the action of the half-trained soldiers who had straggled away from their companies during the battle, and who once the retreat began "threw away their muskets, blankets and knapsacks and ran as if their lives depended on their speed." Hours after the battle ended, they streamed across the Long Bridge, tired, sodden in the rain that began to fall toward dawn. Raymond noted how on street corners and barrooms "each speedily became the central point of a steadily swelling crowd, who learned the bloody history of this awful battle from the lips of these heroes."

Raymond's battle story was finished hours before the eyewitness accounts of the fighting got their barroom editing. He hurried his copy to the telegraph office, expecting that the wire would take it to New York for the morning editions of the *Times*, but unbeknown to him, the government censor, who had still to learn of McDowell's unhappy day, struck the dispatch from the "all right" file. Not until two days after Bull Run was the *Times* able to publish what would otherwise have been an exclusive story. By this ill wind the *Herald* instead of the *Times* had a chance to tell New Yorkers first of what had happened on Sunday at Manassas.[4]

V

The *Herald* beat was hard to bear, and not only for itself. Ever since Raymond began his tour as correspondent, the *Herald* had been ridiculing him, belittling his achievements during the Italian war, recalling with impish delight the "elbows of the Mincio" and the "race to Castiglione." "The Hon. Jefferson Brick" the *Herald* had also called him,

[4] The editors, disbelieving the facts of young Henry Villard's dispatch, cut it so hard that he thought it ruined.

identifying him with the pallid, ineffectual editorial assistant whom Dickens portrayed unforgettably in one of his American chapters of *Martin Chuzzlewit*.[5] Raymond was no stranger to this sort of thing, particularly in regard to the *Herald*, and he himself not so long before had given Bennett so sarcastic a ribbing that the old man had sued. He did not really mind when the *Herald* called him "poor little Brick, of Mincio and Solferino remembrance." He had taken no notice when shortly before Bull Run the *Herald* said that "poor little Jefferson Brick was patiently waiting a chance for another horseback ride from some Virginia Solferino." Now it almost seemed that Bennett's editorial insight included ability to forecast the turn of events that led to another "race to Castiglione." There had been no need for a stupid censor to make Raymond seem indeed as ineffectual as the Dickens character.

The *Herald* made the most of it, in fourteen couplets entitled "Ye Plaintive Ballad of Jefferson Brick":

> It was a July morning when Mister Jefferson Brick,
> All thought of danger scorning, marched in the double quick . . .
> Quoth he "I am a soldier who has at running drilled!
> I drilled at Solferino—my boots with fame are filled . . .
> So come along McDowell, and limber out each gun;
> 'Tis you must do the fighting, and I will do the run" . . .
> McDowell peppered bravely from dawn till set of sun,
> The while one Jeff. Brick noisily let out to make his run . . .
> Didst ever see a mortar let fly at battery gun?
> If aye, you have an aye-dear of how our Jeff. Brick run.

Raymond got little fun out of that sort of thing, but he buried his real feelings within himself. For the moment it seemed more important to assess the causes of Union defeat and to insure against a repetition while urging the nation forward to greater efforts in its struggle for survival. It was a task for which he felt the *Times* eminently fitted. He set about its accomplishment, urging with all his editorial eloquence: "With offenses of the enemy unpunished, with faith in the final triumph unshaken, with resources not exhausted, hardly touched even; with armies springing to the field, with national ardor unabated, the United States will go boldly and cheerfully in the bloody path of war ahead, assured of [the] complete and enduring success of 'Liberty and Union.' "

[5] In 1859, *Leslie's Illustrated Weekly* asserted that Raymond had been the original Jefferson Brick, and the assertion has often been repeated. Yet there is no evidence that Dickens saw Raymond during his 1842 visit to the United States when he gathered material for *Martin Chuzzlewit*. Raymond never alluded to any meeting with Dickens at that time, and never mentioned that he had been the original Jefferson Brick, although at a New York dinner for Dickens in 1868, Raymond made a speech in which such reference and allusions would have been very much in order.

CHAPTER

—17—

Battles and Leaders

I

SIX DAYS after the defeated, broken men of the Army of the
Potomac straggled into Washington in the summer rain, a dy-
namic young officer was called from western Virginia to take
command of the forces at the capital. His name was George Brin-
ton McClellan, a colorful, self-confident West Pointer who was not yet
thirty-five. A brilliant organizer, an officer who knew how to inspire
loyalty and devotion, he quickly brought into order the near chaos that
followed Bull Run. He had his faults, not least an arrogance and rudeness
that did not except even the President. In the late summer and early
autumn of 1861, men overlooked such unhappy qualities while McClellan, dashing dramatically about the capital on the horse he called Dan
Webster, restored a nation's faith in its armed might. That McClellan
was hesitant in action to the point of timidity was undreamed of as he
paraded his disciplined and newly equipped divisions in brave shows that
excited the admiration of all who watched. It was after seeing one of these
grand displays that Julia Ward Howe poured out "The Battle Hymn of
the Republic."

The nation, still unbelieving that the making of an army took time,
soon grew impatient with McClellan's reviews and his pompous headquarters where the Comte de Paris, pretender to the throne of France,
and his brother, the Duc de Chartres, were among the ornaments. As it
had in the weeks before Bull Run, the cry went up for an advance into
Virginia that would humble and sweep away the Confederacy. Popular
impatience was reflected in demands by members of Congress that Mc-

Clellan do something, and because the general was a Democrat, many a Republican began to whisper that the reason for inaction lay in his unwillingness to destroy the South. Pressed by the politicians, Lincoln urged, then ordered, the commander of the armies to attack, and when McClellan did move out to the muddy field of Manassas it was only to find the Confederates withdrawn beyond the Rappahannock and wooden guns guarding the earthworks that he had argued were stoutly held.

All the while, the general had pressed stubbornly for his own plan of attack, a great expedition that would move against the rebel capital at Richmond by way of the Chesapeake and the peninsula between the York and the James. Ultimately he persuaded Lincoln, but only after promising that Washington would not be left unguarded, and in March, 1862, the ships began to gather in the Potomac to move 100,000 men and more to the peninsula. McClellan himself left for Fortress Monroe, glad, he wrote his wife, to quit "that sink of iniquity" which was Washington. He felt certain of success, even though Lincoln and Secretary of War Edwin M. Stanton had detached from his force a full corps just as he was sailing. The two civilians, fearful always of a Confederate attack on the capital, were to do worse, for the 35,000 men of McDowell's corps upon whom McClellan had counted were to be kept from him.

Whatever the criticism of McClellan among Republicans, the *Times* supported him staunchly, and as the peninsula campaign got under way saluted him as a commander in whom the army had great faith. "The enemy will be followed until he is found," said the *Times*, "and if he chooses to try the hazard of battle, there is everything in the skill of the General, and the character and perfect armament of the men, to afford us a moral certainty of success." If the *Times* with its elaborate maps of Virginia and the peninsula was optimistic, so now was the nation. McClellan at last was moving to the grand attack, and the East would have victories to equal those of the West.

Northern optimism was mirrored in Southern pessimism. Joseph E. Johnston, the Confederate general facing McClellan, despaired of holding the peninsula, and favored abandoning it along with Norfolk and its important navy yard. There were counsels to counter his, but for the South as a whole the outlook was grim indeed at the beginning of April, 1862. In the West, Grant had won the bloody battle of Shiloh, and Union forces had captured Island No. 10, on which the Confederates had staked their hopes of controlling the upper Mississippi. Before the month was out, Farragut was to run the forts below New Orleans and capture the city, largest in the Confederacy. If McClellan could take Richmond, there would not be much left.

At the end of April, Raymond came down from New York to watch the campaign's progress. He brought with him as a companion the hand-some Leonard W. Jerome,[1] a wealthy, worldly stock plunger, whose flashy company, so different from that of the intellectuals Raymond had once preferred, held peculiar fascination for him. Jerome, who earlier had been a newspaper publisher in Rochester, had bought enough shares in the *Times* to become in January, 1862, a consulting director of the paper. On the peninsula, Jerome's role was wholly that of a visitor, but Raymond, on a busman's holiday, intended to observe and report. Since the *Times* already had three correspondents on the spot, there was not much that he could add to the dispatches of Crounse and the others, but for readers his comments on the military situation and his personal ob-servations had interest because they came from the editor himself.

Fruit trees were in bloom when Raymond and Jerome reached the front lines where McClellan was besieging Johnston in historic York-town, and Raymond noted the pinkness of the blossoms as he rode out to inspect the trenches that the troops had dug. For two days he was much in the company of General Daniel Butterfield, a wealthy young New Yorker who had been a businessman before he became a soldier, and sometimes he climbed into the trees to watch the rebels lob shells into the Union works. There was less to see than to hear, and having heard, Ray-mond sent to New York a strong defense of McClellan that was especially critical of the Administration's refusal to release McDowell's corps to reinforce the army, and of the navy's failure to send its gunboats up the James behind the rebel lines. He defended McClellan's sticky slowness as strategy calculated to save lives at the same time that, by avoiding rash action, it insured final victory. Besides, he asked, and the words sounded almost like McClellan's, what other strategy was possible when the army had been deprived of forces on which it had counted? "If [McClellan] had been allowed to carry out his original plans," wrote Raymond, "he would have . . . been in Richmond by now."

Because of a week end in Washington, Raymond missed Johnston's un-expected withdrawal from Yorktown on May 4, but he was back the next day and in mud often a foot deep he inspected the abandoned rebel defenses. He thought them strong and well-placed. As usual, there was rain—"the weather is infamous," said McClellan—and the marshy penin-sula mired wagons, batteries, and horses until often they could not be re-trieved. When Raymond rode from Yorktown to the general's head-quarters in Williamsburg, a pleasant old house that Johnston had recently occupied, he spent five hours covering twelve miles, so deep was the mud. It was mud that explained in part the slowness with which the

[1] Whose daughter Jennie was to marry Lord Randolph Churchill and become the mother of Britain's famed Winston Spencer Churchill.

Union force followed Johnston in his retreat toward Richmond, for except at Williamsburg, where there had been a spirited rearguard action, there was little contact between the armies.

Like many a man North and South, Raymond now thought that the war was "substantially over." So hard had Johnston been pushed at Williamsburg that he had left his wounded behind in the rain, a fact that Raymond reported while reporting also that the poor boys, for they were hardly more than boys, were attended by Northern surgeons who disregarded what uniform the wounded wore. On May 10, the Federal troops which Raymond had watched sail from Fortress Monroe entered Norfolk, where the Confederates hastily blew up the *Virginia*, the ironclad that had done so much damage to Union men-of-war until halted by the *Monitor*. With Norfolk's fall, Union gunboats steamed up the James, and in Richmond the government began to pack its archives.

Lincoln, who had come down to Fortress Monroe with Stanton and Chase, two of McClellan's most bitter Cabinet enemies, was said to have directed the Norfolk attack and to have sent out the gunboats, but if he did, Raymond seems not to have known it. Nor did he seem to be especially impressed by the extraordinary delegation from Washington. Perhaps, out of loyalty to the harassed McClellan, he would not admit in the *Times* what he knew, or confess that the official visitors meant trouble for the general.

Meanwhile, the army's advance postponed the trouble, and for several days before returning to New York, confident that McClellan could take Richmond when ready, Raymond and Jerome rode about the peninsula on horseback like a couple of tourists. Raymond was deeply moved by the impact of war. "The inhabitants of this part of the peninsula are on the verge of starvation," he reported. "The Southern soldiers had absolutely swept them bare of everything, and now the National troops come to gather up the gleanings. Their corn, their cattle, everything they had for themselves and their slaves has been consumed; they have no crops for the coming season and their condition is truly deplorable." Sometimes, when provisions ran short, Raymond and Jerome stopped at Negro cabins to beg hoecake for their supper. Sometimes they met the commander of the Army of the Potomac galloping along the road, for whatever his faults, McClellan was no desk general, and day after day he was out inspecting, conferring.

Because it was hard to justify staying indefinitely at the front, Raymond returned to New York in mid-May for a month of work before another visit to the peninsula and what he expected would be the final act. By the time he saw the Army of the Potomac again, it was within five miles of Richmond. Except for the inconclusive battle at Seven Oaks on June 1, when Johnston had been wounded and Robert E. Lee had taken command, Raymond had missed little action. Now, after all the rain, the roads were drying out and he saw that artillery could be brought up easily. That seemed significant, but while anticipating anxiously the military climax, Raymond reported: "No movement yet—nor any signs of movement. This unbroken quiet is becoming oppressive. Almost every day something occurs which renders it almost certain that there will be a general action tomorrow. Tomorrow comes, and scarcely a gun disturbs the peaceful air. . . . Everybody is desperately tired of this inactivity, yet everybody is perfectly confident that it is all right." With other correspondents, he lived at Michie's farm, a comfortable place where his Southern host served excellent food even in wartime and had a julep at a man's bedside before he arose in the morning.

On June 26 Lee attacked at Mechanicsville to open the Battles of the Seven Days that saved the Southern capital. When the fighting ended, a defeated McClellan had fallen back to the James. Lee reproached himself for not having destroyed the whole Army of the Potomac.

How much of the Seven Days fighting Raymond witnessed is uncertain. Military censorship prevented the sending of anything but the briefest dispatches while the battles were in progress, and these revealed little of what was happening or of its meaning. Presumably Raymond was present throughout, for he would scarcely have left the field after the attack began, and he had gone to the peninsula expressly to attend the campaign's conclusion. In any event, while New York was still in the dark as to what had happened, Crounse and another *Times* correspondent, who was probably Raymond, reached the city from the battlefield. Together they wrote a comprehensive account of the fighting and the retreat that on the morning of July 3 gave New Yorkers the first story of the disaster that had befallen.

All that day the *Times* offices were crowded with anxious, weeping parents seeking news of their sons, wives seeking news of husbands. Copies of the paper sold as soon as they were in the newsboys' hands, and extras that poured from the presses by the thousands did not meet the demand. On ferryboats from Brooklyn, in crowds that milled in Park Row, in hotel lobbies and along the bar of many a saloon, no topic except the news brought by the *Times* could be mentioned or discussed. Of events that day, the paper said soberly: "It was the good fortune of the *Times* to present the first and best account of the battle; it was all the *Times* could do, but the people wanted more, and many came insisting that there must be more and secret information, which if made public would console the great grief of the people or overwhelm them with disgrace." Later reports only confirmed what the *Times* had told, and

George Jones

Louis J. Jennings

Leonard Jerome

Raymond, the National Chairman

VANITY FAIR.

THE THREE BELDAMS.

Herald.—Posters of the Sea and Land
    We three travel hand in hand ;

Tribune.—Of each secret expedition
    Letting out the sealed commission ;

Times.—So that nothing private here
    May vex the rebel privateer.

All.—Double, double—nay, we treble
    Aid and comfort for the rebel !

A cartoon from Vanity Fair, Oct. 5, 1861. Northern newspapers were often criticized f
printing military news that could give information to Southern leaders and commande

over New York, as over the nation, fell gloom unequaled since Bull Run. Said the *Times:* "It is the heaviest week since the war began."

II

From the day that Jasper telegraphed from Charleston that war had begun, the *Times* had correspondents in the field. Some of them, like Fitz-James O'Brien, who in April, 1861, wrote vividly and brilliantly of the march of New York's fashionable Seventh Regiment from Annapolis to beleaguered Washington, were writers and reporters who had put on Union blue and doubled occasionally in the role of soldier and war correspondent.[2] Others were men who laid aside the grubby reporting of civilian life to dramatize army life and the crash of battle for readers of the *Times*. As the war pursued its bloody course, these correspondents, their identity usually hidden behind pen names or initials, told of it in dispatches written often by candlelight with a tree stump for a table, and hurried by telegraph, by post or courier to Park Row and the waiting compositors.

Raymond, who would have enjoyed it, could hardly devote his time to war correspondence, and except for the exciting days at Manassas, contented himself with occasional visits to the front where, as on the peninsula, he supplemented the more detailed dispatches of the regular correspondents. He had a good team, and was always alert to recruit new members for it. There were men like Lorenzo Crounse, who after Manassas and the peninsula, went on to report many of the war's great battles— Antietam, Chancellorsville, Gettysburg, Lookout Mountain. Twice he had horses shot from under him. Once he was wounded and briefly he was a Confederate prisoner. William Swinton, who like Crounse spent most of the war with the Army of the Potomac, was so diligent in newsgathering that toward the war's end he almost got himself shot as a spy when caught eavesdropping on a secret discussion between General Grant and General George Meade. H. S. Winser sent the *Times* the first full account of the fall of the forts below New Orleans in April, 1862. Walt Whitman now and then reported on the hospitals and the suffering of the wounded. When, late in 1864, the Union forces routed the Confederates in a cruel battle at Franklin in central Tennessee, the *Times*, thanks to its skilled correspondent Ben C. Truman, got the news four days ahead of the War Department.

That was the kind of work Raymond appreciated. He wanted the

---

[2] Adam Badeau, who had been a *Times* reporter before he became a member of General T. W. Sherman's staff during the expedition against Port Royal, South Carolina, in 1861, felt no embarrassment in combining military service with correspondence for the *Times*.

news, and whenever possible he wanted the *Times* to have it first. That was why he paid a man like Truman the generous salary of $100 a week. He did not always pay so much, but he always paid well, and he never let unusual achievement go unrecognized. On a young correspondent named Franc B. Wilkie such treatment made an impression that lasted all his life.

In the summer of 1861, Wilkie was watching the war in Missouri and sending to a paper in Dubuque, Iowa, letters that told of what he saw. Somehow one of them got Raymond's attention. He liked it, and soon, on the promise of $7.50 a column and expenses, Wilkie was writing for the *Times*. "Galway," as he signed himself, was still new to the assignment when in September, 1861, the Confederate General Sterling Price trapped and besieged a sizable Union force at Lexington on the Missouri. Wilkie set out for Lexington with a Union column that had been ordered to raise the siege, but when the column turned back, unwilling to attack Price's strong positions, Wilkie kept on. He had a wild idea—it had been born, he admitted, in a drinking bout—and it was nothing less than to enter the rebel lines for an eyewitness account of the siege. Wilkie knew that even if he escaped being shot or hanged as a spy, his chance of being allowed to see any of the battle was slim. Luck was on his side, and his hare-brained scheme worked.

As soon as the Union troops surrendered, Wilkie hurried to St. Louis to get off his exclusive story of the Union defeat. Even then the *Times* almost missed it, for Wilkie, short of money, had to turn to a famed *Tribune* correspondent, Albert D. Richardson, for a loan. He got instead the offer of $125 in gold for his Lexington dispatch. It was more than three times what Raymond would pay for it, and the temptation was great. Wilkie put it behind him, and Raymond got the story.

Many times afterward Wilkie told how delighted Raymond had been and how he had shown his delight: "He sent a substantial draft to my wife as a present. He gave my feat at Lexington a half-column editorial, in which he warmly commended my daring, my devotion to the interests of the *Times*. . . . He did more; he raised my pay to a salary of $30 a week [which seemed enormous to Wilkie], all my expenses, and gave me charge of all military operations in the West." During the next two years, while Wilkie followed the armies in the campaigns that led to the capture of Vicksburg, his salary was increased from time to time, but it was the pleasant relationship with Raymond rather than salary that tied him tightly to the *Times*. Said Wilkie: "I never saw Mr. Raymond, [but] I learned to respect, admire and esteem him above any other public man whom I knew. He wrote me many letters, some of instructions and others complimentary to my work. I never wrote a letter which pleased him that was not responded to by return mail, with his thanks and a compliment. He surely was the most appreciative, kindliest, and most courteous of journalists."

For Wilkie, as for all correspondents with the armies, a chief problem was getting dispatches to the paper. The unpredictable censorship of telegrams, as Raymond had learned so unhappily after Bull Run, could mean that a dispatch was held up indefinitely or cut to nothing. Nor were the mails always secure. After the Union defeat in the Battle of Chickasaw Bayou in December, 1862, Wilkie sent a long account by mail to Cairo, with instructions for forwarding to the *Times*. His letter never got to Cairo. The Union commander, General William T. Sherman, had it taken from the mail bag. Couriers, without whom many a dispatch could not have been delivered, were often unreliable. The *Times* missed Wilkie's account of the fall of Vicksburg because the man who was taking it to New York got drunk on the way.

Sherman and many another general hated newspapermen, complaining over and over that they revealed military information to the enemy, and the charge was not unfounded. After Halleck in May, 1862, had expelled all correspondents from his army in the West, other generals considered following the example. Such action set the *Times* quivering with anger. "More harm would be done to the Union," it cried, "by the expulsion of correspondents than those correspondents now do by occasional exposures of military blunders, imbecilities, peccadilloes, corruption, drunkenness and knavery, or by their occasional failures to puff every functionary as much as he thinks he deserves." But the *Times* was no stranger to charges that the Northern press printed information of value to the South.

When the Port Royal expedition commanded by General T. W. Sherman was about to sail in October, 1861, the *Times* published a detailed account of the number of troops and ships involved. It did not give the expedition's objective, which after all was the information the South needed most, but the very fact that the *Times* told as much as it did, and ahead of other papers, set off an explosion. Treason, cried the *Tribune* and the *Herald*, which surely would have published the news if they had had it. Samuel F. Du Pont, naval commander of the expedition, wrote bitterly to Assistant Secretary of the Navy Gustavus Fox: "Everybody is much disturbed here by the publication of the expedition etc. in the New York *Times* . . . under the villainous assumption that we had sailed. Of course it is all going over the Southern wires by this time and may add some four or five thousand lives to the list of casualties, but what does the *Times* care for that if it can be in advance of rival sheets." To all of which the *Times* answered enigmatically: "This publication of the departure and composition of the expedition is made with the knowledge and assent of the proper authorities."

A few weeks later, the *Times* published a six-column map locating the lines before Washington and detailing the divisions defending them. When General McClellan saw the paper, he got off an excited and angry letter to Secretary of War Simon Cameron demanding suppression of the *Times*. What the paper had printed, he charged, "is clearly giving aid, comfort and information to the enemy, and is evidently a case of treasonable action, as clear as any that can be found. You will remember that this same paper did its best to aid the rebels by publishing full details as to General Sherman's Expedition before it sailed. I have therefore to represent that the interests of your arms require the suppression of this treasonable sheet, and urgently recommend that the necessary steps to suppress the paper may be taken at once." Cameron, refusing to get excited, sent the general's letter to Raymond with the suggestion that in the future the paper might be more careful.

As was to be expected, Raymond rejected McClellan's accusations indignantly. He pointed out that the map of the works around Washington could be bought in any capital bookstore, that the names of the forts had been given in one of McClellan's own General Orders, that the *Times* had printed only the names of the commanders, not the size of their divisions. As for the Port Royal expedition, he recalled to Cameron that the story had been released to the *Times* by the commander at Fortress Monroe. "I repel in the strongest terms," wrote Raymond, "every intimation in Gen. McClellan's letter that the *Times* made either, or any, of these publications with any treasonable intent, or with any desire, purpose or thought of either aiding the enemy or embarrassing the operations of the army under his command."

III

Raymond's close and friendly relations with Lincoln and his support of the Administration developed only slowly, and even when the *Times* had become the Administration's defender in New York it regarded itself as free to blame as well as to praise. The famous "Wanted: A Policy" editorial on the eve of the firing on Sumter marked the high point of Raymond's uncertainties about Lincoln. Thereafter, he stood behind the President whenever he could. He supported arbitrary arrests and the suspension of *habeas corpus* because "the existence of the government is in peril. . . . If this government is overthrown, civil and political liberty must perish with it. . . . The temporary surrender of these rights is a small price to pay for their permanent and perpetual enjoyment." When Lincoln modified General Frémont's proclamation freeing the slaves of rebels in Missouri, abolitionists raved, but Raymond, on sober second thought, admitted that Frémont had acted without legal right and upheld the President.

The occasions for such support were many. In a special message to Congress on March 6, 1862, Lincoln outlined a plan for gradual and compensated emancipation. A conservative scheme, it put the burden of compensation on the Federal Government, the task of emancipation on the states. Because Lincoln wanted no sudden disruption of the social fabric, he forecast that the working out of his proposals would require a generation, and while many a radical opposed compensation to slave-holders, Lincoln defended it like the conservative he was at heart. "The liberation of slaves is the destruction of property," he said. Across the country, except among abolitionists, Lincoln's message was praised and for once the New York *Herald* and the New York *Post* found them-selves on the same side. But the *Times* restrained its praise, for while it liked the general idea, it thought the scheme as a whole impractical.

Such lukewarmness in the New York paper that called itself his friend, brought a quick protest from Lincoln. "Your paper," he wrote Raymond, "intimates that the proposition, though well intentioned, must fail on the score of expense. I do hope you will reconsider this. Have you noticed the facts that less than one half day's cost of this war would pay for all the slaves in Delaware at $400 per head—that 87 days' cost of this war would pay for all in Delaware, Maryland, the District of Columbia, Kentucky and Missouri at the same price? Were those States to take the step, do you doubt that it would shorten the war more than 87 days, and thus be an actual saving of expense? Please look at these things and con-sider whether there should not be another article in the *Times*."

Raymond, who was absent from New York and had had nothing to do with the *Times* editorial, acted quickly on Lincoln's prompting. "I telegraphed the office," he told the President, "to sustain the Message *without qualification or cavil*." For his own part, he was wholeheartedly behind Lincoln's proposal. "I regard the Message," he wrote him, "as a master-piece of practical wisdom and sound policy. It is marked by that plain, self-vindicating common sense which, with the people, over-bears, as it ought, all the abstract speculations of mere theorists and confounds all the schemes of selfish intriguers,—and which, you will permit me to say, has preeminently characterized every act of your Ad-ministration. It furnishes a solid, practical, *constitutional* basis for the treatment of this great question, and suggests the only feasible mode I have yet seen of dealing with a problem infinitely more difficult than the suppression of the rebellion. It shall have my most cordial and hearty support."

Raymond gave similar support in August, 1862, when Lincoln, in response to Greeley's "Prayer of Twenty Millions" demanding immediate freeing of the slaves, put the *Tribune* editor in his place by writing: "My paramount object is to save the Union, and not either to save or to destroy slavery. . . . What I do about slavery and the colored race, I do because I believe it helps to save this Union; and what I forbear, I forbear because I do not believe it would help to save the Union." Antislavery men were angered by this Presidential rejoinder, but Raymond hastened to applaud: "He could not have said anything more satisfactory to the country. . . . All loyal men everywhere will say Amen."

Support of the Administration could never in Raymond's mind halt criticism when criticism was needed. In the freedom to speak out, he believed, lay the real strength of democratic government, and he intended to exercise that freedom. So it was that he demanded Cabinet changes, attacked the draft as a "muddle" and a "disgrace," accused Secretary of War Edwin M. Stanton, who in January, 1862, had succeeded Cameron, of making "buncombe his god." He had supported McClellan against partisan attacks, but when the general was removed from command after his defeat on the peninsula, it did not seem out of order to say some nice things about John Pope, who replaced him. "You worship the rising sun," snapped *Vanity Fair*, "your consistency is an affectation, while your aim is a reputation for sagacity." Raymond had heard that sort of thing before, and, remembering the months that he had defended McClellan, he resented it less than *Vanity Fair*'s unkind cut: "When have you shown a patient and untiring devotion to an unpopular man or cause?"

For Raymond, men were far less important than the Union, and as the war moved ahead what he wrote and said was guided primarily by the possible benefit to the Union. Thus he could write in the midsummer of 1862: "The time has come which is to decide the fate of this rebellion and of this Union. If the war is to be prosecuted for the year to come as it has been for the year past, the success of the rebellion is a foregone conclusion. We can never crush it by the policy thus far pursued or with the means thus far employed. We must have larger armies, bolder councils, better leaders."

This independence of mind, as so often in the past, stirred Raymond's enemies to attack him. During the New York State campaign of 1862, the Democratic organ at Albany, the *Argus*, printed two columns of extracts from the *Times* that pulled together many of Raymond's critical views on policy and policy makers, a summary that to the unthinking seemed devastating. "Behold," cried the *Argus*, "the record of treason to the government, spiced by abuse of President Lincoln, slanders of our armies, and assaults upon our generals, furnished by [Raymond's] own pen." For Lincoln and Seward and others who knew Raymond well this evidence carried little weight. They understood the workings of his mind. Besides, his war record was above reproach.

IV

The *Times* had scarcely saluted the rising sun of John Pope before that pompous braggart had met with overwhelming defeat on the old field of Bull Run. Quickly he was removed and McClellan was brought back for long enough to give the North a bloody but inconclusive victory on the banks of Antietam Creek. He failed to follow vigorously Lee's withdrawing columns, and an exasperated President, confronted again with what seemed to be McClellan's ingrained dilatoriness, summarily removed him in favor of Ambrose E. Burnside, an officer who had already twice declined the responsibility now thrust upon him. Seemingly whoever the commander, the Army of the Potomac was tagged for disaster. On December 12, 1862, a little more than a month after Burnside had taken over, the army crossed the Rappahannock to storm the heights of Fredericksburg in a futile slaughter that left Union dead deep upon the winter fields. In the *Times*, the names of the fallen filled many tragic columns, and somehow it seemed as though the very listing of these dead spelled out the national despair. Burnside, "dazed, grief-stricken," commanded an army in which morale was low and officers had lost all confidence in their general. William Swinton, whose dispatches to the *Times* once so enraged Burnside that he threatened him with the guardhouse, reported that the army was unpaid, bored, disgusted. A "melancholy muddle," he called the situation, and commented: "The Administration looks with distrust upon the Army of the Potomac. . . . It might be added that the Army of the Potomac looks with distrust on the Administration."

It was this disaffected army that Raymond visited in mid-January, 1863, when he spent more than a week at Burnside's headquarters. News, false news it proved to be, that his younger brother James had been killed while serving with the 24th Michigan Regiment, had brought him down from New York. After a fraternal reunion, Raymond made the most of the opportunity to learn the state of the army. A horse and orderly were put at his disposal, and with William Swinton as company he rode from one division to another, talking to officers and men. He saw General James S. Wadsworth, who had once chided him for supporting McClellan and who now blamed disaffection among the officers on the desire of some of them to see him reinstated. Raymond refused to take his old friend Wadsworth too seriously, for he doubted his military capacity, and suspected that morale in Wadsworth's own command was none too high. One day Raymond dined with General Edwin Vose Sumner, an aging veteran of the Mexican War, who was "full of talk and keen loyalty" but who told Raymond little, even after they had drunk his excellent champagne. Another time he visited the commander of his brother's regiment, to whom he put the question of the state of the army. "He said," Raymond recorded in his journal, "there was a good deal of dissatisfaction—or, rather, despondency—among the officers and men, due mainly to a want of confidence in General Burnside. I asked him why they lacked confidence in him. He replied, because he had no confidence in himself." Burnside showed Raymond the medal's reverse, complaining bitterly "that he found it extremely difficult to carry any operation into effect for lack of cooperation among his officers." Finally, Raymond had seen and heard enough to send his conclusions to the *Times:* The officers were demoralized and responsible for whatever disaffection existed among their men. "They are a source of discouragement, of discontent, of disheartenment to their subordinates and to the ranks."

Of Burnside's self-distrust and the insubordinate, if not traitorous, conduct of his officers, Raymond got firsthand knowledge in the military incident that went down in history as the "mud march." In an effort to redeem his reputation, Burnside had decided to cross the Rappahannock again with a view to outflanking Fredericksburg and striking against the Confederate rear. For hours the night before the troops were to move up for the attack, General W. B. Franklin, on whom Burnside blamed the Fredericksburg defeat, and General William Farrar Smith argued with their commander against the movement, protesting that the enemy was too strong, that the Union troops were not ready. Raymond, reading in his tent, could hear the loud voices at headquarters as the generals vainly pressed their views.

On the morning of January 20, a cloudy morning with a northeast wind that threatened rain or snow, the files began to move. Raymond thought the troops seemed in good spirits. That evening, shortly after he had retired to his tent, "it began to rain . . . ; soon the wind rose and the rain became a driving sleet, and . . . the tempest fairly howled around and through the tent, and I spent nearly the whole night in thinking of the poor fellows who had left their camps, and would be compelled to bivouac . . . on the cold, wet ground."

All next day it rained and blew steadily, and Raymond, rather than venture out needlessly, waited in his tent for the cannon that would announce the start of battle. Late in the afternoon a frustrated Burnside returned to headquarters to admit that mud had hopelessly bogged the forward movement. Cannon and wagons had sunk so deep that twenty horses could not pull a single caisson. Hundreds of mules and horses had died in harness. About the best Burnside could do was to order up a whisky ration for the troops. He still had hope that the operation could be salvaged, though Franklin sent word that "success was impossible," and others echoed his opinion. William Swinton took Raymond aside to whisper that he had heard General "Fighting Joe" Hooker openly denounce the movement as absurd, "the commanding general as incompetent, and the President and government . . . as imbecile." What the country needed, said Hooker, who had made himself a military reputation on the peninsula, was a dictator, and the sooner the better.

Such talk and such outrageous insubordination shocked Raymond, who had been "greatly impressed by General Burnside's frankness, simplicity and noble truthfulness of character," and thought he had the stuff of a good soldier and successful commander. He recognized Burnside's self-distrust, but attributed much of it to want of support in Washington. Raymond could hardly believe it when told that General Halleck, general in chief of the armies, had refused to confer with Burnside on extricating the mired movement, which he had approved when it was in the planning stage. Surely, thought Raymond, that was no way to run a campaign or to inspire a general.

Snubbed by Halleck, flouted by his own generals, Burnside struggled to make up his mind what to do. At first he thought he would dismiss his disputatious and disloyal generals and simultaneously resign. Then he decided to resign and leave the fate of the generals to the Administration. At that point Raymond, privy to the soul searching, intervened. "You have planned a military movement," he said to Burnside, "which I take it for granted will stand military criticism. You have been thwarted in its execution by the insubordination of your generals. Why should you relieve them from the responsibility of their conduct by assuming the blame of the failure yourself—for this is practically what your resignation will imply?" Half convinced, Burnside hesitated, by next morning had decided not to resign. Instead, starting with Hooker, the darling of the more radical Republicans, he would dismiss his generals "as unfit to hold a command." He told his adjutant general to issue the orders of dismissal at once. "It is time," he said to Raymond, "to see whether patriotism or unprincipled selfishness rules the army."

Such resolution frightened Burnside's closest aides, who pleaded with him to show the orders to Lincoln before issuing them. Despite Raymond's warning that in such an event the orders would never be issued, Burnside took his aides' advice, and early on the evening of January 24, set out for Washington with Raymond as a companion. For a while they rode in an army ambulance, but when the driver got lost in the foggy night, they pushed ahead on foot, stumbling across the Virginia fields in inky blackness, falling over broken caissons and dead mules until they finally came to a railroad. Here they found an engine that took them to Aquia Creek, where they got a steamboat to the capital.

Burnside hurried to the White House, joining Raymond later for breakfast at Willard's. It was not a very cheerful meal, for the interview with the President had gone badly, and Burnside was starting back to the army with a sense of failure deep within him. After he had gone, Raymond, greatly alarmed by the sorry state of the Army of the Potomac, wasted no time in reporting to members of the government what he had learned. He called on Seward. He went to see Chase, a great Hooker man who only half believed what Raymond told him. Later, with Chase and his magnetic daughter Kate, Raymond attended a levee at the White House, and watching his chance, managed to get Lincoln away from his guests long enough to tell him about the army and Hooker's rash talk. Lincoln "put his hand on my shoulder," Raymond remembered, "and said in my ear, as if desirous of not being overheard, 'Hooker does talk badly; but the trouble is, he is stronger with the country today than any other man.'" That told Raymond how the land lay. Two days later, "Fighting Joe" Hooker was given the command of the Army of the Potomac, which he kept until June, when George Meade superseded him after the disaster at Chancellorsville.

V

As the war lengthened, Raymond's diminutive figure and well-groomed whiskers became increasingly familiar in the lobby and dining room at Willard's. Sometimes he came to Washington on business directly connected with the *Times* (hope for the repeal of the duty on newsprint had brought him on one occasion), but more often his visits were those of an editor anxious to keep in close if not always intimate association with members of the Administration and members of Congress. He had known many of them during his years on the outskirts of national politics, and they helped him now to keep informed on policies that were shaping and being shaped.

A witty and wise conversationalist ("he has a great fund of anecdotes, knows exactly where the point of a story lies and when it is reached"), he was a congenial and welcome guest in Washington's wartime drawing rooms and at its dinner tables. Sometimes he was at Chase's, where the sprightly Kate presided and one met members of Congress and men like Governor Andrew of Massachusetts. At Moncure Conway's he sat down with Henry Wilson and Charles Sumner and a variety of anti-slavery men whose views were far more radical than his own. At Seward's, long-time friendship made him welcome always, whether at company dinners or at breakfast with the family, and once after such a breakfast Raymond and Seward walked across Lafayette Square to see the President in the White House. Lincoln, thought Raymond at first, "seemed jaded and tired," but soon the President was laughing with Seward over a private feud that Raymond's old boss, General Webb, now Minister to Brazil, was having with the British Minister in Rio. Raymond decided that Lincoln was "in good spirits" after all.

Often the talks with Seward or Stanton or Chase affected the *Times* editorial page. In February, 1863, Seward rejected a French proposal for mediating between the North and the South, and the day before making public the long letter which he had sent the French Minister, he showed it to Raymond. This diplomatic document spurned all idea that the South, "an insurrectionary party . . . adjacent to the shore of the Gulf of Mexico," should be recognized, and it pressed the springs of patriotism when it asserted that Americans must settle their disagreements in their own way. Seward, always the advocate of a vigorous foreign policy to distract from troubles at home, had written his note partly for domestic consumption and hoped that it would strengthen Northern determination to press forward with the war. He urged this view on Raymond, who was easily persuaded. "I told him," said Raymond, "I would telegraph the *Times* to back it up very strongly." Said the *Times* next day: "Mr. Seward . . . upholds with splendid power the national honor, and puts in the clearest light the national spirit and purpose."

Rejection of French mediation did not lift the shadow of Napoleon III from the American landscape, and in the late winter and early spring of 1863, rumors of French intervention circulated everywhere. In New York men stopped Raymond on the street to ask what he knew about it, and others told him fantastic stories when he lunched or dined in the walnut-paneled dining room of the Union Club. It was not all idle talk, for Seward wrote Raymond that he was anxious lest France seek to break the Union blockade of the Confederacy, and in Paris Consul General John Bigelow, who had once worried himself half sick because he thought Raymond wanted the consulship, watched imperial policy closely, fearfully. Not until the Union victories at Gettysburg and Vicksburg in July could Seward and Bigelow and the others rest soundly.

Raymond's membership in the exclusive Union Club, which had a reputation for putting "wealth and fashion above character and culture," marked the place he had achieved. Journalism and politics had given him prominence, influence. Now wealth had been added, and when he lunched on the club's famous black bean soup with men like Leonard Jerome, he was recognized for what he was, a brilliantly successful man of the world who kept his own horses. He was in demand, as always, as a speaker. He held honorary posts on public committees like that which arranged for a great Academy of Music ball to entertain the officers of the Russian fleet which steamed into the harbor in September, 1863. Raymond, said the *Tribune's* Junius Henri Browne, "is in no sense an ascetic or puritan, but much of a practical optimist, who thinks the world was made for our enjoyment, and that work is necessary to pleasure no less than to health."

Raymond worked hard. Frequently he was at the *Times* until well past midnight, and whenever he was out of town his mind was seldom off the paper. The war had added to his burdens. At first he had been worried about its effect on finances, for the firing on Sumter had been followed by a brief business depression that cut hard into the paper's advertising at the very moment that public interest in the war boosted circulation. Costs zoomed. In November, 1862, the *Times* told readers that the price of newsprint had risen 5 per cent in three months. Correspondence was costing $25,000 more a year than before the war, and expenses generally were up $75,000. One way of overcoming costs was to raise the price of the *Times*, and in December, 1862, it was advanced from two to three cents for the daily editions, from three to four for the Sunday.[3] Advertising was already picking up, and much to the *Herald's* disgust, the *Times* had been made the official city printer, a plum worth about $20,000 a year.

Hard times did not last long, and as the war boom got under way, the *Times* had more advertisements than it could handle. For all its seeming preoccupation with the war, the North went about the business of making money with a zeal and a success reflected in new factories, new houses, new school buildings, new hospitals, and reckless, ostentatious spending.[4]

Bank clerks, hard hit by war's inflation, could complain in letters to the *Times* that a salary of $400 a year was no longer enough, but if white-collar wages did not rise, profits did, and wartime profiteering spawned a new class, the "shoddy aristocracy," whose only standard was the dollar. In reviewing the fall fashions of 1863, the *Times* remarked that

---

[3] In July, 1864, the daily went to four cents, and in September, 1865, the Sunday went to five.

[4] On a wartime visit to the United States, Anthony Trollope was struck by the "persistence in the ordinary pursuits of life," and went on to philosophize that "the truth is . . . that we, all of us, soon adapt ourselves to the circumstances around us. Though three parts of London were in flames I should no doubt expect to have my dinner served to me if I lived in the quarter which was free from flames."

"the question is not so much what is new, what is the best taste, as what costs the most money." For the *Times* that was as much news as the letters that young Henry Adams had sent from his father's London embassy and that early in the war, before the fact of Adams's authorship was disclosed, Raymond had been glad to publish. Adams's letters had been political, and so were many of the letters that arrived unsolicited at the *Times*, but neither politics nor war could keep the paper from following the intellectual and cultural interests that had been Raymond's since he was a boy. For suitable articles he turned as in pre-war days to the facile Evert A. Duyckinck, whose knowledge was broad enough for him to move swiftly from a review of a Dickens novel to a discussion of Theodore Parker's theology. When Thackeray died late in 1863, it was Duyckinck who wrote the three-and-a-half-column obituary for the *Times*.[5] Nor were art and dramatic criticism forgotten. The workers in that field were several and most of them were not much good, but one of them Raymond thought "really superior." He was Charles Godfrey Leland, who long after he had made a lasting reputation by his study of gypsies, remembered that during his brief service as a critic for the *Times* he "was paid in full in good money."

The planning of the paper, the arranging for contributed articles like those of Duyckinck's, the writing of editorials and sundry notes, explained why Raymond spent long hours in his office, where his pen seemed never to stop. ("If the days were a little longer he would write up the whole paper," some of the men in the shop used to say.) On work for the *Times* other business intruded. From friends, acquaintances, and often strangers came letters appealing for aid in securing political appointments. Sometimes there were letters of rebuke or rejoinder. Raymond tried to answer them all, most of them in his own hand, and many a time he put aside other work to send to the White House a personal plea that this man or that be given a place in the government service—a postmastership, perhaps, or military command.

Though usually considerate and kind, he took umbrage occasionally at the unreasonableness of his correspondents. Henry Bergh, who went on to found the Society for the Prevention of Cruelty to Animals, gave such an occasion when he assailed Raymond for failing even to acknowledge his request for a letter recommending his appointment as secretary of the American legation in Russia. "The mistake you have made," wrote

[5] On January 11, 1864, Duyckinck wrote in his diary: "For this [the article on Thackeray] and another on the [Pierre Irving] *Life of Washington Irving* Mr. Raymond today sent me sixty dollars—a recompense for such a service quite inconceivable from a newspaper not many years since."

the angry Bergh, ". . . is in having included me among the numerous political mendicants who daily importune you for assistance." Now it happened that Bergh's original request had gone astray, and when his letter of rebuke arrived, Raymond felt that Bergh deserved nothing more than the courtesy of an icy reply. He wrote: "I regret exceedingly that you should have deemed it necessary to assume towards me such a tone, and to put upon a trifling accident such a construction as to forbid my doing more than to acknowledge the receipt of your communication."

Such incidents were part of the day's work, but they were not necessarily typical nor the kind of business that Raymond thought worth recording. The matters that he emphasized are suggested by the entry in his journal for March 2, 1863:

> At the office all day. For the last few days I have been in a controversy with the *Tribune* on their assertion that Mr. Seward had sent dispatches from the State Department in the President's name, without first submitting them for his approval. As I had conversed with Mr. Seward about this I denied it, and he confirmed the denial in a telegram which I published. The *Tribune* . . . persists in its statement. The root of the whole affair, I believe is this: Mr. Sumner discovered a short letter from Seward to [Ambassador Charles Francis] Adams in the volume of Diplomatic Correspondence for 1862, marked "confidential" and saying that the pro-slavery secessionists and abolitionists seemed combined to bring about a servile insurrection. This stung Sumner, and it was said at the time that he went to the President about it and that he disavowed all knowledge of it—*Voilà tout*. Read Law on financial history of England during wars of 1792–1815.

VI

Chancellorsville had been fought and lost, and Lee at the beginning of June, 1863, began to maneuver his Army of Virginia for an invasion of the North. Lincoln called for additional men, and the *Times* printed an elaborate map to explain the movement of the rebel armies. Alarm swept the North, but Raymond was not dismayed. He saw in Lee's invasion a chance for Union victory. "If our Government and Generals are equal to the occasion," urged the *Times*, "this rebel campaign will close with their army broken up, Richmond captured, and the rebellion, already damaged by so many blows, will receive the blow of death." It was not easy for most Northerners to be so optimistic, and when Lee's gray soldiers crossed the Potomac and moved on into Pennsylvania, something close to panic swept the Union.

The two armies came together, almost by accident, in the wheatfields and peach orchards of Gettysburg, and for three days under the July sun cannon roared and rifles cracked until Lee fell back in defeat. Crounse told of it in his dispatches to the *Times*. So did another of its correspondents, Samuel Wilkeson, who in a long, detailed account of the battle included a personal and poignant note: "Who can write history of a battle whose eyes are immovably fastened upon a central figure of transcendingly absorbing interest—the dead body of an oldest born, crushed by a shell in a position where a battery should never have been, sent and abandoned to death in a building where surgeons dared not stay?"

Wilkeson like many another parent mourned the dead of the Northern victory, but amid the mourning there was rejoicing, for the day after Gettysburg, Grant took Vicksburg and the war's end now seemed close indeed. Bells pealed in Northern steeples, and buildings everywhere were illuminated. In Washington people massed outside the White House to serenade the President, and then followed the band to Seward's residence and that of Stanton.

The war was far from ended, and within ten days what the *Times* called the "left wing of Lee's Army" was terrorizing New York in the murder and arson of the draft riots. The draft law, an imperfect one and manifestly unfair, had caused much agitation among the working classes of New York, many of whom blamed it all on the Negroes, whom they saw as rivals for jobs. The first drawings caused the eruption. The provost marshal's office at Third Avenue and Forty-sixth Street was destroyed, and a mob, ever growing in size and strength, moved out from Third Avenue's wilderness of shanties to burn, loot, and kill. On upper Fifth Avenue the colored orphan asylum was destroyed; downtown, Brooks Brothers was sacked, and on side streets many a private dwelling was destroyed as riotous rowdies roamed the streets. Young Edward Mitchell, who watched the rioters from his housetop, saw one band of "men, boys and women, the very dregs of ragged terrorism, armed with guns, clubs, brickbats and all sorts of improvised weapons . . . led by a hag with straggling grey hair, howling and brandishing a pitchfork. She might have come directly into Fifth Avenue from among the *poissonnières* of the French Revolution."

The police, who did what they could before the troops moved up from the Pennsylvania battlefields, helped to save the *Tribune*, which on the night of July 13 had been attacked by a gang that did its best to set the place afire. Though the *Times* had been spared, Raymond prepared to resist attack if any there should be. He had the building illuminated so that its lights would flash warning of the *Times*'s readiness, and besides, the lights might serve to keep away rioters seeking to raid from behind the barrier of darkness. From somewhere he obtained two Gatling guns, which he mounted in the first-floor publication office where they commanded the streets to the north from which attack would presumably come. He took charge of one gun, Leonard Jerome of the other, and members of the staff stood by waiting to take on the mob that never came.

"Crush the Mob!" cried the *Times* when the first outbreak occurred, and in succeeding days, as the rioting waned and finally ceased, it hammered home the need for government to assert authority. Governor Seymour, no friend of the draft, was accused by his political enemies of being soft and ingratiating toward the rioters when vigor and force were demanded, and the *Times* joined the denunciation: "The duties of the executive officers of this State and city are not to debate, or negotiate, or supplicate, but to execute the laws. To execute means to enforce by authority. That is their only official business. Let it be promptly and sternly entered upon. . . . It may cost blood, much of it perhaps; but it will be a lesson to the public enemies whom we always have and must have in our midst. . . . The issue is not between Conscription and no-Conscription, but between order and anarchy."

Though the *Times* opposed suspension of the draft, arguing that it would signify submission to the rioters, the draft was halted on July 15 and this probably had almost as much to do with calming mob passion as the arrival of the troops. The "left wing of Lee's Army" had unwittingly aided the Confederacy, for the withdrawal of troops from Meade's Army of the Potomac handicapped pursuit of the retreating rebels. Meanwhile New York had damage to repair and injured to aid. To help the Negroes, chief victims of the riots, the *Times* urged special Sunday collections in the churches, and it went out of its way to help further a special fund for the police and firemen who had done such valiant work until soldiers took up positions on New York's streets and avenues.

18

"Union for the Union"

I

ON THE red walls of Bible House, flickering light from towering bonfires drew weird patterns that were repeated on the brownstone of Cooper Union across the way. Occasionally, a rocket etched the sky, and all the while men massed in Astor Place cheered for the Union and called for speakers to sound its praise. On this night in October, 1861, the People's Union party was holding a rally that had overcrowded the great hall at Cooper Institute and spilled into the streets. From inside the hall seeped now and then the music of a band, but those outside heard none of the patriotic eloquence exciting those within.

For Raymond, who had pleaded steadily for a wartime end to party politics, it was a great night. When Northern spirits were lowest after the disaster at Manassas, he had urged that Union Democrats be taken into the Government, and he had been overjoyed when the Republican State Committee in a move unprecedented invited Democrats to join in putting in the field a Union ticket pledged to "a more vigorous prosecution of the war." As a party, the Democrats had been unwilling, but many a man broke away to join the movement that early in September, 1861, had brought a People's State Convention at Syracuse and a Union ticket for the fall elections. Republicans accepted the ticket as all over the state men got to work organizing what ultimately would be the Union party. In New York, Raymond threw himself into the work, giving his time to committees, his voice to rallies. For him now, as he said over and over again, the sole question to be asked was not to what party a man belonged, but whether he would support and defend his country's flag.

Behind the Union ticket were men like Thurlow Weed and Horace Greeley, their partisanship momentarily dulled by patriotism. There was more than patriotism to Raymond's attitude. In less critical times, he had been ridiculed and assailed for suggesting that blind allegiance to party did not necessarily assure the nation's welfare. Now many men had come around to his views; he swam with the tide, and found the experience exhilarating. When he stepped forward on the platform of Cooper Institute to urge "Union for the sake of the Union," he got applause such as he had never known. "All parties for the moment are laid aside," he cried. "Not that we surrender party convictions or attachments permanently, but simply that now and here we recognize a higher necessity, a nobler duty, a louder call, that comes from the heavens above, and tells us that parties are nothing when the government is in danger." The cheers rolled out until it seemed that solid walls would not contain them.

At Jefferson Market three nights later, after the stalls had been cleared of fish and fowl, of fruit and vegetables, the People's party in Raymond's district came together to nominate him unanimously for the State Assembly. He accepted gladly, and he could hardly have declined, for as one who had advocated the Union ticket from the start, it would have been unthinkable that he should step aside. The prospect of his election set the *Herald* foaming. "One of the original anti-slavery agitators who have brought this country into its present trouble," it labeled him. It accused him of having helped to break up the old Whig party; it charged that he had been disloyal to Lincoln's Administration. On a single day it assailed his honor and integrity in twelve different editorial items, and when the election returns showed that Raymond, come January, 1862, would sit at Albany, the *Herald* growled that his election was a "disgrace to the city."

Though in part a personal tribute, Raymond's success belonged to the statewide victory of the Union ticket. The Democrats had been soundly beaten, and the legislature at its coming session would be in the hands of Union men, whether chosen as Republicans or as representatives of the People's Union party. It was almost more than Raymond had dared to hope.

II

Three days after the election, Thurlow Weed sailed on the *Arago* on a special Presidential mission designed to counter in both England and France dangerous sympathy for the Confederacy. For the first time in years, he would not be in Albany to pipe the tune during a session of the Legislature.

Weed left behind him a political situation little to his liking. To the Union movement in the campaign just past, he had given his blessing. He had worked for it, written for it in his *Evening Journal*, where in an amazing abnegation of partisanship he had said: "It is humiliating to find men only thinking of party when the Country is in peril." With President Lincoln he was on excellent terms, and the Weed forces had received many a choice patronage plum. Yet in New York the omens were inauspicious.

When Republicans in January, 1861, were maneuvering to pick a Senator for Seward's place, Raymond had described Weed as "the Sampson of the State," and had recklessly prophesied that he always would be, since "with Sampson's strength he has Solomon's wisdom." But as though a Delilah had been snipping at "Sampson's locks," Weed almost lost the senatorship to the party's hated Greeley wing.[1] His prestige suffered sorely, and the resulting decline of power and influence had been registered in the fall of 1861 when Weed men were kept off the Union ticket for the principal state offices. There was more to come, for soon after Weed landed in France, he learned that New York had chosen as mayor his personal and political enemy, George Opdyke, a Republican who at Chicago in 1860 had been hand-in-glove with Greeley.

Amid all these evidences of political decline, Raymond's election to the Assembly provided some solace, for the Dictator had real affection for Raymond and admiration for his powers, although he must have often wished that as a political partner he was easier to keep in line. By long-time association as well as personal inclination, Raymond was counted in the Weed camp, but it was an undisciplined association, and whenever principles or beliefs so indicated, Raymond broke away. He showed just that sort of independence when he supported Opdyke for mayor, and while Weed might have been persuaded that the course was necessary, since the alternative to Opdyke was the notorious Fernando Wood, he did not understand why Raymond had to be conspicuous at the great reception in Opdyke's Fifth Avenue mansion after the latter's victory.

Enemies accused Raymond of working both sides of the street, but his apparent willingness to be both Weed and anti-Weed did him no harm when at Albany he entered the contest for the Speakership. He had Weed men with him, as expected, and he also had men more radical than Weed and Seward on questions like emancipation. All groups knew that

[1] When his candidate, William M. Evarts, faced certain defeat, he had reluctantly accepted the anti-Greeley Ira Harris.

in experience as well as all-round ability he was the member best qualified for the job, and after he had been chosen, even the *Herald* tipped its
hat in tribute, while commenting sourly that Raymond would probably
use the place less to advance his party than to push himself toward a
senatorship.[2]

In the filling of committees, he had a chance to show what he meant
by standing above partisanship, and though members and lobbyists be-
sieged him at his rooms in the Delavan House and at the Capitol, he kept
his own counsel until in the end as hostile a paper as the *Herald* conceded:
"The committees are Raymond's and not the work of outsiders." He
had picked men from all parties. Some of the disappointed grumbled that
he had given Weed men the best assignments, but in general there was
approval for what he had done.[3]

Raymond had also tried to find for the committees men able to resist
the blandishments of the lobby, which had so corrupted recent legislatures that it had become almost a rule that on the passage of a bill money
changed hands. It was this sort of corruption, so often blamed on Weed,
that had done Seward harm at Chicago. Raymond intended to end the
business. Committee make-up was an essential first step because in committees legislation was shaped and often originated. Committee selection
was followed by denunciation of corruption from the Assembly floor.
The *Times* went into action, and ultimately Raymond so disorganized
the lobbyists that Albany newspaper correspondents noted in their home-
town dispatches that "money was scarce." Raymond had given the lie
to the *Herald*'s charges that under his Speakership "peculation and
plunder" would flourish, and had done much to make the 1862 Legislature the most honest in many a year.

Chauncey Depew, a new member that session, remembered until his
old age that Raymond was "by far the most interesting member of the

---

[2] Said the *Herald*: "Raymond, with the strategical ability which distinguished him
among the elbows of the Mincio and at Manassas, has gone up to Albany and entrenched himself in the Legislature, where the main, decisive battle [for the senator-
ship] will be fought."

[3] As Speaker, he was plagued with all sorts of minor matters, including the selection of messenger boys. He wrote his ten-year-old daughter Lucy: "I have had a
great many little boys come to see me. They all want to be appointed errand boys in
the Assembly where I am, because those errand boys get a dollar and a half every
day, and this will do a great deal towards supporting their mothers and brothers and
sisters. Nearly all of them have no father to earn money for them. In a great many
cases there are six or seven children whose father and mother are both dead and
there is nobody to take care of them all but one or two of the children as old as
Henry and Mary [Raymond's fourteen-year-old son and twelve-year-old daughter].
There is one very bright little boy not much bigger than Walter [Raymond's seven-
year-old] who has no father or mother and nobody but himself to earn money & get
food for him. He is one of the best boys here. . . ."

legislature. . . . The better I knew him the more I became impressed with his genius, the variety of his attainments, the perfection of his resources, and his ready command of all his powers." Intellectually, Raymond was a giant among pygmies. He spoke easily, brilliantly, and his longer speeches followed his custom of buttressing argument with careful analysis of cause and effect. He knew world history as well as he knew that of the United States, its Constitution and the debates that had preceded its adoption, and he brought his knowledge into debate so effectively that if votes had been won only by facts and logic he would have been generally on the winning side. In the give-and-take of the Assembly, he knew how to silence critics and to squelch the querulous. For his best sallies, he was sure of laughter, and applause regularly greeted his telling climaxes. No one who sat in the Assembly's semicircle that session ever forgot what a contemporary described as Raymond's "power as a debater, the politeness of his badinage, the refinement of his cutting sarcasm, and the gentility of his wit."

Raymond's ability to do two things at once caused Chauncey Depew to marvel. Said he: "I have seen him often, when some other member was in the chair of the committee of the whole, and we were discussing a critical question, take his seat on the floor and commence writing an editorial. As the debate progressed, he would rise and participate. When he had made his point, which he always did with directness and lucidity, he would resume writing."

More than the brilliance of a Raymond was needed to bring the session to life and to give it significance. Not a single important law was passed during that dreary winter in Albany. Debate dealt less with legislation than with the divisions of party and the ambitions of individuals. Behind these divisions were similar ones apparent in the Congress at Washington, where Republicans were separating into those who wished to use the war to abolish slavery and those who saw its primary purpose to restore the Union, into those who already talked of treating the South at the war's end as a conquered province and those who believed such a course unconstitutional. At Albany, Raymond belonged among the moderates, for while he hated slavery, he was never willing to accept the war's purpose as other than to preserve the Union. What happened to slavery was incidental. Since the war was being fought to deny the right of secession, he did not see how it was possible to regard the South as ever outside of the Union and therefore subject to a conqueror's peace. His ideas were still taking form in 1862, but they were fixed enough for him to oppose those extremist Republicans in the Legislature who looked outside to Horace Greeley for leadership.

Divided sentiment among the Republican-Unionists made more difficult the whole Union party idea that was so close to Raymond's heart. The radical elements pulled one way, the moderate another, and to Raymond's dismay his own friends in the Seward-Weed camp showed a disquieting tendency to chuck the Union party and to get back to politics as usual. He went to work on them. Ex-Senator Daniel S. Dickinson, a lifelong Democrat and one of the leaders of his party, sought to hold in line the Union Democrats. There were legislative caucuses in which differences were thrashed out and from which there emerged ultimately an able, stirring address that praised the Lincoln Administration and called upon Republicans and Union Democrats to banish "the heart-burnings and bickerings of party" while seeking the preservation of the Union and the restoration of the Constitution. Without Raymond's energetic diplomacy, the address would probably not have been adopted and the Union party idea might have been lost. Success in averting such an outcome was his greatest achievement in the legislative session that finally droned to a close in April, 1862.

"Political affairs in this state were never more promising," Raymond wrote Lincoln a few weeks later. "A thorough union on *principle* has been effected between the Republicans & the Union men, New York next fall will sustain your Administration by 100,000 majority." The results were to be quite otherwise, but in May Raymond had been unable to foresee the military and political events that would combine to make him a poor prophet.

III

The Union State Convention that came together at Syracuse in September, 1862, met against a background of military defeat and disappointment. The public still had fresh memories of the peninsula campaign, which Weed had called "Bull Run without the dishonor," and of Pope's disastrous defeat on the old field of Manassas. Only a week before the convention, McClellan had struck hard at the Confederates under Lee, and while the North hailed Antietam as a Northern victory, it did not escape the more discerning that Lee's forces had been stopped but not destroyed. Five days after Antietam, Lincoln issued the Preliminary Emancipation Proclamation.

Radicals like Greeley hailed it with joy, and Raymond was not far behind. Unwilling as he might be to make the war an abolitionists' war, he was glad if emancipation could be used to save the Union. "A weapon of warfare," he called the proclamation, and added that it held out "the promise of reestablishing the Constitution in all its old supremacy, and at the same time of removing that dreadful evil which has weakened its authority." That was not the talk of a Radical—the term was beginning to be capitalized—but neither did it place Raymond among Conservatives like Weed and Governor Morgan, who deplored the proclamation and were genuinely alarmed. Like many another Conservative, Weed feared that emancipation would serve only to unite the South and to make more bitter divisions already present in the North.

Every delegate at Syracuse knew that the shadow of military defeat would fall long across the political campaign so soon to open, and that the coalition of Republicans and Union Democrats would be hard-pressed to answer the arguments of Democratic regulars that the Lincoln Administration had failed both to save the Union and to win the war. Every delegate also understood that in the convention emancipation would be an immediate and telling issue dividing the followers of Weed from those of Greeley and accentuating the struggle for party control.

Greeley got to Syracuse early to perfect his strategy and to push the candidacy for governor of General Wadsworth, an abolitionist Republican. Governor Morgan, who knew that his hostility to emancipation made his cause impossible, declined to seek renomination, and, with Morgan out of the running, a gloomy Weed was supporting John A. Dix, a Union Democrat who as Secretary of the Treasury in the last days of the Buchanan Administration had earned immortality of a sort by his order to a New Orleans Treasury official: "If anyone attempts to haul down the American flag, shoot him on the spot." Raymond, who had first favored Wadsworth, shifted to Dix, so he told the convention, because he had been convinced after talking to other delegates while on his way to Syracuse that his friend Wadsworth could not win if nominated. Weed may have been the one who persuaded him that Dix, a War Democrat who would bring in Democratic votes, was the stronger candidate, and while Raymond disagreed with the Dictator on emancipation, he tended to stand with him in the struggle for power. Moreover, Dix appealed to Raymond as a symbol of the "Union for the Union" that he had made the cornerstone of his house.

As Speaker of the Assembly, Raymond had been described as the "most skillful, ready and efficient presiding officer in the State," and the widespread recognition of this ability explained in part why he was chosen president of the Union State Convention. There was another reason. He might be accused of attempting to carry water on both shoulders, and yet he did stand midway between the extremes of Greeley and Weed. Linked to Weed in some things, he was as sympathetic to emancipation as the Greeley Radicals. Both groups could support him; both did.

Raymond's opening address gave the convention and the campaign a keynote. He denounced the Democratic party, which a short time before had named Horatio Seymour for the governorship, as the party of "treason." He attacked Seymour as a man "whose sympathies have been with the South" and whose election would "give aid and comfort to the enemies of our country." "Treason," said Raymond, "lurks at our doors. . . . It seeks to clutch the political power of this great State, and throw it virtually and practically into the scale of the rebellion." It was a political attack that was a good deal less than fair to Seymour and his party, and it is hard to believe that Raymond really believed his own words when he spoke them at Syracuse or when he reiterated them in the weeks of campaigning that followed. Perhaps with an eye to the military record of the Lincoln Administration, he saw no other way of carrying the election than to make the issue one of loyalty *versus* treason.

If Raymond was disappointed in the defeat of Dix and the nomination of Wadsworth, and the rout of the Weed forces that it signaled, he gave no sign. He threw himself into campaigning with greater vigor than he had ever shown before. Night after night he spoke to New York City rallies, at least once in company with Greeley, and in late October he went upstate to swing through the chief cities and towns on a tour that must have taxed all his energies. Sometimes he spoke for two hours or more, pleading "Rally, boys, once more, for the glorious Stars and Stripes," urging that "we must strike blows at the rebellion—not at the Government," building over and over again emotional appeals on the theme that "a vote for Seymour [is] a vote for the Union's death." When all the hecklers had been silenced and the torches had gone out and the cheers had died away, Raymond came home to forecast victory, although by then he must have known that it was most unlikely.

Election night, the crowds began to gather early before the *Times* in Printing House Square, where clerks every few minutes pasted the latest returns on the bulletin boards. At Republican headquarters there was only gloom. The Union ticket had been defeated by more than 10,000 votes. In seeking an explanation, many a politician blamed Weed and Morgan, accusing them of having knifed the ticket, although Weed had given his support and had been called in at the eleventh hour to raise funds when the State Committee found its treasury bare. A better explanation lay in the field of war. That was where the *Times* found the basis for its verdict, the verdict that has been history's: the election was "a vote of want of confidence" in Lincoln's Administration.

After pondering the results of the election further, Raymond began to wonder if emancipation might have had more influence on the outcome than he had at first believed. Finally, he wrote Lincoln a long letter in which he outlined suggestions for removing what he feared would be the harmful political consequences of the permanent Emancipation Proclamation that the President was scheduled to issue on New Year's Day. "I think it clear," he wrote, "that any attempt to make this war *subservient* to the sweeping abolition of slavery, will revolt the Border States, divide the North and West, invigorate and make triumphant the opposition party, and then defeat *itself* as well as destroy the Union." If emancipation were used wholly as a military weapon, thought Raymond, the whole North, including the border states, would support it. "I suggest, then, that the Proclamation to be issued in January, *take the form of a Military Order,*—commanding the Generals of the Army, within every designated State and part of a State in rebellion, *to deprive the rebel forces of the aid direct and indirect derived from their slaves, by setting them free and protecting them in their freedom.*"

Raymond argued that his plan had definite advantages: "1. It avoids all cavil on points of legality and constitutionality. 2. It avoids the public odium and dissension inevitable in a more sweeping and less guarded movement. 3. It will free just as many slaves and thus attain the same practical results, inasmuch as no Proclamation can operate beyond the lines of our armies." Aware of the abolitionist pressure on Lincoln, Raymond added that "the only drawback I can think of is that such a mode of reaching a result will not suit those who deem the *mode* of more importance than the result itself."

Just how Lincoln regarded these suggestions is unknown. He was getting much unsolicited advice on his Proclamation, from both its greatest advocates and its chief opponents. In any case, he hewed to the line he had laid down at the start, and on New Year's issued the Proclamation that he had promised a hundred days earlier. Raymond accepted it without further questioning.

IV

Raymond first knew the United States Senate in the days of its giants when men like Webster and Clay and Benton filled the little oval chamber in the old Capitol with their eloquence. Time had brought new names and new faces, and the Senate had moved to a more spacious chamber in the new north wing, but the red mahogany desks were the same and some Senators still pinched snuff from the black boxes beside the chamber entrances. To be numbered among the members of this legislative club was an ambition that for Raymond was as hard to explain as to escape. Twice his name had come up in New York senatorial elections. Twice he had got nowhere, but the future was not wholly dark, and in 1863 opportunity rose again. The term of Preston King was running out. Weed's choice this time was Edwin D. Morgan.

Twice governor of New York State, chairman of the Republican

National Committee in 1860, Morgan had much of the influence and prestige and money needed to send him to Washington. With the rout of the Greeley wing in the 1862 elections, much of Weed's former power had returned. With Weed's backing, Morgan's election would have been certain had he not alienated party Radicals by his opposition to emancipation. Moreover, everyone knew that he had been lukewarm in his support of Wadsworth the previous fall, and whatever the truth, he found it hard to turn aside the charge that he had actively worked against him. Morgan was not much of a debater, and men were saying that he would not carry weight in a Senate engulfed by the problems of war and menaced by the dark issues of reconstruction. When his assets and liabilities were balanced, the chances of his being nominated on an early ballot looked slim, and should the balloting be prolonged, there was a good possibility that the party's Conservatives and Radicals would unite on a compromise choice, and one that Weed would approve. Raymond's friends convinced him that he was the man; persuaded, he went to Albany to look after his interests.

On the steam cars as he rode northward, he found a traveling companion in Horace Greeley, still smarting from the Wadsworth defeat and aware that for the present his own political power and influence were crippled. Greeley was interested chiefly in blocking Morgan's election. It would even old scores and rebuff Weed, and he was ready to use any instrument to gain his end, although at the showdown he could not bring himself to back Raymond. Greeley and Raymond must have made a strange pair as they rode together, one a disheveled bundle of ill-fitting clothes, the other neat and the tip of fashion. Though Raymond never held a grudge against Greeley for attacks upon him, he seldom had much use for Greeley's ideas, and no more now than in the days when Greeley had been preaching socialism. The two had disagreed editorially of late over Greeley's advocacy of foreign mediation to end the war, a position that Raymond regarded as little short of treason, especially since advocacy of mediation had brought Greeley into close relations with Ohio's notorious Copperhead, Clement L. Vallandigham. Yet the two men discussed the subject while they sat together. "You'll see," said Greeley, "that I'll drive Lincoln into it." Such ideas, thought Raymond, helped explain Greeley's loss of influence among staunch supporters of the Administration.

At Albany, Raymond settled into the familiar surroundings of the Delavan House, where Greeley and a good many other Republicans and Unionists also registered. Under the spell of the optimistic and reassuring words of the anti-Morgan men who called to see him, he gained hope and confidence, and he found further confirmation of his chances in the fact that some of the leading lobbyists were working for him. They wanted to be on the winning side, he thought, for he had not sought their support or indicated that he would grant them favors.

Prospects would have been bright indeed if Raymond could have counted on Weed's help, but an evening's visit with his long-time friend made it obvious that Weed would do nothing for him. It was one of Weed's blacker periods. The Dictator was not only out of sympathy with Radicals like Greeley and Sumner and Chase, but out of step with the Administration at Washington. He still found it hard to accept emancipation. His suggestions on policy seemed to fall on barren ground, and he complained to Raymond that his political influence was largely gone. Only a few days before Raymond's call, Weed had resigned his thirty-three-year editorship of the *Evening Journal* in a long and moving editorial that confessed: "I differ widely from my party about the best means of crushing the Rebellion. That difference is radical and irreconcilable. . . . The alternative of living in strife with those whom I have esteemed, or withdrawing, is presented. I have not hesitated in choosing the path of peace as the path of duty. If those who differ with me are right, and the country is carried safely through its present struggle, all will be well. . . ."

In his view of slavery and its relation to the war, Weed did lag behind his party and public opinion, yet his political sun, while past its zenith, was far from set. He was a good deal less than forthright when he told Raymond that he had written Morgan that he could take no active part in the canvass, and Raymond was too old a hand at this sort of business not to understand, for the word was being generally circulated that Morgan was Weed's man. Nor was Raymond deceived when the old man said that Raymond or Morgan, it was all the same to him so long as the Radicals were blocked. When he added that he thought that this objective had been already assured, Raymond knew that Weed would go all-out for the former Governor. The subject was dropped, and when Raymond dined next day with Weed and his family the senatorship was not mentioned.

Raymond refused to be discouraged. His friends brought good reports, and as he listened to their accounts of maneuvers planned, objectives sought, and the relation of all to the final purpose, he thought his chances good. Before long, however, he began to hear strange dissonance in what had been a pleasing harmony. Legislators came to ask for pledges. Some, and they must have known that Raymond would have none of such a bargain, promised to support him if he would agree to war on Weed. Raymond was willing to admit that he did not see eye to eye with him on many questions and to assert that as a Senator he would not be under his influence. Farther than that Raymond could not go except to agree that those who voted for him would be entitled to the same consideration as any friend. Any politician would probably have done the same, but Raymond had not long to worry about it. Warned that Morgan's friends were spending money for votes, and spending it freely, he was urged to start spending too. On it, he was told, depended his election. He indignantly refused.

When the Republican-Union caucus met on Monday evening, February 2, Raymond had no illusions. He had failed to build up a following, and since the anti-Morgan men had failed to unite on him or on anyone else, he knew that Morgan would win. On the first ballot, the former Governor lacked only five votes for the nomination. On the second he was chosen, and the next day he sent Weed a revealing note of thanks for "this renewed evidence of your friendship." The *Times*, rather half-heartedly, gave Morgan its blessing, and Raymond, with a pen dipped in the bitterness of disappointment, wrote in his journal that his only regret was in having been a candidate at all.

V

If the political cards had been dealt differently, and Raymond had gone to Washington in 1863 as a United States Senator, he would have found himself among men for whom his phrase "Union for the Union" held no magic. With the Senate Republican leaders, men like the haughty Charles Sumner of Massachusetts, Zachary Chandler of Michigan, and tough old Benjamin Wade of Ohio, he would have had no common ground. They hated the idea of party coalition, and their hatred was matched at the other end of the Capitol by that of the vindictive Thaddeus Stevens of Pennsylvania. These men and those drawn to them were the Republican Radicals, men who detested the old Southern aristocracy as much as they loathed slavery. They wanted to abolish slavery; some of them had been abolitionists before they were Republicans. They wanted to destroy the old Southern ruling class and its way of life so that the South might become a greater market for Northern industry and perhaps an industrial province of the North itself. To them the Civil War was more than an armed conflict; it was a revolution, and they intended to make the most of it.

Party coalition by its very nature meant compromise, but among the Radicals—the Jacobins, as Lincoln's secretary, John Hay, called them—there was not an ounce of compromise. To pursue it would lessen the chance of making their revolution real. Besides, the architects and supporters of the political coalition represented by the Union party movement were moderates and Conservatives, and the Radicals had long ago made it clear that they wanted to drive such men from influence in the party and the Administration.

Raymond had seen this at first hand, for he had been in Washington in December, 1862, when a Radical cabal, seeking a scapegoat for the Fredericksburg disaster, had tried to oust Seward from Lincoln's Cabinet. On Seward, and unjustly, they pinned the blame for counsel that had led to one defeat after another. Only his removal, they argued, would restore confidence in the Administration. Seward immediately offered to resign, but Lincoln delayed acceptance. When Secretary of the Treasury Chase, a Radical, rashly offered his resignation too, Lincoln had, as he said, "a pumpkin in each end of my bag." If the moderate Seward went, the Radical Chase would go too. He then refused both resignations. His neat spiking of their intrigue left the Radicals embarrassed, loving neither Lincoln nor Seward the more for it.

Seward had told Raymond the inside story of the Radical intrigue, who in turn told it to *Times* readers with a fullness and authority lacking in the heavily censored dispatches in the other papers. The episode—a political crisis of the first order, it had set Washington by the ears—outraged him, and in a long *Times* editorial he denounced the action of the Senators as an unconstitutional invasion of the independence of the executive branch of the government. What made him still more indignant was the threat to the Union party movement, for Raymond was convinced that if the intriguers had driven Seward from the Cabinet, they would also have driven from support of the government the moderates, Republicans and Democrats alike, who had become a mainstay. "Success," said he, ". . . would have been a public calamity. . . . It would have been regarded by the country as a factious movement, as aiming rather at a personal triumph—the victory of opinion on minor points—than at the consolidation of the North in hostility to the Rebellion. . . . The substantial union of the great mass of the loyal people of the country has been our strength thus far in the prosecution of the war."

In the fundamental quarrel between Conservatives and Radicals, Raymond for a long while sought to remain aloof. He recognized that the war would bring changes in the country, and he admitted freely that slavery would not survive. But at first he refused to concede that before the war was won there was need to lay down principles and policies for rebuilding the disrupted nation. He had written in the summer of 1862: "The great question in hand is fighting—and fighting only. The question what we are going to do with the rebels, or with the property of the rebels after the war is over, is wholly irrelevant and untimely." After the Seward crisis, he sounded a similar note: "The question now is not . . . how can the nation exist, but how can it exist at all. Death threatens it. . . . Relief must come quickly or never. . . . The prime concern is not whether your remedy is called Conservative or Radical, but whether it will be effective." Under such circumstances, Raymond believed, it was no time to talk party. Rather was there greater need than ever for all loyal men to work together to put down the Rebellion. In that cause, he was ready to place all his energies. It was as a public speaker that he could best serve.

Sometimes he made his plea at public dinners or in smoky party club rooms. More often, he was on the platform of great public meetings. In March, he joined 4,000 Republicans and Democrats at Cooper Institute, where almost eighteen months earlier he had first made the appeal, "Union for the sake of the Union," that he now reiterated. On a raw, gusty April afternoon, he was among the speakers who aroused the thousands packed in Madison Square for New York's greatest war meeting. "We are to have the Union preserved!" cried Raymond, while the aging, ailing General Scott, wrapped literally in the Stars and Stripes, listened from the Fifth Avenue Hotel's balcony. "If this Administration cannot save the Union," he shouted, sounding a note of party heresy that must have outraged every Radical, "then I pray God in Heaven send us another that can, whether it be Democratic or any other!" He was not renouncing Lincoln, but he was placing country above party. At the Union State Convention in Syracuse in 1863, he wrote into the party platform a plea that there "be no intrusion of the old partisanship," and when the Union ticket swept the state, he boasted in the *Times* that "it is not partyism, it is patriotism, that has gloriously carried the day."

The issue of reconstruction could not be evaded forever. Already the advance of the Federal forces had made pertinent the question of what to do with the peoples and territories brought under the Union flag. The problem was now not how to save the Union, but how to restore it.

As early as February, 1862, Charles Sumner had put forward his doctrine that in seceding the Southern states had committed suicide, destroying by their ordinances of secession all rights and privileges that they had enjoyed as members of the Union. In short, even if the Confederacy were destroyed, the South had no longer any place or part under the Constitution. This conquered-province doctrine was popular with the revolution-minded Radicals, but moderates like Raymond rejected it summarily. At Syracuse, Raymond had written in the Union party platform, and the party had approved, that rebels "may at any time resume their place in the American Union, subject only to such pains and penalties as they may have incurred by violation of its laws." Substantially, that meant support for the principle being advocated by many speakers on Northern platforms: "The Union as it is and the Constitution as it was."

The principle was expounded and developed by Raymond many times as he swung around the political circuit in the autumn of 1863. "We want the old Union provided by the Constitution, in which every State shall have control of its purely local affairs, and in which all the States shall yield to the authority of the general Government in those matters of common interest confided to its sovereign supervision. . . . It is that for which we are fighting." He used his voice in the New York campaign, and because of his spreading reputation as a protagonist for the Union party, he was called to speak in other states. He went into Pennsylvania, the first time that he had made political speeches there, and rendered what the Philadelphia *Press* called "effective service to the friends of the Union cause." There were several speeches, one of them in Independence Square, where the nation had been born, and one night members of the Union League and the National Union Club serenaded him at the Continental Hotel, where he was staying.

In Delaware, a slave state, the Union party was out to elect a Congressman, and to insure victory it brought up a battery of outsiders. Raymond was one of them. He took the occasion of his address at the City Hall in Wilmington on November 6, 1863, to answer with all his intellectual power and logic the Radical doctrine of state suicide. As a statement of constitutional theory, the speech was historic, and it was more than that. Reprinted, widely circulated, widely read, it did much to lift Raymond from a local to a national figure and to place him among the leaders of the moderates. What he said at Wilmington branded him forever as an enemy of Radicalism.

Despite its vigor, Raymond's speech was good-natured, good-mannered. He attacked ideas, not individuals. He refused to debate the issue of slavery; slavery, he said, was dead, and all that remained was to decide the manner of burial. The real issue was how to restore the Union, and to that he directed his powers. "It has been argued with ability and force in some quarters," said Raymond, "that the rebel States, by seceding from the Union, have committed suicide. . . . I do not find any support for this theory in the Constitution." In words that echoed the letters he had written to Yancey in 1860, he denied that secession was constitutionally possible. "The Constitution," said he, "has almost nothing to do with States as such. . . . It does not depend upon them for execution of its laws. It deals directly and exclusively with individuals. It makes a law, and it requires every individual within the scope of its authority to obey that law. That law is the supreme law of the land. . . . No State can release a citizen from obedience to the government's laws." That brought him quickly to secession. "No State," he argued, "can possibly take any one of its citizens out from the jurisdiction of the National Government; still less can it take them all out. In other words, no State can possibly secede. . . . Any act or ordinance which any State may pass for such a purpose is simply null and void."

If Raymond was right that from the point of view of constitutional theory secession was impossible, how did he explain the fact of the Confederacy? He had an answer, and it was fundamental to his position. Not the states, but their citizens, had withdrawn from the Union and set up the rebel government. The states had not flouted national laws; the citizens were the guilty ones who had taken up arms and thus committed treason. "The Constitution," said he, "does not impose positive obligations upon States, but only upon their individual citizens. It is, therefore, the individual citizen of a State, and not the State as such, that is to be punished for crimes against the United States. The State of South Carolina cannot be hung for treason, though every individual living in South Carolina may—and perhaps ought to be. . . . One of the penalties of treason is disfranchisement; but that is a penalty to be inflicted like all others upon individual criminals, and not upon aggregates or communities or States. A State cannot be disfranchised any more than it can be hung."

To make his position the stronger, Raymond argued that the whole war was being fought "on the assumption that [the rebels] still rest under a supreme obligation to the Constitution." "They are still citizens of the United States," he contended, "offenders against its laws, rebels against its authority. . . . The obligation of obedience to the national law remains unimpaired—and with that obligation goes every right which the Constitution recognizes or confers. Every citizen of every State is entitled today to every civil right which he enjoyed before the Rebellion broke out, unless he has forfeited it by some crime for which deprivation of his rights is the prescribed and acknowledged penalty; and in that case he can be restored to the enjoyment and exercise of his lost rights only by the remission of that penalty by the proper authority. But upon such remission he at once resumes them."

Raymond called for penalties. He wanted the guilty to be punished. He wanted also an oath of allegiance so that the Union could distinguish Southern friend from Southern foe. He had no wish for men like Jefferson Davis to sit again in Congress—he had told a New York audience that "Jefferson Davis would make a better Senator after being hung"— but he did not believe that the Senate and House of Representatives

The New York Historical Society
Andrew Johnson

The New York Historical Society
Gideon Welles

Frederic H. Meserve Collection
Thaddeus Stevens

The New York Historical Society
Edwin D. Morgan

Raymond's New York Residence at 12 West Ninth Street

would ever let the Confederate leaders return to Capitol Hill. For the rank and file of Southerners, the chief test should be acceptance of the Union and the Constitution. Said he to the listeners packed in Wilmington's City Hall, and here, in fact, he was talking directly to the rabidly partisan Radicals in Congress: "We seek to restore the Union. We have a right to insist that none but loyal men . . . shall have part and lot in the conduct of its affairs. . . . We cannot insist upon any party test. We cannot require adhesion to any party platform, or to any specific opinion on any subject of legislative action as a test of loyalty and a condition of exercising political rights."

Raymond had now fixed the pattern of his thought on reconstruction. What he said helped other men to fix the pattern of their thinking. Said the St. Louis *Union:* "The doctrine of State suicide advanced by Sumner and his followers is handled in masterly manner by Mr. Raymond, and its sophistry fully exposed. . . . All men of every party, who are genuine Union men and desire its restoration, and who are opposed to any adjustment of our difficulties that looks solely to the triumph of any political party or opinions, should early array themselves against these dangerous theories, and in the speech of Mr. Raymond they will find material for battling these false doctrines." Connecticut's Senator James Dixon, a moderate, called Raymond's arguments "unassailable," and the Indiana Congressman Schuyler Colfax, who was far closer to the Radicals, wrote Raymond that the speech was "one of your best."

The words were Raymond's, but the tenor of his arguments reflected the views of Lincoln and Seward, and with Seward at least Raymond must have discussed reconstruction many times. At Auburn that autumn of 1863, Seward had inflamed the Radicals when in discussing reconstruction he had said: "I am willing that the prodigal son shall return. The doors, as far as I am concerned, shall always be open to him." Essentially, that was what Raymond said at Wilmington. Lincoln's Proclamation of Amnesty and Reconstruction, which accompanied his annual message to Congress in December, put the official seal on Raymond's speech, for it offered to all Southerners, upon the taking of an oath of allegiance, full pardon and restoration of all property rights except in slaves. Only the Confederate leaders and a few others were barred.

With the amnesty came also a plan for restoring state governments. It provided that whenever one-tenth of the qualified voters in the Presidential election of 1860 had taken the oath of allegiance in a state "wherein the national authority has been suspended," they could establish a new state government which the Chief Executive would recognize. Admission of its representatives to Congress was, of course, beyond Lincoln's power, a fact that enabled the Radicals ultimately to force through many of their schemes. Meanwhile, it was significant that in bringing forward his plan for reconstruction Lincoln had not only challenged the Radicals but had ignored their doctrine of state suicide. The *Times* applauded: "We long ago took decided ground against all schemes of provincializing the rebel States. . . . The President's plan of restoring our Federal system to its normal operation, therefore, finds us already thoroughly committed to it in every essential particular."

To Schuyler Colfax, who was about to be chosen Speaker of the House of Representatives, Raymond wrote that "the task of reconstructing the Union will be better performed by Lincoln than by anybody else." Probably Colfax had some doubts, and certainly the Radicals with whom he associated were opposing Lincoln's reconstruction plan and calling it "silly." They opposed a second term for Lincoln, meanwhile booming Secretary Chase as a possible successor. On that issue Raymond also split from the Radicals, for Lincoln was his man. He intended to do all he could to help him win renomination and then reelection. That effort was to carry Henry Raymond to the pinnacle of his political career.

19

Lincoln and Johnson

I

E ARLY IN MAY, 1864, Raymond sent to the publishers Derby & Miller the completed manuscript of his *History of the Administration of President Lincoln*. Each morning for many a week he had risen early to work on it for an hour before breakfast, but now it was done, a fat book of almost 500 pages in which the President's messages and proclamations, many of his important letters and telegrams, stood beside Raymond's commentary on the Lincoln years. Though the enterprise and weary hours of writing had been Raymond's, the history had had Lincoln's help and approval, for the book was designed wholly and frankly to promote his nomination and reelection.

By the time the green cloth volume came from the press, Lincoln's nomination was practically assured. It had not been when Raymond began writing—"compiling," he modestly called it, and with considerable truth. During the winter and early spring anti-Lincoln Republicans throughout the North had talked of ways of blocking the President's nomination, and in papers like the *Tribune* much of what they said echoed in the columns of the editorial page. Chase, who had seemed at first the most likely man to beat Lincoln, had clung to his hopes for the nomination until in early March his friends persuaded him that he was getting nowhere. Greeley, after an ardent flirtation with the ambitious Chase, had then switched his interest to Frémont, behind whom some Radicals were lining up. He told Raymond that he was unalterably opposed to a second term for the President, yet Greeley, like many another Radical, did not want to get too far out on a limb. That could be dangerous politically, and as the months passed such men saw more and more clearly that their dislike for the President and his policies was not shared by the public. By the time the national Union convention met in Baltimore on June 7, their opposition had been cut to a whisper.

Such an outcome had grown steadily more certain after the Chase boom was pretty well punctured by the publication on February 20 of the "Pomeroy Circular," a manifesto issued by Senator Samuel C. Pomeroy of Kansas, that called for replacing Lincoln with Chase. The "Circular" met with angry protest. "The efforts to weaken the trust of the people in Mr. Lincoln," cried Raymond in the *Times*, "or to intimidate them into the support of some other candidate by threats of an independent nomination are vain. . . . The people, we believe, have their hearts firmly set upon being served for another term by him who has so faithfully and wisely served them." An embarrassed Chase offered to resign as Secretary of the Treasury, a course that Raymond urged, but Lincoln let him stay and one day when Raymond was at the White House told him why.

"Raymond," said the President, "you were brought up on a farm, were you not? Then you know what a chin fly is. My brother and I were once ploughing corn on a Kentucky farm. I was driving the horse, and he was holding the plough. The horse was lazy; but on one occasion rushed across the field so that I, with my long legs, could scarcely keep pace with him. On reaching the end of the furrow, I found an enormous chin fly fastened upon him, and knocked it off. My brother asked me what I did that for. I told him I didn't want the old horse bitten in that way. 'Why,' said my brother, 'that's all that made him go!' Now, if Mr. Chase has a presidential chin fly biting him, I am not going to knock it off, if it will only make his department go."

All the while, state legislatures and conventions, with New Hampshire in the van, had been adopting pro-Lincoln resolutions. The Union State Committee in New York called for his renomination. Lincoln clubs were formed in New York City, and committees and associations dedicated to his candidacy sprouted like seedlings after a spring rain. The *Times*, which at the start of the year had called for the President's renomination ("the public interests require the continuance of Mr. Lincoln at the head of affairs"), forecast that "before the National Convention meets in June the popular earnestness for the renomination of Mr. Lincoln will have expressed itself so emphatically that the delegates will find their business to be little else than a registration of a popular decree."

Just before the Union State Convention met at Syracuse on May 25 to pick the New York delegation for Baltimore, Preston King wrote Raymond that upstate he had found sentiment almost unanimous for

Lincoln. When Raymond got to Syracuse and had a chance to talk with Roscoe Conkling, Chauncey Depew, Weed and many another, he learned how accurately King had read the signs. He soon learned also that among the 300 delegates in Shakespeare Hall support of Lincoln was about the only thing upon which there was agreement; for the delegates, though Lincoln-appointed officeholders were prominent among them, were deeply split into Conservatives and Radicals, a perpetuation of the old feud between the Republican party's Greeley wing and that of Seward and Weed. As spokesman for the Conservatives, Raymond did his best to block Radical control of the convention, but when he failed he lost nothing in the old Dictator's eyes. Weed, who had hesitated long before coming out for Lincoln, at the moment was chiefly concerned with a convention endorsement of the President; if he could get that he was willing to postpone settlement of factional quarrels until necessity ordered. He was unalarmed by Radical control of the convention, because on the essential business before the house, the Radicals were on his side, a fact that the *Herald* noted when chiding Greeley for allowing Weed to win the game.

Further evidence of Weed's victory was given by Raymond's election as a delegate-at-large to the National Union Convention. He was slated to head the New York delegation, which with its sixty-six votes would be the largest at Baltimore, and that position alone assured him of an important part in the convention's work. Raymond's influence had a broader base than that. Some of it rested on his skill as a parliamentarian, his power as an orator, his broad tolerance and suavity. His ties with Seward and Weed and the friendships made in the years of political activity increased the weight he exerted as editor of the chief Lincoln paper in New York City. Most important of all, as the official biographer of the President, he could be regarded in some things as speaking for Lincoln himself.

II

At Baltimore, the New Yorkers set up headquarters in the famed Eutaw House, the city's best. Because of the war, there was none of the flamboyant hospitality extended at Chicago in 1860, and with the President's renomination a certainty, there was no need for the flowing champagne and marching bands with which Weed had tried to put across the Seward candidacy. John G. Nicolay, the Lincoln secretary who had come to Baltimore to whisper Presidential messages in the proper ears, was surprised at the small amount of drinking and the absence of roistering.

Though not a delegate, Weed hovered about the New York headquarters, his stooped figure and whitened head a constant reminder of the Conservative power that the Radicals so feared and hated. Senator Morgan, chairman of the National Committee, had come up from Washington to open the convention. Among the delegates were many officeholders and unknowns, but there were also distinguished men like Chauncey Depew, Preston King, and Daniel S. Dickinson. Of them all, none got the attention paid Raymond as he bustled in and out of the New York headquarters, talking to this man and that, and then moving on to buttonhole delegates at other hotels. Rumor, which events proved false, said that he would be president of the convention when it got down to business on June 7 in the old Front Street Theater.[1] Many an observer believed that he was the real master of the convention.

For hours before the Second United States Regiment band struck up the overture that signaled the convention's start, the New York delegation wrangled over a suitable running mate for Lincoln. Weed had favored Hannibal Hamlin's renomination, but sentiment was against it, and word circulated that a War Democrat was to be selected. Raymond had been pushing that idea for months—it was a natural part of his Union party professions—and he had come to Baltimore convinced that he knew just the man for the job. His candidate was Andrew Johnson, military governor of Tennessee, who had the unusual assets of being a War Democrat, a Southern foe of secession, and a man radical enough to please Radicals, but not so radical as to frighten Conservatives. A good many delegates were convinced that Lincoln had told Raymond that Johnson was the man, and while that was something Raymond kept to himself, the belief persisted.

Raymond's advocacy of Johnson split the New Yorkers, many of whom insisted that their own colleague Dickinson was best qualified to stand with Lincoln. The division followed the now familiar line of Conservative and Radical (Weed labeled the Dickinson men as "ultra abolitionists . . . radical demagogues"), but there was more to the division than political philosophy. It had been noised about that if New York got the Vice-Presidency, it would lose its Cabinet seat, and that meant Seward's retirement as Secretary of State, something Weed & Co. would not willingly accept. When Raymond called the Dickinson candidacy "a move to break up the cabinet," a Radical retorted that he did not think that that would be "a very serious calamity." Sometimes

---

[1] After the convention Raymond was inclined to minimize his influence at Baltimore. He told a New York City rally: "I have been perfectly astonished to find how many things I did that I never dreamed of, how many things I said, I never thought of saying, and how many most intricate, complicated and far-reaching motives I had for what I thus did and said."

the debate was pitched on a higher plane, permitting Raymond to develop his theme that the naming of a Southerner for the Vice-Presidency was "a pledge that the great Union party was what its name imports it to be, a party without sectional prejudice, ever ready to give the clasp of friendship to every loyal man from the lakes to the gulf." In the end, while he convinced many of the New York delegates, he failed to get a caucus majority for Johnson, though Johnson did get the most votes in a show of strength that impressed the convention considerably.

At one in the afternoon of June 7, Senator Morgan called the convention to order in the Front Street Theater, where the Democratic party in 1860 had picked Stephen A. Douglas for the Presidency. Nearly 500 delegates crowded the flag-festooned auditorium, in the pre-summer heat a steam bath that the committee on arrangements tried to make more comfortable by removing all scenery from the stage and leaving the back of the theater open. This thoughtfulness may have lowered the temperature, but it only increased the convention hubbub, for to the noise within was added the noise of the street outside, the rattle of carts, the shouting of drivers. Because the Reverend Robert J. Breckinridge of Kentucky, who was chosen temporary chairman, had so poor a voice that he could not be heard above the din, the convention was soon bogged in confusion.

Simon Cameron of Pennsylvania started things off by moving that the roll of the states be called for the presentation of credentials. A simple motion, it was quickly so tangled in amendments, withdrawal of amendments, votes of approval and disapproval, motions and countermotions, that the bewildered Breckinridge confessed that he had no idea of where matters stood. Andrew White, shortly to be the first president of Cornell, remembered that "when there came a lull of despair, [Raymond] rose, and in a clear, strong pleasant voice, made an alleged explanation of the situation. . . . He began somewhat on thesewise: 'Mr. President: The eminent Senator from Vermont moved a resolution to such an effect; this was amended as follows, by my distinguished friend from Ohio, and was passed as amended. Thereupon the distinguished Senator from Iowa arose and made the following motion, which with an amendment from the learned gentleman from Massachusetts was passed; thereupon a resolution was moved by the honorable gentleman from Pennsylvania, which was declared by the chair to be carried; and now, sir, I submit the following motion,' and he immediately followed these words by moving a procedure to business and the appointment of committees." Quickly adopted, the motion transformed into a convention what Raymond had only a few moments before described as "a mass meeting."

Raymond, a veteran in the drafting of political statements and resolutions, was a natural choice to draft the platform. Working presumably in close harmony with Lincoln and men like Weed, he soon had ready eleven resolutions that had something for everybody. While avoiding the pestilential issue of reconstruction, the platform called for fighting the war until the unconditional surrender of the rebels. It pleased the Radicals by demanding a constitutional amendment prohibiting slavery. It spoke for the Conservatives when it praised Lincoln and approved of all that he had done to save the Union. It did not overlook the soldier vote when it thanked the armed forces for their sacrifices and promised "some permanent recognition of their patriotism" and "permanent provision" for the wounded and disabled. An ambiguous plank calling for "harmony . . . in our national councils" was presumed to be an attack upon Lincoln's Cabinet, more especially Seward and Postmaster General Montgomery Blair, the particular targets of Radical critics of the Administration. Finally, in order to unite the interests of ail, the platform called for a railroad to the Pacific, increased immigration, government economy. It ended with a denunciation of the French adventure in Mexico and Mexico's puppet-emperor, Maximilian.

The convention quickly gave the platform its unanimous approval, and its praise to Raymond. "This man's talent is of national fame," an admiring *Tribune* reporter wired New York, forgetting that Greeley was no Raymond friend. "His work was done in the brightest style of art, and portions of it received a tribute of admiration which mere art never commands. The resolution demanding the extirpation of slavery off this continent caught the convention as it were around the waist and flung it into the sea of enthusiasm. . . . The resolution of honor and respect and love to the soldiers who fight and who bear wounds and lie in honored graves, brought the convention to its feet and drowned the orator's voice and suspended the proceedings."

With the platform out of the way, the convention, which as Nicolay told John Hay had "remorselessly coughed down the crack orators of the party," was ready to name the candidates. The irrepressible Cameron moved a ticket of Lincoln and Hamlin, to be chosen by acclamation, but the anti-Hamlin men would have none of that, and when Cameron tried to settle for Lincoln alone, Raymond opposed on the grounds of political harmony. Said Raymond: "It is very well known that attempts have been made . . . to convey the impression that the nomination of Abraham Lincoln is to be rushed through this convention by some demonstration that will not allow the exercise of individual opinion. Is it wise, under the circumstances, to take a vote by acclamation, which cannot possibly change the result . . . but which may give rise to misconstruction?" He had won the convention to the traditional form of nomination: a call of the roll of states. Within minutes Lincoln had been named. The band struck up "Hail Columbia" and the delegates shouted themselves silly while throwing their hats and canes in the air. A bemused Washington correspondent named Noah Brooks watched Raymond and the Tennessee Congressman Horace Maynard alternately shake hands and hug each other in a disregard for dignity uncommon to either.

The way for Johnson's nomination as Vice-President had been opened by Preston King, chairman of the committee on credentials. He had approved the seating of a Radical delegation from Missouri, and then had balanced it by admitting delegations from Tennessee, Louisiana, and Arkansas. All that flew in the face of the Radical doctrine that the seceded states were out of the Union, and made old Thaddeus Stevens growl. With the admission of Tennessee, Johnson became available as a candidate, and thereafter Raymond's missionary work among the delegates paid off. Johnson got the nomination on the first ballot.

By astute generalship, the Conservatives had come through the convention triumphantly. They had lost battles, but had won the war. Almost as a ratification of their victory, Raymond was chosen the new chairman of the National Union Executive Committee, a party post of paramount importance. Raymond, said Lincoln, "is my lieutenant general in politics."

III

Though the convention had left him exhausted and ill, Raymond lost no time in laying his lines for the campaign, and in setting up headquarters in the Astor House, close by the rooms occupied so long by Thurlow Weed. "Union men," he said in the *Times*, ". . . must prepare for the contest forthwith. . . . In every State and city and town and school district of the North, they should organize and carry on the struggle with unflagging energy until the sun goes down on the day of election. Documents should be distributed, speeches should be delivered, and private appeals should be made."

In the early summer, with active campaigning still two or three months away and the Democratic convention postponed from June to late August, planning had to be preliminary and tentative. Raymond started right away to compile lists of speakers and to arrange for campaign documents. "I suppose," he wrote the Illinois Congressman Elihu B. Washburne, "there will be some Members of Congress whose whole time will not be required in their own districts, and who will be willing to enlist for service, more or less protracted elsewhere. Can you give me the names of those whom you think best fitted for such work?" To Edward McPherson, clerk of the House of Representatives, he got off a request for a pamphlet "to show how steadily the Democrats have opposed the war in Congress—on propositions for men, money, colored troops, etc., etc." Raymond's own life of Lincoln, with a sketch of Johnson added, was being pared down to pamphlet size with a view to wide distribution.

Soon Raymond was in touch with Congressional campaign committees so that work could be coordinated. With state chairmen like Simon Cameron of Pennsylvania he drew close ties, and to Cameron he wrote in mid-July: "The delay in military movements and the postponement of the Democratic nominating convention seem to have suspended action & checked enthusiasm in regard to the Presidential canvass, throughout the country. We feel anxious, however, (I speak for the Nat. Union Committee) to know as well as we can how matters look especially in the States where the contest comes off first & will be the most doubtful. . . . I would like to hear from you in regard to Pennsylvania—how far your organization has been completed—when the active canvass will open and what help our Committee will be expected to give. . . . To what extent will you probably rely on us for Speakers during the campaign? What kind of documents can we get up that will be of most service in your State? Does your State Committee expect to make exclusive assessment upon Federal officeholders within the State for purposes of the canvass, or is our Committee to go over the same ground?"

It was well to have started early, for unless the armies achieved spectacular successes, Raymond and his committee would be called upon for superhuman efforts to reelect the President. War-weariness had seeped through the North, a feeling that the South could never be defeated, least of all if the Lincoln Administration retained the job of doing it. At the bar of the Astor House and along the verandahs at Saratoga—despite the war the resort was having a good season—men grumbled about Lincoln and his generals, and their grumbling drew strength from the tears of wives and widows whose men had died or disappeared in the months of endless war.

IV

In early May, Grant had struck across the Rapidan to launch his Wilderness campaign against Richmond, and while the official reports were optimistic, they hid much that was happening. On the day that the National Union Convention met in Baltimore, William Swinton told readers of the *Times* that at Cold Harbor four days earlier the Army of the Potomac had met with bloody disaster. At first the news was hard to accept—the *Herald* charged the *Times* with untruth—but by mid-June the facts of Cold Harbor and the failure of Grant's campaign had to be acknowledged. In a few short weeks the North had lost more than 50,000 men in futile fighting in Virginia.

To tragic disappointment was added humiliation when the Confederate General Jubal Early on the third day of July swept out of the Shenandoah Valley on a raid that carried him to the defenses of Washington. The raiders ripped up railway tracks, cut telegraph lines, burned bridges and farmhouses, and might have plundered the capital if they had known the weakness of its defenses and the incompetence of its defenders. The sour old Secretary of the Navy, Gideon Welles, wrote in his diary: "The waste of war is terrible; the waste from imbecility and mismanagement is more terrible and more trying than from the ravages of the soldiers. It is impossible for the country to bear up under these monstrous errors and wrongs."

At that moment, with volunteering almost halted, Lincoln called for 500,000 draftees to fill the gaps in the wasting armies. Many a politician was appalled, seeing certain ruin of the President's chance for reelection. It was all very well for Raymond to urge in the *Times:* "Let every man who cares for the deliverance of the country from its terrible dangers know no purpose but to do his utmost toward reelecting the President who is charged unreservedly never to yield to the rebellion." National chairmen were expected to talk that way, but it would take more than words to win votes from a war-weary public.

On July 7, Horace Greeley wrote Lincoln: "I venture to remind you that our bleeding, bankrupt, almost dying country . . . longs for peace —shudders at the prospect of fresh conscriptions, of further wholesale devastations, and of new rivers of human blood; and a widespread conviction that the Government and its prominent supporters are not anxious for peace . . . is doing great harm now, and is morally certain, unless removed, to do far greater in the approaching elections." On the Canadian side of Niagara Falls, he informed Lincoln, were two Confederate commissioners with full powers to talk peace. Greeley thought that the Administration should see what they had to offer.

Pressed by Greeley, Lincoln empowered him to bring to Washington "any person anywhere professing to have any proposition of Jefferson Davis, in writing, for peace, embracing the restoration of the Union and abandonment of slavery." Greeley set out for Niagara, was soon in contact with the Southerners, Clement C. Clay of Alabama, and James Holcombe of Virginia, neither of whom, he discovered, had credentials. Greeley, who had failed to tell the Southerners of Lincoln's terms, was still negotiating when John Hay arrived at Niagara with a reiteration of Lincoln's conditions, which now for the first time were disclosed to Clay and Holcombe and the public. The disclosure abruptly ended the talks. In a statement that supplied Lincoln's enemies with potent propaganda, Clay and Holcombe made it appear that the President had been ready to sue for peace, but that on second thought, perhaps under the influence of his more intransigent advisers, had imposed conditions that destroyed any chance for successful negotiation.

Those Northerners who prayed for the war's end were depressed by the fiasco. Those who wished to get on with the fight were no happier, for they believed it betokened a weakening of the President's resolve, and where, they asked, did this leave the Union party war plank so recently adopted at Baltimore? Raymond, who in a weak moment of his own had asked whether the President was wise in making "abandonment of slavery" a prerequisite for negotiation, since that made the war seem an abolitionist struggle,[2] denounced the "Niagara tomfoolery," labeled "any dealings with such vagabonds as these self-constituted emissaries of Jeff. Davis . . . peculiarly unfortunate." Let us have "no more back-door diplomacy," he urged, a remark that enraged Greeley, who was already smarting under public criticism of his role in the fatuous episode.

In replying to Raymond, Greeley so far forgot the truth as to say that Lincoln had started the Niagara negotiations. He also insisted that he had not been "required to impose any such 'conditions' as those embodied in Major Hay's rescript." Raymond, to whom Seward or perhaps Lincoln himself had shown all the documents in the case, knew that Greeley was lying, and he urged the President to publish the letters and telegrams that had passed between him and the *Tribune*'s editor. "It seems to me," said Raymond, "that the public interest would be served—& certainly your action would be vindicated, which amounts to the same thing."

Lincoln was willing, but he wanted to omit Greeley's defeatist sentences about the "dying country" and the "rivers of human blood." Because Greeley insisted on all or nothing, Lincoln reluctantly abandoned the plan, though he sent Raymond the correspondence, marking with a red pencil the portions he had asked withheld from publication. "I have concluded," he told Raymond, "that it is better for me to

[2] Charles Eliot Norton, an editor of the *North American Review*, wrote George William Curtis: "What does Raymond mean . . . ? Is he hedging for a reconstruction with slavery? If so, he is more shortsighted and more unprincipled than I believed. I never fancied, indeed, that he had principles, and I thought he had learned enough not to confess such bad ones."

submit for the time to the consequences of the false position in which I consider he [Greeley] has placed me than to subject the country to the consequences of publishing their [the letters'] discouraging and injurious parts. I send you this and the accompanying copy, not for publication, but merely to explain to you, and that you may preserve them until their proper time shall come."

If Greeley's meddling had contributed to the country's depression and despair and to the Administration's political uncertainties, he had allies among the Radicals whose maneuvers emphasized the division within the Republicans and Unionists. At Baltimore, the Radicals had seemed to join in the sense of party destiny, but the appearance was illusory, and among diehards there was soon talk of calling another convention and making another nomination. Weed hailed Chase's resignation as Secretary of the Treasury at the end of June as a "gleam of sunshine," but the Radicals were infuriated; the loss of their chief Cabinet representative meant increased influence for the Seward-Weed element. A few days later, when Lincoln pocket-vetoed the Wade-Davis Bill that sought to make law a Congressional plan of reconstruction, Radical anger knew no bounds.

The Radicals waited for more than a month and then, with the nation's morale at low ebb after the summer defeats in Virginia and the abortive Niagara peace talks, sent to the *Tribune* the amazing document that history knows as the Wade-Davis Manifesto. Signed by Senator Benjamin F. Wade of Ohio and Representative Henry Winter Davis of Maryland, the Manifesto assailed Lincoln for his veto of their bill, accused him of usurping the powers of Congress by insisting on his own plan for reconstruction, of using his plan to place "the electoral votes of the Rebel States at the dictation of his personal ambition." In rash, rough words, the Manifesto asserted the supremacy of Congress, hinted at impeachment of the President. "The assaults of these men on the Administration may break it down," said Secretary Welles, and in Raymond, as in many a Lincoln friend, stirred a great fear lest the Radicals tear the Union party in two and make impossible the President's reelection.

V

From state chairmen and from other correspondents, Raymond got only discouraging reports of the public temper. "I find everywhere," he told Cameron, "a conviction that we need a change, that the war languishes under Mr. Lincoln and that he *cannot* or *will* not give us peace. . . . The country is tired & sick of the war & is longing for peace: at the same time I believe they would scorn & scout any peace that involved disunion; but the faintest hope of peace *with* union is hailed with infinite satisfaction. I fear that the desire for peace, aided by the impression or suspicion even that Mr. Lincoln . . . is fighting not for the Union but for the abolition of slavery,[3] and by the draft, the tax, the lack of victories, the discontent with the Cabinet and the other influences that are swelling the tide of hostility to the Administration will overbear it and give the control of everything to the Opposition."

When the National Committee met at the Astor House on August 22, Raymond could report only gloom and despair in every quarter. He canvassed the situation with the other members, then sat down to tell Lincoln that "the tide is setting strongly against us. Hon. E. B. Washburne writes that 'were an election to be held now in Illinois we should be beaten.' Mr. Cameron writes that Pennsylvania is against us. Gov. Morton writes that nothing but the most strenuous efforts can carry Indiana. This State, according to the best information I can get, would go 50,000 against us tomorrow. And so of the rest."

The President's political lieutenant general thought he knew the reasons for the popular dissatisfaction, and in one of the frankest letters he ever wrote Lincoln told what they were: "The want of military successes, and the impression in some minds, the fear and suspicion in others, that we are not to have peace *in any event* under this Administration until Slavery is abandoned. In some way or other the suspicion is widely diffused that we *can* have peace with union if we would."

Then the worried Raymond laid before Lincoln a proposal so extraordinary that the President must have wondered if the national chairman had let his fears run away with his wits. It was for nothing less than the appointment of a commission "to make distinct proffers of peace to Davis, as the head of the rebel armies, on the sole condition of acknowledging the supremacy of the Constitution, all other questions to be settled in a convention of the people of all the States." Raymond, who had won the National Committee to the idea, argued that the Confederacy would be certain to reject any such proposals—an unofficial mission had been told only a few weeks earlier that the Confederacy's first demand was for independence—and that rejection would immediately

---

[3] Charles A. Dana, then Assistant Secretary of War, disputed Raymond's contention that Lincoln should have omitted "abandonment of slavery" from his conditions for the Niagara negotiations. Dana wrote: "If the President had left slavery out of his letter, he would have done himself and his party a great injury, hopelessly alienating the great part of the Radicals. As you are very well aware, he is more or less under suspicion of a want of earnestness upon this supreme question and if in such a communication he had omitted all reference to it, people would have taken for granted that he was willing to sacrifice his emancipation proclamation and let the Southern States come back with their old power."

dispel the "delusions" about peace so widely held in the North. The whole scheme, said Raymond, is "calculated to do good—& incapable of doing harm. . . . It would rouse and concentrate the loyalty of the country &, unless I am greatly mistaken, give us an easy & a fruitful victory."

Lincoln wanted no more peace talks, but he could hardly brush aside proposals that Raymond as national chairman brought forward. He decided that Raymond, if he thought his scheme so sound, should go to Richmond to "obtain, if possible, a conference of peace," and with his own hand Lincoln drafted the instructions. Then he talked the plan over with some of his Cabinet. They opposed it, and when Raymond arrived in Washington to urge his ideas in person, convinced him that instead of strengthening the Administration's position, his wild plan would do irreparable harm.[4] Lincoln folded the instructions that he had drafted and quietly put them away.

That day, August 25, the National Committeemen met in Washington amid rumors that they were going to win the Administration to a policy of peace. They arrived, Lincoln's secretaries recalled, in "depression and panic." Lincoln, however, persuaded them that the outlook was not so dark as they supposed. For one thing, the Wade-Davis Manifesto had not won the support that its authors had expected. Moreover, there was still chance for victory in the field: Sherman was close to Atlanta, and the country had taken heart from the recent destruction of the famed Confederate raider *Alabama* and the naval successes in Mobile Bay. In the end, "encouraged and cheered," the committee issued an optimistic statement of confidence in Lincoln's reelection (though the President himself thought reelection unlikely), and the *Times* next day denied that the Government had had any thought of peace negotiations. "Its sole and undivided purpose is to prosecute the war until the rebellion is quelled."

VI

"The political skies begin to brighten," said the *Times* on September 6. "The friends of the Government, the defenders of the Constitution, the supporters of the Union ticket are full of courage and confidence." The pealing bells after Sherman's capture of Atlanta on September 2 had heralded the new day, and from the popular rejoicing over the year's first great victory, the North took on fresh hope, fresh assurance. In that

---

[4] Welles wrote in his diary: "Calling on the President near eleven o'clock, I went in as usual unannounced, the waiter throwing open the door as I approached. I found Messrs. Seward, Fessenden and Stanton with Raymond . . . in consultation with the President. The President was making some statement as to a document of his. . . ."

dawn the demand for peace adopted at the Democratic Convention on August 30 looked abject indeed, and no amount of amendment by General McClellan, the Democratic candidate, could make it seem otherwise. Already, the Radicals were creeping back to the Union tent. "The tide has been strongly in our favor since the erection of the Rebel platform at Chicago & the fall of one at Atlanta," James G. Blaine, the Maine state chairman wrote Raymond. "Our gains are continuous, daily and large."

Raymond, plugging away at campaign organization, knew that one military victory would not necessarily win an election. He had to get his speakers onto the platform, his pamphlets into thousands of hands. Most of all he needed money for expenses. Appeals for funds kept coming to him, but the committee treasury was embarrassingly empty, and the Administration was doing little to help him out. "I have spent the best part of four weeks at Washington," he wrote Schuyler Colfax on September 20, "trying to get the Government to help elect itself . . . but to no purpose." In his diary John Hay wrote that "Raymond went away a good deal discouraged about money matters."

Following established custom, Raymond wanted to assess Federal employees for political contributions, but the arrangements proved difficult to make, although under pressure the War and Treasury Departments and the Post Office ultimately fell into line. The Navy Department gave him a lot of trouble. Secretary Welles, a man with an Old Testament prophet's hatred for the Seward-Weed machine, had no use for Raymond. "An unscrupulous soldier of fortune," he snorted, "a political vagabond." "The *Times*," said Welles, "is a stipendiary sheet; its principal editor, Raymond, mercenary, possessing talent but a subservient follower of Weed and Seward." With a moralist's view of politics, he had as little sympathy as understanding for Raymond's money-raising problems.

"I met R. some days since at the President's, with whom he was closeted," said Welles on one occasion. "At first I did not recognize Raymond, who was sitting near the President conversing in a low tone of voice. Indeed, I did not look at him, supposing he was some ordinary visitor, until the President remarked, 'Here he is; it is as good a time as any to bring up the question.'" Raymond wanted to discuss the Brooklyn Navy Yard, where the commandant had been blocking party collections, and he urged that for the good of the cause the commandant should be removed. Later he argued, at least so Welles interpreted it, that the yard should become "a party machine," that it should employ "men to elect candidates instead of building ships." "I am amazed," said Welles, "that Raymond should debase himself so far as to submit such a proposition, and more that he expects me to enforce it."

Again and again Raymond tried to persuade Welles to cooperate. Failing himself to win the bearded patriarch, he sent one agent after another, but Welles was adamant. The system of assessments Welles detested. "To a great extent," he growled, "the money so raised is misused, misapplied, and perverted and prostituted. A set of harpies and adventurers pocket a large portion of the money extorted." To his diary he confided: "I am not sufficiently ductile for Mr. Raymond. He says I am unapproachable, a wall that he cannot penetrate or get over."

How far Raymond was ever able to move in on the navy yards is hard to tell, but that he made some progress is certain, for in the weeks before election men were let out in the Brooklyn Navy Yard because they were supporting McClellan. Meanwhile, at least in New York City, he was having much more success with the post office and custom house.

At the beginning of September, Lincoln had removed Hiram Barney, who as collector of the port of New York had been regarded as too friendly to Chase, and replaced him with Simeon Draper, a long-time friend of Weed, though the two men were momentarily estranged because of Draper's increasing Radicalism. He also shifted Abram Wakeman, another Weed follower, from the postmastership to the surveyor's office, and put James Kelly, still another Weed man, at the post office. All that business made it easier for Raymond to make his assessments; custom house employees were told that they were expected to ante 5 per cent of their annual salary. "Raymond," said the *Herald*, "walks into the Post Office and Custom House and collects his bills like one having authority." He did not stop there. In addition to dunning business houses—Phelps, Dodge & Co., the New York metals firm, sent him $3,000, with the promise of more if it were needed—he asked for help from contractors who were making money from government work. "The need of funds is pressing," he told one of these, "and the time for using them is short." "Every man who sells a pound of pork or a dose of medicine," gibed the *World*, "is expected to walk up to the office of the committee and hand in his contribution." Raymond, the *Herald* sneered, is "a kind of political Mosby,[5] whose greatest exploit consists of making home raids on the Post Office, medical contractors and the Custom House for funds to carry on the election."

However reprehensible in the eyes of a Gideon Welles, such practices began before long to fatten the party purse. "We are not in funds at present," Raymond had written Cameron in late summer, "but hope to have enough for useful purposes in time." Despite the moments when such assurance seemed vain boasting, Raymond was able to promise Cameron by mid-September that he would do everything possible to

[5] John S. Mosby, best known and most spectacular of the Confederate raiders.

help the party in Pennsylvania. He added wryly: "That State *ought* to furnish money enough to supply her own wants & give some help outside." When Speaker Schuyler Colfax complained that he was having a hard time in his Indiana district, Raymond sent him $500, told him that he could have $500 more if he needed it for the "final pull." "Your scalp shan't adorn the rebel wigwam if we can help it," Raymond wrote him confidently.

Though the National Committee dispatched $4,000 to New Hampshire, William E. Chandler, the state chairman, whined that it was not enough. "By close economy," he said, "by paying . . . speakers . . . almost nothing, we can just manage to pay our printing & telegraphing, our speakers' bills; & here & there very sparingly help a very close town." Chandler's report was so pessimistic that Raymond sent him an additional $5,000. To Indiana went $25,000 ("If you don't carry the State it won't be *our* fault," Raymond told E. B. Washburne), to Maine $3,500, and to doubtful states and districts everywhere went offers of help. "We should be very glad of anything we may properly have of sinews of war," replied Roscoe Conkling from upstate New York, and Raymond found in few quarters party leaders so confident or so proud that they spurned money when offered.

As the campaign got up a full head of steam, hardly a night passed in Northern cities and towns without a Union rally and a patriotic address. Many of the speakers had been recruited by Raymond. "Will it not be possible for you to make a trip North & East during the canvass and make a few speeches at the most important points?" he asked Andrew Johnson, who answered by swinging through the Middle West and the border country. "I wish very much that you would come into our State for four or five days about the middle of October," Raymond told the Massachusetts Governor, John A. Andrew, who was soon making a spectacular progress from Albany to Buffalo, speaking to thousands at every stop. Though pressed to lend his own voice to the campaign oratory, Raymond kept his speaking engagements as few as possible, and tried to limit even those to New York City meetings where he would not be too far from the Astor House.

Reports from the campaign were growing more and more optimistic, and on October 11, Pennsylvania, Ohio, and Indiana, following in the steps of Vermont and Maine, gave Union majorities in their state elections. "The great States of Pennsylvania, Ohio and Indiana," crowed the *Times*, "yesterday gave their popular verdict in favor of the Union, the prosecution of the war against the rebellion to its successful conclusion, and in favor of the present administration of the government." Though Raymond later said that these elections gave certain portent of "what was to be the result in November," he was not so sure at the time. "Take care," he warned, "that the very splendor of these victories does not betray you into fatal inactivity."

For him, as for every other commander in the political warfare, there could be no rest until election day. The soldiers' votes had to be assured. The party organization had to be kept at high pitch. Always the Democrats had to be countered, and how much Raymond knew of the high-handed measures that were sometimes used, he never told. At a roaring rally in Cooper Union shortly after the October elections and after General Philip Sheridan's sweep through the Shenandoah Valley, Raymond set off a demonstration of his partisans when he cried: "We have at last fallen upon the era of victories." He intended to do everything in his power to make that era lasting.

VII

"I have . . . a small matter to attend to in my own Congressional District," Raymond wrote Cadwallader Biddle of Philadelphia on October 29, "and propose to devote as much of the time remaining as possible to that." Earlier in the month he had been nominated for Congress, and had straightway found himself in a pretty mess. It was bad enough that the district was generally regarded as a Tammany stronghold, although with two Democratic candidates contesting for the seat, Tammany's grip was not as tight as it had been in years gone by. In fact, Raymond would have looked with delight at quarreling foes had he not been the victim of division within his own party.

The same night that a convention called by the Union Central Committee had nominated Raymond, a rival convention called by the Union General Committee had named the dashing Colonel Rush C. Hawkins, who at the start of the war had raised a regiment of Zouaves that had won battle honors at Roanoke Island and elsewhere along the North Carolina coast. The existence of the two committees made as little sense as their insistence on naming rival candidates. William A. Darling, chairman of the Central Committee, was a Weed man, but so until recently had been Simeon Draper, the chairman of the General Committee and the newly named collector of the port. Unquestionably Draper knew that Raymond and Weed had opposed his appointment to the collectorship, had favored Postmaster Abram Wakeman instead, but all that was past.

Raymond and Draper were working hand-in-glove in the assessment of Custom House workers for the Lincoln campaign, and in the *Times* Raymond had been lavish with praises for the way Draper had tackled the collectorship. Any desire for personal revenge would have seemed easy to repress, and political wisdom should have dictated suppression of the factionalism that was jeopardizing the party's chances in the Sixth Congressional District.

When accepting the nomination, Raymond had reserved the right to withdraw if withdrawal would further party harmony, and almost immediately he started negotiations with Hawkins with a view to ending what was fast developing into a most unhappy feud. Negotiations got nowhere, and perhaps it was too much to expect that they would, although Raymond had been conciliatory until convinced that Hawkins, a hothead who thrived on controversy, had no intention of agreeing to anything. Meanwhile, the press took up the row. While the *Herald* blasted Raymond, praised his rival, the *Tribune* did its best to stay neutral. The *Post*, for all its hostility to Weed & Co., inclined toward Raymond. In distant Massachusetts the Springfield *Republican* pointed to Raymond's "national reputation and eminent qualifications for service in Congress," and deplored the "singularly bad habit" of New York Republicans of "throwing away their opportunities."

The unprofitable character of this sort of business was apparently borne in upon Simeon Draper and many of the men who had originally supported Hawkins, for on election eve they switched to Raymond. "His strong attachment to the cause of the Union," they said in a public circular, "his learning and eloquence, and his parliamentary experience, point him out as the one among all the candidates who is pre-eminently fitted for the place in times like these." Though late, the endorsement was gratifying and probably more helpful than Raymond would have wanted to admit.

He had been unable to give as much time to his personal campaign as he might have liked, for there was no letup to the work of the National Committee. Just before election he had had to spend several days in Washington, and he had been among the speakers at a great rally in Bridgeport that had brought together Connecticut Republicans and Unionists from as far away as New Haven in a procession that stretched five miles between illuminated and flag-draped factories and houses. But as a long-time resident of his district, almost twenty years, and a public figure to boot, he needed no introduction to the voters, and he had stated his position on the issues of the campaign so often on the platform and in the *Times*, that there was little he could add.

His campaign opened with a district rally in the Bleecker Building, only a few blocks from his Ninth Street home. His supporters put on a good show, with men and women packing the hall, their cheers echoing in the fall night when Raymond came out to pledge: "I shall support the President in all measures deemed essential to a vigorous prosecution of the war. I shall favor the prompt readmission to the Union of those now in rebellion whenever they shall lay down their arms, and renew their allegiance to the Constitution and laws of the United States, and I shall advocate and support all measures of legislation, just in themselves, and calculated to secure equal rights to every section, freedom to every citizen, and the permanent unity and prosperity of this great Republic." In the days that followed, there were other meetings, other rallies. Generally, Raymond talked more of Lincoln than of himself, though once he came out specifically for a Constitutional amendment against slavery, a stand that must have surprised his critics of the summer just past. On November 8, he had done. The city, the state, the nation, were ready to make known their decision on the Lincoln Administration and the party that was its chief support. However intent he might be on the national returns, Raymond would not have been human if he had not been just as keenly interested in what happened in the three wards of his own district.

VIII

In New York City that election day, a heavy fog hung over the harbor and the gridiron of streets; rain fell occasionally. Special precautions had been taken against the possibility of trouble—the ban on liquor sales curbed much of the traditional rowdyism and drunkenness—and the damp, dreary day passed quietly. ("The quietest city ever seen," reported General B. F. Butler, whom the War Department had sent to New York to guard against disorder.) In the rooms at the Astor House where Raymond had planned and directed the campaign now ended, the long day of hope and uncertainty wore on until with evening the committee was ready for the open house planned should there be victory. Across the park, as night fell, a crowd jammed into Printing House Square to read the bulletins posted by the *Times* and *Tribune* of success here, failure there.

In Washington that night, Lincoln and John Hay went early to the War Department for the returns. "The night was rainy, steamy and dark," Hay wrote in his diary. "We splashed through the grounds to the side door of the War Department where a soaked and smoking sentinel was standing in his own vapor with his huddled-up frame covered with a rubber cloak. Inside a half-dozen idle orderlies, upstairs the clerks of the telegraph. . . . Despatches kept coming in all the evening showing a splendid triumph in Indiana, showing steady, small gains all over Pennsylvania, enough to give a fair majority. . . . Guesses from New York and Albany which boiled down to about the estimated majority against us in the city, 35,000, and left the result in the State still doubtful.[6] . . . Towards midnight we had supper. . . . The President went awkwardly and hospitably to work shovelling out the fried oysters. He was most agreeable and genial all the evening. . . . We got later . . . a scattering despatch from the West giving us Michigan . . . and one, too good for ready credence, saying Raymond . . . had been elected in New York City."

Lincoln had carried the country by 212 electoral votes to 21. In New York State, he had only 6,749 more votes than McClellan, in the nationwide poll only 411,428, but it was enough. His Administration had been ratified by the people, and to the securing of that ratification Henry Raymond could feel that he had contributed in not insignificant measure. He had won his own campaign, too. By a minuscule plurality of 464 votes, he was entitled to sit in the Thirty-ninth Congress.

[6] Early in the evening Raymond wired Lincoln: "Democratic majority in the city will be 34,000 not over 35,000, no returns from interior yet."

—20—

Victory

I

ONE NOVEMBER night, shortly after the election, a file of men behind a band paraded down Fifth Avenue to West Ninth Street, where it wheeled and halted before Raymond's four-story brownstone. The Veterans Union Club had come to serenade the victor and one of the architects of victory. Long before they had done with song and music, Raymond came out to speak briefly and to express his thanks. As he finished, cheers from the serenaders' throats reverberated from the house fronts on the staid, substantial street.

The serenade, a simple thing but heartwarming even for a sophisticate like Raymond, was quickly over. The gaslights went out behind the French windows of his parlor, and Raymond returned to the work and worries of politics, his newspaper, and his family. There was not much time for serenades in his crowded days, for though the campaign's end had lifted much of the burden borne as national chairman, Raymond was deep in the business of patronage. Most of the appointments he sought were routine rewards for party service, but one was personal. He had set his heart on securing for his friend Charles L. Benedict [1] of Brooklyn the coveted judgeship of the newly created Federal Judicial District of Eastern New York. A University of Vermont graduate like himself, Benedict had once lived in the Raymond household. He had been Raymond's legal adviser, a political associate (as a member of the New York Assembly in 1862 he had been described as one of Speaker

[1] Whose lawyer-brother, Robert D. Benedict, had married Mrs. Raymond's sister Frances. For many years, R. D. Benedict was the law reporter for the *Times*.

Raymond's "right bowers"), a fellow delegate at the Baltimore Convention. Benedict, a brilliant lawyer, was a man whom Raymond could promote without prejudice, and though many another sought the place, when Benedict was finally named, no man spoke against him.

From the moment that he became national chairman, gossip had it that Raymond's own reward was to be the French mission, and when Minister William L. Dayton's death left the post vacant in December, 1864, the rumor-mongers marched out in force. Gideon Welles was certain that Raymond wanted the place.[2] So was Senator Morgan, who as a close associate of both Raymond and Weed should have known better. In the end, Raymond shut off the talk by a public statement that he had sought no office at home or abroad, that he had had no sign from the Administration that it "was willing to give him one if he did desire it."

There was no reason why Raymond should have desired an appointment. He had just been elected to Congress, and the prospect before him was bright and alluring. He had neglected the *Times* for many a month, and if he was to remain in control of its editorial content and policy, now was the time for him to take up the reins again. Any appointment, especially one abroad, would dictate a general rearrangement of business at the *Times*, as well as his resignation as Congressman and chairman of the National Committee. The chairmanship in particular was a place that Raymond wanted to keep. To exchange all that for a foreign post was unthinkable, whatever the promptings of Mrs. Raymond, who looked back fondly to European residence in the Fifties and was only awaiting the war's end to take up where she had left off.

II

One did not need to be a military expert to forecast that the war's end was near. Sherman, who had burned Atlanta on November 15, was slashing through Georgia on the march that gave the North Savannah as a Christmas present. In one of the bloodiest campaigns of the war, the Federal forces had driven Hood from the muddy fields of Tennessee in late November, and though Grant could claim no victories in Virginia, he was pounding tirelessly at the gates of Richmond, which were soon to open for his greatest triumph. The South, noted Raymond, was "rapidly and fatally failing."

Despite the imminence of the collapse, the Government in March, 1865, issued a new draft call, and in New York Raymond's name was on

[2] Welles wrote in his diary: "Intelligence of the death of Mr. Dayton, our Minister to France, creates some commotion among public men. . . . A numerous progeny has arisen at once to succeed him. John Bigelow, consul at Paris, has been appointed chargé, and I doubt if any other person will be selected who is more fit. Raymond of the *Times* wants it, but Bigelow is infinitely his superior."

the lists. He was unconcerned. "The present draft is merely a measure of precaution," he told a patriotic rally in his home ward, and he knew he spoke the truth. By then, with Sherman's armies deep in the Carolinas, the Confederacy had been pretty well dismembered. Already, Charleston, cradle of the rebellion, had fallen. Once more the Stars and Stripes waved over Sumter. Then suddenly it was Grant's turn. On April 3, he took Richmond, the goal toward which McDowell had set out almost four years earlier with Raymond tagging along. When the telegraph flashed the news, the North went wild with jubilation, for now only Lee's surrender was wanting, and it came at Appomattox within the week. That day of final victory—in New York a spring storm washed out the celebration—Raymond sat down in his office above rainswept City Hall Park to write a fervent leader for the *Times:* "The great struggle is over. . . . The great rebellion is crushed. The Republic is saved. Peace comes again. To Heaven be the praise."

Appomattox made acute the struggle already so bitter over how the South should regain its place in the Union. The issue, said Lincoln to serenaders celebrating the victory, "is fraught with great difficulty," and that was understatement. The Radicals, who from the moment he set out his plan for reconstruction in the Annual Message of 1863 had opposed his moderation and magnanimity, had been in no mood to surrender after his triumphant reelection. There had been a brief honeymoon when Lincoln threw his weight behind a constitutional amendment abolishing slavery, a measure dear to the Radicals, but it was soon over. The strident voices of the Radicals assailed the President in both houses of Congress, and when the Senators and Representatives from reconstructed Louisiana appeared on Capitol Hill, the Radicals tore into Lincoln's reconstruction policy with bitterness and vituperation until all but the most deep-dyed Jacobins were embarrassed and ashamed. "Why in heaven's name," Raymond protested to Speaker Colfax, "can't men . . . rise above party feeling—(I don't mean party relations but the *spirit* of *partisanship*) and save the country first!—I don't like the political drift of things overmuch."

He was too staunch a supporter of the Administration to take pleasure in the Radical attacks upon it, even if he had agreed with the political philosophy behind them. His backing for Lincoln's reconstruction policy had been firm from the first, and he had seen no reason for change. Coldly intellectual Raymond might seem when arguing his position in speeches and editorials, but he had a heart as well as a mind, and temperamentally he was far closer to the Lincoln of the Second Inaugural than to the snarling Radical spokesman Ben Wade, who had charity for none and malice toward all.

On April 11, two days after Lee's surrender, the White House grounds were crowded with people come to celebrate with Lincoln the victory in Virginia. The war-torn President came out to speak to them, and the words he spoke that spring night told all who desired to know that he intended to contest with the Radicals every deviation from his elected path of "a righteous and speedy peace" that would soon find the seceded states "safely at home." Three nights later—Walt Whitman observed that in that early spring the lilacs were in bloom—Lincoln rode away from the White House for an evening at Ford's Theatre and a martyr's crown.

III

The war's end loosed a rush of Americans to Europe—they jammed every outgoing steamer—and now Mrs. Raymond could indulge her love for travel. "We go to New York tomorrow to reside in Mr. Raymond's house," Weed wrote John Bigelow [3] in late May, 1865. "Mrs. Raymond, with her children, left for Havre on Friday." Raymond had seen them aboard the French liner *Europe*, and they made quite a party —his wife, the three daughters, ten-year-old Walter, and a maid—when the steamer dropped down the North River in the early morning light. They planned to be away for several years. Mrs. Raymond wanted to place the children in European schools again, but first they all tarried briefly in Paris ("I had the pleasure of seeing Mrs. Raymond and one of your daughters—an absurd likeness of you, only a thousand times handsomer," Bigelow wrote Raymond), then went on to Switzerland for the summer, where they settled into the same hotel at Vevey where Aimee had been born in 1857.

The children wrote their father often, as he did them, sent him little presents that bespoke their great affection for him. He loved them just as deeply—when Arthur, his youngest child, died late in 1864 he had been heartbroken—and despite the time-consuming demands of the life he led, he had never permitted his career to breed neglect of his boys and girls. When his children were away from home, his house was empty and lonely, and never more so than now, although his son Henry, a youth of seventeen and ready to enter Yale in the fall, had stayed behind when the family went abroad.

To Raymond his children's love helped to compensate for the estrangement that had grown between him and their mother. A brilliant woman, and a beautiful one, Juliette Raymond was also a strait-laced puritan with a temper of classic proportions. Her outbursts were so violent that

[3] After being on tenterhooks for months, Bigelow had finally been named Minister to France.

Raymond feared to cross her lest he bring on a tantrum and be abused by his Xanthippe's cruel tongue. According to John Bigelow, George Jones, a red-faced witness of one of these episodes, told Mrs. Raymond when it ended "that he wished he had her for his wife for about a fortnight." "Well," said she, stepping up to him fiercely, "what would you do?" "I would break your back, or I would break your damned temper," Jones replied. More and more Mrs. Raymond opposed the social entertaining that her husband liked so much and that had once characterized their household. Raymond enjoyed whist; his wife would not have a pack of cards in the house. He was fond of both the opera and the theater; she disliked them, refusing to accompany him when he went to the Academy of Music or sat in his box at Wallack's. They still shared interest in certain public-spirited undertakings, but such interest did nothing to lessen their increasing incompatibility.

The failure of his marriage, to which his own protracted absences from home must have contributed greatly, had gradually accentuated the melancholy that had always been part of his character. On the surface he was the gay companion, the man of wit and charm, but behind the polished façade, he suffered from a soul sickness that made it easier to wander in paths he once would have thought forbidden. One evening during the war there had been a scandalous scene at a Washington musicale when Mrs. Raymond insulted a lady present whose name gossip had linked with Raymond's. Sometime later, Raymond had been in grave danger of being named corespondent in a divorce suit, but the danger was averted, and Raymond went his way while the *Herald* mumbled something about a modern Abelard.

"I am perfectly conscious that within the last two or three years," Raymond wrote Jones rather enigmatically in the summer of 1865, "I have lost interest in many things that used to enlist my ambition and have become indifferent—(perhaps reckless would be a better word,) to considerations which really were entitled to weight. I have fallen (and no one knows it half so well as I do,) into a cynical mood,—prizing very few things as worthy of much effort and thinking of very little of what people in general prize most. This affects my action more or less in all directions and exposes me in some to dangers which I should avoid. Perhaps I shall get over it—at any rate I shall involve others as little as possible in my misfortunes."

Jones, a good friend as well as a partner, understood. During the war when Raymond's personal life had been complicated and tangled, he had written him: "I do most fervently hope you may be able to lift this heavy weight that has so long been pressing down upon you. . . . I cannot understand how you bear it so patiently—so uncomplainingly.

I therefore believe there will be some way out of this trouble." But Jones also probably realized that Raymond's soul searching could well be the result more of mental and physical weariness than of spiritual breakdown, for as usual Raymond was driving himself hard.

IV

Derby & Miller had waited scarcely for the long Lincoln funeral procession to reach Springfield before they broached to Raymond the possibility of a definitive life of the martyred President. Raymond hesitated, unsure that he could do it properly. Finally persuaded, he set to work with a view to completing the job as quickly as possible so that the book might come from the presses on the flood tide of Lincoln interest. He hired a couple of assistants, for he could not devote all his time to the book, and set about collecting documents that should be part of it.

From Paris Bigelow wrote him: "I am glad the biography of poor Lincoln is in such good hands. Let me beg of you not to attempt a hasty book for a temporary sale. You have the range of more material than any future biographer can hope to have; why not utilize it and give the whole story at such length as to have nothing in the way of facts to be added? There is no danger of the subject growing stale, and if you do the work deliberately and thoroughly your book will have a large and continuous sale, not to speak of the fame it will confer upon the biographer." But Raymond, whatever the prospect of fame, had a rush job to perform, and while he hoped that he would write a lasting book, he knew that his publishers were more interested in promptness than completeness.

Just as he had done with the first version of his Lincoln, he rose early in the morning, writing and rewriting in the fresh hours before he breakfasted. ("If a man would take an hour before breakfast," Raymond told Chauncey Depew, "and concentrate upon his subject, he would soon fill an entire library.") Although the campaign biography gave Raymond something to start from, the new book was not just a revision and expansion. He rewrote from beginning to end, added much new material and many new documents. He tiptoed around the controversies that had marked Lincoln's Administration, discussing them so as to make no political enemies for the biographer, at the same time making sure that they did nothing to detract from the late President's stature. Despite Raymond's close connection with much of what he told, he kept himself out of the story except for two or three anecdotes that served to point up the personality of his hero.

By midsummer, he had finished a big book of 808 pages, and for all his haste, he had written a biography that was worthy of its subject and a tribute to its author's literary skill and sense of history. Later biographers were to salute it as the best of the contemporary Lincoln lives. "I am glad I wrote it and am *very* glad it is done!" Raymond told his daughter Lucy when he sent a copy to the family in Switzerland.

With the book out of the way, Raymond was ready to vacation. He felt listless, "used up," he said, "not so much by hard work as by city air and confinement." For a holiday he went north to Saratoga, where Judge Benedict soon joined him for one of the gayest seasons the resort had known since before the war. He registered at Union Hall and, seated behind the span of bays he had brought with him, was soon a familiar figure on the fashionable drives and at the track, where Leonard Jerome was president of the racing association. Thurlow Weed and his daughter Harriet were at the spa. So was Raymond's political friend Governor Curtin of Pennsylvania. Franklin Pierce, the sad and broken former President, mingled among the guests on the Saratoga verandahs. Raymond also found in town a young Englishman named Louis Jennings,[4] Washington correspondent of the London *Times*. Men of similar tastes and interests, they ultimately bound tight the ties of friendship.

Racing had become as important at the watering place as the daily promenade of men and women of fashion, but at night there were parties and theatricals and concerts, and when General Grant came to Saratoga there was a great ball in his honor, with Raymond prominent on the committee of arrangements. Raymond thought the change from New York life was doing him good, but he complained that he was not really enjoying himself. If his family could have been with him, it would have been different. "How I wish you could all have been here too!" he wrote one of his girls. He missed his family badly, and if Jones had not picked that particular summer for a European trip, leaving Raymond to watch over the *Times*, Raymond would undoubtedly have spent a few weeks in Switzerland with his children after his book was done. Saratoga distracted, but did not satisfy, nor was it any better when he was in New York, for with the Weeds out of town, it meant that he came home to an echoing house where only the servants were present to keep him company. "I shall be glad when the time comes to go to Washington," he said, "for I am lonesome here—whenever I have time to think about it."

V

In the summer of 1865, the *Herald* got hold of Treasury Department figures on newspaper income, and shouted for all to hear that its name led all the rest. In the year ending May 1, 1865, the *Herald*'s gross income had been more than a million dollars. The *Times*, though second

---

[4] Later London correspondent of the New York *Times*, and in 1870, after Raymond's death, editor of the paper.

on the list, was far behind with $368,150; the *Tribune* tagged along in third place with $252,000. Raymond wrote Jones: "The *Herald*'s show of receipts for circulation, etc., puts them terribly ahead—but we stand next, though the *Tribune* has been trying to explain this away. I have said nothing—because there was nothing to be said."

Raymond was not too worried about the *Herald*'s lead. He was more concerned by its purchase of the corner of Broadway where Barnum's Museum had been a famed fixture until a recent fire destroyed it. "It is the best place in the city," remarked Raymond, "and we may be eclipsed. Still we are doing well enough, and can hold our own ground." It was true. *Times* stock, when it could be purchased, sold for $5,000 a share, and Raymond's chief regret was that his expensive family made it impossible for him to expand his holding. The *Times,* whose circulation had bounded from 45,000 to 75,000 in the first weeks after the firing on Sumter, had more advertising than it could print. The paper, said Raymond modestly, "stands well in public estimation."

Raymond was doing his utmost to keep it so. He kept up a steady fire at his foreign correspondents. He sent Ben C. Truman and other correspondents into the conquered Confederacy for graphic and colorful accounts of "the South as it is." He found time to congratulate staff members like E. L. Godkin when they left the *Times* for wider fields, and to talk to aspiring young men. One of the latter was named William Dean Howells. Though only twenty-eight, Howells had already lived five years abroad as the American consul in Venice. In the fall of 1865 he wrote for the *Times* occasional editorials on European politics and literary topics. "They paid me well," said Howells, "and more than well; but I was nowhere offered a basis, though once I got so far towards it as to secure a personal interview with the editor-in-chief, who made me feel that I had seldom met so busy a man. He praised some work of mine that he had read in his paper, but I was never recalled to his presence; and now I think he judged rightly that I should not be a lastingly good journalist. My point of view was artistic; I wanted time to prepare my effects."

Whatever Raymond's reason for passing over Howells, it surely was not because of the artistic point of view, for Raymond had gladly published, though belatedly, Walt Whitman's magnificently moving account of Lincoln's second inauguration, and for all his editorial keenness for news, he had never lost his delight in well-turned phrases and polished prose. He wanted the *Times* to be highly readable, and while it often missed that goal, the goal remained, to be attained on occasions that were sometimes notable.

Editorially, Raymond gave Andrew Johnson the same sort of support that he had given Lincoln. But Raymond was not blind to the fact that the political storm which had threatened Lincoln now endangered the Administration and policies of his successor. "Public matters," he told Jones, "are getting *foggy*. Pres't Johnson is said to be sick—seriously so, while others speak mysteriously of his *habits*. The general opinion is that he is going too *fast* in his policy of reconstruction and that the rebel states must rest awhile longer under military rule."

VI

Reconstruction had become the dominant issue of American politics. For a few weeks after Lincoln's death, the Radicals had thought that Johnson was going to be with them in treating the South as a conquered province, but they had been soon and abruptly disillusioned. When Johnson at the end of May announced that "if a state is to be nursed until it again gets strength, it must be nursed by its friends, not smothered by its enemies," he hoisted a signal that his course was to be that set by Lincoln. On May 29, he issued an amnesty proclamation almost identical with that issued at the end of 1863 by Lincoln. His proclamation for restoring state government in North Carolina repeated the Lincoln pattern already applied in Louisiana and Arkansas.

Similar proclamations pressed hard upon one another, and in Mississippi, the first state to act, a convention assembled in mid-August to meet the requirements established for organizing civil government. Other states fell into line. If the President had his way, reconstruction would be an accomplished fact by the time the Thirty-ninth Congress met in December. But as Raymond had observed, the President's policy was meeting criticism. The speed with which Johnson had acted was not the real reason for it. Gideon Welles noted among the Radicals "an exhibition of hate towards the Rebels which bodes mischief." In Maine, Massachusetts, and Pennsylvania, the Union state conventions condemned Johnson's policy, and Welles thought such action proof enough that "extensive operations" were afoot "for an organization hostile to the Administration." "It is the old Radical anti-Lincoln movement . . . with recruits," he said.

If New York Radicals, Horace Greeley prominent among them, had had their way, the Union state convention that met at Syracuse on September 20 would also have condemned the President. But the extremists, though in the majority, were poorly led and no match for the political skill of Weed and Raymond. From his rooms in the Syracuse House, Weed directed the Conservative strategy, in which patronage had an important part. At the moment he had plenty of jobs to give away, for his fellow Conservative Preston King had just replaced the Radical

Simeon Draper as collector of the port of New York, and that put the Custom House in Weed's pocket. Moreover, his influence in the Johnson Administration had been growing steadily, a fact not missed by many a job-hungry delegate.

On the convention floor, Raymond was Weed's chief lieutenant. Because of his party post and his acquaintance with the President that stemmed from his fight for him at Baltimore in 1864, Raymond had a good deal of power and prestige in his own right. He impressed, perhaps sometimes awed, and skilled parliamentarian that he was, he knew just how to make the most telling points in debate, how to marshal the Conservatives at a critical moment, how best to block the Radicals. It meant that in the end Chauncey Depew, a Conservative, was chosen convention president, that Raymond himself was made chairman of the resolutions committee, and that Conservatives were nominated for the principal offices in the state's off-year election.

While Weed wanted to put his men in key posts and maintain control of the party machine, he was equally anxious for the convention to endorse Andrew Johnson and his work. It was Raymond who carried the burden. He drafted the convention's resolutions, for two hours defended them in committee, accepting minor changes when compromise was indicated, scratching out altogether a vague plank in favor of Negro suffrage. Late in the evening, when the tired delegates were ready to vote for anything so long as it let them go home, Raymond read his resolution: "We recognize in Andrew Johnson . . . a statesman of ability, experience and high-tone patriotism . . . and renew to him in his administration those assurances of cordial and effective support, which were tendered by us in his nomination and election." It brought the weary delegates to their feet cheering, and the shouts were renewed when he reached the resolution— Greeley thought it "timid and windy" —calling for reconstruction in "the spirit of equal and impartial justice." There were more cheers, and then at midnight the convention adjourned, leaving Weed's men victors on the field.

In the state campaign that followed, Raymond called up all his strength to help the Union party to victory, for success could be expected to speak in loud, emphatic tones to the President's opponents. New York's endorsement of Johnson and his policies implicit in a state victory would surely strengthen the hands of his supporters in the coming Congress, might even weaken the determination of his foes.[5] As party chair-

[5] Wrote William E. Chandler, Assistant Secretary of the Treasury: "We had better have lice and locusts than the revival of the Democratic party; and if your election is carried, it does seem to me that they will give up. All lingering doubt of the policy of certain parties here will vanish if your State is carried for the Union ticket."

man, Raymond once again faced the business of fund-raising, and as in the previous year, he tangled with Gideon Welles over assessment of navy yard employees. ("Weed and Raymond," said Welles, "are . . . mad with me for cutting off supplies.") He spent hours in party conferences and with party correspondence, was ever on call to party workers and hangers-on. "Now that Mr. Weed and I are both in the house," he wrote a daughter, "it seems to me the door bell rings *all* the time. I always find three or four people waiting for me when I go down to breakfast, and they keep coming in steady stream. There it goes again —that's the second time it has rung since I commenced this letter! . . . I am so busy & so badgered with people that I sometimes don't know whether I stand on my head or my heels."

Probably his most important speech of the campaign was made at Albany, where on October 10 he spoke to a big rally in Tweddle Hall. It was a difficult and embarrassing speech to make, for Raymond, so long the advocate of an end to partisanship, planned to reject the support of the President and his policies pledged by New York Democrats at the same time that he called for popular support of Andrew Johnson. Raymond based his case on the war record of the party that had spurned the Union party idea and had often seemed to oppose the very prosecution of the war itself. Had the Democrats really been converted to nonpartisanship now? Raymond doubted it. How, he asked, could one believe in Democratic sincerity? Was it not enough to point out their war record and the incongruity of their support of Johnson's reconstruction policy, which was essentially Lincoln's, but which in his lifetime had had no good Democratic word? Raymond concluded that the real objective of the Democrats—he made much of their harping on Radical devotion to Negro suffrage—was to split the Union party by setting Radical against Conservative.

Raymond wanted Union party victory. He was ready to welcome into the house all men who stood by that party's purpose. Said he: "I do not wish to reject any honest and sincere support which the Democrats may offer to President Johnson. I welcome all such support. I believe that Andrew Johnson deserves it all. I believe that his administration is one that commands, and that ought to command, the heartfelt support of the American people. I believe that if all men could act without distinction of party, they would support it."

Whatever his inner doubts about Johnson, he was unwilling to speak them publicly. "Andrew Johnson," he cried, "will lead you and the country in the path of progress toward the equality of all men before the law. . . . All that we, who stand by the administration, who desire to see the Union restored, and to see, among the people of all sections of the country, mutual respect, mutual regard and mutual interest in each other's welfare, have to do, is to go steadily forward—kindly and generously, but steadily and firmly—insisting always upon what is right and never upon anything that is wrong." The cheers in Tweddle Hall burst upon the night, and before a month was out had been translated into the votes that gave the Union party its New York victory.

The Albany speech—printed as a pamphlet, it was sown across the state—was only one of Raymond's many. On party business he shuttled between New York and Washington. He spoke in strategic centers. "I am going to Washington this evening . . . for two days," he wrote his daughter Lucy on October 17, "then next week I shall go & make some speeches in Western N.Y. . . . Then I hope to stay still until I go to Congress."

He looked forward with great confidence and self-assurance as well as keen pleasure to the opportunity to sit in Congress. It was not only the allure of public office. He enjoyed being part of a lawmaking machine—"it was a privilege," he said later, "to feel when you answered the call of your name that your voice was a determining factor in the government of the Republic"—and he liked to rub elbows with men who were shaping a nation's destiny. After years of being an observer and reporter of Washington, he was now to be part of it, and this at a time when he could tell himself that a man of his moderation had a contribution to make and a place to fill.

If he had uncertainties, he kept them secret. Rashly perhaps, but optimistically, he had told the partisans in Tweddle Hall: "The next Congress will be wise and patriotic, not disposed to push any abstract doctrine to dangerous extremes [he meant Negro suffrage]. . . . I believe that they will act conscientiously, fairly and justly, and will impose upon the Southern States only such conditions and requisitions as fall within the Constitution. . . . I am perfectly convinced that we shall wisely and speedily do hereafter as we have done hitherto, follow the lead of the wise and practical statesman, who stands at the head of the Union." At the end of November he moved on to Washington to meet the unhappy fate of many a man who hazards prophecy.

—21—

Disillusion

I

AT NOON on December 4, 1865, the rapping of a gavel at each end of the United States Capitol announced the convening of the Thirty-ninth Congress, one of the most famous in the country's history. To watch the legislators start work that balmy, almost springlike day, the chief men of government, diplomats, and Washington society leaders crowded the corridors and galleries, sharply aware that the curtain was going up on a tragic struggle over the rebuilding of a divided nation.

The actors had taken their places. First among them was President Johnson, whom the new Congress pointedly slighted when it failed to send him the traditional notice that the nation's Legislature was open and ready for business. If Johnson had any illusion that the new Congress intended to rubberstamp the policies he had laid down to insure speedy restoration of the Union, he was shortly to be disabused. In the Senate, men like hard-bitten Benjamin Wade, the uncompromising Charles Sumner, and old Zach Chandler, the same men who had so added to Lincoln's crushing burdens, stood solid as a roadblock against him. He had his friends, Dixon of Connecticut, Doolittle of Wisconsin, Cowan of Pennsylvania, but such moderates and Conservatives were no match for the overbearing Radicals. And the House, where the cynical Thaddeus Stevens was tightening his dictatorship, was no different. The men, and Raymond outstanding among them, who stood with the President were soon to find themselves incapable of stemming the Radical tide.

Raymond's position of course was peculiar. His political partners, Seward and Weed, were close to the President, and he himself, though there was little truth to it, was regarded as Johnson's spokesman in the House. He enjoyed the further prestige conferred by his post as Union party chairman. He had known Speaker Colfax for years, and was friendly with Union-Republicans in both House and Senate, many of whom were beholden to him for patronage and election favors. Why should he not have supposed that on such a foundation he could build a bridge between the President and the House? In the past, he had often mediated between extremes, and now there seemed to be a supreme chance, a supreme need too, for the mediation of a moderate like himself. In anticipation of the influence he would wield and the prominence he would hold, he rented a comfortable house at 264 I Street, installed an old family servant as cook, and got ready to dispense a generous hospitality.

On the opening day Raymond was a man to be pointed out from the galleries. "Few members," said his colleague James G. Blaine, "had ever entered the House with greater personal prestige or with stronger assurance of success. He had come with high ambition—an ambition justified by his talent and training. He had come with expectation of a Congressional career as successful as that already achieved in his editorial life." With him that day sat others whom history would not forget. The future presidents Rutherford B. Hayes and James A. Garfield were among the Union-Republicans. Speaker Colfax would be Vice-President of the United States before he was driven from public life by the same Crédit Mobilier scandal that wrecked Oakes Ames, the famous Massachusetts shovel manufacturer who was also a member of the Thirty-ninth Congress. Two former Massachusetts governors were on the floor: George S. Boutwell, a Radical and a vindictive, and the moderate Nathaniel P. Banks, the bobbin boy who had been Speaker of the House before he was a general in the army. Among the Radicals was the New Yorker Roscoe Conkling, a brilliantly able man but one of such vast conceit that Blaine, who hated him, was inspired to describe unforgettably his "haughty disdain, his grandiloquent swell, his majestic, super-eminent, overpowering turkey gobbler strut."

Then there was Stevens, the real master. Though physically broken at seventy-three, he retained the biting wit, the sarcasm, and the parliamentary skill that made him feared by most and loved by none. A gaunt, clubfooted figure whose ill-fitting wig was often askew, Stevens lived near the Capitol in a dilapidated house kept for him by a mulatto woman who gossip insisted had been for many years far more than a housekeeper. Such talk might have ruined the political life of lesser men, but Stevens paid it no heed, nor did it prevent his reelection term after term to the House, where since early in the war his power had grown steadily.

House and Senate came together with the memory of the war and its dead still green. For a majority of members, the South was a land of treason and its people traitors who had been conquered but not reconciled to the Union they had fought so hard to destroy. While reconstruction was recognized as the paramount problem of the hour, the method was even more the immediate issue. Congress, ever since passage of the Wade-Davis Bill in 1864, had been asserting that the method was its own to determine. Assertion of Congressional power as superior to the President's was a natural reaction to the Chief Executive's exercise of his war powers, but more than political theory was involved.

It was hard to accept as fellow Americans the men so recently in Confederate gray and who now, under the Presidential reconstruction plan, were claiming seats in Congress. Moreover, their admission would open the way for restoration of the Southern branch of the Democratic party, and thus endanger both the rule of the Union-Republicans and the economic policies they sponsored and pursued. A far stronger man than Andrew Johnson would have found it difficult to dominate a Congress in such a mood. Hesitant by nature and politically weak, Johnson's lot was hopeless almost from the start. He had no personal following. Despite the help of Seward and Weed, he had no party organization loyal to him, and as a former Democrat he was always open to the suspicion that his ties were stronger with the Democrats than with the Union-Republicans who had picked him for Vice-President in 1864.

II

A couple of days before the convening of Congress, a Union-Republican caucus agreed upon a resolution creating a joint Senate and House committee of fifteen that would decide when and if any Southern state was entitled to representation in Congress. Stevens fathered the scheme as a means of blocking Johnson's plans for reconstruction and of insuring Congressional control of the remaking of the Union. Somehow, he made need for the committee seem so plausible that Raymond missed its real import. He both voted for the proposal and joined with Radicals like Stevens in drafting the enabling resolution. He voted for it when it was presented to Congress, and in the *Times* defended the committee as "an orderly and dignified" way of meeting a controversial question. It was the greatest mistake of his political career. How anyone of his experience and astuteness could have failed to comprehend Stevens's strategy is hard to answer, and Raymond himself never had any explanation, except the lame one that he had not fully appreciated what Stevens was up to. But the fact of his action cut away much of the influence that he might otherwise have wielded and made hard for him the justifying of his later course as the session slowly unwound.

Meanwhile, Tennessee's delegation was demanding that it be seated. Prominent among the Tennesseeans was Horace Maynard, who in 1864 had cheered with Raymond when Lincoln was named at Baltimore. He may have thought that as a staunch Unionist throughout the war he could expect special consideration, but if so he met bitter disappointment. When he tried to plead his cause, Stevens cut him short. To consider Maynard's plight and that of the other Tennesseeans, Raymond brought a group of Congressmen to his house, where he sought to persuade them that Tennessee's restoration as a state should be immediate. Just how far his colleagues were prepared to go is now forgotten, but all agreed with him that the taking of the oath to the Constitution should be enough for the admission of a state's delegation. To start action, Raymond raised in the House on December 12 the question of seating Maynard and the rest. Though Stevens snorted that "the State of Tennessee is not known to this House of Congress," Raymond got the question referred to the Committee of Fifteen, from which he apparently expected a favorable report.

More than that he did not expect, for he saw where the committee was tending. "Things do not work smoothly in the House," he told Weed. "I think they will admit Tennessee *early*,[1] as a matter of expediency, & keep all the rest out indefinitely. Thad. Stevens seems to have the whole party under his control. Colfax's Committee [of Fifteen] is thoroughly Radical. A few of us will try & make head against them but it is rather a 'forlorn hope.'"

On December 18, his gray eyes sparking but his pallid face grim and bleak, Stevens rose in the House to attack the President's theories of reconstruction and to assert with finality his own position toward the "conquered provinces." He assailed the "theory that the rebel States for four years a separate power and without representation in Congress, were all the time in the Union. To deny that we have a right to treat them as a conquered belligerent, severed from the Union in fact, is not argument but mockery. Whether it be our interest to do so is the only question hereafter to be considered." He insisted that to Congress belonged the power to decide how the South should again function as part of the Union, and he laid down the terms he wanted to impose. They added up to Congressional supremacy, continuance of Republican ascendancy through enfranchisement of the Negroes, and basic to it all,

[1] It was July before Tennessee was admitted.

subjugation of the South. Let its people, cried Stevens, "eat the fruit of foul rebellion."

Three days later, for his first major speech in Congress, Raymond elected to reply to Stevens. He prepared carefully, as he always did, but as usual he spoke from the briefest notes, and even then referred to them but seldom. Word that Raymond was speaking soon filled the galleries and brought to the floor many a member who had been anxious to get away for the Christmas recess that was due to begin at the day's end.

Blaine watched Raymond closely that day. His "intellectual acuteness and alertness" were at full power, but Blaine thought he detected strain and "mental weariness" in Raymond's still youthful face. He attributed it to the "prolonged and exacting labor of his profession," without apparently suspecting that Raymond's face betrayed his appreciation that he was fighting a losing cause. Still, it was a good speech, perhaps even a great speech, and Stevens could have gained by being on the floor to hear it.

Before an audience of partisans who interrupted again and again, Raymond rose above partisanship to plead his tolerant and statesmanlike case for a united nation. At times he turned from the logical arguments that so often characterized his political oratory and let emotion have its head. He began by reasserting his denial of the theory of the "conquered province," the denial that he had repeated so many times since Wilmington. His argument, however much it might differ from the counter-argument of Stevens, lacked freshness to anyone who had followed his speeches and editorials on reconstruction. It was in the peroration that Raymond hit new and eloquent notes that stirred the mind and heart.

"I am here," he said, "to act with those who seek to complete the restoration of the Union. . . . I shall say no word and do no act and give no vote to recognize its division, or to postpone or disturb its rapidly approaching harmony and peace. . . . We have great communities of men, permanent interests of great States, to deal with, and we are bound to deal with them in a large and liberal spirit.

"I would exact of them all needed and all just guarantees for their future loyalty to the Constitution and laws of the United States. I would exact from them, or impose upon them . . . proper care and protection for the helpless and friendless freedmen. . . . I would exercise a rigid scrutiny into the character and loyalty of the men whom they may send to Congress. . . . But I would seek to allay rather than stimulate the animosities and hatred, however just they may be, to which the war has given rise. . . ."

Now, his attackers momentarily silenced by the suavity and good manners with which he met their bitter railings, he reached his climax.

"We have been their enemies in war," said Raymond of the defeated rebels; "in peace let us show ourselves their friends. Now, that slavery has been destroyed . . . there is nothing longer to make us foes. They have the same aspirations that we have. They are one with us; we must share their sufferings and they will share our advancing prosperity. . . . I hope and believe that we shall soon see the day when the people of the Southern States will show us . . . that they have returned, in all sincerity and good faith, to their allegiance to the Union; that they intend to join henceforth with us in promoting its prosperity, in defending the banners of its glory, and in fighting the battles of democratic freedom." [2]

III

With the applause of the House a pleasing memory, Raymond rode up to New York for the Christmas recess. He had defied Dictator Stevens, but he had not gone so far as to break with other members of the party. He was still speaking for Union-Republican moderates and for the Johnson policies; he still might find a way to bridge the gulf between Radical and Conservative. He was worried a little because the Democrats were so open in support of Johnson, and he had been vexed when a Democrat had spoken in defense of the President the very afternoon he made his own defense. Yet he hoped that he had made it clear that he wanted no help from men who belonged to the anti-war party. It was important to make it understood that neither he nor the Administration sought help from Democrats except in so far as it might benefit the Union party.

Firmly convinced that the country was behind Johnson, Raymond may well have put his forebodings aside and congratulated himself on having made a good beginning. Even the Committee of Fifteen might turn out all right. The next few weeks would tell, and meanwhile it was good just to be away from Washington, a city that was muddy when it was not dusty, and where company so largely masculine tended to grow wearisome.

Because the Weed family had filled the Ninth Street house for the holidays, Raymond stayed with the Jeromes in their big house on Madison Square. Though he joined in their celebrations—the Jerome children and their friends made the parlors gay, and Jerome's lovely daughter Jennie played the piano for him—it was a lonesome Christmas with-

[2] As usual, Gideon Welles refused to accept Raymond at face value. "Raymond," he wrote in his diary, "went off at first with Stevens and the Radicals, but after being harnessed in that team, he has jumped out of the traces. Interest, patronage, Seward's influence have caused this facing about and may compel him to act with the Administration; but he is unreliable. I have so told the President, yet I am glad to have him move in the right direction."

out his scattered family. Henry was with friends in Connecticut, where his father visited him before returning to Washington. Walter and Lucy were in school in Paris, while Mrs. Raymond and the other daughters were on the Riviera.

Raymond did not have much time for sentiment. It had been all very well to edit the *Times* by remote control, but it was much better to be at the office every day. During the past two years, he had been absent so often and so occupied with other matters that, although he laid down general policy, much of the paper he never saw until he read it. Weed told John Bigelow that "Raymond almost every morning is as surprised at his editorial columns as the hen with a brood of young ducks." But the paper was doing well. It was fat with advertising, and just before the end of the year it added a column to its page size, a move that made possible a boast that it had the largest page of any paper in the country and equaled the London *Times*. The change brought out a lot of praise, and even papers politically opposed to the *Times* said pleasant things about it and about the man who in less than fifteen years had made it a major force.

With Weed, whom Raymond had persuaded to join the *Times*'s editorial staff, there were political problems to discuss. Not least was that of the New York collectorship, for Preston King, who had held it briefly, had loaded his pockets with shot one day and jumped from a North River ferry. Its rich patronage made the collector's office the citadel of party power in New York; it was essential to find a man who would strengthen the Weed machine. There were many applicants. Chauncey Depew wanted it and thought that he had Raymond's support. Chester A. Arthur also wanted it; and Charles A. Dana put in a bid, promising if selected "to render you every proper service of a friendly nature." Raymond and Weed went over all the candidates, but none seemed just the man, nor did later discussion in Washington with the President speed the decision. Only months later, in an effort to appease all political factions in New York, did Johnson make an appointment: a banker named Henry A. Smythe, who pleased none and strengthened the President and his close political friends not at all.

IV

Raymond was in his seat when Congress reassembled on January 5 in a city trying to recreate some of its prewar gaiety. At the White House, where guests had an annoying habit of snipping the curtains for souvenirs, there was an elaborate calendar of receptions. Cabinet officers, members of Congress, diplomats, and many a prominent resident brought together in their homes the varieties of political opinion. Dried-up Alexander H. Stephens, Vice-President of the Confederacy and a Senator-elect from Georgia, was a guest at General Grant's one night, where his presence discomforted Radicals like Senator Trumbull and Thad Stevens, who were doubly embarrassed by meeting President Johnson and his daughters face to face. There were also dinners for Raymond to attend, and when actresses like the popular Rose Eytinge played at the Washington Theater or the National, he was often among the gentlemen who gossiped in the greenroom.

Though Blaine remembered him as a charming host, Raymond was too busy to be as hospitable as he had planned or to enter prominently into the capital's social life. His correspondence was vast, and many of the letters he answered in his own hand. They came from constituents, from strangers, from old friends. Every day he saw a procession of visitors who came to talk policies and political practices or to ask for favors. General Webb, on leave from his post as minister to Brazil and suffering from gout, presumed on old association to badger Raymond for a new political plum. There was always the *Times* and its affairs in the capital to watch over. The Associated Press took his time, and when the day was done, the Congressional reports and documents that accumulated on his desk awaited study.[8] Only occasionally could he push them aside to read his favorite Macaulay.

In the House, where the poor marksmanship of tobacco chewers was rapidly ruining the carpet, Raymond was increasingly unhappy. He hated a zealot at any time, and particularly now when he believed the greatest need to be forbearance, moderation, and magnanimity. The *Times* echoed his view. "The very term compromise," it said, ". . . is odious in some quarters. It implies moderation, which to the incurable ultraist is the unpardonable sin. It implies mutual concession, which the genuine Radical is rarely disposed to make."

Even if Raymond had accepted the aims of the Stevens dictatorship, he could not have accepted the fact. He was too independent to bow to any dictator, and he believed too firmly in democracy to admit that a dictator could be part of the American system. He deplored the constant use of the party caucus at which Stevens snapped the lash of party discipline to compel support of his program. He was equally opposed to any procedure that limited debate, and in the *Times* complained: "There has scarcely been any expedient known to parliamentary usage left untried by the majority of the present Congress to

---

[8] The A.P. reports of debates in Congress caused him concern. "Since I have been here," he complained early in 1866, "I have had an opportunity to judge with some degree of accuracy; and I cannot help seeing that the reports do not give any just idea of what is done, or the arguments advanced by the different speakers. . . . [They] are not creditable to the enterprise of the Associated Press. . . ."

prevent a frank and full discussion on points affecting the restoration of all the States to their proper relations within the Union."

For all that he had helped to set up the Committee of Fifteen, he now attacked it for exceeding its powers. His attack gave his enemies another chance to charge him with unreliability, but that did not dissuade him from pointing out that the committee had been created solely to decide the issue of Southern representation in Congress. The arrogation of power to draw up a comprehensive plan for reconstruction seemed only added proof that Stevens and his followers intended to do about as they pleased, without regard for rules, laws, or the Constitution of the United States.

It was on the Constitution, of course, that Raymond based his argument against the conquered-province theory. His case had been attacked by Samuel Shellabarger of Ohio, and he knew that many of his colleagues thought that Shellabarger had the best of the argument. He himself was not shaken, and when on January 29 he had a chance to reiterate his views, he did not hesitate.[4]

Just as he arose to speak, General William T. Sherman was discovered in the hall. The House hastily recessed for five minutes while Sherman was escorted to the speaker's rostrum for a flowery introduction. By the time the House got back to work, the galleries were filled in both seats and aisles; Raymond had the biggest audience of his Congressional service. He knew what to do with it. For two hours, calm and cool despite Gatling gunfire of interruption, he developed his case. He was the constitutional lawyer at one time, the impassioned pleader at another, and as in his maiden speech, he closed on the high note of a united nation.

"The gigantic contest is at an end," he said, his full voice rich with feeling. "The courage and devotion on either side which made it so terrible and so long, no longer owe a divided duty, but have become the common property of the American name, the priceless possession of the American Republic through all time to come. The dead of the contending hosts sleep beneath the soil of a common country, and under one common flag. Their hostilities are hushed, and they are the dead of the nation forevermore. The victor may well exult in the victory he has achieved. Let it be our task, as well as our highest glory, to make the vanquished and their posterity to the latest generation, rejoice in their defeat."

Blaine thought it a clever speech—"every intellectual effort of Mr.

[4] The Supreme Court later upheld his position. Said the Court in 1868 in Texas v. White: "The Constitution, in all its provisions, looks to an indestructible Union, composed of indestructible States."

Raymond exhibited cleverness"—which "to some extent influenced public opinion," but he made the telling point that it affected Republican
action in Congress not at all. Stevens expressed the Radical contempt.
"Was there ever blasphemy before like this?" he cried. "If the loyal
dead, who are thus associated with the traitors who murdered them
. . . could have heard the gentleman they would have broken the cere-
ments of the tomb and stalked forth and haunted him until his eye-balls
were seared."

V

Soon after the Christmas recess, the House took up a long-debated
resolution of confidence in the President. In its final form it was at best
a lukewarm endorsement, but Raymond and his New York friend William A. Darling were the sole Union-Republicans to vote for it. If anything more were needed, this overwhelming and humiliating defeat told
Raymond how completely he had failed to build a band of followers.
It told him, and the Administration too, how small a chance there was
of winning head-on battles.

Increasingly, Democrats were supporting the President, and as Raymond had foreseen, that made political capital for the Radicals. Though
Johnson told Raymond that he would never go over to the Democrats,
that he was first and last a Union party man, the fact of Democratic support could not be denied. It was being used to weaken the Administration among Conservative Republicans. Raymond, ever fearful lest the
Union party coalition crumble, saw the President's role as crucial in
the preserving of it. That meant a willingness at times to compromise,
but it also assumed that the Radicals likewise would give way upon
occasion. Apparently Raymond still hoped to show the way.

In that spirit he voted for limited Negro suffrage in the District of
Columbia—Johnson opposed it—and for the Freedmen's Bureau Bill
that passed the House on February 6. The bill, an outrageous measure
which gave the bureau's commissioners judicial and probably unconstitutional powers to defend the freedmen against discrimination, had
been accepted by many moderates like Raymond. There is some evidence that they did so as a *quid pro quo* for the admission of Tennessee's
delegation. In any event, shortly after the bill passed the House, a subcommittee of the Committee of Fifteen recommended the admission
of the Tennesseeans, and the recommendation seemed likely to be accepted. It turned out quite otherwise.

Basing his stand on constitutional grounds, Johnson on February 19
vetoed the Freedmen's Bureau Bill, and to Radical chagrin, the Senate
sustained him. The Committee of Fifteen hastily pigeonholed the admis-

sion of Tennessee. Because the Senate acted first, the House did not go on record, but that Raymond would have voted to sustain the veto, there can be no doubt. The President's appeal to the Constitution would have been enough, but he saw in addition that if the veto meant open warfare between Johnson and the Radicals, he had to stand with Johnson. The *Times* came out flat-footed for him: "The choice is between the President and the whole Union and the Radicals and a broken Union—between the President struggling to uphold the Constitution, and the Radicals who would overturn the Constitution."

To celebrate the sustaining of the veto—it was Johnson's last victory over the Radicals—a great meeting was called for Cooper Institute in New York. Seward, Postmaster Dennison, Raymond, and other Administration stalwarts came up from Washington to speak for the President. The anti-Johnson *Tribune* said that the rally "bore the unmistakable marks of an old-fashioned Democratic gathering," but to Raymond and Seward and the others, the cheers that night were so thundering that they thought they signaled popular ratification of Johnson's policies, and the *Times* next morning so interpreted.

While the chief speakers spoke in Cooper Union's great hall, other speakers addressed the thousands gathered outside in Astor Place. Red flares burned, but even before their glow had faded, stories were being spread through the city that President Johnson that evening had got off a drunken and disgraceful harangue to serenaders at the White House. The *Times*, which alone had a full report of what the President had said, denounced the false and scandalous stories spread by his enemies, but once started they were hard to halt. "The extremists are angry," wrote Welles in his diary, ". . . and their operations through the press are prolific in manufacturing scandal [against the President]. No harm will come of it if he is prudent and firm."

The Radicals did not halt with scandalous stories. Before the House was a Civil Rights Bill—the Senate had already passed it—which forbade the states to discriminate between citizens on grounds of race or color. The Radicals were determined to push it through and to make it law, regardless of any veto. Debate was long, bitter, often scurrilous, and Thaddeus Stevens used the occasion to put into the record a sentence from the New York *World* that described Johnson as "an insolent drunken brute in comparison with whom Caligula's horse was respectable."

Raymond spoke out against the bill on March 8 in a speech that even the ever-hostile *Tribune* admitted won the respect of many a colleague. "I cannot and will not vote for any bill," he said, ". . . unless my judgement is satisfied that it is a constitutional bill," and the Civil Rights Bill did not meet that test. He assailed its provisions empowering the Federal Government to penalize state judges who enforced state laws. "Have we the power," he asked, "to say that the judge of a state court shall be punished by fine and imprisonment for enforcing a state law? . . . If he does not enforce it, he is subject to punishment as an officer of the state by the government of the state. If he does enforce it, he is to be punished by the Federal Government. . . ." That, he said, seemed a direct violation of both state and Federal constitutions.

Raymond, as he repeated many times later, did not disagree with the bill's purpose. "I hold that the national government is not only bound to protect the freedmen from oppression and unequal laws, but that justice and good policy alike require that all persons, without distinction of race or color, should be equal before the law." To him the bill seemed the wrong way of doing the right thing.

He spoke for twenty-five minutes, and probably for all his logic and eloquence changed not a vote. Aware that his negative would make no difference, Raymond was in New York on *Times* business when the bill came up for vote on March 15. The triumphant majority pushed the bill through easily. The anticipated Presidential veto was soon forthcoming.

Johnson, after detailing many an objection, summed up his veto on constitutional grounds that differed little from those cited during debate by Raymond and men who thought like him. Logic meant nothing to the Radicals, who promptly and with great care set about marshaling the votes needed to make their bill law. One moderate after another capitulated; in the Senate even Morgan fell into line, surprising and distressing Administration members like Welles, who described Morgan's action as "one of calculation, not of conviction." On April 9, after the Senate had overridden the veto, the House acted. The vote against the President was nearly three to one, and of New York Union-Republicans, only Raymond voted to sustain. "Poor Raymond," wrote William Cullen Bryant to his daughter, "seemed in great perplexity to know which way to turn. He supported the veto, but his paper commended it but faintly."

For Johnson, the action of Congress signaled the final break between the Administration and the Union party majority. For Raymond, it marked the end of all real influence. He would carry on, gamely but ineffectively, but he understood that short of a miracle the Administration was lost, and he had not much faith in the miraculous. "Things do not improve," he wrote Weed. "I think you had better come on here for the purpose of having a talk with the President about the general policy of his Administration. He seems, I think, a good deal depressed by the passage of the Civil Rights Bill, though I could not detect any symptom of yielding. Unless he is wise, it seems to me he is ruined."

VI

At the Cooper Union rally for Johnson, Raymond had confessed the regret he felt at separating himself "on great public questions from those personal and political friends" with whom he was allied by party and long-time association. He did so, he said proudly and defiantly, because he believed that the welfare of the country demanded it. Many a man praised him for his independent and patriotic spirit, and Raymond placed in the *Times* columns of excerpts from letters of commendation he received. In one of his gayer moments he wrote a friendly correspondent that "what you say of my part in Congress delights me and does something to correct my overweening modesty—which possibly may have escaped your attention. I am fond of debate—feel more at home there than in most other places—but my taste for that is subject to some drawbacks here to its full indulgence. To begin with there are 150 gentlemen quite as fond of it as I am—& we interfere with each other somewhat."

It was heartening to read a Southern paper's editorial citation for his "manly" stand for "those broad and liberal principles which have added so much to his good repute, and removed him from mere sectional influences." But Southern praise only weakened him further in Congress, and for every letter he got from New Yorkers like James W. Beekman —"my thanks for your renewed and patriotic efforts for the good of the country as a whole" [5]—he had scores from men like his constituent Sinclair Tousey—you vote "in company with the most bitter and uncompromising enemies of [your] party and its doctrines." The London *Times* correspondent, Louis Jennings, who lived in Raymond's bachelor hall, noted that Raymond's "breakfast table was covered with letters, every one of which contained a sting," and that others awaited when he returned home at night.

His record did look bad, and he knew it. There was no surprise, then, when the *Herald* said: "The constituents of Hon. Henry J. Raymond are somewhat puzzled to define his position in Congress. According to the *Times*, he is a staunch advocate of President Johnson's policy; but according to Mr. Raymond's votes in the House of Representatives, he is sometimes on one side, sometimes on the other, and occasionally miss-

[5] Wrote William Appleton, head of the publishing house of D. Appleton & Co.: "I hope I may be allowed to say that personally I have admired your course since in Congress, have read all yr speeches, and hear but one opinion from all I meet. If the people could have the opportunity of expressing their opinion Mr. Stevens would be *nowhere*."

ing." The most disturbing attacks were those from his constituents, and while friends at a district organization meeting managed to squelch a resolution against him, he recognized that politically he was very insecure.

It would have been easy to have conformed. Despite their political differences, he and Stevens, who sat near each other in the House, got along well personally. Jennings remembered that "when Mr. Stevens was in sportive humor (which happened more frequently than one would have judged from a mere look at his face), he would put his foot on his desk (always the club foot with characteristic cynicism) and beckon to his adversary. Then the two would quietly laugh and talk until the call of battle sounded in their ears again." Stevens was not only willing but apparently anxious to bring Raymond into the Radical camp. "You would be worth all the world to us if you would only fight within the lines," he told him. "But this plan of insisting on working out your own line of battle is a great mistake. Don't stop there in the cold—come over to us." But Raymond did not intend to surrender. Quixotic his stand might be, but there he was, let his foes ridicule him as they would.

Ridicule him they did. On one occasion, desiring to leave town, he tried to arrange a pair, and finally appealed to his friends on the floor to help him. Stevens, as the California Senator William M. Stewart told it afterward, "looked around sarcastically and remarked that he did not understand why the gentleman was asking for a pair; he had observed that the gentleman found no difficulty in pairing with himself." The gibe at his seemingly contradictory record hurt, and the hurt was only aggravated when the House roared with laughter.

He tried to be good-natured, sometimes succeeded. "My friend from New York," said a Wisconsin member, ". . . started out this session . . . with one foot on the shoulder of Andrew Johnson and the other foot on the shoulder of the gentleman from Pennsylvania. These two gentlemen have been diverging, and he is still trying to keep his feet upon them both. God knows what will become of the body if they diverge much further. His legs I do not find elongating much . . ." Countered Raymond: "I am in the condition of the obstinate juror who wondered how it was that those eleven obstinate fellows would hold out against him."

Raymond had a good idea where all this was leading. To his partner George Jones, who had so long disliked his part in politics, he wrote: "I rather think I don't stand much chance of coming back to Congress! *You* will like this I know."

He had said all along that his opposition to the Civil Rights Bill was based on constitutional grounds. The Fourteenth Amendment met this objection, and when the amendment came before the House on June 14 Raymond voted for it. "His ringing response," said Blaine, "elicited loud applause both on the floor and in the galleries." But to many a party regular, Raymond's vote was further proof that he was too independent for good politics. Others questioned his sincerity, reiterating the now familiar charges that he tried to carry water on both shoulders, for how else could he oppose the Civil Rights Bill and yet vote for the Fourteenth Amendment, which sought the same goal and which was equally disliked by Johnson? Trimming, his critics called it, and Secretary Welles, who never ceased to regard him as "a whiffler on public measures," interpreted his vote as betrayal of the President.

VII

Although the unceasing tug of war between President and Congress had all along threatened to disrupt the Union party, Raymond refused to take the dark view that the party could not be saved. Passage of the Fourteenth Amendment, he believed, had removed a primary cause for disruption, and now if even a single Southern state, more especially Tennessee, were allowed representation in Congress, he foresaw a bright day dawning. He wanted to save the party because it was his party. More than that, he wanted to make the Union party national, a party as strong in the South as in the North, for along such lines he was convinced lay the best guarantee against the political sectionalism that had helped bring the disaster of civil war.

He told the House exactly where he stood. "The great political necessity of the day," he said, "is to nationalize the party that has saved the nation. . . . Let it plant itself upon national ground, discard all sectional feeling, extend its organization into every state, make the interests, rights, honor, welfare of all sections its own and it will stand forever! . . . It is the hope of such a result that has prompted my action on this floor during the present session. It is that which had led me to seek so strongly and so steadily to maintain harmony of action between the President and the majority of Congress, for I knew then, as I know now, that in all the essential principles of their political action, both were united. . . . I indulge the hope that when we adjourn, standing upon ground which we hold in common and referring to the people the decision of questions on which we differ, we shall go to the country united in purpose, and having the cooperation of the President whom we placed in power."

Radicals like Stevens, who had always distrusted the wartime alliance of Republicans and Democrats in the Union party, who had no desire to associate themselves with the President in policy or deed, had no ear for Raymond's words. After all, they were addressed to moderates, and spoken, few listeners doubted, with the President's approval, perhaps even at his urging. Actually Raymond had not consulted with Johnson about the speech and learned only later that he agreed with every word of it, but he had discussed the Union party with the President too many times to have any question about the Administration's views. Though Johnson had told him that he thought politics was "in a strange transition state," he had always urged the need to bring the South into the party. "Under a wise and judicious policy," Raymond reported Johnson as having said, "half the Southern States at least will vote and act with the Union Party. Why should we by hostile action drive them back into their old alliance with the Democratic Party of the North?" That was just what Raymond was trying to impress upon his colleagues.

The trouble was that Congress under Radical domination had been neither wise nor judicious. Nor had Johnson himself, for besides antagonizing the men on Capitol Hill, he had done nothing to link the party rank and file to the Administration by shrewd use of patronage and political favors. The collectorship of New York had been a case in point.

As a means of nationalizing the Union party and at the same time building support for the Administration, men close to the President were already laying plans for a national convention. Raymond heard about it first from Weed, who called at the I Street house to discuss political complexities. Seward told him more while urging that as Union party chairman he was the man to draft an address to the country that would be both a call for a convention and an argument for speedy restoration of the Union. Raymond hesitated, and by the time he had persuaded Seward that any such argument would be stronger if it came from the convention itself, Senator Doolittle had already prepared the call. Raymond criticized it as too broad, since it would admit to the convention men who had fought or had sympathized with the South, an element sure to alienate much support in the North.

For the general purpose of the proposed meeting he had only good words. "I went to New York a few days afterward," Raymond recorded in his journal, "and while there wrote and published in the *Times* an article in favor of a National Convention for the purpose of adopting, if possible, a platform of principles upon which the Northern and Southern States could take common political action." It was a strong leader, the essence of which was that "new necessities demand new action, and the first of these necessities is to place the Union Party on ground which it can hold in every State and every section." Four days later, on June 26, a call for a convention to meet in Philadelphia on August 14 was made public. Raymond did not sign it, probably because he was increasingly uneasy lest the Democratic party take over the convention and use it for its own ends.

He poured out his fears to Seward, urging that Democratic support of the convention was already weakening the movement among Union men. "I told him," he said afterward, "I did not feel inclined to attend the convention. He asked why. I said that it seemed likely to be in the hands of the former rebels and their Copperhead associates, and to be used for purposes hostile to the Union Party, of which I was not only a member, but in which I held an official position." Seward argued with him, for it was most important that the movement have the Union party chairman's support, and finally drove with him to the White House to talk it over with the President.

The three men sat down together in the White House library. "Mr. Seward," Raymond recalled, "said to [the President] that we had come to talk about the Philadelphia Convention—that I had expressed fears lest it should fall into bad hands, and that he had told me that was what they wanted me to prevent. The President said yes—it was important that the right direction should be given to it. It ought to take national ground in harmony with Union principles, and in favor of a speedy restoration of the Union. . . . His sympathies, he said, were with the party which had carried the country through the war—that party ought to restore the Union, and although it ought not to repel Democrats who were willing to act with it and to aid it, he did not wish the Democratic Party to get control."

Raymond countered that he had become confused as to the exact purpose of the convention. Was it to create a new party, or was it to influence the election of a Congress favorable to the admission of loyal representatives from the South? Creation of a new party, he argued, would help only the Democrats. But the second objective he favored. "I thought great good might be accomplished," he said. Johnson agreed. The President told him that "he did not want any new party, nor did he want the Democratic Party restored to power." He thought that the very fact of a national convention "would be a great step toward the restoration of the Union" and that the holding of such a convention "would have a very salutary effect on public sentiment, and would cause the leaders of the Radical movement to pause." He ended by urging, "with a good deal of earnestness," that Raymond ought "to take part in the convention."

Under such pressure, Raymond gave in, adopting Seward's position that if Union men stayed away from Philadelphia, they would be playing into Democratic hands. The important thing, he said, was "to prevent this result, if possible, and I accordingly decided to do what little I could in that direction."

VIII

The convention movement got under way amid heightened political tension. At the beginning of June, Raymond had written the *Times* that President and Congress might be close to settling their differences: "There is a more openly avowed desire on both sides for harmony of action, or if that cannot be had, for the avoidance of needless and useless conflicts." The bright prospect soon dimmed. On June 22 Johnson told Congress that he was opposed to amending the Constitution during the absence of Southern representatives. Though Cabinet members like Welles applauded, moderates like Seward were appalled, and Raymond must have wondered just where this left his carefully reasoned analysis of increased harmony. Radicals were delighted. The President's seeming intransigence against any amendment, and the Fourteenth in particular, cost him most of the remaining support among Congressional moderates. In July, a veto of a revised Freedmen's Bureau Bill was easily overridden; Raymond was one of four Republicans to support it.

To the triumphant Radicals, the Philadelphia Convention loomed more and more as a scheme for organizing support for Johnson and obstruction to Radical policies. As Raymond had feared, Democratic enthusiasm for the convention was being translated by the Radicals into proof that the whole idea was a plot to destroy the Union party. They made effective propaganda, and meanwhile, although the summer heat was the most burning in recent Washington memory, they kept Congress in session with a view to blocking the President at every turn. In such a mood Union-Republicans—few Senators attended—caucused in the House chamber on the suffocating evening of July 11. Though the ostensible purpose was to fix a date for adjournment, Stevens and his lieutenants were out to portray the President as a man so dangerous that Congress should sit indefinitely lest he turn the country over to the rebels. They also intended to destroy the Philadelphia Convention.

"We had a caucus last night," Raymond wrote Weed the next day, "full, venomous, reckless, the worst yet. The ruling sentiment was to sit all summer, so as to prevent the President from making appointments.[6] . . . Stevens submitted a resolution denouncing the Philadelphia movement and reading out of the party any one who has anything to do with it. The Radicals are terribly excited. . . . The stories of the

---

[6] Even Thad Stevens sometimes lost a fight. A second caucus fixed July 23 as the date for adjournment; Congress finally shut up shop on the 28th.

Tribune, World and *Herald* about my remarks are utterly false." These stories—the *Times* described them as a "shady and malicious vilification"—bothered Raymond, and rightly; and as so often happens, truth was unable to overtake falsehood.

The difficulty was that the press had been barred from the caucus which itself was pledged to secrecy. A *Herald* reporter, however, had slipped past a drunken doorkeeper to hide beneath a gallery bench, a vantage point from which before he was discovered he had heard much of the violent language of men who should have known better. Of what went on after his eviction, he could only guess, and so it was that he reported inaccurately that Raymond supported the Stevens resolution against the Philadelphia Convention. The *World* sneered that "his faith as a party man and his honor as a gentleman were pledged to oppose a movement of which, up to that hour, he had been the most prominent patron and promoter." Welles noted in his diary that Raymond had "again played the harlequin." Yet the whole story, as Raymond had written Weed, was false.

What had happened was quite otherwise. In the course of the caucus, Representative Kelley of Pennsylvania denounced the Philadelphia Convention as "a conspiracy of traitors" which the President had got up "for the purpose of destroying the Union Party." That, he continued, was why some papers in New York supported it, and while the *Times* had not gone quite so far, it was nevertheless behind the movement. Though conscious that he was almost alone against the pack, Raymond had jumped to his feet to defend his paper. No one, he challenged, had the shadow of right to accuse the *Times* of seeking to break up the Union party, and as for himself, he believed that, properly managed, the convention could do the party a lot of good. "Whenever he saw reason to believe that it was to be used to destroy the Union Party neither the *Times* nor its editor would support it."

There was no stopping the Radicals. Stevens now offered his resolution reading out of the party any man who supported the convention. Once again Raymond fought back. No stenographer took down his words, and probably his own account lost nothing in the telling, but if the third-person story that he wrote in his notebook and later published in the *Times* was close to the truth, he surrendered nothing at the same time that he dared his enemies to destroy him.

"He presumed," he said at the start, "he was not guilty of any undue assumption in supposing the resolution was aimed in part at least at him. He regarded it as a menace, and so far as it was a menace he regarded it with contempt. He was not responsible, financially, professionally or politically, to the gentleman from Pennsylvania [Stevens], nor to the delegation from Pennsylvania, nor to the Union members of Congress. He held position in the Union Party by favor of his constituents and by the appointment of the National Committee. When either of these authorities saw fit to expel him, he would give heed to it. But the action of that caucus was a matter of entire indifference. When the Philadelphia Convention was summoned, he believed it would have a good effect in nationalizing the Union Party. He could never conceal his conviction that unless the party was thus nationalized it would be short-lived, and he had therefore looked with favor on the call for the convention. Whenever he saw reason to change his opinion as to its effect and object he should act accordingly."

He must have known from the start that he was wasting breath on the angry men around him, for if a few among them had accepted his statement as honest and sincere, these dared not defy the terrors of the Stevens dictatorship. When the Stevens resolution came to a vote, only Robert S. Hale, Raymond's old college friend, opposed it. To Raymond, who sat silent in his chair, the resolution was as a premonitory flash of lightning across his darkening political skies.

CHAPTER
22

Disaster

I

IN THE muggy heat of the Philadelphia summer, carpenters swarmed over a great "wigwam" being built in a goat pasture on Girard Avenue to house the first truly national convention in America since before the war. A plain, two-story structure, nearly square, and topped with a 100-foot flagpole, it was planned to seat 10,-000 people, with delegates on the floor, spectators in the galleries that stretched around three sides. The workmen had only a fortnight to complete it, and by August 14, when the convention was called to order, the wigwam's roof was but half finished, though the seats were in place, the bunting was up, and over the flag-draped platform had been strung a great banner: "1776–1866: THE UNION AND THE CONSTITU-TION."

Delegates—they represented the thirty-six states and the territories, too—began to gather early, jamming hotels until in some places they slept three and four to a room. Southerners got the attention of the curious, for after the years of war they were almost strangers in their own land. Their clothes were shabby, out of style—a *Times* reporter wrote: "I saw one delegate from the sunny South with a dress coat whose tails weren't of the same length"—and summer showers did great damage to the white cotton trousers many wore. A lot of them—and among the delegates they were not peculiar in this—were short of money, a fact dismaying both to the swarming pickpockets and to the Philadelphians who had hoped to profit from selling ginger beer, watermelon, cigars, and whisky outside the wigwam.

Raymond stayed away from Philadelphia until the night before the convention, and he pointedly avoided the executive committee, which was sitting at the Continental Hotel, by putting up at the Girard House. For all his promise to the President and to Seward, he wanted no part in the business, entered into it even now with utmost reluctance. In the *Times* he had given the movement enthusiastic support, though warning always that it must be kept out of Democratic hands, but he had not attended the Saratoga Convention, where New York's delegation, headed by the Democrat Samuel J. Tilden, had been picked. He knew, of course, that he could not avoid being named a delegate, but he could leave to Weed and others the convention preliminaries. He brought to Philadelphia the fear that had pursued him all along—fear that the convention would wreck him and his cause—and his fear was well-founded.

Raymond knew at first hand the temper of the Radicals, and he could hardly forget the rough talk in the recent July caucus in the House chamber. Secretary Welles had noted that "the Philadelphia movement is . . . encountering tremendous and violent opposition from the Radicals." In New York State Federal officeholders were restless, and the Albany postmaster, for one, had denounced as renegades all who favored the convention. In mid-July Raymond had said privately that the Union party in his state was almost unanimous in opposing the movement. Then, as though prearranged, a political row in Louisiana over Negro suffrage flared into ugly riots that, scarcely a fortnight before the Philadelphia meeting, had left scores injured and close to forty dead, most of them Negroes. General Sheridan called it "an absolute massacre"; Welles thought Radicals from the North had instigated it, but whatever the facts, the tragedy was just what the Radicals needed to prove that the South was neither repentant nor regenerate. In Philadelphia, backwash from the riots provoked such hostility to the convention that the militia was mobilized and marines at the navy yard alerted.

Despite the bad omens, Welles, who talked with many Southern delegates as they passed through Washington, found that most of them seemed "in good spirits and cheered with the prospect of a restored Union." Many an observer, North as well as South, looked optimistically toward Philadelphia and its wigwam. Benjamin Curtis, a leader of the American bar and a former Supreme Court justice, wrote the scholarly George Ticknor: "Neither you nor I have much confidence in 'conventions'; but in the present state of our country, I have hope from all *honest* expressions of popular feeling, and I do not despair that this may be such an expression." And in an open letter to Orville

H. Browning, a moving force at Philadelphia and soon to be a member of the Cabinet, Curtis argued that the Southern states should be recognized as members of the Union, and thus put himself behind the issue that above all others had brought the convention together.

It was the *Times* that sounded the ringing notes that both moderates and Conservatives wanted to hear: "The world has no grander or more inspiring spectacle than that which is presented by a people who having passed through all the agonies of civil war are sitting down in council once more. . . . No quarrel is so bitter as a quarrel between kinsmen, and none requires so much forbearance. . . . The work of the Philadelphia Convention is preeminently a Christian work. . . . It is an impromptu Congress summoned in the midst of great perils—perils made imminent by rash politicians who do not know how to forgive and whose love of power blinds them to the welfare of the people. It is emphatically a council of the people who have begun to tire of sectional hostility and who think that the peace won by the sword should be a reality."

After the fashion of conventions, the one at Philadelphia was late in getting started, and because the street railways failed to put on extra cars, delegates found it hard to get to the wigwam at all. Private carriages were few; hacks were expensive. Yet somehow the trip was made, and the wigwam was crowded when Postmaster General Randall rapped for order—the gavel had been made from timber from the frigate *Constitution*—and bawled: "Gentlemen of the Convention, I have to announce to you the approach of the delegates from Massachusetts and South Carolina, arm-in-arm!" The bands boomed "Hail Columbia," the packed galleries cheered lustily—in the excitement a blond-haired army officer named Custer was seen to throw his hat in the air—and with South Carolina's Governor James L. Orr and General Darius Couch of Massachusetts in the lead, a long procession filed into the vast hall. As the hundreds of delegates who symbolized a united nation found their places, spectators wept—perhaps now the war was really over—and the bands swung into "The Star Spangled Banner," "Dixie," and "Rally Round the Flag." General Dix, Raymond's personal and political friend, was chosen temporary chairman; Senator Doolittle, who had written the convention call, was made permanent chairman. Committees were named, and then, just as a heavy shower broke through the wigwam's unfinished roof, delegates adjourned to their hotels for impromptu speech-making and serenades by marching bands.

On the convention eve the atmosphere of brotherly love had been chilled by the presence of three delegates who had been notorious Copperheads: Fernando Wood of New York; Clement L. Vallandigham of

Ohio; Henry Clay Dean of Iowa. "The feeling was very strong," said Raymond afterward, "that the admission of men who had been so hostile to the Government during the war, and who, though Northern men, were thoroughly identified by the public mind with the rebel cause, would be of serious injury to the Convention by alienating the sympathies of Union men and by affixing to the proceedings the stigma of having been dictated to or influenced by Copperhead counsels." In hotel lobbies and private rooms, argument over the presence of the three stimulated what Raymond called "turmoil and heat," and he was in the middle of it, for if he had any influence at all, he intended to use it to keep Copperheads away, even though to do so might step on Southern toes. Wood withdrew first. Then, "after the proper amount of swagger and bravado," Raymond recalled, Dean followed, though not before he had asserted with noise and insolence that he wanted no part of a convention where men like Raymond dictated the terms of admission. In the end, Vallandigham, too, caved in. This first success presumably raised Raymond's hopes that the convention might still turn out all right.

If he and his group could determine the nature of the convention's address and its resolutions, then final victory could be assured. The way was opened when to no one's surprise, and surely not to Raymond's, he was placed on the resolutions committee, where as so many times in his political life his job was to draft an address and a platform. Forewarned, he had written an address in advance, and when the committee met in Parlor C at the Continental the first convention afternoon, he was ready to read the forty-three pages of his letter-size manuscript. "It was listened to respectfully," he said, "and without comment, but I could hear [Senator] Garret Davis of Kentucky, who sat near me, now and then say to a gentleman near him, 'that's not true,' 'not a word of truth in that,' etc." Some of the opposition was louder, for there were members who preferred Copperhead sentiments to Raymond's middle-of-the-road position, but in the end the assignment was passed to a subcommittee where Raymond was left to defend himself against the predominating Southern members.

Together they worked out an acceptable address. It was essentially Raymond's, although he was obliged to tone down some passages in the original, to cut others, and, regretfully, to omit all reference to the pending constitutional amendments which he himself supported but which many committeemen—and they were in tune with the Administration—hated virulently. Then the resolutions were taken up. Several drafts were offered and rejected, and finally Raymond drew from his pocket a draft he had scribbled out the previous evening and for which he had gotten Weed's approval. Once more there was argument; there was cutting, rewriting, compromise. Senator Cowan, committee chairman, said that Raymond, if not the committee's soul, was "its intellect, by the wonderful manner in which he gathered the views of the members, digesting them and expressing them with a clearness and elegance which satisfied all." In little more than three hours, the work was done. "I hear it remarked by many who were accustomed to severe mental labor," said Cowan, "that it was the most extraordinary performance they had ever known to be performed in so short a time." From Raymond's point of view, the important thing was that the extremists had been blocked, and a relatively moderate document drafted. Even so, it was probably stronger than he had really intended, and Radicals soon showed that in their eyes it was a revolutionary manifesto.

Raymond brought his address before the delegates on the convention's third and final day. "We are again people of the United States," he shouted in his best voice, "fellow citizens of one country, bound by the duties and obligations of a common patriotism, and having neither rights nor interests apart from a common destiny." A roar of cheering and applause burst in the overcrowded wigwam, and again and again cheers interrupted him as he continued with an address filled with patriotism and expressions of loyalty to the Union. He recognized and accepted the changes wrought by war: the end of slavery and the doctrine of secession, the integrity of the Union, the inviolability of the public debt, the repudiation of Southern debts incurred in fighting the rebellion. He upheld the Constitution, its principles and practice, reasserting with full eloquence the stand he had taken so many times during the recent years of debate. Then he moved onto dangerous ground, for with startling vigor and vehemence he assailed Congress for its refusal to admit loyal representatives from the South, and threw out the Congressional theory of reconstruction as unconstitutional, as a dangerous usurpation that left "the very existence of Congress and the Union" dependent "solely and entirely upon the party and sectional exigencies and forbearances of the hour."

The address went further: it called for the election to Congress of men who, "whatever other differences may characterize their political action, will unite in recognizing the right" of every state to representation in Congress and "who will admit to seats . . . every loyal representative from every State in allegiance to the Government. . . ." In such fashion the Union party could be remade along the national lines Raymond had pleaded for in Congress and through editorials in the *Times*. The resolutions put in briefer form what had already been said in the address, and the roar in the hall now reached its climax, for as

Raymond finished, Tilden stepped forward to call for three cheers for Henry J. Raymond. The work was done, and Raymond thought it well done.

"I have never seen a convention made up of better men, or animated by a better sentiment than this one," Raymond said. The *Times* put it more formally: "The Convention has been a splendid success. . . . It has materially advanced the work of reconciliation, has hastened the return of sectional harmony and has given an impetus to the National Union movement which cannot be easily overestimated. The movement is from this day a power, which will command the confidence of conservative Unionists, and will eventuate in victory." Secretary Welles, who talked again with many Southerners on their return from Philadelphia, wrote: "All in good spirits and patriotically disposed." Then he put his finger on the nub of it all, perhaps without foreseeing where events would lead: "Most of these men, as well as those whom they represent, have been connected in some degree with the Rebellion, but they submit and acquiesce in the result with grace, and I believe with sincerity. But the Radicals are filled with hatred, acrimony, and revenge toward them, and would persist in excluding not only them but the whole people of the South from any participation in the government. For four years war was waged to prevent them from going out; now the Radicals would wage as fine a war to shut them out."

II

If the Radicals were "filled with hatred, acrimony, and revenge" before the convention met, they were in a blazing fury by the time it adjourned. It was not only the declaration of principles that excited them. They had flouted constitutional theory before with impunity, presumably could do so again. But the appeal to the country to elect a Congress that would toss aside the Radical program was something else. If heeded, it might indeed destroy Radical power, and that was a chance not to be taken. The Radical press brought up its guns. The convention was attacked, ridiculed. The "arm-in-arm" convention it was dubbed, and with biting sarcasm the wigwam was likened to a Noah's Ark, into which there went "in two and two," "of clean beasts, and of beasts that are not clean, and of fowls, and of every thing that creepeth upon the earth." Cartoonists got in their licks. Radical orators cleared their throats to shout denunciation, and to counterbalance the Philadelphia movement Radical leaders organized three different national conventions that in September did much to shape public opinion against the President and in favor of Congress.

In the swift, violent reaction to what had been done at Philadelphia,

Raymond was a prime target. It was the doctrine that Congress had no right to bar the loyal Southern representatives that drew the lightning. Blaine remarked that Raymond's "personal friends and admirers, who were not confined to any one party, were amazed at the recklessness of his position," and it was true, as Blaine said, that the doctrine was one certain to arouse the ire of Union veterans who were fast becoming an instrument of political force. And though Raymond, as Radical-minded *Harper's Weekly* pointed out, had taken this position many times before, he had never had it adopted by a national convention imbued with political purpose. Perhaps the fatal error had been in accepting the convention's prevailing hostility to the constitutional amendments. If these had been endorsed at the same time that the issue of representation was expounded, the address would have seemed less inflammatory. Yet to have endorsed the amendments would have been to go counter to the President, and opposition to them had been omitted from the convention call only to assure Raymond's support. Now Raymond had been caught in the middle.

He might have been able to withstand editorial assaults and oratorical vilification—Stevens lashed him in a speech dripping with words like wild, wicked, brazen, frenzied—but he was now faced with an attack that put his political life in jeopardy. Even before the convention gathered, *Harper's Weekly* had called for his resignation as national chairman. It accused him then, and it renewed the charge after the convention, of calling in the party's enemies to remake the party, of working with the Democrats to defeat good Unionists for Congress. What *Harper's* was saying, others were thinking, even if they kept their own counsel. Action was not long delayed.

Before the month was out, four anti-Raymond men on the National Committee called a special meeting to oust him and others who had been in the Philadelphia movement. The date: September 3. The place: Philadelphia. Raymond countered with a call for a meeting at the Astor House on the same day, and under the committee's rules only his call or that of the secretary had standing. Promptly, New Jersey's Governor Marcus L. Ward, a Radical member, wrote him a public letter. He denounced him: "You have deemed it wise and proper to abandon the great Union Republican Party of this country, and to connect your name and influence with a new organization designed to destroy and defeat the cause with which I sympathize." Ward announced that he would go to Philadelphia: "I cannot acknowledge your right to use the title under which the [Astor House] meeting has been called."

Only eight members showed up at the Astor, seventeen at Philadelphia. At neither were there enough to transact business, but the seventeen did not let that stop them. Without delay they resolved that Raymond had vacated his post because of his "abandonment of the principles of the National Union Party and affiliation with its enemies." Though he protested that he had done nothing of the kind, that their action violated committee rules and was therefore null and void, his protest was futile: two days later the Union State Convention at Syracuse ratified his dismissal.

Raymond knew when he was beaten. Though some of his constituents, praising his ability and integrity, urged him to run again for Congress, he declined—he knew he had no chance of election—in a long letter that gave him the opportunity to review and defend his work in Congress and at Philadelphia. He made no apology, insisting that whatever he had said and done had been according to principles that he had made clear to his constituents from the start and according to what he believed to be the principles of the Union party. (On a later occasion, he said that he had never left the party, that it had left him.) Finally, and it seemed almost to echo Webster's words in the famous "I am a Whig" speech of so many years before, he ended his letter with defiance to his foes: "I am now as I was when elected two years ago—as I have always been, and shall always remain—a member of the Union party, holding the faith as declared in its conventions, seeking its welfare, and striving for advancement and reform in everything touching the public good, through its agency. *With the Democratic party, as it has been organized and directed since the Rebellion broke out, I have nothing in common*, and . . . should regard its re-established ascendancy in the government of the country, State or national, as a public calamity."

III

For Raymond, the fall of 1866 was a trying time. Whatever personal loyalty he felt toward the President was sorely battered by the unhappy incidents during Johnson's speaking tour across the country, the famous swing around the circle. Raymond had long believed that Johnson had been obstinately wrong in opposing the constitutional amendments, but that was a difference of opinion that could be tolerated. There could be no tolerance for the President's undignified conduct at the great public rallies he addressed as he moved from city to city, and the *Times* did not hesitate to rebuke him for it: "President Johnson in his speech at Cleveland remarked that he did not care about his dignity. In our judgement this is greatly to be regretted. The American people care very much about it and can never see it forgotten or laid aside without professed sorrow and solicitude."

The Radicals, of course, were doing their best to make the Presidential tour a fiasco, and Raymond undoubtedly knew it. But that was all the more reason for Johnson to be on guard. His unseemly behavior as he took on hecklers, his reported drinking, were playing into Radical hands and making it difficult for men like Raymond to support him. Furthermore, he was squandering whatever good the Philadelphia Convention might have accomplished.

So far as Raymond was concerned the last hope for the Philadelphia movement lay in the meeting of Democrats and moderate Republicans that came together in Albany on September 11 as the National Union State Convention. The name meant little—all factions tended to use the word Union so that party labels were inextricably confused—but the convention promised to translate the Philadelphia idea and purpose into reality. The answer would depend on the platform and ticket for the state's fall elections. Raymond, who wanted Dix to be named for Governor, did not go up the river, but Weed, who was also for Dix, was present and led the moderates. He was ineffectual—"an old, played-out stump," a Tammany delegate called him—and his impotence reflected pitifully the political failure of the once powerful firm of Seward, Weed & Raymond.

If at the start there was a bow to the idea of a Union-Republican-Democratic coalition, it was soon forgotten as the convention became a Tammany show. There was disorder, egged on by the Tammany-packed galleries. There were shenanigans and disgraceful skulduggery as the convention, after making the Philadelphia platform its own, nominated for Governor the handsome and popular John T. Hoffman, Democratic Mayor of New York. Dix never had serious consideration. It took Raymond no time to realize that in New York State the Philadelphia movement, for whatever it was still worth, had been captured by the Democrats, who intended to use it solely for their own advantage. It was what he had feared all along, and yet to avoid it he had joined the movement in the first place, and at what sacrifice!

Whatever qualities Raymond may have lacked, courage was not one of them, and he now did not hesitate to denounce the Albany ticket as a travesty and to swing the *Times* behind the Radical Republican ticket headed by Governor Reuben E. Fenton. Amazed, his enemies and critics attacked him for it, charging him again with trimming; Horatio Seymour told a Democratic rally at Cooper Institute that Raymond, trusting "in his dexterity to ride upon many animals at once had been so tossed upon their horns that neither he nor we can tell upon what spot he will fall." Few seemed to understand how difficult the change in course must have been, or how disappointing it was to Raymond to scrap his cherished ideas for a restored Union and a Union party truly national. "The 'purposes' of the Philadelphia Convention the *Times* has renounced," the paper eventually explained in an editorial that Raymond probably wrote. "It renounced them when they became clearly impracticable—when the extraordinary declarations and demonstrations of the President's Western tour so confirmed the general distrust of his wisdom and self-command as to array the people against any system of measures he was known to favor—and when the eager selfishness of the Democratic Party betrayed its purposes to use the Convention merely as a means of replacing power in the hands of those leaders who had arrayed it as a party against the war. . . . The 'ideas' of the Convention neither the *Times* nor its Editor has ever renounced."

Throughout the fall campaign the *Times* did all it could for Fenton, and when the November elections brought victory to him and to the Radicals generally, the paper viewed it with the realism that had so often characterized Raymond: "The people have given their support to Congress and its policy as against the President and his policy. . . . President Johnson has a thousand times expressed his confidence in the people. . . . It can, therefore, be no violence to his principles of character to listen to their voice and obey it."

IV

For the second and short session of the Thirty-ninth Congress, Raymond got to Washington a day late, well aware that whether he appeared or not made no difference to the Radicals running the House. Only a year earlier—it seemed longer—he had been pointed out as the most promising freshman member, as a man of power whose favor should be cultivated. The interest in him now was wholly different. He embodied the fate that overtakes one whose political independence prevents his running with the pack. For all his efforts in the New York election just past to realign himself with his party, he remained outside, in the eyes of many an unregenerate apostate.

The reversal of Raymond's political fortunes was reflected in his style of living. He had never entertained on the scale that he had anticipated when he rented the I Street house, and now, with the need for show and hospitality much reduced, he gave up the place and took rooms at Crutchett's, the boardinghouse where General Scott had lived before the war and where on the eve of the first Bull Run he had explained to Raymond his anaconda policy. It was no hardship to live at Crutchett's, for the house boasted one of the best chefs in town. What Raymond had lost was the prestige of an establishment of his own.

He had returned to Capitol Hill determined to be regarded as a Union-

Republican, but his right was challenged the moment he appeared at the first party caucus. Had he not been warned, demanded the violently Radical Ashley of Ohio, that all who supported the Philadelphia movement would be expelled from party membership? Surely that had been the sentiment of the caucus that had met that hot July night when the convention was still in the planning stage. Had Raymond forgotten? Raymond had his answer ready.

He insisted, as he had in his September letter to his constituents, that he had always been a good Republican and Union party man, and still so regarded himself. He defended his record: he had joined in the Philadelphia Convention because he had thought it would be good for the party and the country; he had never thought it a movement to create a new party, and when he had been convinced that the movement was falling into Democratic hands, he had cut loose from it. Raymond had said all this so many times that he must have been getting tired of explaining; perhaps he hoped that repetition would convince even those who intended to remain unconvinced. Then Stevens spoke up. Did Raymond still adhere to the Philadelphia address? The answer was a resounding yea—so far as its principles and sentiments were concerned—although Raymond had only to cite the election returns to make his point that the Philadelphia movement was cold and dead. Hale and Darling spoke for him. With wit that was not wholly unfriendly, Morrill of Vermont argued: "While the lamp has oil to burn, the vilest sinner may return." Probably because a lot of Republicans liked Raymond personally and still others believed him sufficiently punished, it was finally left to his own conscience as to whether he should sit in the caucus. Presumably he did, although the record is unclear; to have stayed away would have been to admit guilt that he did not feel.

His position was bound to be anomalous. Unless he accepted Radical party policies without reservations, he was suspect. But, in the light of his past, if he did accept them he stood forth unprincipled. As a matter of fact, Raymond intended to act without thought of party discipline, just as he had in the previous session. At the same time he was ready to recognize that situations, not theories, were often at issue, and he had become somewhat philosophical, he said, to the extent at least that he was now prepared to accept the inevitable even should it clash with his views of right and wrong.

"I say frankly," he told the House, "that I am still of the opinion that if [loyal Southern representatives had been admitted] at an early stage of the controversy, promptly, cheerfully, generously, by the party that ruled the destinies of the country at that time, it would have restored peace, and healed to a great extent all the troubles of the body politic.

But because I believed and still believe that to have been the best policy then, I do not feel bound to maintain that it is the best policy now. A physician may prescribe a gargle for a sore throat, and if his prescription is thrown out of the window, the sore throat may develop into an inflammation or into a raging and consuming fever; but he would be regarded as wanting in sound judgement and in common sense if for the sake of consistency he should feel bound to prescribe nothing but gargles during the whole course of the disease."

The situation had indeed changed. The New Orleans riots and Southern failure to ratify the Fourteenth Amendment had convinced Raymond of the need for new policies. The fall elections, he kept repeating, could not be ignored, for they proved that the President was getting nowhere with his ideas. Moreover, Congress came together with many members talking of impeaching him. Though Raymond now regularly criticized the Administration, he was no friend of impeachment. He voted against the impeachment resolution, put the *Times* against it, and presented to the House batch after batch of anti-impeachment petitions sent him by New York business groups. Yet he was so convinced that conditions in the South were rapidly deteriorating, that something must be decided and quickly, that he was ready to accept any reasonable plan of reconstruction Congress could devise. Unhappily, no reasonable plan was likely to pass the House.

On January 3, 1867, Thaddeus Stevens brought in a Military Reconstruction Bill that proposed virtual military dictatorship for the South, and while it provided for the creation of new state governments and for eventual restoration of the South to a place in the Union, it did so in a fashion that made law the conquered-province theory that Raymond had always fought. To Raymond, with a true democrat's fear and hatred for military government, the bill was nothing more than an outrageous use of police power. In the last great debate of his Congressional career he joined with a handful of moderates to fight it.

In a long speech filled with examples of the fate that had overtaken civil governments that abdicated to military dictatorship, he surveyed the situation in the South, admitting the excesses of many unreconstructed Rebels at the same time that he denied the existence of a situation critical enough to excuse the suspension of habeas corpus. "Because we cannot devise any thing of a civil nature adequate to the emergency," he said, "it is argued that we must fly to the most violent measure the ingenuity of man could devise. . . . This has been the history of popular governments everywhere, the reason of their downfall, their decadence and their death." What was needed, Raymond insisted, was civil government backed, if necessary, by military force.

"What I object to in this bill," he cried, "is not the presence of the Army; not the protection to be extended by the Army over loyal citizens, black as well as white. But I object to clothing the military officers of that Army with power to make just such laws as they please, to establish their own definitions of the rights of liberty and person and property, which are to be protected by them and the forces under their command. . . . What I insist upon as fundamental, unless we are to abandon all pretense of self-government and republican institutions, is that we shall not clothe subaltern officers of the Army with the unrestricted power of life and death, with absolute authority over the liberties and the property of our fellow citizens."

The Indiana Congressman George W. Julian, a long-time Radical, was so impressed that a decade and a half later he recalled in his memoirs that Raymond had "analyzed and exposed" the bill with "great ability." His "arguments," said Julian, "were unanswered and unanswerable." John Hay, who listened to the debate from the gallery, was not so sure. "Went to the House again," he wrote in his diary. "Raymond talked a little—clever and fluent as ever, and impressing nobody."

The bill passed the House easily, with Raymond among the handful opposed, but in the Senate it was considerably changed and in its final form so many of the features that Raymond had attacked were omitted that he felt he could vote for it and did. The *Times*, while urging Johnson to sign the bill, confessed to disliking it on the grounds that it was "at war with the Constitution and hostile to the dictates of a wise and considerate statesmanship." On the other hand, with all the bad features, the plan was "preferable to prolonged uncertainty or delay," and it had to be admitted that the war had so altered public sentiment that what had once been the rules of statesmanship no longer seemed to apply. Besides, if the Southern states could once be organized and recognized as states with constitutional rights, they could set about arranging their houses to suit themselves.

For Raymond, playing the game to the end, the debate on military reconstruction must at times have seemed purely an intellectual exercise, and so with many of the other legislative questions in which he participated. He had things to say on inflation, on the tariff, on taxes. (One of his speeches on taxes, including a plea for a graduated income tax, filled pages of the *Congressional Globe* and was reprinted as a pamphlet.) But it all got him nowhere, and if his spirits sagged, it was with reason. Sapped by political disappointment and hard work, his health was poor, and often illness kept him from Capitol Hill.

The session ended on March 2, and Raymond must have welcomed it as release from purgatory. Yet if the term in Congress had been filled with disappointment, had ended in the shadow of political disaster, he could at least justify it to himself in the assurance that he had tried to follow his own principles, that he had never been mean or cowardly, and that his mistakes were the mistakes of a very human man. In a period of the most bitter partisanship, he had been almost alone in placing country above party, a fact that men would long remember and some day praise. Now, as he took the steam cars to New York, there was no rancor in his heart. He looked forward, he said, to enjoying "an independence of judgement and of criticism much more agreeable to myself and I think more useful to the public, than any mere subservience to the dictates of party convention or party leaders. I propose to continue the enjoyment and exercise of that independence. When I 'give advice' at all, it will be such as I deem wise and judicious. Whether it is accepted or not, is the business of other people—not mine."

V

Six weeks after the close of the Thirty-ninth Congress, President Johnson, without consulting him, nominated Raymond to be United States Minister to Austria. The honor was not unmixed, for Raymond's name was the fourth Johnson had laid before the Senate in an effort to fill a vacancy created by the summary removal of John Lothrop Motley as Minister the previous January. Each nomination the Senate had speedily rejected, and the *Times* immediately forecast that Raymond's experience would be similar. It was. Within a week his name was tabled, and that meant rejection. John Hay wrote about it to Bigelow: "The Senate is of late gone clean daft in Presidentophobia. . . . They confirmed Dix [as Minister to France], who was the Philadelphia Convention, obstinate and unrepentant, and smothered Raymond, who did more than any mother's son of them to defeat the nominee of that movement [for Governor of New York] and elect Fenton."

Just how Raymond really felt about the episode is uncertain. Publicly he stated that he had not sought the place—which was true—did not want it, and could not have taken it if confirmed. He wrote his daughter Lucy that he could have had the job if he had wanted it. Did he believe that, or was he avoiding an explanation of the complicated political situation to a fifteen-year-old girl? In his letter to the President thanking him for the nomination can be detected a wistful note, as though he almost wished that he might have had the post: "I beg to tender you my most cordial and sincere thanks for the honor you have done me. . . . It is not likely to be confirmed nor could I probably accept it, if it were. But I shall always feel profoundly grateful for the regard and consideration implied in the compliment you have paid me."

Raymond's name had been mentioned so often in connection with diplomatic appointments that perhaps he had periodically let it be known that he was available, but whatever his desires in that regard, the Austrian nomination was the closest he ever came to service abroad. Even if he did not want the Austrian post, he probably would have liked confirmation, for, anticlimactic though the Senate action was, the tabling of the name of the former national chairman of the Union party emphasized in humiliating fashion the full measure of Raymond's political debacle.

23

Into the Valley

I

RAYMOND was forty-seven when he came home from Congress. He looked scarcely forty. His face was almost unlined, and years of hard work, poor health and political heartbreak had only touched with gray his bushy side whiskers and his thinning hair. In the fast-growing city of 1867—buildings were going up everywhere and Fifth Avenue seemed lined with the mansarded mansions of millionaires—he might have been mistaken for a man about town, what with his eyeglass and gold-headed cane, his well-cut clothes, his fondness for driving a span of neat bays in Central Park. The head waiter at Delmonico's knew him well, and he was often in a box at the theater, at the popular Wallack's in particular. He enjoyed the races and fashionable company at newly opened Jerome Park, the magnificent course in Fordham that had been named for his sportsman-friend and had given America its Longchamps. After watching Raymond in the luxurious precincts of its clubhouse one afternoon during a spring meet, John Hay remarked that "he has great talent for talking to women," and he might have added "to men, too," for Raymond, who had for years made almost a business of dining out, remained as always a congenial companion at the Union Club and at the banquets and receptions characteristic of New York's more important male society. "Raymond is very sociable," said a *Times* colleague, "likes company exceedingly, and when he has nothing to do, which is seldom, enjoys conversation and story-telling as well as any journalist in New York."

However much an eye he might have for a pretty woman, however much he might enjoy feminine society, Raymond was too much a man of the world to be only a man about town. Besides, there was not enough time for it, and if there had been, no real intellectual sympathy. Meanwhile, despite his worldliness and his enjoyment of society and its entertainments, he retained an interest in simple pleasures. When he first returned from Washington, he lived at the Astor, and often as he passed back and forth between the hotel and the *Times*, he paused to lean against a fence post and watch the urchins playing with bat and ball in City Hall Park, even as he had once played in the fields of Lima.

Raymond was a busy man. He was a director of the National Life Insurance Company of New York, and in the affairs of the Associated Press he was the mover and shaker that he had been since its founding. Most especially, for the first time since 1860, he could focus his best interest and energy on his paper. "I want to make the *Times* as strong as possible, in merit and interest," he said, and straightway set about doing so. On the editorial floor, in the business office, and in the composing room where the printers filled their sticks under the gaslight, his voice became as familiar as in the *Times*'s early years. With colleagues, with friends like Judge Benedict, he talked about the possibility of making the *Times* the first truly national paper in America, just as he had already made it what E. L. Godkin of the *Nation* later said was "nearer the newspaper of the good time coming than any other in existence."

On the eve of the Civil War, Raymond had set down as his guiding journalistic principle—he had always tried to adhere to it—that a paper's "proper business is to publish *facts*, in such a form and temper as to lead men of all parties to rely upon its statements of facts, and then to discuss them in the light of truth and justice, and not of party interest." Throughout his political life he never swerved far from that principle, nor did he now, however great the temptation to use the *Times*'s columns to justify his course and political philosophy. It was that attitude, and Raymond might have wished that he fully deserved the accolade, which made the Springfield *Republican*'s famous Samuel Bowles call him the "prophet" of "the spirit and power of the future journalism of America." Not many editors of the period could have kept themselves and their private concerns out of their papers as successfully as Raymond. Bowles praised him for it. "No paper," he said, "can hope for the first position in American journalism until it has learned to recognize and enforce the truth of this example."

Just as Raymond refused to use his paper to further himself, so he shied from the identification of himself or any other person with its news and views. "There is a popular impression," he said soon after resuming full-time editorship in 1867, ". . . that the editor of every paper writes everything there is in it, whereas, in point of fact, he can only supervise what is written by others, and see that it is what he needs and conforms in general sentiment to his own opinions. He is responsible to the public for the character of the paper and his reputation for integrity therefore is important to the public and to the journal he edits. . . . We are inclined to think it will be a sad day for journalism when the names and reputation of individual writers become a matter of more interest than the principles they espouse and the opinions they express. Just in proportion as the profession becomes personal, does it become trashy, gossipy and worthless."

He had made the *Times* a landmark in journalistic decency—"at its foundation," said a contemporary, "it had almost a monopoly of decency"— and dignity and courtesy had always belonged to it. In these it mirrored Raymond. When he called names, which he did occasionally when under great provocation, he usually ended by wishing that he had not so far forgotten himself. He was no Colonel Diver, and the *Times* no *Rowdy Journal*, and if his example had raised the tone of American journalism in the sixteen years since the paper's founding, that was a matter of self-congratulation, for Raymond held the good of the profession as well as of the *Times* close to his heart.

In a politically minded age, it was the political independence of the *Times* that set it really apart. Given Raymond's character, the quality was inevitable, but he was ready to justify it, and did so again and again. "There is but one agency through which the people can be enlightened as to the real nature of the tyranny of politicians by which they are ruled," he said, "and that is the newspaper press. If that press becomes the mere tool of the politicians it is, of course, the ally and accomplice of the tyranny from which the people suffer. It is only as it is independent of the ruling political hierarchy . . . that it renders service of the slightest value to the country." In this somewhat exaggerated statement, Raymond expressed his sense of journalistic mission.

He gave point to it on the editorial page. "We shall continue to support the Republican Party," the *Times* said, "so long as we deem its ascendancy, in spite of its errors, on the whole better for the country than that of any party arrayed against it." That left plenty of freedom for criticism. "This journal," readers were told, "has never claimed or consented to be the organ of the Republican Party or any other. . . . Whatever the [Republican party] may do or propose to do, at war with the supreme authority of the Constitution, or with the settled peace and harmony of the Union, or with the dignity, honor and permanent prosperity of the country, we shall not hesitate to warn it of the dangers it will incur, or to resist the evil it may inflict upon the public welfare."

Despite his definition of editorship, Raymond wrote much of what was said on the editorial page, and until form and style were fixed, he also wrote many of the "Minor Topics," a new and immediately popular department instituted in 1867 in order to treat with wit and pungency news not important enough for full-dress leaders. He kept a close eye on the news columns, and knew what he wanted. "When a chance for a telling book review offers," he wrote an out-of-town contributor, "that will be a good topic. Sometimes a sketch of a prominent man—letters on Literary, Political or Social movements—or whatever may strike you as capable of effective treatment, will be of value to us. We want mainly articles to command attention by timeliness of topic, style and strength of statement. . . . I shall deem it a special favor if you will send us such articles now & then—*Especially when you feel savage* about something or other, for then you, like others, are apt to be most effective."

He assigned William Swinton, the *Times*'s best-known war correspondent, to a three-month reporting tour of the South. He watched always for good men to add to his staff, for its improvement was a constant goal.[1] For foreign news, the *Times* used the new Atlantic cable more and more, and Raymond was in the market for free-lance reports from abroad—Russia sometimes, China, or wherever a roving correspondent might chance to be. When the imperial adventure in Mexico neared its final tragedy on the hill at Queretaro, Raymond drew on his limited leisure and his own knowledge of recent diplomatic history for a three-installment story for the *Times* on how the adventure came about and of the course it ran. "I work very hard—stay till late at night just as I used to," he wrote his absent family. "I should like to stop but cannot just yet. Bye and bye I'll take a rest."

II

The rest Raymond had in mind was a European trip that would include the relaxation of a sea voyage, the stimulus of new surroundings and, best of all, reunion with his children. He hoped that rest at sea would halt the prostrating headaches to which he had become increasingly subject, but the trip would not be wholly vacation. He was anxious to use this opportunity to arrange for better coverage of the foreign news that had always been essential to the *Times*. By early summer he decided that he could leave the paper long enough to go.

[1] To Frederic Hudson, who had left the *Herald* because of ill health, Raymond wrote on April 13, 1867: "I should like to make you a proposition to join the *Times*. . . . We want somebody to watch for *points of news*—especially at a distance—and to have a sort of fatherly oversight for the concern! Drop me a line, please, and I will write you more fully—if it is any use!" Hudson could not be persuaded.

His son Henry, who was making a good record at Yale and to whom he sometimes sent the advice of a Polonius,[2] was eager to accompany him, and Judge Benedict was ready to make the party a threesome. Before they sailed on the *Ville de Paris* on July 13, Raymond's friends and colleagues staged rounds of farewell parties that told a little of the affection in which many held him. The witty General Halpine (Miles O'Reilly), a one-time *Times* editor, wrote a special poem "to toast the health and safe return of him who rules the *Times*"; Dana, soon to buy the *Sun*, reminisced about their friendship in the days of the early *Tribune*, and Raymond in a serious moment revealed a corner of his soul. "There are few things in the world worth impatience," he said, "and still fewer worth anger." Such mildness of spirit his intimates long had known and appreciated, but only gradually was it being borne in upon those who, because they knew him only casually, thought of him as reserved, cold, and not a little calculating.

That summer of 1867—it was the year of the great exposition Napoleon III had staged in Paris—Europe was again filled with Americans. Raymond saw them everywhere, although at first he had little time to give them. In England, his days were filled with Associated Press business with the cable companies, and because of it he had to forego the uncertain pleasure of a call on Senator Sumner. Then there was the matter of English correspondence for the *Times*. In Paris, where the cultured Charles Seymour, the *Times* art and drama critic, was one of the American commissioners to the exposition, Raymond was just as busy, for here he aimed to set up a general business and editorial office for the paper.

The more he studied the problem, the more he was convinced that for the backbone of its foreign news the *Times* should rely on a news service. Anything else would be too expensive, and Reuter's, he urged in a letter to George Jones, was the one to buy. "With that," he said, "and a liberal arrangement for cable dispatches of general interest we should have all we want." As for the Paris bureau, that would be needed also, and he set about making the final arrangements. He hired his man, and gave him instructions for acting both as general European correspondent and as business agent. The instructions tell a good deal of what Raymond regarded as news and of the system he had set up for its gathering.

We shall expect from you, twice a week, by the steamer likely to arrive earliest [Raymond wrote the new man], summaries of Paris, French & general news in all departments—such as your general knowledge of the wants and

---

[2] "*Don't run up bills,*" Raymond once wrote him. "That always ends in debt and lavish expenditure. Let me know what you want, and I will give you the means of paying as you go. That will be cheaper & better in every way, for tradesmen always charge for the risk they claim to incur by trusting."

interests of such a paper as the *Times* may suggest. Dr. Johnston [Malakoff]
. . . who has been our correspondent for many years will continue to write
—but will discuss special topics rather than attempt a summary of general
news. Your letters may be prepared without reference to him: but you will
find him at all times ready to consult with you on matters of interest to the
paper. He knows Paris very thoroughly and is on good terms at the U.S.
Embassy. I need not say that everything relating to Americans and American
topics & interest in Europe is especially desirable.

I shall be glad to have you keep a lookout for events of special importance
that are likely to happen in other parts of Europe and to make suggestions to
our other correspondents, by Telegraph or letter, in regard to their going to
write specially about them. Mr. A. J. Jones, care of Marquand & Co. Florence,
is our Italian correspondent and will go at any time wherever his service may
be desired. Col. O. Irvin, Frankfort on the Main, will do the same in Germany. . . .

As a general thing we do not want at present to receive special cable dispatches; but if you hear anything of special importance, worth a dispatch in
your judgement, you have authority to send it. . . . You may also telegraph
to other correspondents asking information on special points and either go
yourself, or send others to points of special interest for news & letters. . . .

As soon as Raymond had the *Times* business well in hand, he went by
train ("railroads are now so finished . . . that traveling here is very
rapid & easy") to Mozart's Salzburg, where his wife, with Mary, Lucy,
Aimee and Walter, awaited Henry and him in the story-book town that
clustered along the Salzach below the castle-crowned hill. They had
been separated for more than two years, crowded, eventful years, and
while letters had passed back and forth among them all, it had seemed
sometimes as though they never would be together again. As he walked
about with his boys and girls, or drove with them over the town's cobbles, Raymond experienced the joy of a doting father once more with
long-absent children and the paternal pride of being able to show them to
his countrymen, for the Raymonds were not the only Americans in
Salzburg. Dr. Bellows, founder of the Sanitary Commission, was there
with his family; so was the scholarly Robert C. Winthrop, one-time
Senator from Massachusetts, and there were many others: "a host,"
Raymond said.

Probably because he could not resist seeing the legation that he might
have headed, he took the family to Vienna for a few days—John Hay,
who had come out as legation secretary, arrived while they were there
—and then returned briefly to Salzburg before moving on to Innsbruck
and finally across the Alps into Italy. The weather was perfect, and
Raymond's holiday was marred only by the misery of the headaches
which relentlessly pursued him. "I have suffered a great deal . . . since
I landed," he told Jones, "and I attribute it to the fact that I was not

seasick during the voyage and thus had no chance to work off the bile."
The family reunion was soon over, and while Mrs. Raymond got
ready to winter in Germany, Raymond finished the last details of *Times*
business in Paris. Early in September he and Henry crossed over to England and sailed for home on the *Arago*, which he knew so well. Despite
his headaches, he felt refreshed and ready for hard work again. Moreover, he was confident that the new arrangements for foreign news
coverage had completed the groundwork for the stronger *Times* he had
set himself to build.

III

While Raymond was out of the country, he had been named without
his knowledge as a Conservative delegate to the Republican State Convention that met in Syracuse late in September, 1867. He did not attend,
and knew only at second hand of the Radicals' rejection of all Conservatives and of their efforts to treat men like Raymond as renegades. He
used the occasion to reiterate his position. "Mr. Raymond," said the
Times, "considers himself out of politics, certainly out of all party com-
binations and movements, and intends, moreover, to remain so. When
he declined a reelection to Congress a year ago, it was with the purpose
of devoting himself wholly to the Editorship of the *Times*, a position
which is much more to his taste than any other he has filled, and which
carries with it quite as much of influence, honor and substantial reward
as any office in the gift of Presidents or of political parties." He was
trying very hard to believe it.

During the fall and winter—the winter was bitter, with one storm close
upon another—Raymond was noticeably absent from meetings and
public dinners that had any tinge of the political, and toward political
questions he wrote in the *Times* as he pleased. When the fall elections
showed significant Democratic gains, the blame was pinned on the Republican party and its leaders: "We regard the defeat . . . as simply
a *lesson administered to the Republican Party*. They are admonished
to be wiser, more discreet, less arbitrary and extreme in their measures,
less arrogant and overwhelming in their tone." And somewhat later, in
an echo of the days when Raymond had pleaded in the House for
magnanimity, for patriotic fellowship, the *Times* charged that "the great
mistake in what has been done since the war closed is that it has been
done in the spirit and temper of conquerors dealing with a conquered
people." To Raymond, such a spirit and temper had been always as
foreign in politics as in private life—he hardly knew the meaning of the
word vindictive—and the evil of it, which he preached, remained stubbornly unrecognized when his voice was forever stilled.

Toward Johnson, Raymond had not softened, and he was depressed by what seemed to him to be a time of small men. "None of our Congressional politicians commands national confidence," said the *Times*. "Not a man stands up in the Senate capable of leading the country wisely and safely. There is nothing but wrangling and turmoil. Passion and partisanship completely rule. . . . When the President failed on one side, no one appeared as leader on the other." Though Raymond opposed the Tenure of Office Act, which Congress had passed to hamstring the President, he deplored Johnson's defiance of the law by his summary dismissal of Stanton, for he foresaw quite accurately that this action would make impeachment certain. Conviction of the President, he feared, would overturn the Constitution by destroying the division of powers basic to the American system, and thus, if on no other grounds than its threat to the Constitution that he had so often defended, he opposed impeachment. When the House voted to impeach, the *Times* thundered: "Reason, judgement or patriotism has nothing to do with the purpose now proclaimed. In its inception and in its exercise it is partisanship, worked up to the point of frenzy and aggravated with a personal hate, of which many who yesterday voted for impeachment will shortly be ashamed." In Raymond's eyes, only the Senate barred the way to what amounted to revolution, and when the long, drawn-out trial ended in failure to convict, he jubilantly hailed the verdict as having saved the nation.

Though impeachment dwarfed all other news that winter, New York life had to go on and much of the pattern was familiar. Lucy Stone was lecturing on women's suffrage—once it had been Amelia Bloomer who defended women's rights. Darling, Raymond's friend and Congressional colleague, was defeated for mayor by the Tammany candidate, John T. Hoffman. At Wallack's, the dark-eyed Rose Eytinge was receiving critical acclaim and popular applause, and while *Times* readers may sometimes have thought their paper too attentive to Miss Eytinge's triumphs, the knowing whispered that maybe it was because of close friendship with the editor, for it was common talk that Raymond had more than a spectator's interest in the Wallack star. It was this winter, too, that Charles Dickens returned to America. One evening the aging Weed went to Steinway Hall to hear this impressive, bearded figure, a gold chain doubled across his waistcoat, read of his Doras and Little Nells while a sympathetic audience wept happily.

The climax of Dickens's American tour—he was half sick from the exhaustion of it—was a great dinner given by the New York Press Club at Delmonico's on Fourteenth Street. Greeley presided, with Dickens on his right, and Raymond next to Dickens. It was the first time in months that Raymond had appeared at an important public dinner, and because the *Times* had of late been reading Greeley a lesson in good editorial manners (the *Tribune* had called Governor Seymour a liar), many a club member had feared that Raymond would not attend. They did not know their man, for despite their public feuds Raymond was fond of Greeley. ("Horace Greeley may attack me as much as he thinks proper," he once said, "but I shall never be able to get over my old liking for him.") The evening at Delmonico's belonged to Dickens, but Raymond, who spoke for the press, shared the honors. He was in his best form as he reminisced about other famous guests of the club— Kossuth, who in that long ago had unknowingly made circulation for the *Times*, Richard Cobden, Thackeray. His polite wit crackled. He displayed urbanity, good taste, and his customary excellent command of language. His fellow newspapermen were proud that he was one of them.

IV

For a brief holiday and another reunion with his family, Raymond went to Europe again in the summer of 1868, but for the first time in his life foreign travel failed to stimulate him or rub out the fatigue of incessant work. "I wish I was back in N.Y. and shall be very glad when I again find myself there," he wrote Jones from London. "There's nothing at all going on here—or anywhere else so far as I can see." London was broiling in a heat wave that made a city normally cool almost as brutally torrid as the New York that Raymond had just left. He went out very little, although one week end he rode down to Gad's Hill to be with Dickens and he saw a lot of Louis Jennings, who was now prospering as a free lance in London. He would have hired him for the *Times* if he had not set his price too high; as it was, he had to be satisfied with Jennings' promise of occasional English letters for the *Times*.

In England, Raymond had been joined by his daughter Mary, a beautiful girl of eighteen, frail after long illness and unable to go about much. Mary's health worried her father, and he was also depressed about himself. The disappointments of his private and public life were much on his mind that summer, and his troubled mind was part of a troubled body. His eyes were badly inflamed—he did not know why, overwork perhaps—and bothered him greatly. He had developed a trembling in the right hand and a disconcerting twitch of the facial muscles. Jennings, who had always regarded Raymond as a sparkling companion, now found him "languid and difficult to rouse." Alarmed, he urged his friend to consult one of London's eminent physicians, but like many another man, Raymond hated to bother with doctors, refusing to admit that his health might be precarious, and ultimately he left London without seeking medical advice.

With his adored Mary, he crossed to the Continent, where he eventually caught up with the rest of his family. Mary had made him happy by announcing that she wanted to return to New York with him, and now greatly to his surprise, Mrs. Raymond decided to come home also, bringing Walter and Aimee with her. Lucy would remain in school on the Isle of Wight. Late in August they sailed, and for Raymond the event must have been as tonic, for his spirits revived and he apparently put aside any worries he may have had about his physical condition.

Before long, now that the family was back, the Ninth Street house was again filled with life and laughter. Carriages bringing relatives and callers and other guests wheeled before the house, and Mary, soon no longer a convalescent, was in demand for the city's gayest balls and parties. Raymond had money to give his family comfort, even luxury. In a report on income tax payments published in the *Times,* his income for 1868 was listed as $25,000, but it must have been much more. The paper, and it was not his only source of income, was so prosperous that for years it had never paid less than an 80 per cent dividend—and he owned thirty-four shares at his death.[3] At the beginning of 1869, his salary, which had been $4,000 after 1860, was raised to $10,000. Yet his debts were heavy, too; in 1868 he owed E. B. Morgan, one of the paper's original stockholders, $30,000, which he repaid, apparently, by turning over five shares of the *Times.*

In a letter written a few months after they all were reestablished, Raymond told Lucy of returning happiness and of a happy family. "Things go on with us very much as of old," he said. "We are having very cold winter weather and you know how cold the large rooms of the old house *can* get when they try. But we are pretty comfortable on the whole. . . . Mother is better than she used to be, though she seldom comes down to breakfast with us. She used to go out riding every day till the coachman had a spree . . . and now she is afraid. Besides it is too cold. She has a large nice carriage. Aimee is as jolly and full of frolic and fun as ever. She is a good deal as you used to be when you were of her age, and I call her Lucy half the time at table by mistake. Walter is grave and solemn as ever. He is studying hard and is a real good boy. Mary has my old room—the blue room—& Mother has the front room upstairs. The one she used to have is a spare room.

"I wonder if you will come home next summer. I hope so. It doesn't seem complete—it isn't quite *home* while you are away, though it is so

[3] They were sold by his heirs for $375,000, which was reported to amount to about a third of his estate.

much better than it used to be when you were *all* away, that I am contented by contrast. . . . No matter how far away you are, be sure I always think of you and always love you very dearly."

Peculiarly enough, revival of Raymond's family life coincided with his political rehabilitation. It was overdue, for the *Times* since late in 1867 had been campaigning for Grant for President. "He would . . . be able, far beyond any other man," the *Times* said almost a year before Grant's election, "to restore peace to the country, put an end to sectional strife and enable us to legislate for the common good of the common country." In words prophetic of Grant's laconic letter accepting the Republican party's nomination, the *Times* urged: "We want Peace—not only in form but in fact; Peace that shall involve harmony of sentiment, unity of purpose and of feeling among the people of the sections lately at war." It was a theme reiterated many times in the months of the Presidential year; it became, though the responsibility of the *Times* is debatable, the watchword for Republicans.

As the campaign progressed, Republican Radicals and Conservatives came together in temporary proof of party unity, and it was in that spirit that Raymond was invited to make the chief address at a Grant rally in Cooper Institute in September, 1868. No man could have better symbolized wounds healed, past differences forgotten, and as he began to speak he was met with such cheering as he had not known since the ill-starred convention at Philadelphia. He was suave, he was fearless. He defended Seward before an audience that hated Johnson and the men around him, and was hissed for his defense. He spoke out for his own position: "I have never been hard on the South. Some of you think my sin has been on the other side. . . . It may have been weakness, but it was from kindness." Most of all, and this of course had been anticipated, he upheld Grant as his candidate, as the candidate of his party, as the candidate who would do most for the nation. The rally's rockets bursting above Astor Place might have been interpreted as dazzling salutes to Raymond's return to the party.

If any further proof of his rehabilitation was needed, it came in the form of an invitation to speak at a Grant rally in Cleveland on October 8. Because of other engagements he had to decline, but he used the occasion to send to the Cleveland organizer a reiteration of his faith in Grant and Grant's victory. "Everything indicates the determination of the people to make Grant their next President," he wrote, "and I think they will do it by an overwhelming majority. They have faith in his firmness of character—in his justice, generosity, practical good judgement and entire devotion to the public good, and they know, too, that it is upon these qualities, rather than subservience to the wishes or necessities of any political party, that the country must rely for the restoration of peace and prosperity."

Grant's victory over the Democrat Horatio Seymour⁴ delighted Raymond, and soon after the election he told of his pleasure to Colonel Badeau, the former *Times* war correspondent who was now a close adviser of the President-elect. "What a glorious, cheering victory has been achieved," he wrote. "And how nobly, *greatly* [Grant] has borne himself through the contest. I do not generally pay much attention to the cant about *Providence* managing our politics—but in this case *somebody* has been doing very great things for us, and with a wisdom which, whether *Superhuman* or not, certainly is not *common!*" Raymond, who had never abandoned the hope that his party, Union, Republican, or whatever its label, would become truly national, and who hated the division within its ranks, now forecast a happier day. "I look for an entire reorganization of political parties," he said to Badeau, "—not to be brought about by management or plan, but to *grow*, as a natural result of Grant's action & policy, out of his administration, so that long before his term is out he will have the cordial support of all that is wise, and sensible & moderate & patriotic in all parties. The less done with *direct reference* to this result the better—but it will come!"

Raymond did not live long enough to appreciate how poor a prophet he had been, and meanwhile, to further the ideal of unity, he accepted the presidency of the city's Union Republican Central Committee. He had been led to believe that he could bring the warring factions of Conservatives and Radicals together, but when a few months later he realized that he was getting nowhere, he resigned, an action that brought him praise. Even the recently hostile Albany *Evening Journal* applauded his "integrity of purpose." Whether the events of 1868 had reawakened his political ambitions is impossible to know. Certainly Jones hoped that his partner would not be drawn again into political adventure. In a discussion of *Times* affairs early in 1869, he reminded Raymond: "We have run down the circulation arising from the fact of our not being in accord with the great bulk of our leaders—that cause has gone by I hope forever. . . . This has not however as yet hurt our revenues. I feel sure nothing can ever get us into exactly such a fix again."

Whatever his political views or personal interests, Raymond intended to use political friendship to further the *Times*. Badeau offered this opportunity to lay pipe into the White House, and Raymond made the most of it. "I am distracted," he wrote him, "by *two* desires—first, to have a talk with the General which may guide the *Times* somewhat in

⁴ "The Democrats made a good nomination in Seymour," Raymond had said the previous summer, "i.e., better than they might have made, but they can't elect him."

being useful to him; and next *not* to bore or bother him just now when so many thousands stand ready to do both. I would go to Washington but for the latter feeling. . . . I don't want any office, which fact will, I am confident, soon make me distinguished. But I do want very much to know *in what tone and spirit to write* in order to shape public sentiment for his active guidance of affairs. I am not so absurd as to want or to expect to know *what* he will do, whom he will appoint to office etc. etc. But I should like to know a little of the direction he will give to government policy—and the general tenor & tone which he will adopt towards sections, parties, cliques & factions. Will it be asking too much to ask you to drop me a few lines on this matter?"

What Badeau answered is unrecorded, but Raymond and the *Times* did have excellent news sources in the Grant Administration, and when Hamilton Fish became Secretary of State, it was almost as though Seward had stayed on. News was what the paper wanted; often that news could be used for patriotic purposes, and one of Fish's lieutenants recalled that "the sec'y had given Raymond his confidence in one or two important matters, which was judiciously used for the interests of the country."

Though the Grant Administration had the editorial support of the *Times*, it was not a month old before Raymond was privately expressing strong misgivings that it would not live up to his hopes for it. Some of the doubt may have arisen from the muddle over Grant's Cabinet appointments, or from his willingness to compromise on repeal of the Tenure of Office Act. More important was the fact that somehow, somewhere, Raymond had early sniffed out signs of corruption. "I am grieved and disappointed to learn of your want of faith in Grant's Administration," Jones wrote him on April 6, 1869, "and that we are to have the same corruption and disgraceful jobbing & plundering that disgusted every honest man with Johnson's rule. One feels like running away from his country and hiding in the back woods away from all contact with the thieves and robbers that fill its highest places."

It was a time of corruption everywhere, spurred by the promise of easy money and lots of it from highhanded stock manipulation, from fraudulent contracts, from bought legislatures. The Tweed Ring, which everybody knew was looting New York City, and which the *Times* after Raymond's death had a big part in destroying, was at the height of its thieving power. Tweed himself was hand-in-glove with Jay Gould and James Fisk, Jr., in the plundering of the Erie Railroad. In editorial after editorial, the *Times* denounced the swindlers and robbers, sounding the alarm that it hoped would arouse public opinion against the corruption ravaging city government and extending to Albany and Washington. The *Times* tangled with Fisk over the outrageous stock-watering of the Erie, and while Raymond escaped the libel suit and night in jail that were inflicted on Samuel Bowles because his Springfield *Republican* said of the Gould-Fisk operations that "nothing so audacious, nothing more gigantic in the way of real swindling has ever been perpetrated in this country," he was subjected to the threat and bluster of Gentleman Jim, and the *Times* reporter who had written about the Erie scandal had to skip lively to keep away from the bailiff.

It was one of the risks of being a newspaperman, and one that Raymond had no more wish to avoid than he wanted to escape the more apparent and pleasant duties and responsibilities of his profession. He was proud of that profession, and he was always conscious, as an editor must be, that what was said in the *Times* on a particular morning might have unforeseen effects on some phase of the nation's life. If the present time of loose economic morals was capable of reform, then a *Times* editorial or news story might conceivably be the agent of reformation. That was why it was easy to shrug off Jim Fisk's complaint about "the slanderous assaults made upon me in the columns of your journal," and to retort to his brazen request for help in locating the offending *Times* reporter with a crushing "I am not a professional detective & decline to serve you in that capacity."

V

"I expect to spend the summer in New York pretty hard at work," Raymond wrote Jennings in the spring of 1869. His mention of hard work could scarcely have surprised Jennings any more than it would have others who knew him well, although Theodore Tilton, an editorial neighbor on the *Independent*, noted that Raymond's industry "was more for the work's sake than for the reward. To have nothing to do was with him to be miserable. His muscular intellect craved perpetual activity." Once James Parton had spoken penetratingly of Raymond's desire to open the world oyster, and if that ambition now seemed lost, perhaps it was because Raymond had learned too much of the oyster's nature or had come to suspect that it contained no pearl.

The soul weariness he had confessed to Jones in the summer of 1865 had never lessened; if anything, it had grown worse. Outwardly, in little social gatherings, in meetings with friends, or at the succession of dinners—even Raymond must have tired of them sometimes—he seemed the self-sufficient, well-poised man of achievement, a man who had mellowed as he grew older and became more resigned to life's buffeting. Though less seldom than formerly, he still showed at times almost a boyish enthusiasm for new things and new ideas, but it was not lasting. Failure in Washington and in his party had only served to ripen in him what Tilton described as "Solomon's desolate conviction that all things are vanity." Nor, surprisingly, was the conviction weakened by the prestige and success of the *Times*. More and more often he displayed openly a melancholy that once had been revealed only to intimates. Occasionally melancholy deepened into depression, and in the late winter of 1869 it caused him to talk seriously of selling the *Times*. ("I feel that to give up the Paper would be very hard to do, harder for you than for me," Jones remonstrated.)

Although only forty-nine, he must have felt sometimes as though he had outlived his era, at least in politics. That was one of the penalties for having started young. Many of the men with whom he had made political history of a sort had already retired; some like Preston King, Daniel S. Dickinson, and, most recently, Thaddeus Stevens were dead. Lincoln had been quickly swept into folk myth and legend. In March, 1869, Seward stepped out as Secretary of State and out of public life forever. On his way home to Auburn, he paused briefly in New York, where Raymond and other old friends joined him for a little celebration ("a sumptuous dinner," Seward's son Fred described it) at the Astor. It was one of the last times, perhaps the very last, that Raymond talked with his great political mentor who, as fate decided it, was the subject of the final editorial Raymond put on paper. Weed was missing that day at the Astor. Broken in health, some said from a stroke, he was in the South seeking strength. Bigelow saw him when he returned, thought him "feeble," and recorded in his diary that "Raymond called while I was there." It was natural that Raymond should call at Weed's West Twelfth Street house, for the fallen Dictator remained a close friend, a friend who despite a weakened body retained a clear, sharp mind, and from whom Raymond could still draw guidance and advice.

Some of the guidance he sought that spring was beyond Weed's capacity to extend. In late February, fourteen-year-old Walter Raymond had sickened and died. His father, who had already buried two sons, was deeply shaken by this loss of a third, a lad in whom he had put great store. Once he might have drawn consolation from the rigid tenets of the orthodox Presbyterianism in which he had been reared, but he had long ago put aside that sort of faith, and while he always loved to debate matters philosophical and metaphysical, he had grown to take religion lightly and formally. Bigelow remarked that "Raymond had but imperfect notions of the efficacy of prayer." Raymond's father had died only a few months earlier, and now the death of his beloved boy left Raymond spiritually unprepared. He began searching for support.

His hunt brought him to a new and popular book, *The Gates Ajar*, by Elizabeth Stuart Phelps, the scholarly young daughter of a professor at the Andover Theological Seminary. She had written it out of her own grief for a lover who had died in the war, and its purpose was definitely to comfort the war-bereaved. A book of conversations and biblical quotations, it scrapped orthodox conceptions of life after death, presenting instead the prospect of a pleasant, happy heaven where the dead, unchanged from their earthly form, awaited reunion with those left behind. This promise of reunion beyond the grave comforted an ever-widening audience, and for Raymond *The Gates Ajar* seemed to have peculiar fascination. He read it over and over, and discussed it with his friend, the Reverend Henry M. Field, editor of the *Evangelist*, who called at Raymond's house not long after Walter died. Raymond, recalled Field, "thought our ideas of the future life were too shadowy and dim, and he seemed to be groping after something more definite and real in his conceptions of the invisible world. Little did he think he was soon to enter it; to pass within the veil, and to know the great mystery." That *The Gates Ajar* afforded Raymond all the help he wanted is most unlikely; he was not the sort, even under emotional stress, to accept uncritically such a popularization, but it seems to have given him at least temporary consolation while he tamped down his grief as best he could.

Death continued to pursue him. In May, the charming and brilliant Charles Seymour, who had been on the *Times* almost from the beginning, died suddenly, and Raymond served as pallbearer at a funeral that brought together all the principals in the city's musical and dramatic life, Rose Eytinge among them. Only a few months earlier General Halpine had died accidentally from an overdose of chloroform. Raymond, who stubbornly refused to heed the warnings of his trembling hand and twitching face, was to die next. Meanwhile, he kept to his accustomed tasks, maintained his accustomed pace.

One afternoon in June, he ordered out his carriage and horses, and with Mary drove pleasantly to beautiful Greenwood in Brooklyn to select a spot for Walter's burial after the removal of his body from a temporary tomb. Because they had been in no hurry, it was six o'clock by the time they got back to New York. Raymond stopped at the *Times* for a few minutes before driving uptown for a family dinner and an evening with callers in the high-ceilinged parlor. About ten o'clock he excused himself to go to what the *Times* euphemistically described as a "political consultation." Someone remembered later having seen him outside Wallack's, and from there he apparently went to see Rose Eytinge. Henry Ward Beecher told John Bigelow that Raymond's visit was for the purpose of ending his friendship with the star. George Jones was not so sure.

Sometime after midnight that same night, a carriage rounded the corner into West Ninth Street, halted before No. 12. Two men supporting a third—it was Raymond—got out, climbed the stoop, rang the bell for admittance. The servant who answered tarried only long enough to turn the key, and then because she was in nightclothes fled. Raymond's unconscious body—he had apparently had a stroke—was deposited on the floor; the two mysterious escorts hurried away without doing more. The stertorous breathing of her stricken father was soon heard by Mary, who investigated and then, terrified, roused the sleeping household. Someone rushed for help at General McDowell's, next door; someone else was sent for a doctor. A few hours later in the early summer dawn of June 18, 1869, Raymond died.

VI

In New York flags flew at half-staff for the founder of the *Times*, and the *Tribune*, so long an unrelenting critic, hastened, however belatedly, to make amends.

In the great newspaper offices [said the *Tribune*], in the club-houses, in Wall Street, in committee rooms, in all places where men of culture and of affairs meet together, a little whisper of news came yesterday which awed the bravest and saddened the lightest heart. It was only the news that is told every day of some man well known to his fellows; only the news that a kindly face would be no more seen among them, a heartsome voice would be no more heard, a firm step would no longer ring down familiar ways. And yet few faces could be more missed than this one lying upturned in such dreamless sleep; few voices die out of more listening ears; few steps fail whose coming had brought assurance of a friend's approach to a greater host of friends. "Governor Raymond is dead," said the brief report. But no man who heard it, repeated it in that form. "A great journalist is dead," said one voice. "An able politician is gone," said another. And so multitudes remembered him, each giving him honor for some distinctive power, but all adding, in softer voice, "and he had no enemies." It is a good record to have left.

As the newspapers, so many of which had regularly scourged him in their columns, prepared their tributes and organizations drafted resolutions, the question circled, what sort of man was Raymond? He lacked the colorful eccentricity of Horace Greeley, the vanity and vulgarity popularly associated with James Gordon Bennett. More principled than Bennett, he was also more stable than the erratic Greeley, and personally far more likable than either. A solid, respectable citizen who resembled a successful businessman, and in a sense that was what he was, he had none of Greeley's zeal for reform, and yet he was no reactionary. Greeley said that in England Raymond would have been at home among the Gladstonian Liberals.

There was much in Raymond's character that had aroused dispute and controversy while he was alive, but with death he was thought of only kindly. At his funeral, members of the Press Club agreed that among them there had been "no brighter companion, no friend more faithful, no truer master of his craft." Jennings, who knew him so well, wrote to Jones out of grief and bereavement: "You and I know how tenderhearted he was towards others, how eager to assist the unhappy, how gentle and forgiving in his disposition. He was the most lovable man I ever knew, and his high principles and conscientiousness could not but make an impression on all who lived with him. . . . He confided most of his plans and secrets to me at one time, and I know that he was as guileless and generous-hearted a man as ever breathed." Such sentiment, and it was echoed by many, may have arisen in part from a desire to speak only good of the dead, and yet the unanimity suggests that it was more genuine than conventional. "He was never more kindly regarded," said *Harper's Weekly*, "than when he died. . . . No man in the editorial fraternity will be personally remembered for more friendly acts, for a more constant kindliness of nature."

Raymond had a good and well-trained mind, though not a very original one, and even the *Times*, though his creation, was not something that sprang full-armed from the head of Jove. It represented ideas that Raymond had drawn from others—from the *Tribune*, the *Herald*, the London *Times*—and then had infused with his own philosophy of fairness and moderation until it became something new and different among American newspapers. The *Times* was his real monument, and the American press, conscious of it, put the chief emphasis of its valedictories on Raymond as an editor. While the Brooklyn *Eagle* said that he had "probably" been the nation's greatest journalist, many another paper gave him first place without qualification. From all over New England, the chorus sounded: Boston, Springfield, Providence, New Haven—Raymond had "inaugurated a new era in American journalism." In Pittsburgh, the *Chronicle* said that he had "held up as a mirror before us a paper which could deal with the most exacting topics without compromising its character for courtesy, firmness and honest argument." As Judge Benedict later told the University of Vermont alumni: "The thousand voices of the press began to repeat the lesson which he had sought to teach. Words of sorrow for his loss indeed were heard on every hand, but with them also words of thankfulness that he had lived. What he had always inculcated was repeated as acknowledged truth in regard to journalism, and his example in the management of that great power, the public press, was everywhere presented as the best model of an honest, an able, and a fearless journalist."

On Raymond's political service there was less unanimity. Some dismissed it as total failure, as final evidence of the folly of a man's trying to wed a career in journalism to one in politics. Others, without wholly disagreeing, saluted him nevertheless as one who had been able to put country above party, as one who had adhered to his convictions regardless of the winds that tore at him. Already, with political passion less high, some of his contemporaries were beginning to wonder if possibly his views toward the South and toward the Constitution might not after all have been right. History was so to believe, and before long the moderate and peace-loving Rutherford B. Hayes was to remark that the difficulty with Raymond was that he was "ten years ahead of his party." Now that he was dead, he was praised for his qualities of moderation, his ability to see both sides, and many a former foe retracted the charge of trimming that had dogged him for so long. "His misfortune," said Elmer Davis many years later in the *Dictionary of American Biography*, "was not only that he was a temperamental non-partisan in an age of bitter partisanship, but that he was a temperamental non-partisan incurably addicted to party politics."

Raymond had spent so much of his energy in trying to win men to his nonpartisanship that it was symbolically fitting for men of all factions and political creeds to come together at his funeral. Weed and Greeley put aside their enmities to act as bearers, along with James Watson Webb, George William Curtis, editor of *Harper's Weekly*, and Senator Morgan, who had broken with Seward, Weed & Raymond. Mayor A. Oakey Hall, a Tammany Democrat, was a bearer; so were the War Democrats John A. Dix and Judge C. P. Daly. Admiral Farragut and General McDowell represented the armed services, while from the world of trade came the merchant prince A. T. Stewart and Moses Grinnell, the newly named collector of the port. There were prayers at the Ninth Street house, and then while the heavens darkened with the approach of a summer storm the cortege traveled slowly the few blocks to the University Place Presbyterian Church, where Henry Ward Beecher delivered a final tribute to "a man without hate . . . without animosity, a man the nearer you came to him and the better you knew him, the more you esteemed him." Outside the church thunder rolled and lightning flashed while torrential rain drenched men and women massed in the narrow street to honor Henry Jarvis Raymond.

Some Notes on Bibliography

FORTUNATE it is for the biographer of Henry J. Raymond that he and his journalistic contemporaries lived much of their lives in the pages of their newspapers. Without that open though often contradictory record of acts and ideas, the life of Raymond in particular would remain largely untold, for the private records of what he did and said and thought are widely scattered and often disappointingly scanty. He peers from the yellowed pages of the *New-Yorker*, the *Tribune* and the *Courier and Enquirer*. For nearly eighteen years the New York *Times* both mirrored much of what he was thinking and presented his attacks or counterattacks in the many controversies into which he was drawn with his neighbors on the *Tribune*, the *Herald* and other papers. When the *Times* did not report his goings-out and comings-in, the *Herald* in particular was apt to fill the gap, and if the details were sometimes too colorful or too inaccurate, then the *Times* promptly sought to set them right. From a balancing and checking of such conflicting reports ultimately emerges what seems to be a close approximation of truth.

The tracking down of Raymond's private papers was a project that spread across the country—from the Widener Library at Harvard to the Huntington Library at San Marino. Some places the finds were significant. At the New York Public Library are a good many Raymond letters. Some are catalogued separately; others are in the Horace Greeley Papers, the Bryant-Godwin Papers, the Evert A. Duyckinck Papers, the Schuyler Colfax Papers, the Papers of Rufus W. Griswold and of James

R. Doolittle. There are also a few but important Raymond letters at the New York Historical Society in New York City. At Harvard, the E. J. Wendell Bequest contains a variety of letters that throw light on Raymond's editorial career, and the Charles Sumner Papers also contain items of interest. The Boston Public Library has Raymond material in its collection of Rufus W. Griswold Papers. Among the William Henry Seward Papers at Auburn, New York, are Raymond items, and the Thurlow Weed Papers at the University of Rochester are particularly good for Raymond's political activities in the Eighteen Fifties and Sixties. At the Library of Congress, the most important Raymond letters are in the Abraham Lincoln Papers, which supplement the *Complete Works of Abraham Lincoln*, edited by John G. Nicolay and John Hay (New York, 1905). For the story of the campaign of 1864 the Raymond items in the Simon Cameron Papers and the Papers of Edward McPherson, both Library of Congress collections, are interesting and revealing. At the Library of Congress a few Raymond letters can also be found in the Hamilton Fish Papers, the Horace Greeley Papers, the L. C. Garrett Papers, the Andrew Johnson Papers and the E. B. Washburne Papers. These public collections were the ones of most use to me; others, like the Edwin D. Morgan Papers at the New York State Library at Albany, were examined and in some instances contributed facts or facets that furthered understanding.

Despite the wide net cast for Raymond manuscript material, the results would have been very disappointing had I been unable to locate and use several important private collections. To those who opened them to me, I am extremely grateful.

From the start of my research, Mrs. George Lambert of Philadelphia, a Raymond granddaughter, did all she could to assist me, both in the way of making manuscripts available and of opening doors that might otherwise have remained closed. She let me use papers in her possession, most notably letters that passed between Raymond and Seward in the late Forties and early Fifties. She also gave me permission to draw on the unpublished portions of Raymond's journal; the most interesting section is an account of the New York senatorial election of 1863, which Mrs. Lambert's father, Henry Warren Raymond, presumably withheld from publication because it reflected on Senator Edwin D. Morgan, a family friend and executor of the Henry J. Raymond estate.

Among the papers lent me by the Reverend Albert C. Larned of Bristol, Rhode Island, were letters written by Raymond to his daughter Lucy, Mr. Larned's mother. Their simple beauty revealed much of Raymond's deep affection for his children at the same time that they reported details of everyday life that helped a great deal to give Raymond's portrait depth.

The largest single collection of Raymond Papers is owned by Mrs. Seymour Holbrook of Norfolk, Connecticut, who not only put them at my use but unknowingly encouraged me to keep on with the biography when my enthusiasm flagged. The collection, an extremely varied one, covers most of Raymond's adult life and includes such diverse items as these: Raymond's letter to George Jones in the mid-Forties regarding the start of a newspaper, Raymond's notes on a Webster speech, the original copy of a news story Raymond sent from Italy in 1859, McClellan's request to the Secretary of War in 1861 to suppress the *Times*, a bristling exchange of correspondence with James Fisk, Jr. There are also letters to and from Raymond on all sorts of personal, business, and political matters, as well as letters of reminiscence written to Henry Warren Raymond at the time he was editing his father's journal.

Mrs. Gilbert Jones of Morristown, New Jersey, turned over to me the Raymond material in the George Jones Papers, and this has now been deposited in the New York Public Library. Included are letters and memoranda that tell a good deal about the problems of the *Times* and Raymond's part in solving them. There are many letters relating to Raymond's work as Republican National Chairman in 1864. Still other letters, personal in nature, help to make Raymond seem a human as well as a historic figure.

Many other people, far more than I can thank here, have also contributed in one way or another to this biography. Some gave me leads that might have been missed. Others, and Dr. Reinhard H. Luthin of Columbia University chief among them, sent me pertinent facts, even copies of letters and other documents, which they came across during their own researches in the Raymond period. Anyone who has ever engaged in biographical research will appreciate the importance of this kind of assistance. Mr. Arthur Hays Sulzberger, president and publisher of the New York *Times*, placed at my disposal Raymond manuscripts and related material in the possession of the paper. The staffs of the manuscript division at the New York Public Library and at the Library of Congress were willing helpers whenever I called upon them, as were the staffs of many other institutions, and without the facilities of the New York Historical Society, where I spent long hours among newspaper files, I find it hard to believe that the biography could have been completed.

Among published works that are fundamental to the writing of a Raymond life, none is more important than Augustus Maverick's *Henry J. Raymond and the New York Press for Thirty Years* (Hartford, 1870). The only previous biography of Raymond, it includes letters and other source material that have now disappeared, and it is something of a source itself since Maverick both knew Raymond and worked for him. As a book it is superficial at times and badly organized, and yet it is indispensable. Next in importance are "Extracts from the Journal of Henry J. Raymond" (*Scribner's Monthly*, vols. 19, 20). Though some of the entries suggest that they were written considerably after the event, the journal as a whole is an essential source for Raymond's role in public life. A brief but intimate picture of Raymond as a man, an editor, and a politician is drawn by his friend Louis J. Jennings in "Mr. Raymond and Journalism" (*Galaxy*, vol. 8). In the *Eclectic Magazine* (vol. 146) E. B. Wesley recalled both the founding of the *Times* and the personality of his former partner. Among other contemporary portraits are those given in Matthew Hale Smith, *Sunshine and Shadow in New York* (Hartford, 1868), and Junius Henri Browne, *The Great Metropolis: A Mirror of New York* (Hartford, 1869).

In addition to such well-known histories of the United States as that by James Ford Rhodes, certain more special studies have much to contribute to a Raymond biography. For Raymond's years in politics, the most important is De Alva S. Alexander, *A Political History of the State of New York* (New York, 1909). For the Civil War, it is supplemented in detail by Sidney D. Brummer, *Political History of New York State During the Period of the Civil War* (New York, 1911). Dorothy Dodd, *Henry J. Raymond and the New York Times During Reconstruction* (Chicago, 1936) is helpful. Other studies that cannot be overlooked are Harry J. Carman and Reinhard H. Luthin, *Lincoln and the Patronage* (New York, 1943); George Fort Newton, *The Eve of Conflict: Stephen A. Douglas and the Needless War* (Boston, 1934); Roy F. Nichols, *The Disruption of American Democracy* (New York, 1948); T. Harry Williams, *Lincoln and the Radicals* (Madison, Wisconsin, 1941).

To the preparation of this biography the published memoirs of Raymond's friends, associates, and casual acquaintances contributed recollections that were frequently illuminating. To list them all would be like calling an unending roll, but some are too fundamental to be omitted. Among these are: Lyman Abbott, *Reminiscences* (Boston, 1915); Henry Adams, *The Education of Henry Adams: An Autobiography* (Boston, 1918); *The Diary of Edward Bates*, edited by Howard K. Beale (Washington, 1933); John Bigelow, *Retrospections of an Active Life* (New York, 1909), which is supplemented by Bigelow's unpublished diary in the New York Public Library; James G. Blaine, *Twenty Years of Congress* (Norwich, 1886); Frank B. Carpenter, *Six Months in the White House* (New York, 1866). Chauncey Depew, *My Memories of Eighty Years* (New York, 1922), tells a good deal about Raymond, and Horace Greeley's *Recollections of a Busy Life* (New York, 1868) has an obvious importance. *Passages from the Correspondence of R. W. Griswold*, edited by W. W. Griswold (Cambridge, 1898), is invaluable for Raymond's student days and his early years in New York City. Glimpses of Raymond during the Civil War and Reconstruction are caught in *Lincoln and the Civil War in the Diaries and Letters of John Hay*, selected with an introduction by Tyler Dennett (New York, 1939). Nancy Johnson (Minnie Myrtle) gives a thinly disguised description of the Raymond household in *Myrtle Wreath* (New York, 1854). Theodore Tilton's *Sanctum Sanctorum: or Proof-Sheets from an Editor's Table* (New York, 1870) reprints Tilton's reminiscent editorial on Raymond that appeared in the *Independent* after Raymond's death. Despite the diarist's hearty dislike for Raymond, *The Diary of Gideon Welles* (Boston, 1911) gives a detailed picture of Raymond as party chairman and member of Congress. *The Autobiography of Andrew Dickson White* (New York, 1905) contains a graphic picture of the Baltimore Convention of 1864.

Among the biographies of Raymond's contemporaries, *The Life of Thurlow Weed*, vol. I, Autobiography, vol. II, Memoir, by Thurlow Weed Barnes (Boston, 1883–84), is both suggestive and informative. *Hamilton Fish: The Inner History of the Grant Administration*, by Allan Nevins (New York, 1936), touches on phases of Raymond's life. For background and interpretation three studies of Greeley are most useful: Ralph Ray Fahrney, *Horace Greeley and the Tribune in the Civil War* (Cedar Rapids, Iowa, 1936); Jeter Allen Isely, *Horace Greeley and the Republican Party* (Princeton, 1947); James Parton, *The Life of Horace Greeley* (New York, 1855). Other aspects of Raymond's political career are touched upon in C. E. Hamlin, *Life and Times of Hannibal Hamlin* (Cambridge, Massachusetts, 1899); J. G. Randall, *Lincoln the President: Springfield to Gettysburg* (Indianapolis, 1945); Carl Sandburg, *Abraham Lincoln* (New York, 1939); Stewart Mitchell, *Horatio Seymour of New York* (Cambridge, 1938); Frederic Bancroft, *The Life of William H. Seward* (New York, 1900); Frederic H. Seward, *Seward at Washington* (New York, 1891); Alphonse B. Miller, *Thaddeus Stevens* (New York, 1939); James Woodburn, *The Life of Thaddeus Stevens* (Indianapolis, 1913).

Many books have information about Raymond as a newspaper man. Among the histories of American journalism, two were especially useful to me: Frederic Hudson, *Journalism in the United States* (New York, 1873), and Frank Luther Mott, *American Journalism* (New York, 1941). Hudson's book has added interest because it was written by a man who knew Raymond. For particular chapters of Raymond's journalistic career, these books are valuable: Oliver Gramling, *A.P.: The Story of News* (New York, 1940); Victor Rosewater, *History of Cooperative News-Gathering in the United States* (New York, 1930); Charles F. Wingate, *Views and Interviews on Journalism* (New York, 1875); *A Cycle of Adams Letters 1861–65*, edited by W. C. Ford (Boston, 1920); Ernest Samuels, *The Young Henry Adams* (Cambridge, 1948); C. L. Brace, *Life of C. L. Brace* (New York, 1894); Rollo Ogden, *Life of E. L. Godkin* (New York, 1907); W. H. Dunn, *The Life of Donald G. Mitchell, Ik Marvel* (New York, 1922); E. C. Stedman, *The Battle of Bull Run* (New York, 1861); George A. Townsend, *Rustics in Rebellion* (Chapel Hill, 1950); Franc B. Wilkie, *Pen and Powder* (Boston, 1888) and *Personal Reminiscences* (Chicago, 1891).

Finally, Raymond's own writings must be considered. For nearly twenty years his principal speeches and addresses were published and circulated in pamphlet form. So was his debate with Greeley on Fourierism. His letters to Yancey on the eve of the Civil War were brought together. All tell something of the man as do his two lives of Lincoln, although in those biographies as in the speeches a Raymond biographer must often read between the lines and make his own interpretation.

These bibliographical notes make no pretense to completeness. They do not touch upon many books which helped to build background, upon directories and legislative manuals, the journals of the New York Assembly and such semi-official publications as the *Congressional Globe*. They do, however, indicate the wide variety of material drawn upon in the writing of the book and the nature of the most important works and original sources. The bits and pieces drawn from them all ultimately fell into place. What at first had seemed almost a hopeless jumble of half-related historical and biographical detail took on form and meaning. Then it became possible to tell this story of Henry J. Raymond and his times.

Index